FRANCE AND THE SOUTH PACIFIC SINCE 1940

Also by Robert Aldrich

ECONOMY AND SOCIETY IN BURGUNDY SINCE 1850
AN ECONOMIC AND SOCIAL HISTORY OF EUROPE, 1890–1939
  (*with Frank B. Tipton*)
AN ECONOMIC AND SOCIAL HISTORY OF EUROPE FROM 1939 TO
  THE PRESENT (*with Frank B. Tipton*)
FRANCE IN WORLD POLITICS (*co-editor with John Connell*)
THE FRENCH PRESENCE IN THE SOUTH PACIFIC, 1842–1940
FRANCE: Politics, Society, Culture and International Relations (*editor*)
FRANCE'S OVERSEAS FRONTIER: Départements et Territoires d'Outre-
  Mer (*with John Connell*)
FRANCE, AUSTRALIA AND OCEANIA: Past and Present (*editor*)
GAY PERSPECTIVES: Essays in Australian Gay Culture (*co-editor with Garry
  Wotherspoon*)

France and the South Pacific since 1940

Robert Aldrich
Associate Professor of Economic History
University of Sydney

UNIVERSITY OF HAWAII PRESS
HONOLULU

Published 1993 in North America by
UNIVERSITY OF HAWAII PRESS
2840 Kolowalu Street
Honolulu, Hawaii 96822

First published 1993 in the United Kingdom by
THE MACMILLAN PRESS LTD
Houndmills, Basingstoke, Hampshire RG21 2XS
and London

Printed in Hong Kong

Library of Congress Cataloging-in-Publication Data
Aldrich, Robert, 1954–
France and the South Pacific since 1940 / Robert Aldrich.
p.   cm.
Includes bibliographical references and index.
ISBN 0-8248-1558-0
1. French Polynesia—History.   2. New Caledonia—History.
3. Wallis and Futuna Islands—History.   4. Vanuatu—History.
5. France—Colonies—Oceania.   6. Decolonization—Oceania.
I. Title.
DU50.A39   1993
996.2—dc20   93–6783
                                                   CIP

To Mark Edwards and to the memory of
Michael C. Blad

Contents

List of Maps

List of Abbreviations

AOM	Archives d'Outre-Mer (Aix-en-Provence)
ATNC	Archives Territoriales de la Nouvelle-Calédonie
ATPF	Archives Territoriales de la Polynésie Française
BSEHNC	*Bulletin de la Société d'Etudes Historiques de la Nouvelle-Calédonie*
CEA	Commissariat á l'Energie Atomique
CEP	Centre d'Essais du Pacifique
CFP	French Pacific franc
CFPO	Compagnie Française des Phosphates de l'Océanie
DOM	*Départment d'Outre-mer*
EFO	Etablissements Français d'Océanie
FLNKS	Front de Libération Nationale Kanak et Socialiste
JSO	*Journal de la Société des Océanistes*
RDPT	Rassemblement Démocratique des Peuples Tahitiens
RFHOM	*Revue Française d'Histoire d'Outre-Mer*
RPCR	Rassemblement pour la Calédonie dans la République
SFNH	Société Française des Nouvelles-Hébrides
SLN	Société Le Nickel
TOM	*Territoire d'Outre-mer*
UC	Union Calédonienne

Preface

This book is the companion volume to my *The French Presence in the South Pacific, 1842–1940.* It thus examines the history of New Caledonia, French Polynesia, Wallis and Futuna and the New Hebrides from the Second World War until the present. It also takes up some of the themes of another book, *France's Overseas Frontier: Départements et Territoires d'Outre-Mer,* published in 1992, which I wrote with John Connell. This work does not claim to be a comprehensive history of the French territories of the South Pacific; rather it concentrates on French political, economic and strategic action and its impact on Oceania and looks at the place of the South Pacific in France's international policy. Since the three present-day French *territoires d'outre-mer* in the South Pacific (New Caledonia, French Polynesia and Wallis and Futuna) have not become independent, it also considers a process of change different from the pattern of decolonisation which France pursued in other colonies.

The impact of the Second World War, particularly the defeat of France, the rallying of New Caledonia and French Polynesia to the Free French and the effects on the colonies of the presence of large numbers of American troops, rearranged their political landscape in the late 1940s and 1950s. At the same time, Paris recast the colonial system with the constitution of the Fourth Republic in 1946, the Defferre law of 1956 and the establishment of the Fifth Republic in 1958. All the while, however, France did not envisage absolute self-government or independence for its Oceanic territories, despite the organisation of political parties which, at least in French Polynesia, promoted secession. During this period, the South Pacific was of little importance to the French, a situation that changed with the nickel boom in New Caledonia and the decision to transfer France's nuclear testing site to French Polynesia in the 1960s.

From the early 1960s to the mid-1970s, the territories underwent a veritable economic and social revolution. From the mid-1970s political conflicts again emerged with new contestatory movements and calls for independence. At the beginning of the 1980s, which became a decade of crisis in the French Pacific, France reluctantly assented to the independence of the New Hebrides, previously administered as a joint Franco-British condominium. Soon political tension and ethnic polarisation exploded into violence in New Caledonia, and strife lasted until late in the 1980s. In French Polynesia, Paris and local autonomists worked out an uneasy compromise, but that territory, too, witnessed growing social and economic problems. France's smallest inhabited South Pacific territory, Wallis and Futuna, also felt great change with a massive migration of its residents to New Caledonia and with the effects wrought by new social currents. During the 1980s, France was castigated by neighbours of its territories in the Pacific for continued colonialism, economic exploitation and the pollution created by nuclear testing. Yet French policy was often misunderstood or not fully appreciated, as different governments in Paris experimented with various solutions to problems in the Pacific territories. The various ideologies espoused and strategies deployed by the French governments, as well as by the different political parties in the territories, reveal their different objectives and concerns.

This work is based on archival material, published sources, statistical information and some interviews. Because of the regulation that French archives are not accessible for a thirty-year period, it was not possible to consult archival documents for the period after 1960; in fact, little significant unpublished material is available after the mid-1950s, and even some documents from that time (as well as from the period of the Second World War) remain classified. When more recent archival sources are opened, there will no doubt be further research to be done and new conclusions to draw. I have nevertheless had access to much useful material, much of it unpublished, in Paris, Aix-en-Provence (where the Archives d'Outre-Mer are located), Papeete, Nouméa and Port-Vila.

Several practical notes to the reader are necessary. Much of my discussion of the Franco-British condominium of the New Hebrides (Vanuatu) has been relegated to a single chapter for the sake of consolidating material on this rather odd imperial possession. Similarly, discussion of Wallis and Futuna, on which very little information is available, has also been largely consolidated in several particular passages. Some topics have been treated rather briefly, as a more thorough discussion would have necessitated the sort of lengthy monographic treatment which was not the intention of this book. To simplify nomenclature, I have used 'French Polynesia' throughout the book to refer to that territory which until the late 1950s was officially called the *Etablissements Français d'Océanie.* I have also generally used 'colonial' to describe the history of the French territories before 1946. I have generally used 'Melanesian' rather than 'Kanak' for the indigenous islanders of New Caledonia, although 'Kanak' is sometimes used here to refer specifically to the independence movement or those active in it. I have used 'Caldoche' to refer to long-term French residents of New Caledonia who have an ethnically European background. In neither case is my usage in the least intended to be derogatory. Less simply, but unavoidably, I have usually used 'Polynesian' to refer to those who consider themselves or are considered by others to be ethnically Polynesian; 'French Polynesian', just as 'New Caledonian', refers to all the residents of their respective territories regardless of their ethnic background.

Research on this project has been funded through a generous three-year grant from the Australian Research Council, and I would like to acknowledge their support with gratitude. This funding has made it possible for me to complete research in both the French islands of the South Pacific and in France. It has also provided for indispensable research assistance from, at various times, Ayling Rubin, Olivia de Bergerac, who also compiled the index, and Lola Sharon Davidson. I would like to thank all of them, as well as Julie Manley and Muriel Trouvé, who typed the manuscript. I would like to thank Air Calédonie International for helping to arrange a major research trip to the South Pacific. A number of people in Australia, France, the French Pacific territories and Vanuatu provided assistance, encouragement and hospitality, and I am grateful to all of them. John Connell read the entire manuscript, and his comments were invaluable, and other colleagues provided insights and suggestions on various topics. In particular my thanks go to Kim Munholland for his comments on the chapter on the Second World War and to Keith Woodward and Will Stober for their suggestions for the chapter on Vanuatu. Friends provided the essential support and diversion which makes research both possible and enjoyable.

ROBERT ALDRICH

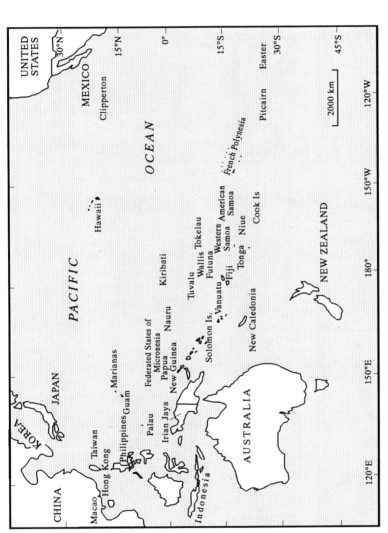

The Contemporary Pacific

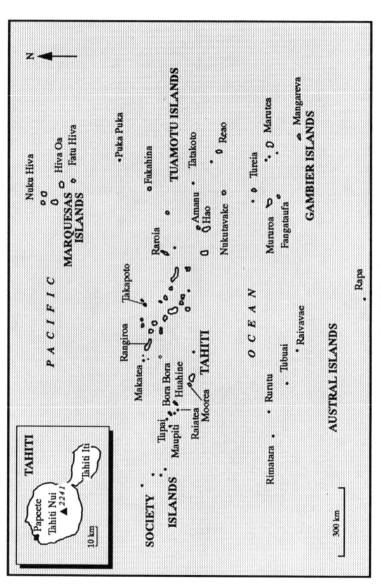

French Polynesia

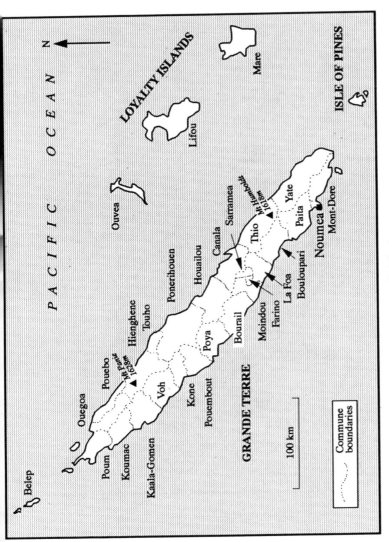

New Caledonia

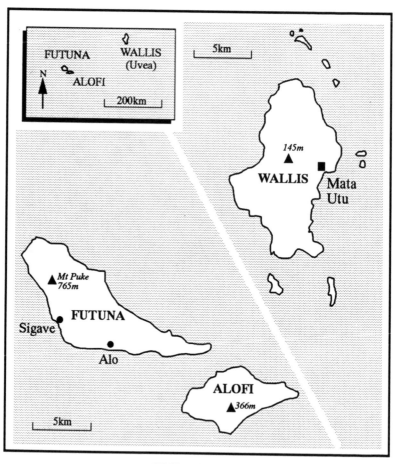

Wallis and Futuna

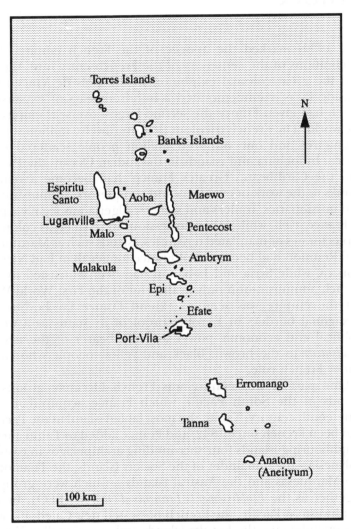

Torres Islands

N

Banks Islands

Espiritu
Santo   Aoba   Maewo
Luganville
Malo   Pentecost

Malakula   Ambrym

          Epi

          Efate
Port-Vila

                    Erromango

Tanna

          Anatom
          (Aneityum)

100 km

New Hebrides / Vanuatu

Introduction: Oceanic France

The 1930s marked the apogee of the French empire. The celebrations of the centenary of the French entry into Algeria and the great colonial exhibition in the Bois de Vincennes, outside Paris, commemorated a hundred years of expansion which had given France the second largest overseas empire in the world. The French tricolour flew over twelve million square kilometres and one hundred million people scattered over Africa, Indochina and islands in the Indian Ocean, the Pacific and the Caribbean. 'Greater France' had become a reality, thanks to the work of explorers and conquerors, administrators and missionaries, traders and settlers. Algeria was legally a part of France itself, while other possessions were ruled as colonies, protectorates or mandated territories. Islands such as Martinique and Réunion had been part of France longer than had Nice or Corsica, while Syria and Lebanon had been entrusted to the French administration only at the end of the First World War. Yet the empire was seen to extend France far beyond its hexagonal borders in Europe, proof of its status as a world political and economic power and the bearer of the *mission civilisatrice* to the brown, black and yellow people who came under French rule.[1]

One part of this empire was French Oceania, groups of islands in the South Pacific which France acquired in the nineteenth century. Tahiti, the most fabled island in the Pacific, had been French since 1842, and France added to Tahiti and its neighbouring islands four surrounding archipelagos in eastern Polynesia – the remainder of the Society Islands, the Tuamotus, the Marquesas and the Austral Islands – which were grouped together as the *Etablissements Français d'Océanie* (EFO). In the southwestern Pacific, the French possessed new Caledonia and its dependencies, the Loyalty Islands and other smaller islands, which were taken over in 1853. Between these two larger territories, the French had Wallis and Futuna, small Polynesian islands over which France established a protectorate in the 1880s. France also owned the uninhabited island of Clipperton,

off the coast of Mexico; in 1931, the very year of the great
colonial exhibition, France's claim to this rocky outpost had
been confirmed by the King of Italy's arbitration in a dispute
between France and Mexico. Finally, France had an interest in
the New Hebrides, a group of Melanesian islands north of New
Caledonia, which had become a 'condominium' jointly ruled
by France and Britain.[2]

The reasons for France's presence in the Pacific were tied to
general imperial rivalry and the scramble for colonies in the
nineteenth century and also to particular attractions the Pacific
islands held. France had been anxious to acquire an outpost in
the South Pacific, although Britain managed to take the two
largest land masses in the region, Australia (in 1788) and New
Zealand (in 1840). France nevertheless succeeded in becoming
the second major imperial power in the South Pacific. The
French Pacific possessions formed part of a chain of islands and
other outposts which encircled the globe from the Antilles to
the Mascareignes, useful commercial outposts and refuelling
stops on maritime routes. In the 1840s, when France took over
New Caledonia, Prime Minister Guizot aimed at acquiring '*points
d'appui*' (support bases) for France's sailing ships, and the
steamships which succeeded them later in the century also
needed coaling stations and sources of provisions.

Economic opportunities in the Pacific Islands were of some
consequence, even if largely indirectly. The islands pro-vided
links between the Americas and Asia and, some hoped, stepping-
stones to the coveted China market. The islands showed potential
for the production of tropical agricultural products, and efforts
were made (although not very successfully) to grow cotton,
coffee and cocoa. The copra produced in the Pacific went to
the French soap and oil industries, and France was the largest
European importer of the dried meat of coconuts in the
nineteenth century. The sea also provided resources, such as
the pearls found off the Tuamotu chain. The French extracted
minerals in the islands, especially the phosphate of Makatea, in
Polynesia, which was useful for fertilisers, and the nickel of New
Caledonia. New Caledonia contained one of the world's largest
deposits of nickel, which assumed increasing importance from
the late 1800s onwards as an alloy for steel, and the territory
also contained deposits of gold, chrome, cobalt and other
minerals. Few of the deposits, however, were known by the

French when they took possession of the islands and so cannot be seen as a reason for takeover.

Missionary activity was probably more important than economics in the French takeover, especially in Tahiti, where the influence of Protestants and a slight to French Catholic clerics provided the trigger for the French declaration of a protectorate over the realm of Queen Pomaré in the 1840s. Missionaries found in Polynesia fertile ground for converts and established virtual theocracies in a number of islands, both before and after they became part of the French empire. Missionaries were among the most ardent advocates of French expansion in the Pacific, seeing the state as a guarantor of their safety in the islands, and the French government – at least until the anti-clerical campaigns of the late nineteenth century – was willing to act as patron to the church's missions.

The French Navy also had interests in the colonies. The French Naval Division of the Pacific Ocean patrolled Oceania, paid courtesy visits to the British domains, made a yearly tour of the Catholic missions and showed the flag in an area of growing imperial competition. Navy captains and strategists in Paris worried first about the English, who took over Fiji and other islands in the South Pacific. Then from the 1880s onwards they saw the Australians as their principal rivals in Oceania, as the Australians cast an expansive eye on New Guinea and the New Hebrides. At the same time, the Germans moved into the Pacific, taking over islands in Samoa, part of New Guinea and outposts in Micronesia, and the Americans annexed eastern Samoa and the Hawaiian islands and defeated the Spanish in the Philippines; both the Germans and the Americans seemed a new menace to the French. The imperial powers coexisted uneasily through the nineteenth century, then Germany was evicted at the end of the First World War. By the 1930s, the enemy was Japan, creating its own empire and flexing economic muscle in east Asia and the Pacific basin.[3]

Lastly, French settler interests maintained the French presence in the islands; in fact, one of the characteristics which distinguished New Caledonia (and, to a much lesser extent, French Polynesia) from most other islands in the South Pacific was large-scale European settlement. One of the purposes of taking over New Caledonia in 1853 had been to set up a prison colony for criminal and political offenders, and thousands of prisoners were exiled there in the last decades of the 1800s. The 'dirty tap-water' of transportation was turned off in the 1890s, but the colony had by then attracted free settlers. Frenchmen also moved to the EFO, albeit in small numbers, and to the New Hebrides, where they came up against Anglo-Australian interests. French settlement in Oceania formed an added justification for a continued imperial presence. Promoters particularly tried to vaunt New Caledonia as a colony of settlement, the only one outside of Algeria in the French empire.

These French interests were disparate and often conflicting. They generally only allied in the face of an internal danger, such as the Melanesian insurrection which shook New Caledonia in 1878, or in the face of an external threat. Only late in the nineteenth century did an Oceanic lobby begin to bring together the various interests. Writers such as Paul Deschanel, a future President of France, championed the Pacific, arguing that the forthcoming opening of the Panama Canal would revolutionise the Pacific and that the Pacific would become the centre of the twentieth century world. Such promotion stirred up renewed interest in the island colonies and, after the end of the First World War, helped in the development of the policy of colonial development ('*mise en valeur*') which saw some of the first concerted efforts to develop the potential of the colonies and erect the infrastructure necessary for a profitable 'use' of France's distant and still poor possessions.

By the 1930s, therefore, various French interests were firmly established in the colonies of the South Pacific. The Catholic and Protestant missionaries had converted many of the islanders to Christianity, a colonial elite (in the EFO the mixed Polynesian and European *demis* and in New Caledonia the white 'Caldoches') dominated the life of the colony, and such companies as the Banque de l'Indochine, the Messageries Maritimes shipping firm and the Société le Nickel, which exploited the bulk of New Caledonia's mineral resources, had changed the economies of the islands. The native islanders, however, had been marginalised: on New Caledonia's mainland, the Melanesians had been confined to reservations which composed only 10 per cent of the land area, while the full-blooded Polynesians in the EFO still lived a traditional life separated from the world of the French or were recruited to work on European properties. However, the main source of labour came from the Asian migrants – Indians, Japanese, Chinese, Javanese, and Vietnamese – which France had recruited for the Oceanic colonies; they worked in the mines of New Caledonia and formed a class of small traders in Polynesia. The arrival of these Asians had added new ethnic groups to the population of the islands; in the 1920s Asians outnumbered the French in New Caledonia, and both that territory and EFO became pluri-ethnic societies. Few of the Asians had any political rights, however, and neither the Melanesians nor most Polynesians had the vote or political representation. Even though the white settlers elected members of consultative assemblies, the political centralism and colonial assimilationism which dominated French ideology meant that Paris kept firm control of its possessions. The exception to the pattern was Wallis and Futuna, where settlers were few, French Catholic priests held the reins of authority and islanders were otherwise little affected by the French presence.

The colonies of the South Pacific were little different from many others in the French empire – they produced pri-mary products, both agricultural and mineral, for the profit of metropolitan companies and local French residents. The military, the church, large companies, government bureaucrats and settlers represented the French presence, and the 'natives' lived in the shadow of foreign domination. The local populations had largely been 'pacified', converted and either integrated into the lower levels of the workforce or kept on the outskirts of settler society waiting for what some Europeans thought would be their eventual extinction. Yet the Pacific colonies remained a small corner of France's vast imperial domains, one unknown to many French citizens, deemed of relatively little importance by most policy-makers, and often seen in the stereotypes of 'good savages' and beautiful maidens with lax morals, or of belligerent and primitive cannibals. Even the white settlers lived with the reputation of New Caledonia as a penal colony and Tahiti, by contrast, as paradise found or lost.

1 The Second World War in the French Pacific

The Second World War brought immense economic and political change to France's colonies in Oceania. The defeat of French armies by Germany in June 1940 posed the question of the future of the colonies, and supporters of the Vichy regime and of General de Gaulle's Free French battled for control of the Pacific possessions. The severing of connections with metropolitan France endangered the economies of the colonies but tightened links between them and Australia and New Zealand, their South Pacific neighbours. The stationing of several hundred thousand Allied troops in the EFO, New Caledonia, Wallis and the New Hebrides provided a great shock to the islands. Meanwhile, soldiers from France's colonies, including Melanesians and Polynesians, fought with the French in North Africa and Europe. In 1944, the Brazzaville Conference heralded a new attitude towards the administration of the French empire. And at the conclusion of the Pacific campaign, the detonation of an atom bomb inaugurated the nuclear age which twenty years later would have great consequences for French Polynesia and thus for France's presence in the South Pacific.

THE 'RALLIEMENT' OF THE FRENCH COLONIES

The defeat of the French forces in Europe and the signing of an armistice between Marshal Pétain and the Germans in 1940 was a humiliating and unexpected outcome to the war that had begun in September 1939. De Gaulle's famous radio appeal for continued resistance on 18 June 1940 provided both a cause and a leader to whom patriots could rally. But it also divided France into those who felt that collaboration with the German victors and obedience to the Vichy government were necessary, and those who wanted to resist the occupiers inside France and to fight alongside Britain. The empire experienced this fratricidal dispute, some colonies, such as Indochina, opting for Vichy, others for de Gaulle; in fact, among the first French

1

administrators to pledge loyalty to the General were the colonial administrators Félix Eboué in Africa and Henri Sautot in the Pacific. But clashes of authority, even within the Free French movement, did not spare the Pacific territories.

The first of the Pacific territories to rally to de Gaulle was the New Hebrides. The French official with ultimate responsibility for the New Hebrides, Georges Pélicier, the Governor of New Caledonia, did not declare his choice of loyalty after the armistice and de Gaulle's message. But Henri Sautot, the French Resident Commissioner in the New Hebrides since 1933, did act. On 24 June he called a meeting, attended by some four hundred Frenchmen, at which he won support for de Gaulle's movement. Pélicier then summoned Sautot to Nouméa to account for his move, but Sautot refused to go. On 20 July Sautot organised another meeting in Port-Vila, at which only three persons out of six hundred who attended did not support the Free French. Two days later Sautot sent a telegram to de Gaulle announcing the *ralliement* of the New Hebrides. Sautot said he would no longer obey Pélicier if he did not also rally to de Gaulle. In all of this, Sautot was strongly supported, and perhaps urged on, by his British counterpart in the New Hebrides' condominium.[1]

In New Caledonia, Pélicier, an unpopular official nearing retirement, had been equivocal after the fall of France, preferring a policy of wait-and-see. The Conseil Général of the colony, however, on 24 June, unanimously voted in favour of continuing the fight against the Germans alongside the British but did not go so far as to join de Gaulle's camp. Since New Caledonia's major export, nickel, was a strategic mineral, the fate of the territory was of particular concern to the French. Most of the nickel recently exported had gone to Japan; some New Caledonians wanted to continue the trade, while others inside and outside the colony worried about the use of New Caledonian nickel for the Axis war machine.

As the government stalled, several New Caledonians independently established contact with de Gaulle. A former president of the Conseil Général, Raymond Pognon, wrote to de Gaulle and suggested setting up a Free French committee in Nouméa. Meanwhile, Michel Vergès, a *notaire*, drew up a manifesto calling for autonomy for New Caledonia. By the end of July, the plan had won the support of the Conseil Général, which also passed a motion criticising Pélicier, who had begun to promulgate Vichy laws and to censor the press and radio. No further action immediately ensued, and so the situation deteriorated in August. After a stick of dynamite exploded outside his residence, the governor became concerned about his hold on the colony. The French warship *Dumont d'Urville*, under the command of a Vichy supporter, then arrived in Nouméa from Papeete – having been unable to forestall the *ralliement* of the EFO – and stood menacingly in the harbour; opponents of Vichy planned demonstrations against the presence of the vessel. Rumours reached Australian diplomatic authorities in London that the Japanese were intent on securing their supplies of nickel. On 28 August, Pélicier resigned, and his deputy became acting governor. By now the Gaullists had massed considerable support in New Caledonia, and Pognon had received an encouraging telegram from de Gaulle.

De Gaulle suggested to the British war cabinet that Sautot be transported to Nouméa to organise forces there. On 30 August, London suggested to the Australian government that the Australian ship *HMAS Adelaide* might do the job. Canberra was less than enthusiastic and only pressure from the British brought the Australian officials round to the idea of entering the fray. Plans were made for Sautot to go from Port-Vila to Nouméa, and the Gaullists in New Caledonia were told to send out a boat to meet him, to marshal support, and to arrange for Sautot to take power. Pognon and his associates did so (although abandoning a plan to kidnap the acting governor). On 19 September Sautot arrived in Nouméa aboard the Australian ship – he had left Port-Vila on a Norwegian tanker and boarded the Australian vessel at sea – and the Australian ship faced off the *Dumont d'Urville* for several tense moments in the harbour. A small boat marked with the Cross of Lorraine came to collect Sautot, who landed to the welcome of the Gaullists. By mid-afternoon he had assumed the powers of government without hindrance or violence.[2]

The Nouméa population, according to Sautot, welcomed the *ralliement* with enthusiasm. In a letter to General de Gaulle, perhaps intended to flatter the leader of the Free French, Sautot explained: 'What can be said about the magnificent population of Nouméa, so patriotic and so vibrant in these days as it acclaimed in you the future liberator of the motherland.

With what a virile accent and patriotic faith the residents of Nouméa intoned the immortal verses of our "Marseillaise", which continually sprang to their lips in their great emotion! How can we doubt that Victory will come to such an ardent population?'[3]

In the EFO, Governor Frédéric Chastenet de Géry had issued a proclamation in June 1940, saying that 'we are all ready to make the sacrifices necessary to safeguard our liberty; we join our allies, in accord with all the other parts of the French Empire, in foreseeing the continuation of the struggle'. The statement satisfied none by its vagueness, and several committees formed to take matters into their own hands. The Comité des Français d'Océanie condemned propaganda against Vichy and Pétain and demanded 'from the authorities a solemn proclamation of loyalty to the Government of Marshal Pétain'; it denounced Communism and Freemasonry and called for all 'half-breeds [*métèques*] whether naturalised or not' to be removed from the administration. Meanwhile a group of anti-Vichy Frenchmen gathered secretly to form a Comité France Libre. The governor responded, on 24 August, with a decree disbanding all clandestine organisations and requiring all public servants to sign affirmations that they were not then members of any such organisations. This measure, coupled with Chastenet de Géry's promulgation of laws issued by the Vichy regime, convinced the Comité France Libre that the administration was far from impartial. The committee organised an informal referendum on Tahiti and Mooréa, in which 5564 voters expressed a preference for the Free French and only 18 voted for Vichy. Consequently, on 2 September members of the Comité France Libre visited Chastenet and forced him to resign as governor. They constituted themselves into a provisional government, and a telegram from London soon gave de Gaulle's recognition to the new leadership.

The Conseil Provisoire consisted of four men. Edouard Ahnne was former director of the Protestant schools in the EFO, Georges Lagarde a customs official, and Emile Martin a businessman; all had been members of the governor's Conseil Privé. The fourth member was the mayor of Papeete and a prominent businessman, Georges Bambridge. The committee which led the *ralliement* included several government officials, businessmen, doctors, and a number of Polynesians, both chiefs and private individuals (the most prominent of whom was Pouvana'a a Oopa, later the leader of an autonomy movement). Most were fairly young; many were Protestants; a number were friends of each other.

Only several weeks after rallying Tahiti, the provisional government on 20 September had to defeat an attempted coup by supporters of Vichy. The Gaullists also had to contend with the presence of a naval vessel commanded by a pro-Vichy captain in Papeete's harbour until the *Dumont d'Urville* left for Nouméa. As well, they had to decide what to do with former pro-Vichy officials. Those seen to be collaborationists were removed from office and the higher-ranking officials, including the former governor, were allowed to board a ship bound for Saigon.[4]

Wallis and Futuna was the last French Oceanic colony to join the Free French. In October 1940, Sautot sent a telegram to the French Resident in the islands, Vrignaud, informing him of the *ralliement* of New Caledonia. Both the Resident and the missionaries were opposed and sent a telegram back to Sautot: 'All the Wallisian Frenchmen gathered together declare that they want to remain loyal to the legal government of France', that is, Vichy. Sautot said he regretted the decision but added that he would continue to send provisions to Wallis and Futuna; he dispatched several other messages trying to rally the Wallisians and Futunans but in November officially recognised the pro-Vichy stance of Wallis and Futuna. He informed Paris that although he had failed to rally Wallis and Futuna, he felt that the islands would eventually join the Free French cause. In December 1940 and in January 1941 ships from Nouméa arrived with supplies for the colony; afterwards, however, Wallis and Futuna went without fresh provisions for seventeen months. Robert Charbonnier – a later French resident with no love lost for either supporters of Vichy or the clergy – reported that 'soon there was no medicine, no coal to fuel the wireless post and, even more serious for the Mission, no more bread to make the communion hosts'. Wallisians and Futunans began to concoct orange wine, used coconut oil for lack of candles and made soap from ashes and coconut. Meanwhile, Vrignaud tried to contact the Vichy colonial government in Indochina, though without success until March 1941; he then also succeeded in contacting the Vichy ambassador in Washington and received encouragement from Vichy authorities in France. Meanwhile,

Sautot continued to try to force the *ralliement* of Wallis and Futuna, suggesting that the Resident be dismissed or even that the British or Australians might send a ship to Wallis to overthrow the pro-Vichy authorities. In May 1942, a Free French warship finally arrived from Nouméa and its commander arrested Vrignaud. The new resident, Mattei, said that the decision to intervene had been taken by the Gaullist High Commissioner for the Pacific, Rear-Admiral Georges Thierry d'Argenlieu, as soon as he had found out that the Americans wanted to occupy Wallis and Futuna because of their strategic location. Since the Americans had agreed to respect the Vichy rights in Wallis and Futuna, d'Argenlieu was trying to affirm Free French control over the islands and forestall any tacit accord between Vichy and the United States. (The American troops arrived in Wallis the day after the *ralliement*, in fact.)[5]

This completed the *ralliement* of the Pacific territories to the Free French movement. The French territories' support for de Gaulle foreshadowed the later *ralliement* of other colonies and the revival of France. Governor Sautot said that the colonies in Oceania would be a bastion of France, and his proclamation of 19 September 1940 indicated the role that the overseas possessions could take in the liberation of France: 'Metropolitan France with its forty million people has been defeated, but its colonial empire of sixty million souls is intact with all its economic and military forces. It is this Empire which must save the mother country temporarily crushed under the German boot'.[6] Sautot's words echoed the general belief that France's salvation would come from a colonial base, an idea current in the war years but which would outlive the war.

The *ralliement* was partly a groundswell of popular opinion, partly the work of dedicated opponents of Vichy such as Sautot. Encouragement from the British, the intervention of the Australians, and the promise of political and economic support from the New Zealand government all played a role. The British prime minister, Winston Churchill, had promised de Gaulle that Britain would extend assistance to French colonies 'on a scale similar to that which we shall apply . . . to colonies of the British Empire', and delegated responsibility for the South Pacific French territories to Australia and New Zealand. Australia was initially hesitant to change the status quo in the region, fearing that any move which could be construed as an Australian occupation of New Caledonia would provide a precedent for Japan to occupy French Indochina and attract accusations of Australian imperialism in Oceania. Nevertheless, Canberra acceded to the British request to transport Sautot to Nouméa and to have the *Adelaide* stand by in case of an effort by the *Dumont d'Urville* to prevent his landing. Australia also proposed economic assistance to New Caledonia; the government signed a contract with the major nickel producing company in New Caledonia, the Société Le Nickel, to purchase approximately half the company's production of nickel matte – New Caledonia's most important export – and agreed to seek markets for New Caledonian coffee, timber and other products.[7] Similarly, New Zealand offered support to the Free French in the EFO. A British ship stationed in New Zealand sailed to Papeete immediately after the *ralliement* to assure the new government of British goodwill. Wellington agreed to purchase much of Tahiti's production of copra, a decision of great importance, as France had previously taken almost all of the copra produced by the EFO and lack of buyers would have plunged the Tahitian economy into chaos.[8]

Given the presence of the British in the South Seas, the distance from Vichy France and the resources of the island, the *ralliement* was not altogether surprising. But it had longer-term implications than just support for de Gaulle. For some who had joined the Free French, the new state of affairs promised a greater degree of self-control of colonial affairs than ever before possible. For the Allies, the decision of the French territories provided important bases for troops in the Pacific theatre.

The *ralliement* did not end political controversy in French Oceania, nor did it immediately silence proponents of the Vichy regime. In New Caledonia, for instance, Governor Sautot reported in January 1941 that the heads of the customs, mines and land-title offices were hostile to de Gaulle, and the following month added that most of the personnel of the Messageries Maritimes, the major shipping company in the colony, were hesitant about the *ralliement*.[9] (By contrast, the employees of the Société Le Nickel were firmly behind the Free French.[10]) Some opponents of the *ralliement*, in the Pacific and elsewhere, were suspicious of de Gaulle and his supporters – or simply doubted their chances of success – while others were sympathetic to the ideology of Vichy. The war provided an occasion for local quarrels to surface, or for personal ambitions to be advanced, as well as for ideological disputes to emerge.

New Caledonia saw great domestic problems at the outset of the *ralliement*. Governor Sautot clashed with many local figures, notably a wealthy lawyer and prominent Gaullist named Michel Vergès. The two men jockeyed for influence in the colony; as Sautot gained the upper hand, Vergès became increasingly embittered and led the governor's opponents. Rumours and charges circulated in Nouméa, made worse by disagreements between the governor and colonists on such issues as the formation of a battalion of soldiers for overseas fighting and fears that the Vichy government would try to reestablish control over New Caledonia. Indications that the United States wanted to station troops in the islands made a resolution of the conflict necessary, and in early 1941 de Gaulle sent Governor-General Richard Brunot to Nouméa. He, his assistants and Vergès all considered Sautot too easy-going (and perhaps too physically unwell) for his job; Sautot, for his part, resented this interference from an outsider. Brunot, whom some charged with behaving as a proconsul, failed to set matters right and left New Caledonia for Tahiti. He was replaced as de Gaulle's emissary by Rear-Admiral Georges d'Argenlieu.[11]

D'Argenlieu was a career navy officer who had distinguished himself in the First World War, then abandoned his career to enter a Carmelite monastery in 1920; he had only left the contemplative life to join de Gaulle's Free French. De Gaulle appointed him French High Commissioner of the Pacific with responsibility for all France's colonies. D'Argenlieu was, therefore, Sautot's nominal superior. The governor reacted angrily to the appointment, which he saw as a direct challenge to his own authority. He wrote to de Gaulle that the High Commissioner might be tempted to meddle in local politics, and, in particular, that it would be impossible for him to preside over both New Caledonia and the EFO – communications and transport between the two colonies were difficult, and 'whether you like it or not, I declare that it is impossible to administer a colonial territory exclusively through telegrams'.[12] Sautot's opponents, however, were happy to see d'Argenlieu and he initially received a warm welcome in the colony.

However, d'Argenlieu quickly became unpopular, not so much because of his actions as High Commissioner and French military commander as for his personality. He was as arrogant and humourless as Sautot was jovial and popular; one writer described d'Argenlieu as a 'caricature' of de Gaulle. He showed little interest in New Caledonia or in cooperation with local politicians and signed a decree restricting civil liberties so severely that magistrates refused to enforce it. He snubbed the American commander on his arrival to establish a base in Nouméa, requisitioned supplies, including houses and automobiles, in authoritarian fashion and lived luxuriously. He provoked the hostility of settlers in New Caledonia, whom he thought had too large a voice in local politics. D'Argenlieu transferred over a million dollars in local currency to the Free French headquarters in London, which created resentment in Nouméa. Yet d'Argenlieu obviously had the ear of de Gaulle.

Five months after d'Argenlieu's arrival in Nouméa, on 29 April, de Gaulle recalled Sautot to London, almost certainly on the advice of the High Commissioner. Sautot at first agreed, then, prompted partly by the unwillingness of his associates to have New Caledonia left in the hands of d'Argenlieu and stimulated by public demonstrations in his favour, asked de Gaulle to rescind the order recalling him. On 3 May, a doctor representing a hastily organised 'New Caledonia committee' visited d'Argenlieu and asked *him* to leave the colony. Two days later d'Argenlieu and Sautot both attended a morning church service. In mid-afternoon, the High Commissioner said that he was still waiting for de Gaulle's answer concerning Sautot's request to remain in Nouméa. Several hours later he made a radio broadcast asking for confidence in de Gaulle, finishing with the words 'Vive de Gaulle! Vive Sautot!' Meanwhile, policemen, on d'Argenlieu's orders, arrived at the governor's residence to arrest Sautot. Several of his associates (and even several of his opponents, including Pognon) had already been arrested. Sautot was soon put aboard a ship out of New Caledonia.

D'Argenlieu's action touched off great opposition in New Caledonia, and a general strike was called in Nouméa. On a visit to a country settlement, d'Argenlieu was harassed and taken hostage (or at least temporarily locked up) by a group of opponents. He eventually backed down and released the arrested men, although Sautot himself would not return to New

Caledonia until after the war. But the episode demonstrated D'Argenlieu's unpopularity, and de Gaulle transferred him to Tahiti. Because of his actions in New Caledonia, and because of his constant bickering with the commander of the American troops in Nouméa, de Gaulle's supporters were happy to see the last of d'Argenlieu. Many saw his sojourn in New Caledonia as another example of France's continued high-handed treatment of the colony and its residents.[13]

The political quarrels in New Caledonia found a parallel in Tahiti. In the EFO, the first Free French governor was Edmond Mansard, who was put into power by supporters of de Gaulle. Recently arrived in Tahiti, Mansard was seen as a leader able to win support from all factions in the politically fragmented Tahitian elite and, as military chief, able to assure the support of the armed forces. Less than a week after assuming office, however, Mansard called in his *chef de cabinet*, the Gaullist Emile de Curton, and admitted having been involved in a plot with several other politicians to pursue a less openly anti-Vichy line and limit the power of the Gaullists. The 'coup' of 18 September 1940 was thus averted by Mansard's own revelation of the plot. Mansard resigned, and de Curton replaced him as governor. De Curton was an ambitious medical doctor and former administrator of the Leeward islands. He immediately dismissed unfriendly civil servants, began mass arrests of his personal and political opponents, and deported three prominent Vichy supporters to the small island of Maupiti – where they raised a fleur-de-lys flag and a banner proclaiming 'Vive le Roi': their Pétainist-royalist adventure lasted until they were returned to Papeete for trial several months later.

Meanwhile, the secretary-general of the de Curton government resigned, denouncing de Curton and declaring loyalty to Pétain; brandishing a pistol, he fled his office and asked for refuge in the British consulate. The British in Tahiti had already been at the centre of conflict when a group of pro-Gaullist Englishmen in Papeete stormed the British consulate, accusing the consul of Pétainist sympathies; London soon replaced him with a more committed supporter of the *ralliement*. These events alarmed de Gaulle, who sent Governor-General Brunot to Tahiti to investigate. Brunot, suspicious and unfamiliar with the Tahitian situation, soon came into conflict with de Curton on questions of policy and authority. He arrested de

Curton and various other politicians and quarrelled with the English consul. De Gaulle himself simply said that 'Brunot clashed, often violently, with bureaucrats who – not without the appearance of reason – imputed to him the intention of establishing himself and his friends in their place. Papeete was the theatre of tragi-comic incidents'.[14]

With the situation still in chaos, de Gaulle sent in yet another representative, Admiral d'Argenlieu, fresh from his controversial mission to New Caledonia. D'Argenlieu was welcomed in Tahiti. He forced both Brunot and de Curton to leave the colony and appointed a new governor, Georges Orselli, a *polytechnicien* and army officer. Orselli's tenure, from October 1941 to December 1945, put an end to a year of political and personal quarrels which had affected Tahiti and finally secured the long-term and unreserved loyalty of the colony to de Gaulle.[15]

The dramas in Tahiti and New Caledonia were tempests in a teapot by comparison with global events in 1940–42. The conflicts reflected the internecine quarrels between supporters of de Gaulle and Pétain in metropolitan France and elsewhere in the empire.[16] They testified, as well, to the personal, political and ideological stakes that were at issue even in small overseas possessions at the beginning of the Second World War and the factionalism which had developed in colonial society. The fall of France and the *ralliement* provided occasions for the settling of disputes, the advancing of careers and the promotion of opinions. The war years also provided an incubator for the post-war political élite. If politicians such as Brunot, de Curton and d'Argenlieu would not subsequently play a role in the politics of French Oceania, men like Bambridge and Pouvana'a dominated politics in Tahiti in the years to come.

De Gaulle's sending of special missions to Oceania, or at least his choice of representatives, was uncharacteristically maladroit, although his probable motive was to assert his own authority over local interests, to coordinate French action in the Pacific, and to put trusted administrators in power just when the Pacific war was beginning. Yet it was also a signal that the colonies, even in the *ralliement*, could not hope for free rein in their activities and that the Free French movement of the General would give little greater autonomy than had pre-war governments.

THE WAR YEARS

After the initial shock of defeat, the disputes between various factions in the colonies and the *ralliement* to de Gaulle, the administrations and residents of the French Pacific territories were faced with the realities of a war which, although initially fought far from their shores, had direct effects on their lives. The Japanese attack on Pearl Harbor and the opening of a battle theatre in the Pacific brought the war home in a frightening manner, but yet before December 1941, the colonists felt the impact of the Second World War. Several thousand men from the islands, including many Polynesians and Melanesians, left Oceania to fight in Europe and North Africa. In the islands themselves, scarcities of some products, fear of attack and, particularly, the arrival of thousands of Allied forces, changed the sleepy life of the colonies. Somewhat paradoxically, a war which caused such immense privations and sufferings elsewhere in the world brought an influx of foreigners, capital and new commodities into the French Pacific colonies. France's Oceanic outposts escaped direct hostilities, and the standard of living in the islands actually rose during the war years.[17]

Despite periodic crises, the war years settled into something of a routine. The correspondence of the governor of the EFO in 1943, for instance, reveals that a year in the life of the chief administrator was in large measure devoted to mundane tasks – considering requests for travel, granting licences for the sale of alcohol and the opening of businesses, deciding on import duties, arbitrating disputes on land titles and questions of inheritance, presiding over meetings and making inspection tours. Sometimes these tasks were broken up by theatrical or musical *soirées*, frequently organised to raise money for the Free French, or, as one letter from the governor noted, by the opening of the first cinema in Papeete. Some problems which the government had to face were not new to the war period. The head of the territory's administration, for example, referred to the isolation of the outer islands of the EFO and the lack of shipping links with them; already before the war, he said somewhat plaintively, this problem 'preoccupied the authorities who, however, were not able to find a solution to it'. He reported on another continuing problem, education in the colony; schooling was 'particularly neglected in certain remote islands . . . The teachers assigned to these islands generally show little hurry to go to their posts and the results obtained by the teachers are most often null or negligible'. But the war had certainly aggravated other problems, such as transportation and communications with the world outside Polynesia. The governor remarked that 'present circumstances have made food provisioning in the colony precarious', a concern which the government made efforts to address with 'administration plantations' and new crops; he wrote to thank the British consul and New Zealand authorities for food aid contributed to the EFO.[18] The governor had to perform duties connected directly with the war. In 1943, he awarded the Medal of the French Resistance to two dozen citizens who had participated in the *ralliement*; he acknowledged the war propaganda films which had been sent from Australia for showing in the new cinema; he wrote regularly to the representative of the Free French in New York to request supplies for the colony; and he decided that only twenty American soldiers per week would be allowed to come to Papeete from Bora-Bora for their recreational leave. Issues of 'foreign affairs' also appeared on his agenda. For example, the governor authorised the recruitment of eighty new workers (and the renewal of contracts for a similar number) from the New Zealand colony of the Cook Islands for the phosphate mines at Makatéa. He had to attend to the trial of a group of Australian sailors who had been arrested for illegally sailing their boat within the waters of the EFO. The issue of foreigners within the colony occasionally came to his attention, as when he decided to permit the Chinese in Tahiti, 'numerous and very rich', to collect donations for Chiang Kai-shek; the governor did worry, however, about the capital which would thereby leave the colony.[19]

In New Caledonia, the governor's schedule included a range of activities similar to those of his counterpart in the EFO. But he also worried about the high cost of living in New Caledonia, 'especially since local merchants must supply themselves almost exclusively from Australia'. The search for markets for New Caledonia's exports was a great preoccupation in the midst of the economic dislocations of the war. The governor wrote the delegate of the Free French in the United States in 1941 to ask if he could investigate the possibilities for sales there. (In the same month the most prominent of New Caledonian mineowners, Henri Lafleur, went to Sydney to study the possibility of chrome exports to Australia.) Yet lack of ships and high costs hindered a revival of trade. By 1942 supplies of certain goods were not always easy to procure in New Caledonia, and the governor wrote to his representative in Sydney asking for such products as automobile tyres, medicine, coffee and cloth. Meanwhile nickel production stagnated, which the authorities blamed on a combination of scarcity of materials, the 'incompetence of management' and the 'lack of goodwill of the workers'.[20]

In the early 1940s, the colony seemed to be in a rather bad way, even with (and partly because of) the arrival of the American troops. Indeed, the surface prosperity brought by American dollars masked political and economic distress. A long report on the political, economic and administrative affairs of New Caledonia was essentially a list of grievances. The report complained about the conflict between Sautot and d'Argenlieu and weak administration in general. This, it said, was extremely dangerous because of the forces arrayed against the powers of the colonial administration. The writer, the secretary-general of the colony, signalled three forces of consequence. The first was large local business, which 'is trying to recover the preeminence which it enjoyed previously, and which must at all costs be avoided, as it was this de facto domination [of the colony] by big business which always hindered the organisation in the colony of a rational economy, since such an economy was absolutely contrary to their business interests'. The second group of which the government must beware was 'autonomist elements, which are trying to gain influence in the hopes of constituting a sort of theoretically independent government, but one which in practice is under American control. This with the idea that the American Government will undertake for the colony an effort at development which the French have not been able to provide (public works projects such as roadways, irrigation, the construction of schools and professional training institutions, the organisation of tourism, etc.)'. The third menace was the 'American command, which is occupying our docks and our quays and our houses, which illegally recruits natives, hides the Annamites and Tonkinese who have escaped and pays excessive salaries to the persons it hires; in short, which is practically disorganising the whole economy'. These forces, and the destabilisation they threatened, could only be countered by a strong French government which addressed the question of who really was in command in New Caledonia.[21]

Such an administration would have to solve multiple economic and administrative problems, the report continued. The American presence had tempted many New Caledonians to abandon their usual work to take employment with the foreign army; 'It is necessary that measures of requisition be taken to get them to return to more essential work'. Furthermore, there was inflation, since 'the money distributed by the American troops piles up without the possibility of being used'. The bureaucracy also received criticism. Some public servants, like New Caledonians in the private sector, had sought lucrative work with the Americans. Others 'generally lack the most elementary skills'. The bureaucrats 'are badly paid and held in disrepute'. Furthermore, 'officers for a certain while now have had the habit of deciding which orders they should accept and which they can ignore'.[22]

The government in New Caledonia was concerned about relations with foreigners during the war years. Governor Sautot wrote to de Gaulle's headquarters in 1940 that it was necessary to maintain good relations with Japan in order to export New Caledonia's nickel. Relations with Australia (and, to a lesser extent, New Zealand), were crucial, since many of New Caledonia's supplies came from these countries. The war meant that direct and closer relations between New Caledonia and its neighbours became necessary. Relations between New Caledonia and Australia had previously gone via London and Paris, but in 1941 the governor considered the possibility of naming a representative of New Caledonia in Australia. Sautot thought, however, that this move had a distinct disadvantage: 'I see in it a danger for the future, which is the risk of indirectly detaching – through a loosening of sentimental links – New Caledonia from the metropole by giving it a character of independence *vis-à-vis* Australia through the nomination of a special representative different from the legal representative of France'.[23]

The war, in short, was stirring up the French Pacific, making the colonial administration aware of its shortcomings and the real or perceived dangers of both particular interest groups inside the colonies and of foreign powers. In the worst possible scenario, foreigners might even collude with disaffected locals to challenge French mastery. The pro-Vichy factions could well be defeated, and the foreign residents of the colonies kept in check – denied citizenship or political rights, or, in the case of the Japanese in New Caledonia, deported after the start of the Pacific war. But the closer ties between the colonies and Australia and New Zealand, and even more significantly, the impact of the American presence, loomed larger as a menace to French supremacy. The American presence, in fact, appeared as the prime cause of change, for better or worse.

ALLIED TROOPS IN THE FRENCH PACIFIC

Military defences in the French islands were minimal at the outbreak of war. Tahiti had only two machine guns and five coastal cannon; New Caledonia had one mobile machine gun available. In Tahiti, the government was able to round up only three hundred soldiers 'of very dubious fighting quality'. In 1939 and 1940, however, Oceania seemed safe from the fighting in Europe, though Japanese incursions in Asia worried French authorities in the South Pacific. The Japanese attack on Pearl Harbor, Hawaii, in December 1941 began the Pacific war. Inhabitants of the French territories, as well as their neighbours, were much more worried about Japanese invasion and occupation of the islands.[24] New Caledonia was a potential target of interest with its deposits of nickel, large land area and proximity to Australia. Australians feared that if New Caledonia fell to the Japanese, it might become a launching pad for an invasion of Australia itself,[25] and the Allies were determined to keep New Caledonia out of the hands of Japanese forces as they expanded in the Pacific and Southeast Asia.[26] Small contingents of Australian and New Zealand soldiers arrived in New Caledonia, but it was clear that neither they nor the French forces there would be able to resist a Japanese onslaught. The United States offered to send troops to the French colonies; this would defend the islands but also give the Allies a base for their Pacific offensive.

In January 1942 a contingent of American soldiers and sailors, Force 6614 or the 'Poppy Force', left New York. The fleet – their final destination was not at first revealed – sailed through the Panama Canal on 31 January and called at Bora-Bora on 17 February to leave 3900 soldiers and 500 sailors whose mission was to establish a refuelling base for flights from the United States to New Zealand. The fleet continued to Melbourne. Meanwhile, Australian, American and New Zealand planes carried out reconnaissance missions throughout the South Pacific, and Canberra warned Washington about the Japanese advance in the Bismarck Archipelago and the New Guinea mainland. On 12 March, the American fleet steamed into Nouméa, preceded by its commander, Major-General A.M. Patch, who had arrived by airplane. Approximately 16 000 GIs disembarked, including the 51st Brigade, two infantry regiments, three artillery battalions, two coastal artilleries, two aviation battalions, a medical regiment and three hospital units, and assorted other communications specialists, staff personnel and military police. The Americal Division – the name formed from 'America' and 'Caledonia' – remained in New Caledonia until the end of the war under the command of Patch, himself under the orders of Vice-Admiral R.L. Gormley, commander of the South Pacific Area, and later Admiral Halsey. From 1942 until 1944, Nouméa served as a forward base in the Pacific campaign, one of the most important Allied outposts in the Pacific. Approximately 22 000 soldiers and other military personnel were permanently stationed in New Caledonia; between half a million and a million GIs passed through on their way to other destinations, for temporary postings or for treatment in the American hospitals there.[27]

Elsewhere in the French territories, 4300 American military personnel were stationed in Bora-Bora and 2600 marines on the island of Wallis; at Port-Vila, on the principal New Hebrides island of Efaté, were stationed 2600 soldiers and 1200 sailors and marines, and on the northern island of Espiritu Santo, 500 men.[28] On 1 August 1942, to take a representative date, over 35 000 American troops were present in France's Oceanic colonies and the New Hebrides condominium. Their stated purposes were to protect these territories from Japanese invasion and to prosecute the war against the Japanese in the Coral Sea.

The stationing of foreign troops, particularly in such large numbers, in islands under French sovereignty produced various clashes of authority, especially in New Caledonia. Admiral d'Argenlieu was concerned that French military commanders had no control over the thousands of foreign troops; he also felt that Governor Sautot co-operated rather too closely with the Americans. The Admiral even claimed that the Americans had conspired to support Sautot and promoted demonstrations in Nouméa.[29] De Gaulle, who relied on d'Argenlieu for his information, agreed that all had been well in the colony until the arrival of the Americans 'gave the turbulent elements in this colony the impression that a game could be played with the foreigner, and unfortunately the American authorities did nothing to cut short this game'.[30] Washington, however, continually assured de Gaulle that it respected French sovereignty and had no designs on the colony.[31]

Nevertheless, French authorities continued to maintain a certain distance from – and display suspicions about – the Americans. Several officials considered the US forces a veritable army of occupation. For example, the governor of New Caledonia telegraphed the official in charge of colonies at the Free French headquarters in 1943: 'Instead of doing something to reduce the inconveniences of stationing around 100 000 men in New Caledonia, the American command behaves as if it were in a conquered country'. He listed a catalogue of complaints against the Americans and concluded that 'the least positive result of all this is an almost unanimous anti-American movement on the part of the population, which is, nevertheless, corrupted by dollars. But the Americans are collaborating with a small minority [of the population], by definition in opposition, and that is the danger in a country as difficult as New Caledonia'.[32] The next year, now in retirement, Governor Laigret repeated his impressions in a report to the Commissioner for the Colonies in Algiers; the major problem facing New Caledonia was the Americans: 'New Caledonia is undergoing a veritable occupation, the disagreeable nature of which is unfortunately reinforced by the attitude of the Allied command, which is often – not to say always – uncomprehending'. He also repeated that the cordial reception given the Americans had now turned into a 'fierce hatred of the Allies'.[33] Some outside observers confirmed that the American presence seemed little short of an occupation.[34]

The presence of large numbers of Americans was obviously not without consequences. The sheer numbers meant that American troops in Wallis sometimes equalled the local population, and Americans totalled about a third of the ordinary population on the Grande Terre of New Caledonia. The Americans first pitched tents along the beaches, then constructed Quonset huts to barrack men and house operations. By the time the Americans were fully installed in Nouméa, according to the governor, 'There is nowhere in the city that is not occupied by the American barracks, complete with cement basements and all possible comforts'.[35] The US command also requisitioned buildings in rural towns. The vast material offloaded from American ships was equally impressive. 'The [New] Caledonians who witnessed these operations had the feeling of finding themselves in a new world: they were flabbergasted by these unknown machines which seemed enormous to them, and especially by the strange vehicles, the "jeeps" that were also called "peeps" [*sic*] (chicks), one of which, to the stupefaction of curious on-lookers, casually climbed the stairway of the hospital'.[36] Whole new neighbourhoods of American military settlement grew up in Nouméa; some of them, curiously, still bear such names as Motor Pool and Receiving.

The American presence injected a large amount of money into the local economies; the Banque de l'Indochine in New Caledonia handled some $20 million in US banknotes during the Americans' stay. The GIs were well paid and had few ways of spending their money in New Caledonia except for food and drink – in such establishments as 'Le Jus de fruit du soldat' and 'Le Sandwich du soldat' in Nouméa – souvenirs and prostitutes. Local shopkeepers did well, and for many restaurateurs and bar-owners the American invasion was a gold mine. Soldiers paid local people to perform various tasks for them, especially to launder their clothes, sometimes at the inflated cost of a dollar a shirt. The Americal Division officially employed a number of New Caledonians, both French and Melanesian, to unload supplies and help in construction projects. Wherever they went, the Americans constructed an aerodrome; the one outside Nouméa, Tontouta, later became the territory's principal airport, and the one on Bora-Bora was the only airport in the EFO. The Americans also constructed new roads, and some of their buildings remained in use long after their departure. (The old American headquarters in Nouméa continues to house the South Pacific Commission.) The Americans provided medical care to the local populations, and many of the products of American consumerism found their way into local hands. The

Americans purchased supplies, especially agricultural products, from local growers, and the Army even became an entrepreneur. In New Caledonia the Army by 1944 planted a total of 521 acres, producing over 229 tons of vegetables for American troops; on these farms, the techniques, including artificial fertiliser and machinery supplied by the American army, were generally much more sophisticated and on a larger scale than those available elsewhere in the islands.[37]

The story was much the same in other parts of the French Pacific. On Efaté, in the New Hebrides, the Americans built a landing base and a village of Quonset huts. By 1944, 100 000 Americans had lodged there. In the Segond Canal of Santo, in 1943 and 1944, an average of 100–150 ships moored each day. (One, however, the *President Coolidge*, sank in October 1942 when it hit a mine.) The Americans built an airstrip and installed electricity, running water and telephones in their camps on Santo, established a 'rest and recreation' base, and opened fifty-four cinemas and thirty restaurants. Vietnamese labourers, as well as 10 000 Melanesians, were hired by the Americans. With salaries of between $350 and $400 a month for an American air force major in the New Hebrides, the money available for spending was great.[38]

In French Polynesia, the Americans who unloaded several tons of material seemed to be bringing manna. Having been cut off from French supplies and finding difficulty obtaining alternative sources of foodstuffs and manufactured products, the residents of Bora-Bora came under the spell of the GIs. As one contemporary testified:

The population is happy to be able to obtain provisions at last: finally there is sugar, milk, etc. – and the cinema. The soldiers brought barrels of candy which they distributed to the children. The local people made souvenirs and the money flooded in . . . . They taught the Tahitians how to distill fruit juice, and the alcohol led to fights. They gave away so much food that people fed their pigs on it. Some was left in the Protestant church because they thought thieves would not dare take it from a sacred place. The wasting of goods was continual: because several cartons of milk were torn, a whole stock of milk was thrown into the ocean. Everyone knew that the American presence was only temporary, so the Tahitians had a good time with all the possibilities offered to them. When the Americans left, no one really minded, for they had hardly become richer. The American presence was of profit mostly to traders and outside merchants. When the last American left the island, what did the residents of Bora-Bora think? They simply said: 'It's all over . . . it was like a dream'.[39]

The Americans employed Polynesians to work on their base and also to perform domestic services for them. The islanders, in return, bought food which they used for their own consumption or sold on the black market of Papeete. Francis Sanford, the Polynesian who served as official liaison between the Americans and the French administration on Bora-Bora, confirmed that legitimate and clandestine trade flourished – even his assistants hid bottles of whisky in petrol barrels sent to the island. The American presence, according to Sanford, 'was a source of unbelievable earnings . . . Thanks to this influx of money, all of Polynesia would live off Bora-Bora for three years. The dollars allowed people to buy rice, flour, and other basic foodstuffs'. These were years of 'abundance'.[40]

The arrival of the Americans in Wallis, according to Robert Charbonnier, 'brought an era of fantastic, marvellous, fabulous, incredible prosperity to the stunned Wallisians'. The Americans opened a cinema and gave the Wallisians free admission, sending trucks around the island to collect them for the screenings. The islanders made money selling handicrafts to the GIs, as well as moonshine liquor and Wallisian pearls of low quality or even fake pearls, boiled fish eyes sneaked into oysters. The Wallisians used their dollars to buy corned beef, lace or perfumed soaps 'which the *coquettes* used for a single ablution, as abandoning a cake of soap almost unused was the height of distinction and good manners'. The Wallisians refused to believe that the Americans would ever leave and that the supplies of dollars would stop; they had diminished their farming activities in the wake of the American largesse.[41]

The wartime presence of Americans created certain problems. Confrontations with local populations occurred. In one incident in the New Hebrides, a group of American soldiers ransacked a chapel on Ambrym, and only the American offer to provide the chapel with new liturgical utensils and vestments smoothed over the resentment. Some observers charged that the army was corrupt, and that everything was for sale; and it was not just in Tahiti that black markets in alcohol, cigarettes and petrol flourished.[42] Liaisons between soldiers and local women also flourished, although the Catholic Vicar Apostolic of New Caledonia forbade inter-racial marriages.[43] Several years after the war, a journalist remarked that 'the land is peppered o'er [*sic*] with half-caste offspring of overseas servicemen'.[44] This was clearly an exaggeration, but one observer estimated that the American soldiers left eighty illegitimate children in Bora-Bora.[45] (In Wallis, however, the Catholic mission kept close watch over local girls; only ten or so half-caste children remained after the Americans left.[46]) The six hundred horses imported by Americans into New Caledonia brought with them a tick, which rapidly spread to the cattle of the colony.[47] In Wallis, a rumour that a local merchant reserved goods for the Catholic Missions angered both soldiers and natives, and another rumour circulated that the missionaries took half of the Wallisians' salaries as tribute. A cross was stolen from a hilltop, and soldiers used the statue of a saint for target practice. An American soldier ('from a segregationist state') killed a young Wallisian in 1942; the following year another Wallisian was shot as he tried to steal goods from an American storehouse; a third died in an accident in 1944.[48] In Bora-Bora, an American soldier killed a Polynesian who had discovered him in his wife's bed; the GI received a death sentence, but the punishment was commuted to his being sent to the battlefront in the Solomon Islands.[49] The governor of New Caledonia reported that four American soldiers had kidnapped a local woman. He also complained that the American command tried to censor radio programmes and that their 'secret service' spied on the New Caledonian population.[50]

Such confrontations and misadventures were probably unavoidable – they were the annoying and sometimes tragic effects of the presence of foreign men, the war situation and ethnic and national differences. But other matters were of more long-lasting concern. One was the effect of the American presence on the Melanesian and Polynesian populations who were exposed to new attitudes, paid employment and a different way of life during the war years.[51] The other concern was possible American interest in remaining in the colony after the end of the war, or even in trying to supplant France as the administering power or to promote New Caledonian separatism. This was particularly true in New Caledonia, where Governor Laigret claimed that the American presence had buttressed autonomist sentiments; among the political elite, 'the most autonomist of them would now agree to swap French control for that of the United States'. Others were interested in some official affiliation with the United States. Laigret played down New Caledonians' sympathy for the Americans, but he did think the Americans were not without designs on the colony. The examples of American heavy-handedness which he reported to Algiers

> make one think that the Americans have not come to New Caledonia solely to fight the war, but that if they came for other reasons, they have here and now lost their psychological battle, because, despite the influx of dollars, there is no population which hates the Americans as much as the [New] Caledonians.[52]

Notwithstanding what Laigret considered their lack of support – which other observers and later events contradict[53] – 'Undoubtedly, these territories interest them [the Americans] both as an advanced base in the Pacific and for their mining wealth. And I am among those who believe that the Americans will not voluntarily leave such territories where they are manifestly installed with the intention of not staying just for the period of the war'.[54] Similarly, the commander of a French infantry unit reported in 1943 that 'the American press is openly discussing the United States taking over from the colonial powers of the Pacific; the name of New Caledonia is mentioned. American officers of whatever rank who become talkative (generally after drinking) say that after the war, their country will establish itself here, as well as in the other European colonies of the Pacific'.[55] Such reports testify to French uncertainty, suspicion and perhaps jealousy of the US might. Any plans for an American takeover of the Pacific colonies remain unproved, and the American forces evacuated New Caledonia, Bora-Bora, Wallis and their bases in the New Hebrides more or less on schedule.

But the very departure of the Americans also created problems. The American base in Nouméa declined in importance from mid-1944, after Allied victories in the Pacific campaign, but the American presence remained; the US Army did not finally evacuate Bora-Bora until June 1946 nor did they return control of the Tontouta air base to the French in New Caledonia until January 1947. The departure of the forces – 12 000 in one month alone – was a serious economic blow, and one journalist reported in 1946 that 'prices of all local commodities have fallen astronomically'.[56] Unemployment rose with the discharge of all those hired by the Americans. Although some American equipment was left behind, much of the material was destroyed. American manufacturers of tractors and jeeps objected to selling or giving the equipment to local people, fearing that this would hurt future sales in the South Pacific; the French, likewise, thought that gifts or sales of American equipment would disadvantage French producers. In an ironic end to the American presence, many tons of material were simply thrown into the ocean. Soldiers were told to jump out of moving vehicles, leaving the motors running, so that they would plunge into the sea. One spot in the New Hebrides, Million Dollar Point, got its name because of the volume of material dumped there. This short-sighted policy deprived local populations of much needed machinery and represented a massive waste of money.

In one incident connected with the end of the war, American evacuation led to a revolt in Wallis. Although most American soldiers left the island in 1944, twelve remained in 1946. Rumours had circulated that the United States was interested in retaining control of the French territory. According to the bishop of the island, Mgr. Poncet, the American governor in Samoa remarked to him, 'Don't you think it would be good if Wallis, Samoa and Funafuti [in the Ellice Islands, now Tuvalu] were under the same flag?', although this may have only been after-dinner conversation. On 25 March 1946, a number of Wallisians marched on the house of the new French Resident, Robert Charbonnier, and asked for American annexation of the island and the departure of the French; they were led by an American captain, whom Charbonnier calls 'Z' but whom Poncet identifies as one Zinchek. Charbonnier says that 'knowing full well the great imprint left here by the allied occupation, there was no reason to be particularly surprised that the announcement of their [the American] departure would provoke an expression of regret or anger'. The Resident, faced with the demonstrators, contacted the Wallisian king, who said he knew nothing of the affair. The Wallisians maintained their siege of the Residence, 'Z' brandished a pistol and again repeated that Wallis wanted to become American, to which Charbonnier replied that those who wanted to be American could leave the island with 'Z'. The Resident agreed, however, to meet with several of the Wallisian leaders, if 'Z' would withdraw. He did withdraw as far as the gate to the compound, and Charbonnier met with eleven Wallisians. He then called 'Z' (without his pistol), the king and the king's chancellor into the Residence and demanded to know why 'Z' had fomented a revolt; the American answered, 'I do not have to render any account to you. As the "Commander of Wallis" I have taken the measures I thought necessary for the Revolution'. 'Z' asked for a plebiscite to be held and threatened to raise the American flag, although he promised to transport Charbonnier wherever he wished to go if he agreed to leave the island. Charbonnier threatened to contact Paris immediately – although he later admitted this was technologically impossible to do. Charbonnier and 'Z' then talked privately and the captain apologised for his action; Charbonnier led 'Z' out of the Residence and forced the American to shake hands with him publicly.

Charbonnier, who thought most of the Wallisians were indeed pro-American, continued to manoeuvre through the night. He went to see Bishop Poncet, whose servant told Charbonnier that the prelate was sleeping and could not be disturbed. Charbonnier insisted, argued with the bishop and demanded that he issue a proclamation marshalling the Wallisians to the French. Charbonnier also sent the king to rally chiefs in a camp located next to the American military base. The following day, 26 March, hundreds of Wallisians gathered, the king affirmed his loyalty to the French (but faced calls for his abdication) and the bishop proposed a plebiscite. On 28 March, the bishop finally declared his loyalty to the French, the king reestablished his authority, and 'Z's deputy told Charbonnier that the American captain had been recalled to Pago-Pago. Tensions remained high for the following two days, and 'Z' kept close contact with a friend and ally, who was the representative in Wallis of the Australian trading company Burns Philp. On 30 March, 'Z' left Wallis on an American ship. One rebel chief, Manuka, however, remained intractable and spread word that 'Z' had simply gone to Samoa to discuss an American annexation of Wallis. Finally, the other American soldiers were evacuated on 9 April, and they presented Charbonnier with a farewell gift of a gun case of cartridges – knowing that the Resident had only an 1886 pistol with three cartridges. At this time, the French High Commissioner in Nouméa, who had titular authority over Wallis and whom Charbonnier had notified, did nothing except ask for clarification of the Resident's message about the rebellion. Charbonnier commented:

> I felt with infinite sadness that, over there, they did not take the situation seriously, that they thought I was exaggerating and that in any case, the tranquillity of their offices had been seriously troubled by our grotesque events [thought to be] induced if not amplified by 'island psychosis', a diagnosis which had often been made in the past when a poor Resident, overcome with difficulties, had alerted his superior authority! And this time calling into question our powerful allies as well! That was probably just too much for them!

The situation deteriorated further with a lack of supplies and a cyclone in Wallis: 'What a situation: Wallisians in revolt, the Americans gone, the island isolated, the Mission discouraged, trade discontinued, dearth threatening, Nouméa silent'.

No ship arrived until 20 September; Charbonnier, a medical doctor, hurried to finish a Caesarian operation to meet it – only to find an American inspector of Marist missions disembarking. His presence prompted several Wallisians to repeat their calls for American annexation, but the ship's commander radioed Nouméa about the seriousness of the situation. In mid-October a French navy ship finally arrived, order was immediately restored, and an exhausted Charbonnier was evacuated to Papeete.[57]

THE EFFECTS OF THE AMERICAN PRESENCE

'Even the early missionaries provoked no such cultural and economic changes as those that have been aroused by the United States troops', wrote a contemporary observer.[58] The Americans, despite destruction of much of their material, left behind airstrips, new roads, buildings, and an arsenal of tractors, jeeps and other equipment which remained in use long afterwards. They had introduced new sorts of scientific farming which increased yields, and their stay had been a 'windfall' for local merchants. The greater circulation of money and supplies had developed the capitalist economy, especially for the islander populations and rural dwellers who had previously lived in a large degree of self-sufficiency. The American construction programme seemed to accomplish more in a few years than the French scheme of *mise en valeur* had achieved in several decades; in New Caledonia alone, the Americans left $US3 million worth of roads and air-fields.[59]

The wartime presence also effected social changes.[60] New Caledonia had been host to some 10 000 indentured labourers from Java and French Indochina before the war. The fighting made it impossible to repatriate them, and the Americans recruited many as employees. The Asians consequently grew increasingly dissatisfied with their indentured status and staged strikes in New Caledonia, to which the French responded with repression. In March 1944, the Asian labourers addressed a letter to the American commander in which they complained of being paid only the equivalent of $5 to $7 per month by the French and of being forced to work 9 hours a day, of being housed in 'filthy huts, 8 to 10 people in a room 2 yards square', even of being refused to be allowed to fight overseas with the Free French. They asked the American commander, 'a citizen of free America and a compatriot of Lincoln', to intercede on their behalf. The American response is unknown, but on 5 July 1945, the French ended the system of indenture and declared minimum wages for labourers.[61]

The effect on the Polynesians and Melanesians was probably even greater. During the war, French officials, particularly in New Caledonia, complained bitterly about the American relations with the islanders and the consequences this might hold for French control. Governor Laigret, never one to spare the Americans harsh criticism, said the hiring of Melanesians and other local labourers 'will be the future ruin of New Caledonia, because they will lose the taste for work and their morals are completely upset, without even mentioning that their fields and herds of livestock are devastated'.[62] A military officer reported that 'the policy of the Americans towards the indigenes is very grave. Without question our allies are trying by every means possible to attract the indigenes to them. They overwhelm the chiefs with consideration and the high salaries they pay to workers will have undoubted repercussions on the future of French colonisation in New Caledonia'.[63] Another contemporary summed up the impact:

> Placed at the disposal of the American construction program, Melanesian labourers received good pay, food and treatment, so that they gained a more favourable impression of such work than they had previously entertained. Formerly they were generally excluded from all political or economic activities, except when employed by the government on public works or by the planters in harvesting the coffee crop. Henceforth, while they may still prefer living in their own villages to working in towns, they will expect to be free to leave home when they wish, and not only on the demand of government authorities. They intend to choose their employers. In return for their manual labour they will expect to earn enough to enable them to buy living necessities, and they will want the same wages as are paid to white workers for similar work. They want also to participate in the political life of their country.[64]

The islanders who had been forcibly marginalised by the French had now experienced contact with wage labour, consumer products, and a different sort of treatment; even the impact of seeing black American soldiers working on an equal basis with white soldiers is not to be underestimated.

A number of islanders also served in the French military during the war – 546 men left New Caledonia to fight overseas, including 68 indigenes, and another 971 Melanesians served in the armed forces in New Caledonia. The French discouraged them from enlisting by using them as labourers or servants rather than as active combatants. But the Battalion du Pacifique served valiantly, fighting in North Africa at the battles of Tobruk and El Alamein, then in Italy and southern France. Almost a third of the Oceanic soldiers died for France. After the Liberation, the survivors marched down the Champs-Elysées and received medals from de Gaulle.[65] Their experiences in the war opened new horizons – most saw other civilisations and the 'mother country' for the first time, they received training and education and earned regular wages. Returning to the South Pacific, the soldiers received a hero's welcome, but few other immediate rewards.

Scholars differ on the overall impact of the war, particularly on the island population. For one French anthropologist, Jean Guiart, the Second World War and the presence of American soldiers had greater effects on the Europeans than the Melanesians. 'The European population lived in unknown prosperity under the sign of the dollar. There resulted a great social mix and a considerable numerical increase in the commercial middle class from which the power-holding managerial European cadres normally emerged.' He disputes the charges of high wages that the Americans gave Melanesians, or the effects money had: 'The dollar manna was little spread in the Melanesian population, which could only benefit from it by the sale of curios, doing laundry if an American camp was nearby and sometimes by prostitution'. In general, he plays down the effects the Americans had on the mentality of the island population:

The easy generosity of the American soldiers who were not spending their own money, the difference in apparent standards of living between the black troops and themselves, the remarkable difference between the salaries paid by the French administration and those that some had been able to get from their American employers in Nouméa and elsewhere, all of that pushed the autochthonous population to become conscious in a new fashion of this abusive and reinforced colonial exploitation. Some have supposed a certain influence by direct contact with the American troops who, in the course of thousands of individual conversations, could have introduced new political notions. The Reverend Father O'Reilly suggested such an hypothesis [in *Pèlerin du ciel*]. I have not been able to discover any real traces. Whole villages were reconstructed with the remains of the American camps and were for a long time furnished with crockery of the US Navy. Were it not for these material proofs of their sojourn, one could believe that the forces of the USA had never passed through, so few traces are there in the spirit, not of the whites but of the Melanesians.[66]

Others, however, see the war period as little less than a revolution. One authoritative study concluded: 'New Caledonia's American-inspired economic boom . . . brought to the island a prosperity such as it had never before known . . . Even after the financial floodgates closed, when the troops left in 1946 and the [New] Caledonians were again subjected to shortages and controls, the island was never again the same as before the war'. Many of the material benefits of the American presence remained, as well as new habits; 'Perhaps, however, the psychological legacy was even more important'.[67] The European settlers may well have reaped the greatest and most immediate monetary advantages, and several prominent families in the present-day French territories trace much of their fortunes to their commercial activities at the time of the Second World War. But the islander populations also felt the long-term effects of fraternisation with the foreigners, wage labour for which they could bargain their services and time spent and the experience gained under arms.[68] Yet they received minimal recognition for all this at the end of the war.

In several parts of the South Pacific the presence of foreign soldiers left a specific legacy in the emergency of 'cargo cults', messianic religious and cultural movements. Seeing the American troops with seemingly inexhaustible money and supplies, transported in gleaming ships and airplanes, many islanders began to believe in the arrival of a saviour from overseas laden with gifts. Such cults often inspired indigenous movements which remained active for decades after the end of the war. One of the most dramatic of these cults emerged in the New Hebrides. The British delegate on the island of Tanna first heard rumours of a new cult in 1940, although such a movement had supposedly been in existence for several years. 'John Frum' – 'John' from John the Baptist and 'Frum' from the English word 'broom' for something which would make a clearing – was rumoured to be abroad in various villages, making appearances in the evening and sometimes performing acts of healing or other miracles. Many Melanesians believed that John Frum would sweep away the British and the French, restore native traditions to islands that had been changed by foreign influence and inaugurate a new society. Rumours of the cult continued through 1940 and 1941, and in April 1941 villagers stormed local stores at a settlement called Green Point. Melanesians stopped working for whites. One 'fateful Sunday', only eight parishioners showed up for Presbyterian worship on Tanna, an island that counted a majority of practising Christians. Two months later, a British official used police reinforcements to arrest eleven Melanesians and burned the houses of the John Frum followers. The dissidents were exiled to Port-Vila, but tension continued. Four weeks later, troubles in another village, Ipeukel, led to a second police raid and more arrests.

The cult still did not die, and the arrival of the Americans revived it. The legend of John Frum was embroidered so that now he supposedly wore a military coat with shiny buttons, and he was rumoured to be the brother of the American president or King of America. The British delegate reported to his superior that all of the Tanna men were eager to work at the American bases; they believed that John Frum was coming from America, so they were only too happy to aid the soldiers. The John Frum cult developed its own songs and emblems, members placed red crosses at strategic locations on the island and in front of their houses and 'soldiers' dressed up in the remnants of old American uniforms for drills. Throughout the 1940s and 1950s, the cult continued to win converts, maintaining the loyalty of a third of the population of Tanna, and colonial powers were unsuccessful in stamping it out.[69]

Cargo cults did not develop in New Caledonia – except among the whites. A number of white settlers, having benefited from the American presence, expressed an interest in New Caledonia's becoming part of the United States. Their attraction found encouragement in one American senator's statement that the United States should try to obtain possession of the island, but the French government quashed all overtures even before they got off the ground. That certain New Caledonians developed a special feeling for the US was evident even forty years later, to judge by the number of American flags painted on the sides of buildings in New Caledonia by those who rejected independence or Melanesian control of the archipelago. Some 1500 New Caledonians even joined an association called 'Americal' (the name obviously came from the wartime designation of the American forces stationed in Nouméa), which proposed that the territory become a state of the United States.[70]

In the French Pacific the contrast with the Depression of the 1930s, isolation and French lack of attention before the war, on the one hand, and the experiences of the war years, on the other, was evident. The Americans arrived when the future of the islands looked bleak and when real scarcities and hardships existed in the French colonies. The prosperity brought by the Americans was both temporary and artificial, but the American presence seemed either the promise or the threat of a new order. In both the EFO and New Caledonia, American money, the years of being cut off from France, and rapid change implicitly challenged French administration and acted to increase demands for greater political autonomy from the *métropole*. After all, as one Australian journalist remarked of New Caledonia in 1940, the territory was now forced 'to meet the sudden change from the status of a French colony to that of a virtually independent country'.[71] Yet the paradox was that New Caledonia's dependency on the outside – although, in this period, on the United States rather than on France – increased during the war. Returning to the pre-war situation, and doing without the money the American presence had brought, would not be easy for the inhabitants of the French Pacific, even if real independence was not on the agenda. For the French Empire as a whole, the Second World War represented a turning point. The *ralliement* of the colonies and the use of imperial outposts as bases for the Free French pointed to new roles for the colonies in post-war France. The fighting in the Pacific, the first use of the atomic bomb, and the geopolitical changes which occurred in its aftermath provided a new context for the French presence in Oceania.

2 Recasting the Colonial Order

The French territories suffered much less during the Second World War than islands where fighting raged, and adaptation to the post-war world brought less dramatic change than, for example, in those islands in Micronesia from which Japan was evicted and administration given to another foreign power. Yet significant dislocation had resulted from the French islands being cut off from the *métropole* for five years, all the while subjected to the American presence. International conditions changed in the Pacific – notably with the detonation of the first nuclear bomb, the defeat of Japan and an increased role for the United States in the region – and in the French empire. At the end of the war, France (and other imperial countries) did not seriously consider the possibility of decolonisation, certainly not in the immediate future, but new conditions warranted a recasting of the old colonial order with the aim of bringing about economic development and political evolution but also at preserving the influence of the 'mother country' in distant domains.

The post-war years saw constitutional changes which altered the relationship between the colonies and the *métropole*, as well as the status of the islanders (and other non-European residents) of the colonies. Political groups organised to demand better treatment for the indigenous populations, autonomy or even outright independence. Scholars expressed great interest in the 'primitive' societies of the South Pacific, while diplomats tried to define the role of Oceania in the context of a different equation of global power. Economic developments, for example the beginning of commercial air service, began to open new commercial possibilities. Colonial promoters, in France and in the overseas possessions, sought a revamped justification for empire. By the early 1950s the modified colonial order seemed securely in place, but continued challenges, especially those emanating from nationalist or autonomist movements, battered this uneasy consensus in the Pacific. Elsewhere wars waged against French colonialism, first in Indochina, then in Algeria, seemed to herald the end of empire. By 1958, the war in North Africa had created a crisis in France, leading to a regime change, a new constitution and further evolution in the colonial system.

VIEWS OF THE FRENCH ISLANDS IN THE 1940S AND 1950S

The war years provided the occasion for observers of New Caledonia and Tahiti, including visitors, residents and colonial officials, to comment on the present situation of the colonies and their future development. Foreign impressions were not always laudatory. A New Zealand colonel who visited New Caledonia in 1943 wrote: 'The island is or was a French colony. The French, however, don't deserve colonies. They are a miserable, backward peasant type here and employ at pittance wages Javanese and Tonkinese who live under worse than slave or farm-animal conditions. Anyway, despite great potential wealth here, and a good climate . . . very little work has been done'.[1] However, Wilfred Burchett, an Australian journalist, visited New Caledonia in 1941 and returned impressed with what he called the 'Pacific treasure island': 'Here is a land, rich in economic resources, with invaluable harbourages, with land and air-bases of great strategic importance within a few hours flight of our capital cities . . . an outpost of French culture'. Such a place would acquire increased importance in the changing world: 'The Pacific is the world of the future. There are signs a-plenty that it is now coming into its own; that as the old Mediterranean world gave way in importance to the wide world of the Atlantic through the development of the Americas, so the centre of *Weltpolitik* is being shifted to the Pacific. . . . The Pacific represents the New World and new ideas'. Yet, he added, 'as far as Australia is concerned, it is a reflection on our parochialism that it has needed the present war and the collapse of France to arouse our interest in this immensely wealthy island, with its unique and diverse population, so close to our shores'. He found a few ageing former convicts with whom to chat about the days of the penitentiary, as well as the daughter of the first white man to settle in New Caledonia; he visited French settlers and toured Melanesian regions. The Javanese in New Caledonia charmed Burchett, and he wrote sympathetically about the

Melanesians – although he could not resist several remarks about their historical cannibalism and their apparent laziness; like many observers of the time, he saw them as relics of a primitive epoch, yet worthy of study in order to understand the early history of the human race. The French had done little to improve the lot of the Melanesians; and 'even to-day, the natives aren't completely satisfied with their treatment – although one must admit that in comparison with our own Australian aboriginals the New Caledonian natives are well off'. Although they had legitimate grievances about land spoliation, 'the most important thing is that their right to live without outside interference is recognized'. They did not seem 'unduly pestered by missionaries', and Burchett felt that 'exploitation of the Melanesians is a thing of the past'. He believed that the main problem New Caledonia faced was the lack of labour, but if this question could be solved, New Caledonia would become a prosperous agricultural and mining country; its location in the South Pacific would also make it what he termed the 'Malta of the South Seas'.[2]

New Caledonia presented a picture of considerable potential but one of surprising underdevelopment to a French official. In 1943 Governor Laigret reported to Paris on the general situation of New Caledonia. He noted the problem of labour but added that the conscripted Melanesian workers on plantations were not sufficient. Medical doctors were scarce, yet leprosy was increasing among Europeans and diseases such as meningitis and tuberculosis were appearing. Roadways were not being kept up. Administration in the countryside was inadequate. Children did not regularly attend classes. The public schools lacked textbooks, teachers and canteens; the teachers were badly housed and lacked the proper qualifications. The mission schools, by contrast, seemed better equipped. Telephone services were insufficient, and to communicate between the *brousse* and Nouméa was difficult. The arrival of the American troops in New Caledonia had had a 'rather nefarious' influence, especially on Melanesians: 'Numerous indigenes have been employed by the allied army for manual labour – this is only a minor problem – but many more natives are happy just to live on black market sales of alcohol or by working as prostitutes'. More surprising to the governor was the situation of the European *broussards*:

In many rural centres, I was shocked to see the conditions in which the settlers live. I shall not dwell on their housing conditions, which are wretched and unworthy of Europeans. I visited several of these houses, where I was received by simple folk – too simple, because they are becoming further and further removed from civilisation. They go about bare-foot and do not give the impression of knowing even the most rudimentary rules of hygiene. Large families are not uncommon; you often meet families of ten or even fourteen or sixteen children. The children usually are in good health, but most of them are totally or nearly illiterate. This is be-cause of the lack of roadways and means of transport. There are some children, in fact, who must travel eight to ten kilometres to go to school.[3]

The chief executive was so moved by his tour of New Caledonia that he sent a telegram to the Minister: 'There is much to be done to save this magnificent country, where there lives a French population of hard-working and deserving small settlers who are gradually dying from isolation, and who lack both doctors and schools'.[4]

If observers of New Caledonia felt that much must be done to develop the considerable potential of the colony, the two best-known writers on the EFO in the 1940s and early 1950s were highly critical of what the French had done in that colony and remained pessimistic about the future of France's Polynesian islands. The title of a work by Alain Gerbault, *Un Paradis se meurt* ('The Death of a Paradise'), indicates his view. Published post-humously in 1949 – Gerbault had died in 1941 – this was the work of an eccentric Frenchman, a champion tennis-player and pioneering aviator, who had visited French Polynesia for several long stays in the inter-war years and on the eve of the Second World War. He made both fast friends and bitter enemies, and, compromised by his pro-Vichy sentiments, left Tahiti at the beginning of the war. In *Un Paradis se meurt* Gerbault summed up an attitude that would later be labelled the theory of the 'fatal impact' of Europeans in the Pacific:

> The religion of these islands has been abolished and the authority of their chiefs destroyed. Nothing remains of their marvellous civilisation of former times . . . . It is no longer

possible today to deny that it was the destructive white invasion which caused all the problems [of these islands] . . . In
central Oceania, white civilisation is a civilisation of absolute
and radical destruction. There has been a gradual destruction by the conquerors of the Maori [*sic*] race, its culture and
history, its dignity and pride – a destruction which will one
day be total if colonial policy is not radically changed.

He railed against tourists who came to Tahiti with 'only one
aim: to procure a native woman', schools which were 'establishments not of education, but of destruction', businessmen who
'above all want to take the indigenes' land', art dealers who
'have stolen all the old artworks', and various other villains.

Gerbault looked more particularly at the few benefits for
France of its rule and the great effects of that rule on the
colony:

What does France get from its Pacific colonies? . . . The
considerable strategic interest of our position in Oceania
and the prestige which our country earns from its presence
in the southern ocean . . . . What do we see here after ninety
years of occupation? Morally, an increasing disaffection with
us among the conquered race. Materially, a budget deficit,
an extremely costly transport service and a very small quan-
tity of French imports . . . . In most of the islands, trading is
totally in the hands of the Chinese, and it seems to me that,
for France, most of the profit of colonisation goes to put up
the large numbers of administrators who come from the
métropole just to earn enormous salaries here.

Gerbault suggested actions for the government to take in this
'exploiters' paradise': the creation of Polynesian reserves and
the prohibition of foreign settlement on some islands, prohibi-
tions on acquisition of land by non-indigenes, measures to end
the indebtedness of Polynesians and to control *métissage*, education of Polynesians in their own language with specially-written
texts, some degree of self-government and particular laws for
the indigenes, better public services, more inter-island maritime links and taxes on business activities. But the aim should
be not only to improve the life of the indigenes but to safeguard
the French presence: 'It is imperative that we improve our

colonial policy in the Pacific if we are to have any chance of retaining this part of our empire'.[5]

Another commentator on French Polynesia was Albert T'Serstevens, a prolific explorer and author. In *Tahiti et sa couronne*, first published in 1950, T'Serstevens tried to correct earlier, more utopian portrayals. He admitted his enchantment by the islands, but he found faults as well. Some Tahitian women were not quite so attractive as legend would have it; Tahitians were indeed far from hard-working, perhaps because the climate and availability of food made strenuous labour unnecessary; Tahitian food, he found, was tasteless and boring; Tahitians lacked an aesthetic sense. T'Serstevens was no less harsh on other residents. The Chinese were money-grubbing merchants who were corrupting Tahitians with their blood, their bargaining and their language. The Europeans were fortune-seekers and adventurers, uninterested in intellectual life – there was no bookshop in Tahiti, he noted – and rapacious in their sexual desire for Tahitians. T'Serstevens was himself not immune to the islanders' charm; a long chapter of his book treats Tahitian sexuality, and he took a tolerant, guiltless attitude to the mores of the South Pacific: 'There is no morality here, just as there is no snow – it's as simple as that'. His conclusion was simple: 'Everything which I have said, or could say, about the Polynesians . . . only points to the different sides of their childlike souls. They are children – and spoiled children at that'.

T'Serstevens remarked on changes taking place in the islands, such as the emigration of Marquesans to Tahiti, and of Austral Islanders to the phosphate mines on Makatéa. Social customs were in flux as well. Alcoholism had become a major problem, and commercialised prostitution was rampant in Papeete. New diversions replaced religious gatherings: 'The opening of cinemas in Papeete and Uturoa (Raiatea) was a heavy blow to the different missions, which saw their congregations desert church services, especially on Saturday night'. Culinary habits were being modified; Polynesians were sometimes ashamed to eat with their fingers in their traditional fashion in front of Europeans, and they were gradually adopting European foodstuffs – 'People thought they were being polite when they served us tinned beef, the height of refinement and luxury for a Polynesian'. The market economy had penetrated even remote islands; combined with the Polynesians' attitudes, it worked odd effects: 'Some of them are so indolent that they won't even go to the trouble of striking a match to make their morning coffee, and instead buy boiling water from the local Chinese shopkeeper for a franc a pot: the practice has set a fixed price'.

T'Serstevens seldom shed tears over the disappearance of old ways, and, in fact, specifically criticised Pierre Loti and others who had lamented the *paradis perdu*. A century and a half of contact with outsiders had inevitably effected the changes he witnessed, and the American influence had completed the metamorphosis. In particular, the American presence had created a monetary economy in the islands. Such changes had been most apparent in Tahiti and Mooréa, even if in more distant places they were less invasive. T'Serstevens, for instance, wrote evocatively about Maupiti that there were no islands where it was possible to be 'more closely in contact with the Tahitian life of last century or even earlier. "Civilisation", as it is called, appears here only in the form of a few utensils, such as a frying-pan, a kerosene lamp and a few articles of clothing. Everything else – the landscape, houses, lifestyles – has not changed, nor, I think, have the people's ways of thinking.' Anaa, by contrast, was 'a civilised atoll', that is 'schooners land at least once a month. There is a wharf, a lighthouse, several cisterns, a few fruit trees, two churches, an infirmary and two Chinese. The chief is a *monsieur*'. T'Serstevens reported some of the anomalies of the colonial order. Visiting a school, he looked through textbooks:

They contain almost nothing which even remotely relates to the life of a Tahitian child. The famous phrase about 'Our ancestors the Gauls' is not a joke – I found it in the first pages, along with Vercingétorix and other mustachioed warriors, which might indeed interest little Oceanians who do not even know the names of their last twenty kings. These schoolbooks talk a lot about wheat, barley, apple-trees, oaks, birches and other natural curiosities, all of which are as mysterious to the Maoris as the *faifai, mpae, upaupautumuore* and *huamati* would be for young Frenchmen. The island brats are taught about the *gabelle* [salt-tax], the *lettres de cachet* [arbitrary warrants of imprisonment in the Ancien Régime] and the revocation of the Edict of Nantes. The unfortunate teachers are even forced to make them learn to recite the fables of La Fontaine, which kids repeat from start to finish without understanding a single word – this at least means they are spared having to ask what on earth are these foxes, crows and frogs which talk like humans and which they themselves have never seen. It would be like talking to a Parisian child about the *moo*, the *tupa* and other Polynesian spirits.[6]

Other books at the time confirmed the paradoxical nature of the French territories in Oceania. One of the few guidebooks available was the *Pacific Islands Year Book*. The 1950 issue remarked on such changes in Tahiti as rising prices and shortages of housing. Visitors were warned that 'Papeete is no longer the place of glamour and romance that it was, and its inhabitants have lost most of their former simplicity'. Automobiles already clogged the streets. Tourism was not much developed, but 'although none of them can be called first-class, the hotels are comfortable enough and their bills of fare are good and varied'. Two or three cinemas and the marketplace provided entertainment, and tourists could buy souvenirs at Chinese shops: 'Chinese influence has gradually extended all over French Oceania'. As for New Caledonia, the authors said Nouméa was picturesque. The Melanesians were peaceful, but 'some of the mountain tribes have still to be watched by the military'. Nickel provided substantial exports, and land was available: 'Land is abundant, and even foreigners, provided they understand French ways and customs, may easily obtain areas suitable for cultivation'. With plans for the repatriation of Asian labourers, need for workers was pressing: 'If there is to be any real development and economic progress in New Caledonia, the Colony must be provided with a labour force. All projects for establishing a new and desirable population in the Colony meet the same problem: Where is the labour force? Where are the markets? The future of the Colony is not easy to foresee.' The labouring classes nevertheless faced difficulties, 'and a sort of post-war apathy seems to have fallen upon all other classes in the Colony'. Canadian nickel competed with that of New Caledonia. Concerning the New Hebrides, the *Pacific Islands Year Book* thought that the condominium was more exotic than other islands: 'The effect of all this Christianising and education work has been the taming of the New Hebrides savages. Even now they are far from being the most lovable natives in the South Seas'. The book remarked on the odd political status of the New Hebrides, and noted statements made in Australia in 1943 and 1944 which indicated 'Australia's belief that the New Hebrides should come under Australian control in a defensive arc of islands'. This, however, would not eventuate, and France would maintain its presence. The guide commented: 'Anglo-French relations are so cordial that French occupation of territory near Australia is no menace to our security, and under the Condominium the New Hebrides are unlikely to become a fortified base. On the other hand, the islands are of no great value to the French, and they might at some time contemplate transferring their interest in them to some other power'. Finally, Wallis and Futuna, perhaps not surprisingly, inspired only a brief account in the guide; any intending visitors were told that the islanders 'seldom see Europeans, and remain unspoiled'.[7]

For those seriously interested in migrating to the South Pacific, a French *Guide pratique pour ceux qui veulent vivre en France d'outre-mer* offered advice.[8] It said that 'New Caledonia is a hospitable country for hard-working and entrepreneurial Frenchmen'. Migrants would adapt easily to the climate and find Nouméa 'a well-tended city of white houses shaded by the luxuriant vegetation which grows along streets and roadways': the inhabitants 'are very welcoming to Frenchmen who come from the *métropole*'. Housing, however, was expensive in Nouméa, and in the countryside settlers would have to build their lodgings themselves. Reassuringly, 'in general, all that is necessary for European life can be easily found in New Caledonia', although the cost of living was higher than in France. In bold-faced type, the guide proclaimed that if the cost of living was double that of the *métropole*, salaries were five times higher and life was thus easy. Medical services, schools and recreation also would be familiar and adequate for the French migrant. Migrants could apply in France to work for the administration of the Société Le Nickel in New Caledonia or they could set up their own businesses. They were warned (again in bold type) that 'unfortunately good land holdings which could be exploited are the property of large companies, which refuse to give them up unless they are obliged to do so'. In conclusion,

'The colony needs new settlers and France can supply them'. Such an infusion of migrants might change the pre-war situation when stagnation and routine habits, supported by egotistical interests, only increased the difficulties faced by business. Before the war, New Caledonia was rightly considered to be a 'private preserve'. Most of the French residents of the island little by little let their active energies be dissipated as they settled for an easy life.

The guide underlined the favourable conditions of climate and hygiene in the EFO and was guardedly optimistic about the chances for migration there: 'Available arable land is scarce, but it is nevertheless possible for young Frenchmen with sufficient capital to succeed in agriculture in these islands'. The financial cost would be high, but vanilla and sugar-cane could become profitable crops. The New Hebrides received an even briefer treatment than that given to the EFO, but the guide spoke encouragingly about 'rich land and huge properties with fertile soil which are appropriate for coffee-shrubs and cacao-trees'. As usual, there was nothing on Wallis and Futuna.

One subject which received almost no attention was the islander population, except to the extent that the author of the guide reassured prospective migrants of the lack of real danger from them. On the Melanesians of New Caledonia, he wrote: 'They are not really suitable for our type of work and live off primitive farming. In former times, they were rather belligerent, but they now respect the authority of the whites and sometimes even work on plantations'. The attitudes towards the islanders was condescending and optimistic: 'The indigenes of the EFO are gradually adapting to civilisation and attend the numerous schools which have been opened since the Liberation. The existence in the islands of numerous *métis* [mixed-blood people] of all races has contributed to the disappearance of all racism'.

In the years during and immediately following the war, the Pacific colonies remained distant, exotic and little known territories of a French empire which still covered almost eleven million square kilometres in Indochina, North Africa, sub-Saharan Africa and Madagascar, plus islands in the Caribbean and Indian Ocean. Writers on the empire gave low priority to the Pacific territories. In a general work on the past and future of the French colonies published in 1943, for instance, Jacques Stern devoted only six of almost four hundred pages to the French Pacific islands, and in 1949 Charles Robequain treated these territories in only four paragraphs in his overview of the empire. A decade later, however, the same author was a bit more expansive in a book on Madagascar and the 'scattered bases of the French Union'. New Caledonia, he said, was a land of great mining potential, but Nouméa was not particularly idyllic: 'One hardly finds here the exotic charm he might expect'. The New Hebrides were insalubrious, and the EFO largely undeveloped since the depletion of pearls; it now sold no exports except coconut products and vanilla. Only a few specialised works provided readers with more extensive information. The famous 'Que sais-je?' series in 1946 published a history of Oceania, written by the eminent colonial historian Charles-André Julien. The Editions Maritimes et Coloniales in 1955 issued Jacques Bourgeau's study of the French islands, a rather thorough account of their history and resources; Bourgeau was optimistic about their future, but he joined other writers in emphasising that much remained to be done to develop them.[9]

Scholars in several disciplines took more interest in the South Pacific in the decade after the war. Several historians examined French policy in Oceania during the first half of the nineteenth century.[10] Patrick O'Reilly, a Marist priest and scholar living in Tahiti, published historical studies, bibliographies, and biographical encyclopedias on the French Pacific territories.[11] One of the most famous scientific expeditions of all times targeted the French islands, when the Norwegian navigator Thor Heyerdahl sailed his raft, the Kon-Tiki, across the Pacific from South America to French Polynesia. Heyerdahl attempted to prove that the first settlers of the eastern Polynesian islands could have ventured there from Peru, and he pointed out certain links between Oceanic and pre-Columbian civilisations. Heyerdahl's thesis was largely discredited, but he became a hero.[12] One of Heyerdahl's travelling companions was a young Swedish anthropologist, Bengt Danielsson; he settled in Tahiti, where he still lives with his French wife, and became an authority on Polynesian culture. He has written on such subjects as acculturation among islanders adapting to the modern world, Gauguin and, more recently, French nuclear testing. In his opposition to such testing, and his support for Tahitian independence, Danielsson has also been a controversial figure in French Polynesia.[13]

Anthropologists of the time studied the structures and cultures of 'primitive' societies before they seemed doomed to disappear but they also tried to separate fact from myth in general perceptions of the island populations and their beliefs. Foremost among authorities on the French Pacific was Maurice Leenhardt, who had first gone to New Caledonia as a Protestant missionary at the turn of the century. Leenhardt's scientific research soon overshadowed his church work, and he returned to Paris in the 1930s to teach – his departure from New Caledonia was welcomed by settlers who felt he was too 'pro-native'. In 1947, seven years before his death, Leenhardt went back to the South Pacific as founder and first director of the Institut Français d'Océanie in Nouméa; in the same year, he published his masterwork, a study of persona and myth in the Melanesian world, *Do Kamo*. One of Leenhardt's students was a young ethnologist named Jean Guiart, who in the late 1940s began to publish studies based on field-work in the New Hebrides and New Caledonia. Guiart, who has continued to write on such topics as Melanesian legends, the Melanesian concept of the chieftainship, social organisation in the Loyalty Islands, Pacific art and Melanesian nationalism, has also been a controversial figure because of his sympathy for Melanesian independence movements.[14]

Leenhardt and Guiart were active in setting up the organisation which became the French centre for study of the Pacific islands. In 1945 was founded the Société des Océanistes, the merger of the Société d'Études Océaniennes organised in Papeete around 1920 and the Société d'Études Mélanésiennes, which Maurice Leenhardt had established in Nouméa in the late 1930s. Leenhardt was elected the first president of the new organisation, with Patrick O'Reilly as secretary-general. Other members of the inaugural council of the society included Roger Gervolino, the New Caledonian delegate to the French Consultative Assembly; Charles-André Julien, a professor at the École Nationale de la France d'Outre-Mer; Marcel Mauss, a distinguished ethnologist and emeritus professor at the Collège de France; Paul Rivet, director of the Musée de l'Homme; Jacques Soustelle, the assistant director of the same museum (and later a French colonial governor and minister); and Charles Robequain, a professor at the Sorbonne – a list of France's most authoritative specialists on the South Pacific, ethnology and the colonies. The first issue of the society's new *Journal*, published in December 1945, included Leenhardt's article on the significance of the mask in Melanesian culture, Pierre Métais' article on ritual gift-exchange in New Caledonia, Jean-Paul Faivre's study of the *ralliement* of the Pacific territories to the Free French, a piece on the development of air transport in Oceania and several contributions on other islands. The book reviews gave accounts of volumes published by Julien, Jore, Leenhardt and Alain Gerbault, among others, and the issue concluded with a lengthy bibliography of works on the South Pacific published since 1939.

Jean Guiart was the co-author, with Hubert Deschamps, a former colonial governor and research director at ORSTOM, of the most comprehensive study of the French Pacific territories published in the 1950s. Deschamps wrote on Tahiti, Guiart on New Caledonia and the New Hebrides. The volume, issued in 1957, summarised the current situation in the territories and exemplified contemporary attitudes about the colonies and their populations.[15] Deschamps in his preface underlined a long-standing difference in perceptions of Melanesia and Polynesia: 'Tahiti remains the prototype of the dream of exoticism, a dream which from the voyages of Bougainville to our atomic age has never ceased inspiring the imagination of people as a paradise lost'. In New Caledonia, 'Melanesians . . . still haunted by the myths and traditions of the Stone Age' in the *brousse*, contrast with the industries which 'concentrate most of [the colony's] life' in Nouméa. The New Hebrides was 'one of the last primitive countries on the globe . . . Melanesians there lead a prehistoric life of bad reputation'.

Writing on Tahiti, Deschamps noted over-population, the importance of the *demis* in political life and of the Chinese in commerce, the 'personal and passionate' nature of local politics and the economic difficulties the colony faced. In many ways, little had changed from the previous century, he implied, and 'much has thus kept its harmonious simplicity. Of course, imported goods exercise a great attraction. But the Polynesian does not let himself become enslaved to money'. Compared with Polynesian islands now dominated by Europeans and Asians,

such as New Zealand and Hawaii, 'French Polynesia remains
. . . one of the most indisputable paradises in the world'.
Nevertheless, the old order could not last. The Tahitian economy
was 'primitive and fragile, at the mercy of world markets'. Urbanisation worked great changes, for 'Papeete is the metropo-
lis, the great city and crucible in which Polynesia is being reformed (some say "deformed") by contact with the influence of
Asia and the West'. The best hope for the future, Deschamps
concluded, was for French Polynesia to maintain its links with
France:

> Politically it seems inconceivable that such a small country,
> islands so scattered and with such a tiny population, could
> form an independent state . . . . The French Union provides
> a great protective structure for it. French Polynesia can evolve
> at its own speed, towards either a certain degree of assimila-
> tion or autonomy . . . . The *métropole* remains necessary for
> the development of the country.

In New Caledonia, Guiart likewise discerned signs of change:
'Melanesians on the Grande Terre are increasingly living a
material life comparable to that in remote European regions'.
As for non-Melanesians, 'Their material life is not always so
different from that . . . of the Melanesians'. Immigration was
growing, but Guiart thought it would neither reach major proportion nor create social upheaval: 'The European population,
which is benefiting from a limited but constant immigration,
has practically no need to fear becoming a minority compared
to the native islanders. Consequently, this results in a relaxed
atmosphere and concord between the two groups in the population which is evident in few territories of the French Union'.
Guiart continued:

> Is not the greatest asset of New Caledonia today the human
> experiment taking place there, the reconciliation which is
> henceforth certain between the autochthone and the con-
> queror in common labour and a prosperity which is increas-
> ingly shared? New Caledonia, a colony of settlement, will not
> have been colonised for nothing. There is being created a
> young, vigorous people, who have already happily joined the

humanism of the French to the solid virtues of the Melanesians.

Since New Caledonia was perceived as a land with a promising future, Guiart gave advice to potential migrants. He first warned that New Caledonia had failed as a country of agricultural settlers: 'For thirty years now, it has been impossible to count the number of those who came from France with the idea of becoming farmers and had to abandon their land and find another job'. Yet a need for migrants existed, especially for skilled technicians, and Guiart did not try to dissuade them from moving. He simply cautioned that the cost of living was high and the obstacles formidable. He also added – a neat comment on the end of the classical colonial era – that 'there is no need to load up with colonial gear, which is here out-of-date and which will make you look a little ridiculous. In particular, do not wear a pith helmet'.

Guiart was less optimistic about the New Hebrides. France currently registered a deficit of 400 million francs a year 'for the safeguarding of the economic interests of a population of French origin which numbers just over 1200 persons'. The tourist industry was non-existent, manganese deposits had not yet been mined, plantations were not doing particularly well and much of the New Hebrides remained unexploited. The migrant was warned to try to negotiate a contract to work for a settler already installed in the islands, to forswear alcohol, take anti-malaria tablets, get accustomed to loneliness, try to learn pidgin and be kind to the islanders. In fact, Europeans must attempt to win favour with the local population: 'The first signs of the emergence of an indigenous middle class can be noticed. Can one hope that the Europeans will have the intelligence not to make it hostile?' As for the political structure of the condominium, Guiart bet on a continuation of the status quo: 'Who wishes for the end of the condominium? Neither the settler, nor the trader, not even the missionary . . . or the native . . . England takes no interest in the archipelago . . . France certainly does not want to withdraw'.

Guiart and Deschamps did not foresee – but then how could they? – that a quarter century after their book was published, the condominium of the New Hebrides would be a thing of the past, that massive European migration to New Caledonia would have reduced Melanesians to a minority and provoked increased ethnic hostility and that French Polynesians could hardly be said to have resisted the lure of money and imported goods bought with subsidies from the French state. The beginnings of economic and social change which they discerned in Oceania in the mid-1950s speeded up dramatically during the following decade. Ironically, most of the large colonies of the French empire gained their independence only a few years after the books of Robequain, Guiart and Deschamps were published, while the more 'scattered bases' of the empire remained under French control.

Ethnologists, colonial promoters, officials of the French administration and foreign visitors did not share the same views of the island Pacific in the 1940s and 1950s. But their ideas were not necessarily contrary to each other. Social scientists' research on the culture of Melanesians and Polynesians suggested the need for an amelioration of their economic situation and a recognition of their political rights. Visitors castigated the French for having done too little to develop the islands, or too much to destroy the islanders' traditions, but these comments were also manifestos for new policies. Global political and military changes provided a rationale for continued French sovereignty at a time when even the ethnologists who were most sympathetic to the native islanders made no demands for independence or even autonomy. Most thought that the 'autochthones' – that word was now preferred to the outmoded 'natives' or 'indigenes' – would and could be integrated into the European economy and polity. Some observers revelled in the luxuriance of the South Seas or pined after paradises lost, others shivered at the thought of cannibalism and convicts, but increasingly note was taken of the need for economic development and a new awareness of the difficult situations of even some European settlers.[16] Such realisations could sometimes turn into diatribes against one or another group, notably directed against the Chinese in Tahiti, but most commentators saw the lack of adequate labour as the major problem for the territories. In the context of the French empire of the 1950s, that problem could partially be solved by migration, and the guidebooks for migrants give evidence that the idea of empire was not yet dead. Some writers still thought, wrongly, that the islands could be turned into prosperous plantation economies for yeoman farmers – an idea dear to nineteenth century colonialists. Many books from this period now seem quaint or ethnocentric with their discussions of the 'natives' and 'savages' and their boosterism and flag-waving; on some points, the imperial discourse of the 1940s and 1950s had changed little from that of the 1800s. These views, which paint a portrait of the colonies in the post-war years, also provide the context for new French policies, and for reaction to French policy in the colonies themselves.

TOWARDS A POST-WAR POLICY: FRANCE'S INTERNATIONAL OBJECTIVES

The Second World War provided an opportunity, indeed an obligation, to rethink many aspects of national policy. These years were the crucible from which many post-war policies in France emerged – economic planning, the constitutional arrangements of the Fourth Republic and the social welfare system. So too with colonialism. The 1944 Brazzaville Conference, held in the French Congo and presided over by General de Gaulle, set down the principles for a recasting of the French empire. The French government rejected any move towards independence, autonomy or self-government in the colonies, but it mandated various changes intended to better the situation of inhabitants – natives and settlers – and to bring about greater development. The meeting called for greater co-operation between *métropole* and *outre-mer*, a reinvigorated but more humane colonialism.

Both at the Free French headquarters and in the colonies comments were made and discussions held to consider the future. Often such views bespoke worry even about the basic French capacity to maintain control of its colonies. Already in 1942, a captain in the French military forces stationed in the South Pacific sent a memorandum to de Gaulle about the EFO in which he expressed concern about the solidity of Free French control and post-war prospects. Although the *ralliement* of the colony had taken place over a year before, he said, strong pro-Vichy feelings remained among part of the population. The Navy and the military doctors in Papeete were 'ultra-Vichyite' and public servants seemed apathetic. Among the French population there were 'several ardent Vichy supporters, even Hitlerites' versus about a hundred committed supporters of the Free French; the Catholic clergy was also pro-Vichy. Only the Protestant pastors were avid supporters of the Free French, and it was their influence which carried the Polynesians along. The mass of the French in the colony were 'amorphous, neutral, and think only of their narrowly personal interests; they are rebellious and impervious to orders'. Such behaviour did not bode well for reestablished French control. Another problem was Anglophilia: 'The old people of this country are too Anglophile, and some of them are linked by marriage to the descendants of the English pastors'; at least their British connections made them supporters of the Free French. But the situation needed to be monitored. Tahiti, he added, was economically dependent on 'Britain' – probably a reference, in reality, to New Zealand. Residents enthusiastically welcomed 'British' warships docking in Papeete: 'How can one deny that their influence grows day be day? . . . It could be envisaged that after the war the indigenous population might demand its independence under the protection of New Zealand, the great Maori country which is a neighbour and friend'. For Captain Rollin, an independence movement was germinating, not unconnected with the British (and New Zealand) presence: 'In every country of the world there is now an "independence party". In existence in Tahiti before the armistice of 1940, since the war, and under the influence of the Anglophile lobby, it threatens to take on . . . a militant and unreasonable character. One has only to recall the Pritchard affair'. Rollin thought that the French government must be extremely careful in choosing administrators for the colony, and in particular must avoid high-handed bureaucrats: 'It is very clear that at the end of the present war, the people of Tahiti will in no way support Vichyite administrators . . . nor these "shore-bound" navy officers who consider themselves to be here in a conquered land'. In an update of his report a year later, the author suggested various measures to be taken. Politically, Tahiti should be given a 'certain administrative autonomy, which, however, will not be prejudicial to French interests'. All French subjects in the colony should be given full citizenship, and a Conseil Général (with competency to discuss the budget and any other matters) should be installed and given the right to choose a representative of the colony in contacts with metropolitan authorities. Economically, a local currency might be created, new inter-island shipping services established, and trading links with other French colonies and the *métropole* reopened.[17]

From New Caledonia the controversial Admiral d'Argenlieu voiced similar concerns. He said that New Caledonian society was fragmented with 'divisions between Vichyites and Gaullists, between New Caledonians and *métropolitains*, between city-dwellers and country folk'. Inhabitants of the colony were 'weak-willed, distracted from their duty by their desire for profit, even content to be dismissed from their jobs so that they can open a shop and earn dollars'. Rebel elements in the population needed to be neutralised, subsidies for planters had to be provided and the big nickel company SLN should be nationalised.[18]

Concern about the future of the colonies was not misplaced given the defeat of France, the presence of the Americans and clashes between various political groups in the islands. Furthermore, articles which came into French hands contained trenchant criticism of the French in the Pacific. For instance, an article in the *Far Eastern Survey*, an American publication which found its way into the French files, said that New Caledonia was an indispensable base for American security. It criticised the French achievements there and speculated on foreign influence in the territory; the French had invested so little in New Caledonia's mines, it claimed, that capital must necessarily come from some other, unnamed source. Yet, in spite of such infusion of capital, mining technology in New Caledonia remained at the stage of the late nineteenth century. The writer thought that Australia and New Zealand considered the South Pacific their sphere of influence, and Australia had after all played a major role in the *ralliement* of New Caledonia. Demands of autonomy in New Caledonia might also conceal efforts to break the yoke of the 'ten families' rumoured to control the territory. Alliance with foreign – perhaps Australian or New Zealand – groups would be one strategy for discontented residents. The article also condemned the lack of suffrage for Melanesians.[19]

US Army commanders had been highly critical of the French colonial administration. In despatches to Washington, Admiral Halsey called the French authorities to task for their inept government of New Caledonia and lack of more cordial co-operation with the Allies. Halsey even told President Roosevelt that 'under no circumstances should New Caledonia be handed back to the French, [since] its administration is a disgrace'. Articles in such widely available magazines as *Time* and *Newsweek*, which were circulated in New Caledonia, reported sentiments in the American military and the Congress that the United States should assume control of the territory after the end of the war, perhaps by purchasing it from France or accepting the islands in lieu of French payment of war debts. Rumours also spread that Australia might be interested in acquiring the islands.[20]

French officials, faced with worrying reports and rumours, began in earnest to consider the post-war future of the Pacific region and France's role in it.[21] The Free French Commissaire des Colonies produced a succinct but broad-ranging analysis in 1944. He remarked at the outset that French influence in the Pacific had already begun to decline before the Second World War; a major concern would be to restore and improve the French position:

> Indochina, New Caledonia and Tahiti constitute practically the only bases from which we can mount an effort to make up for lost ground. French business and French missionary and intellectual activities in China and the Far East may perhaps be able to contribute to the success of this endeavour. Nevertheless, it will be through our three colonies that France will be able to make its presence as a great power once again felt in the Pacific. Our efforts should therefore essentially be directed at securing these colonies, which should at the same time be made into exemplary and energetic countries.

In short, rejuvenated colonies would serve as the basis for France's policy in the Pacific basin. The obstacles to achieving such goals, however, were significant. The Commissaire des Colonies first underlined domestic problems in the colonies. Indochina had remained under Vichy control and then Japanese occupation during the war. New Caledonia 'has been leading a singularly troubled life over the last four years; with the presence of the Americans, local politics has masked the expression of the French instinct'. Tahiti had not been immune to troubles. But external problems had to be faced as well: Britain and the Netherlands, as well as Australia and New Zealand, were colonial masters in the Pacific, but the United States 'claims to impose a [new] moral order in the Pacific and it is known that the colonial principle is contrary to that morality'. (The United States could be seen by different observers to be anticolonial or to have its own expansionist designs.) Nevertheless, the situation in the region, and these rivalries, also provided opportunities for the French to play an important role:

> Once our sovereignty over our possessions has again been established, and once the obstacles which separate us from this goal have been surmounted, then France can usefully take greater initiatives and will be able to develop new policies. It is not rash to think that France will become a force of equilibrium in the Pacific, where the current balance of power is unfortunately unstable, for world peace.

The Commissaire des Colonies then examined big power and colonial rivalries in the Pacific. France must work out agreements with the other colonial states to ensure peace and cooperation, as well as to maintain its territories. The Portuguese in eastern Timor would pose no problem for the French, nor would the Dutch in the East Indies. Holland was moving towards greater co-operation with its colonies, 'towards a tighter or looser union'. 'The effect of this [Dutch] union in the Pacific will be to make Indochina, New Caledonia and the Dutch East Indies a vigorous ensemble in which no territory can jeopardise the others'. The French should nevertheless make certain that the Dutch East Indies and New Caledonia remained complementary not competitive. Britain seemed more of a problem: 'Hitched as England is at present to the American wagon, it is more difficult to expect from her an explicit manifestation of colonial solidarity'. France feared that Britain would adopt the anti-colonial feelings of the United States and not strive to maintain dominion over its own possessions in Oceania. Although the situation remained unclear, it was possible to hope for a 'proposal of colonial solidarity' with Britain. As for Australia and New Zealand, wariness was the appropriate attitude for the French to take:

A certain apprehension about America reconciles these countries with our plans, although their own ambitions distance [them from us]. Towards them we must practise a policy of amicable expectation and make them aware that if, in theory, we have no objections to their projects for the defence of the southern Pacific, it is at present impossible for us to commit ourselves in any way.

After examining France's fellow colonial powers, the Commissaire des Colonies turned to other states in the Asia-Pacific region. From the Soviet Union, 'here and now, and for a long time in the future, we have nothing to fear'; in fact, France needed Soviet support to maintain its position in the area. Japan would be defeated in the war, the report predicted, and would be unable to menace French interests. China was a different matter, particularly considering the ideological ferment and political instability there; this very instability, however, could benefit France by restraining China's overseas activities:

China must not become a great power. Its governments must content themselves with a facade [of power] . . . . Consequently, the traditional anarchy will be favoured . . . . In short, we must flatter China without really letting it emerge from chaos, and without this chaos becoming the exclusive domain of either the United States or Russia.

The principal foreign danger to French influence in the Pacific would come from the United States, because of its superpower status and its anti-colonial position. The Commissaire des Colonies thought that America could be permitted to extend its influence over Japan, although neither Japan nor China should be allowed to become puppets of the United States. Similarly, the Pacific countries, including the French colonies, could remain open to American trade. But France must not encourage any American efforts to retain a military presence in the French colonies, much less to gain control of these possessions: 'In the first place, we must courteously but firmly reject any effort to nibble away [*sic*] any French colony'; in particular, no colony could be ceded and French colonial policy had to be seen in a global context, subject to discussions between nations, rather than based on solely local or regional concerns.

In sum, France must steer a clear course among the other powers in the Pacific, safeguarding its own interests and perhaps playing one rival power off against another. (Japan, for instance, could be 'capable of thwarting Chinese expansion and serving as a factor of stability'.) France could come to some arrangement with other colonial powers to preserve their respective imperial interests and to further co-operation. Furthermore, France must reinforce its position in its own territories, for example, by combating separatist sentiments; in Indochina, 'We must demonstrate that Annamite independence is connected with collaboration with Japan'. To achieve these ends, it was necessary to mount a new social policy as well. 'Without delay a liberal statute must be enacted [for New Caledonia]. At the same time, it is appropriate to promote significant French immigration to the colony. Similar policies should be applied to the Établissements Français d'Océanie.' This would consolidate French control but also ward off criticism of French colonial control: 'We will develop the liberal and unique character of our colonial institutions. . . . This rejuvenation of our colonialism will thereby work to forestall the most serious objections to it which emerge.'[22]

Other documents from the central French administration confirm French determination to play an active role in the international affairs of the Pacific and to reorient colonial policy in order to buttress that position. Commentators underlined the need for a renewed *mise en valeur* of the French possessions, an effort which included psychological and material aspects. An official at the Ministry of Foreign Affairs, for instance, wrote:

As concerns New Caledonia, we should particularly aim to cancel out the feelings of inferiority *vis-à-vis* the *métropole* which this colony feels. By enacting a liberal statute in the context of which the New Caledonians will feel their pride soothed, we will manifest the confidence and esteem France holds for them. We can nevertheless attend to those things which make the population of this island a little backward through education, by facilitating study in France for the largest possible number of boys and girls. With the same goal in mind, we should use all our efforts to increase the size of the white population through supervised immigration. Simultaneously, the indigenous population must be treated with solicitude.

He added that economic policy should lighten tariffs to foster productivity in New Caledonia. Similar policies of education and development were counselled for the EFO.[23] Yet another writer, the chief of staff of the French High Commissioner in the Pacific, warned the Commissaire des Colonies of the stakes in the Pacific:

If the *métropole* continues to neglect these possessions and takes no account of the diverse aspects of the important problems which are emerging in this part of the empire, we are heading towards certain loss [of the colonies]. A loss which will first begin with their total economic takeover [by foreigners], doubtless followed by the human detachment of their populations from a *métropole* which will not have understood them and which took no interest in them or their countries . . . . The question is basically whether or not France wants to keep its rich and fine possessions scattered in a part of the world which more and more is going to be in the centre stage of world developments and towards which the USA is increasingly turning.[24]

In these reports reappear many of the tenets of pre-war policy-makers and colonial promoters: the increasing importance of the Pacific region in international politics and trade, the danger of foreign designs on French possessions, an urgent need for France to reinforce its position and develop the potential of its colonies.[25] Such ideas persisted over the next few decades, despite great changes in Asia and Oceania – changes which the commentators of the 1940s did not foresee, such as the successful independence movements in French Indochina and the Dutch East Indies. Particular recommendations contained in these proposals would have a long life. Recognition of the need for a 'liberal statute' for French territories foreshadowed decades of argument (and occasional confrontation) about the degree of autonomy the colonies should enjoy. Demands for a new 'native policy' became a leitmotif of discussions about France in Oceania. The suggestion for greater immigration from France to the South Pacific colonies remained official policy until the 1970s. These views, circulated in the Pacific and among the Free French movement and provisional government in the 1940s, signalled a basic continuity with pre-war attitudes yet announced the main lines of post-war policy.

Not only metropolitan officials sent to the colony or members of the provisional French government's staff commented on the future of the Pacific colonies. Settlers and their representatives were becoming increasingly vocal and presented veritable lists of grievances to the authorities.

One of the most thorough such remonstrations was a report which the Conseil Privé of the EFO addressed to the Free French Commissaire des Colonies, René Pleven, in 1944. Edouard Ahnne, Robert Charon and their colleagues, prominent Tahitian politicians, began by affirming: 'We want to emphasise that we are not revolutionaries anxious for radical changes, but good Frenchmen, supporters of democratic and republican law and of wise moderation' – this type of prologue marked most colonial petitions during the war and immediately afterwards. Nevertheless, French Polynesians argued that they must take part in the territory's affairs; after all 'the half-breeds [*demis-blancs*] of the EFO are at least as well informed of . . . their duties and their civil rights as are some of the good and true peasants of Normandy and Lorraine'. Furthermore, Pacific islanders had served France in two world wars. This justified a new relationship:

> Because of their strategic and commercial position, the EFO have a right to take their place and play an important role in the French Colonial Empire. But in order for them to do so . . . this colony must no longer be treated as in the past . . . in turn as a simple way-stop [*maison où l'on passe* – a pun, since it could mean either way-stop or whorehouse], as a poor relation or as an insignificant outpost.

In just over sixty years, forty-five governors had ruled over the colony, and the succession of ideas and methods had occurred almost as quickly as the change in chief executives. The other members of the administration left much to be desired, said the petitioners; far better than the envoys from the *métropole* who monopolised the administration would be local appointees. 'Is it not possible to recruit here most of the public servants for junior positions? Our young Tahitians would do the job just as well, if not better than, the incompetents, the crazies and the spoiled kids who are shipped to the Antipodes just to get rid of them.' Local appointments would develop the administrative skills of Tahitians and save money for the government.

The members of the Conseil Privé protested against the quality of bureaucrats but also against the structure of the administration. There existed no elected body in Tahiti; the appointed Conseil Privé had no real powers and was often not even consulted by the governor. The governor held both executive and legislative authority, 'more power than the most demanding dictator would claim and – the other side of the coin – more responsibility than he can reasonably bear'. By contrast it was unacceptable

> that the settlers who have devoted their lives to the development of this colony, and who in the mother country enjoyed all rights of French citizens, here become pariahs and see themselves and their descendants condemned to be deprived of their civil and political rights. Neither is it acceptable that the indigenes, who are French citizens, who pay the largest share of taxes and who contribute their labour for the enrichment of the country, have no right to take part in colonial affairs, no control over employment or in the apportionment of the money they pay into the Treasury.

Finally, the counsellors attacked the Chinese population of Tahiti, whom they accused of 'generally deplorable morals' and of an 'atavism of venality'; they 'sabotage everything they produce', are 'essentially unassimilable and outside French influence, maintain a hateful defiance of France and are clearly partisans of the United States'. The letter, in short, demanded recognition of the rights of the local French and Polynesians against the incursions of *métropolitains* and Chinese migrants.

Appended to their declaration was a list of over twenty suggestions for reform. The EFO should have the same administrative system as that of such colonies as Martinique and

Réunion; a representative *conseil général* would be responsible for appointing public servants. Efforts might be made to recruit and appoint local candidates and to dismiss others who were unnecessary. Tahiti ought to elect a representative to the French consultative assembly. French law must become standard throughout the EFO and various particularistic laws remaining in force from the nineteenth century in some island groups should be abrogated. Freedom of the press must be guaranteed. The 'Chinese question' should be studied. An effort should be made for 'the defence of the indigenous race by the organisation on a large scale of a campaign against substandard housing, tuberculosis, alcoholism, venereal diseases and Chinese-Tahitian miscegenation'. There was need for new schools and more scholarships and for an improved road system. Institutions such as a postal credit bank should be established. The government ought to enact labour legislation and also protect Tahitians against land speculation. A further suggestion was to reopen the French shipping lines and to nationalise the Compagnie Française des Phosphates d'Océanie, a major employer and 'the very prototype of colonial exploitation by international capital for the sole and admitted goal of naked profit'. All of these measures, the writers pleaded, would 'revive in our hard-working populations an appreciation of that which is specifically French. You are so far away from us'. René Pleven wrote back to the counsellors that he was basically in favour of the suppression of the *code de l'indigénat* and restrictions on the press, and he accepted the need for more public works, medical and educational projects. He did not mention the Chinese or shipping, however, and said that the nationalisation of the phosphate company would be 'premature'; establishment of a *conseil général*, he added, would not be appropriate for the EFO.[26]

Such correspondence of the 1940s reveals the variety of suggestions made about the future directions of French policy and, often, the strength of sentiments held. Remonstrances and government reports regularly exalted the loyalty of the colonial population during the war and the sacrifices they made, but grave concerns always loomed about their continued loyalty and about the strength of France in the international arena. Moreover, there appears a distinct disparity between the different perspectives of settlers and metropolitan officials and writers in

French ministries on the other side of the world. The colonists felt that France must act to better their economic and social position and to give them a degree of political power simply as their just due; the ultimate aim of the French government should be to accord them the rights, privileges and material benefits of French citizenship. For the strategists in Paris (and in the Free French headquarters in Algiers before the end of the war) the ultimate objective was the preservation and increase of French influence in the Pacific region and the world in general. Certainly, new rights and more aid should be accorded to the island colonies – both because of their loyalty and sacrifices and also because of their evident poverty and under-development. But such concessions should also aim at defusing separatist feeling and, ultimately, at reinforcing France's international position. The difference of opinion was not quite so simple as the colonies being an end for one side and a means for the other, but the divergence in perspective clearly demonstrated separate priorities.

The French archives of the early 1950s contain relatively few general reports or analyses of French policy in Oceania. French attention was diverted elsewhere, notably to the war in Indochina. French policy in the Pacific islands in these years involved the application and execution of principles established earlier; no need for detailed study or reorientation was felt. The islands of France's Pacific empire were simply too small and remote – and the South Pacific in general too calm – to preoccupy strategists (except to the extent that they had to keep watch over contrary local politicians).

In fact, the colonial order in the Pacific seemed safely in place in the 1950s and, somewhat paradoxically, only in the French islands did local political movements act rebelliously. Yet occasionally some significant modification of the status quo seemed in the offing, and French officials took the occasion to comment. Such reports show that they feared radical change in the South Pacific, especially any change which might affect the French territories, and also, that their prime objective remained the preservation of France's international position.

One notable example is a series of dispatches from France's *chargé d'affaires* in New Zealand which are particularly interesting because New Zealand administered several Pacific island

groups taken over by Britain in the nineteenth century: Western Samoa, the Cook Islands, Niue and Tokelau. The French
reports make it clear that New Zealand and France had rather
different approaches to island administration. In 1952, the
chargé d'affaires notified Paris that New Zealand was setting up
an executive council for its Pacific islands, and the following
year he commented on the New Zealand plan for self-government in Western Samoa. The envoy said that democratic institutions were supposed to respect the 'feudal traditions' in
Samoa, but ulterior motives lay behind the Samoans' demands
for institutional changes: 'One of the aspects of the autonomy
movement is the desire of certain notables to reinforce or to
recapture their traditional power in order to oppose the current tendency towards a more individualistic and egalitarian
life'. New Zealand seemed willing to move towards total independence for Samoa, which the Frenchman thought problem-
atic because of the clash between Samoan chiefs, the *matai*, and
commoners, as well as between Polynesians and mixed-blood
residents (which he terms 'Euronesians'). Furthermore, he said,
Samoans lacked resources, and the Polynesians had no desire
to work. There was also the question of eastern Samoa, a colony
of the United States; the Americans did not now object to New
Zealand plans for Western Samoa, but if there occurred unrest,
Washington might be upset, particularly because of the 'anti-
colonialism and the spirit of the anti-Communist crusade' of
the Americans. The French, he added, were not concerned for
their own interests in Western Samoa – a dozen French nuns
and twenty Marist priests. However, there was a certain danger
from current developments:

> There is the danger of contagion and imitation. Our Pacific
> colonies, New Caledonia and Tahiti, run the risk of being
> seriously perturbed by the creation of a free Samoan state
> and henceforth by the publicity which will be given to it.

The governor of the EFO had always tried to limit contacts
between French Polynesians and Western Samoans, for example, by not inviting Samoan dancers to Papeete for the 14 July
celebrations. But the diplomat feared that the 'contagion' might
not just affect the South Pacific:

> Outside the Pacific, there is our North Africa. Certain people
> will not miss the chance to make it known that in Western
> Samoa, just as in Tunisia and Morocco, there coexist two
> evolved populations [indigenous and European] and that
> nevertheless it is planned to treat them alike, even at the risk
> of subjecting the more developed minority to the less devel-
> oped masses.

In societies of settlement, projects tending towards self-government would endanger Europeans and 'evolved' natives who
were their allies. The envoy went on to criticise not just the idea
of the New Zealand proposal but the way it had been formulated, including consultation with the Samoans, a petition and
a special enquiry; the possibility for such political participation
by islanders 'threatens to lead to the most regrettable sort of
agitation in our overseas possessions'. Finally, he blamed New
Zealand authorities for not taking account of the risks their
actions might have on neighbouring colonies and fellow imperial powers:

> It happens that New Zealand, lost at the ends of the globe,
> lying in the extremities of the southern ocean, forgets that it
> lives on the same planet as others. No country is more insular
> than this one. Certainly it is well disposed, even extremely so,
> towards France. But, if we ignore New Zealand, as we too
> often do, we risk seeing it creating serious problems without
> really wanting to do so.

In subsequent reports to his minister, the French envoy in New
Zealand repeated these arguments. He drew parallels between
the New Zealand trusteeship of Western Samoa and the French
domains in North Africa to underline his point that 'it is in our
Oceanic possessions that the risk of contagion is greatest' and
he accused the American press of spearheading the
'disaggregation of the "French Union"'. The diplomat also
commented on other external territories of New Zealand. He
approved of special legislation for the Chatham Islands; Tokelau,
he pointed out, was not attached to a ministry in Wellington
and was under the direct control of the governor-general 'who,
given a general indifference, hardly concerns himself with it'.

He was dismissive of New Zealand's Pacific colonies: 'If I have used the word "empire" to characterise New Zealand's colonial domain, this is undoubtedly a very big word for it. This empire is Lilliputian'. But he realised that New Zealand's relationship with these small islands was cast in a different mould from that of France with its overseas territories. New Zealand, for instance, had not considered giving the islands representation in the national parliament; furthermore, each island was considered as a separate entity rather than as part of an ensemble. He reflected on the aims of the New Zealand 'empire':

Why in fact is there a New Zealand 'colonial empire'? Its island territories are not an area of interest either for capitalists or for bureaucrats. There are hardly any resources to develop, and even administrative posts are rare. New Zealand only has an empire because Great Britain foisted upon it some of its own responsibilities in the South Pacific. This was to Great Britain's advantage and savings. New Zealand would have happily passed this up – how many people here know that New Zealand has a colonial empire or even where the islands I have listed are located? – but the responsibilities it assumes are the ransom paid for the protection Great Britain affords and for the markets which the *métropole* provides for New Zealand's pastoral products.

Nevertheless, Wellington did gain a few advantages from the islands, including tropical products, bases for meteorological stations and the extension of New Zealand's defence frontier from an arc of Polynesian islands in the north to the Ross Dependency, New Zealand's claim in Antarctica, to the south.

The envoy drew some 'lessons for the French Union' from the New Zealand case:

The New Zealand 'colonial empire' shows us that, with distance, certain imperatives must be respected. Territories which are far away cannot be governed exclusively from the capital. Giving a statute to our *départements d'outre-mer* which makes them as much as possible like our metropolitan *départements* is understandable, because their populations are truly assimilated. But it is necessary if not to decentralise, at least to 'deconcentrate' [administration] so that most decisions can be taken *sur place*. Furthermore, it is appropriate to take account of various differences in the process of evolution. A colonial empire, and a 'union', is a very complex thing. In this regard, Great Britain provides a model to copy [the Commonwealth] . . . . A diversity in institutions must be reflected in different statuses for the inhabitants. A common citizenship cannot be absolute.[27]

In general, therefore, the emissary argued that France should avoid the 'contagion' of autonomist movements or decisions to decree self-government from the centre, but at the same time – and somewhat paradoxically – it must undertake a limited devolution of administration and adapt the legislation appropriate to different overseas territories. His explicit comparison was one of different policies – 'Like all English countries, New Zealand practises a policy of decentralisation, not of assimilation'[28] such as favoured by France. But he also suggested a contrast between New Zealand's and France's international aims in the South Pacific: while New Zealand had taken on its possessions in order simply to satisfy Britain and secure English markets for New Zealand's exports, France had more legitimate objectives of global politics. Although critical of Wellington's South Pacific projects, the envoy implied as well that France must take account of such neighbours to its possessions as New Zealand and develop a more concerted policy for the region.

Such comments point to an important aspect of the history of French Oceania: the changes in French policy concerning the Pacific islands never took place in isolation. Domestic French developments, international considerations, the influence of certain pressure groups and different ideologies all played their part in determining the tenor and direction of French policy. Developments 'on the ground' might affect policy, but so too could metamorphoses of ideology and public opinion. This was particularly the case with the empire, the history of which had been one of shifting pro-and anti-colonial sentiments mixed with a substantial dose of indifference to the conquest and preservation of overseas domains. The evolution of political myths, mass attitudes and the constitutional experiments of parliamentary assemblies provide the framework in which France's Pacific policies must be set.

COLONIAL MYTHS AND CONSTITUTIONAL EXPERIMENTS

The years immediately after the Second World War saw the revival of the myth of empire. 'The future lies in the empire', wrote one author, and another added: 'It is only with the help of its overseas territories that France can hope to become once again a world power'. A *député* told the French parliament that without its colonies, France was only a small power but with them, it was a great one. The *ralliement* of at least some of the colonies, including, in the early months of the war, Tahiti and New Caledonia, helped to preserve French resolve in the face of the German onslaught; the contribution of indigenous soldiers in the Second World War, as in the First, testified to the value of colonial men fighting under the French flag. General de Gaulle set up headquarters for the provisional French government in North Africa. In addition to the wartime contribution of the empire, colonial promoters championed the advantages the empire would give France in peacetime – territory, raw materials, markets and bases for cultural influence.[29]

In reality, the French public was often unaware of the situation in the colonies and showed little interest in colonial affairs: a 1949 public opinion poll indicated that a third of all the French received no regular information on the colonies, and just over a half said they were uninterested; a fifth of those surveyed could not name a single overseas territory. In 1949, three-quarters of all the French had no desire to move overseas, and only seven per cent could envisage ever settling in the French overseas territories. The French public took relatively little note of such events as an insurrection in Madagascar or even the war in Indochina. The struggle between French forces and nationalists in Indochina was also a war of attrition on French opinion; from 1947 to 1949, the proportion of the French more or less resigned to the 'loss' of Indochina grew from 37 to 49 per cent. When the Algerian conflict became more violent, the French took greater notice of colonial affairs, but not all were advocates of *Algérie française*, nor did all believe that Algeria would or could remain French: already in 1956 less than a third of the French polled thought Algeria would still be French five years hence. Such figures indicate that the empire was not a major priority for the ordinary French, most of whom were largely ignorant of colonial life. Many thought the overseas domains would in any case become independent. If four-fifths of all the French in the late 1940s vaguely felt that the empire was in general beneficial to France, and a similar proportion thought that France had brought benefits to Africa, Indochina and its other colonies, most saw the empire as a symbol rather than an important reality.[30]

The political elite meanwhile was engaged in heated debate about the future of the empire. The Assemblée Nationale Constituante, elected in October 1945, put the empire relatively high on its agenda. Delegates from the empire took an active, and generally critical, role in the debate; Léopold Sedar Senghor and Lamine Gueye from Senegal, Félix Houphouët-Boigny from the Ivory Coast, Ferhat Abbas from Algeria and Aimé Césaire from Martinique were among those who castigated French economic, cultural and political exploitation of the colonies. They demanded full citizenship, the right to vote and parliamentary representation for all inhabitants of the colonies (including, in particular, the indigenous populations), suppression of the *code de l'indigénat*, the head tax and forced labour where they existed, and provisions for greater economic and social development. Leftist politicians, who formed a majority in the assembly, supported many of these claims, and even conservatives argued in favour of remoulding relations between *métropole* and colonies. Opinion varied largely on whether the colonies should be fully 'assimilated' into the French system or whether the new empire should be a federation of France with relatively autonomous overseas territories and states, a revival, *mutatis mutandis*, of the old debate on 'assimilation' versus 'association'.[31]

What eventuated was a compromise, the establishment of the Union Française (the French Union) under the constitution of the Fourth Republic adopted in 1946. Under the terms of the new constitution, the *vieilles colonies* – Martinique, Guadeloupe, Guyane and Réunion – became *départements d'outre-mer* (DOMs) with a legal structure and administration which 'is the same as that of the metropolitan *départements*, except for those exceptions determined by law'. The other colonies were renamed *territoires d'outre-mer* (TOMs) and provision was made as well for *États associés* (a statute which was only used, and then only briefly, for the Indochinese Federation). The constitution defined the French Union, the new incarnation of the Empire: 'The French Union is composed, on the one hand, of the Republic which includes metropolitan France and the overseas *départements* and territories, and, on the other hand, of the associated territories and states'. The word 'colony', like 'Empire', was thereby banished from French constitutional usage, symbol of the refounding of relations between France and its former 'possessions'. The underlying principle applicable in the *territoires d'outre-mer* was that, unlike the *départements d'outre-mer*, they were not wholly assimilated into the French system of law and administration. They continued to be administered by a governor (or governor-general), who exercised broad powers much as before 1946. The constitution reserved to the French parliament direct control of such domains as criminal law and political and administrative organisation. Legislation passed in Paris was applicable in the *territoires d'outre-mer* only 'by explicit provision or if it has been so extended by decree . . . after consultation of the Assembly of the Union'. The 1946 constitution further allowed that 'provisions appropriate to each territory may be decreed by the President of the Republic'. In short, both the President and the French parliament could draw up and enact or proclaim measures for each individual colony, and there was only an imprecise constitutional requirement that the assembly of the French Union, itself a strictly consultative body, be asked to give advice. The TOMs elected members to this body, as well as to the French parliament, but through a complicated system of electoral colleges rather than on the basis of universal suffrage; the bulk of the non-Europeans in the TOMs still lacked the vote. Territorial assemblies existed, including ones in New Caledonia and the EFO, but they were restricted to deliberative functions and held no legislative power.[32]

The constitution of the Fourth Republic therefore remained true to the precepts of the Brazzaville Conference and the general French tradition of administrative centralisation. Affairs in Tahiti and New Caledonia would still be decided almost entirely in Paris and by Paris's representatives in the Pacific territories.[33] The assemblies in the two TOMs, though lacking many powers, did enjoy the right to debate issues and to decide on the disbursement of certain funds, as well as act on various questions concerning economic and social issues; as subsequent developments proved, they often exercised these rights in a contestatory (and contested) fashion.

Despite failure to decentralise colonial administration, the constitution of 1946 did significantly alter the legal status of the population of the *outre-mer* (except for those in the *vieilles colonies*, parts of the EFO and in some other colonies where they were already citizens). The constitution and accompanying legislation abolished the *code de l'indigénat*, although one article allowed individuals to retain the 'civil status in common law' if they so desired and, thus, to be judged by customary traditions, such as tribal regulations, rather than French civil law.[34] The constitution of 1946 disappointed the more radical critics of French administration, and it did not effect the decolonisation of the empire. But it represented change from the form of rule which had hitherto existed. Even if not all residents of the empire were granted the suffrage, and thus access to parliamentary politics, the principle of representation at a local and national level had been admitted. The way was opened for further parliamentary measures to adapt laws to specific colonies, for decision-making to be devolved to overseas territories and for the French Union to become a Gallic version of the Commonwealth.

This new legal and administrative structure for the TOMs lasted until 1956, despite the colonial crises in Indochina and Algeria (and problems elsewhere) and the instability of the Fourth Republic – frequent changes of ministries, the rise of extraparliamentary movements and general dissatisfaction with constitutional structures. Governors succeeded each other in Nouméa and Papeete with somewhat less rapidity than in the pre-war period. Meanwhile, political parties were organised and several prominent politicians rose to power in the Pacific TOMs. New political activism, made possible by the constitutional provisions of 1946 and set in motion partly by the effects of the war, provided a serious challenge to the redesigned 'colonial' system. These political changes – the actors who took part, their ideologies and their successes and failures – are the single most dramatic development of the post-war decade.[35] But they were accompanied by other changes as well.

ECONOMIC AND SOCIAL CHANGES

The late 1940s and early 1950s saw much new legislation relating to the colonies, not only concerning their constitutional relationship with the *métropole* but also their economic and social structure. Many of these acts aimed at development of the overseas territories and the underlying principle represented a continuation of the policy of *mise en valeur* inaugurated in the 1920s and 1930s and then cut short by the war. Articulated in a book by Albert Sarraut, an official of the Ministry of Colonies, this policy targeted infrastructural development – roadways, port facilities, education and medical care – to improve the life of the colonists and indigenous populations and to maximise the benefits France could obtain from its overseas domains.[36] Post-war efforts in economic policy also linked up with an increasing role for the state in France, as seen by nationalisations and the setting up of a public welfare system.

Some measures carried out in the *métropole* found no parallel in the Pacific territories. Although several commentators had called for the nationalisation of such large companies as the Société Le Nickel and the Compagnie Française des Phosphates de l'Océanie, neither was taken over by the government. The social security benefits available in the *métropole* were not extended to the colonies; however, the colonists also continued to be exempt from income tax. Several other measures were duly adopted by the parliament and promulgated by the appropriate officials but never applied. For instance, a law of 3 May 1946 aimed at making farming or pastoral activities on property owned by individuals or companies obligatory in the EFO, an attempt to encourage agricultural production was promulgated by the governor but never enforced. In 1948, the French government ended the Banque de l'Indochine's prerogative for note-issuance in the Pacific territories, but that measure also went unenforced and the bank temporarily retained the privilege.[37]

New French agencies also had a great impact on the economic development of the colonies, none more so than the Fonds d'Investissement pour le Développement Economique et Social des Territoires d'Outre-Mer (FIDES). Established in

1947, the agency's mission was to fund public works projects and other activities in the French colonies; it became the main source of capital for many undertakings in the Pacific and elsewhere in the French Union through both loans and out-right grants. Among projects funded by FIDES in the early post-war years were schools, highways, port facilities and dams. Other French agencies, such as the Institut Français d'Océanie, a research organisation which opened in 1948, also played a role in the TOMs.

Technological and commercial innovations affected the French Pacific in the years just after the war, the most obvious of which was air travel. Possibilities for transport of imports and exports, as well as movement of people, had always been crucial for the 'water-locked' islands of the Pacific, and the long distances and high costs of such connections had forever been a handicap to their development. Colonists and administrators had argued unanimously that sea-links were inadequate. The war disrupted all transport between the colonies and France, and the situation did not improve dramatically after 1945 despite the resumption of some services. The Messageries Maritimes, the only French shipper to call regularly at the Oceanic ports, connected Papeete to Marseille once every twenty-eight days before the war, but immediately afterwards the frequency diminished to once every three or four months. (Connections between Papeete and Nouméa were even more irregular.) In 1950, one official reported that in 1900 it had taken thirty-five days to go from Marseille to Nouméa, while in 1950, it took sixty-five days to make the same trip; he added that dates of departures and stops were not always fixed, ships were old and uncomfortable, and most French passengers with sufficient means used foreign lines rather than the Messageries Maritimes. The Minister for Overseas France asserted that such insuf-ficiencies opened the door for foreign companies to gain a toehold in the French territories and that lack of attention to such problems fuelled autonomist sentiment since France seemed manifestly incapable of carrying out its duties as an administering power.[38]

New challenges and opportunities presented themselves with air travel. The American forces had constructed aerodromes in Bora-Bora, New Caledonia, Wallis, and on several of the islands of the New Hebrides during the war, and these remained available for French use; Tahiti, however, had no landing strip. Seaplanes occasionally reached the French islands, but the service was irregular and inadequate. Provisions for better air services seemed a question of both prestige and commerce. As the Director of Political Affairs at the Quai d'Orsay noted in 1949, concerning the EFO: 'Our prestige has been seriously compromised by comparison with what was able to be done during the war years. between the great means of the Americans and the paucity of our own means'. Furthermore, difficulties in selling copra now underlined the economic downturn registered by the islands in the wake of the Americans' departure. Discontent with French rule, the official continued, could create pro-American and autonomist sentiment, and every effort must be made to combat this effect. One way would be through improved air connections.[39]

In 1946 was created a Société Française de Transports Aériens du Pacifique-Sud (TRAPAS), a private company formed with government subsidies. It began service the following year in New Caledonia and the New Hebrides, and in 1948 experimented with services in the EFO. A cyclone then destroyed most of its aircraft, but funding from the state, the Ministry of Overseas France and Air France (which was part-owner of TRAPAS) allowed the purchase of new planes. By the end of the decade, TRAPAS flew from New Caledonia to the New Hebrides and the EFO in Catalina planes; the route also extended to Saigon with flights by Air France. By the early 1950s, passengers could travel once a month on Air France from Paris to Nouméa in less than three days via Karachi, Saigon, Jakarta, Darwin and Brisbane.

Foreign carriers also served the French territories. For several years, the American company Pan Am landed planes in Nouméa, as did the Australian line Qantas. The South Pacific, including the French territories, was beginning to be covered by a network of air links. Nevertheless, TRAPAS registered a large deficit on its operations and discontinued its service to Papeete; Air France hesitated to extend its flights through the Pacific islands. Foreign airlines were interested and entrepreneurial, but French officials worried about political repercussions. Debate on air traffic provided the occasion for an official from the Ministry of Foreign Affairs to report fears of foreign influence and its effect on separatist movements in the EFO:

> The deeply-felt emotional attachment [of residents of the EFO to France] is mixed, for many of them, with aspirations to autonomy which the least error, the least neglectfulness, even the least oversight could crystallise . . . . Certain foreign powers are giving proof of their growing strength. I believe that the cutting of concrete [transport] links with the *métropole* would reinforce the conviction that France is no longer able to fulfil its duties as the administering nation. This would only increase the powers of attraction which are already drawing certain sentiments towards the outside and other and nearer sources of wealth and immense material means. Foreign airlines (the American P.A.A. [Pan Am] and Ruantas [*sic*, i.e. Qantas]), which cannot be kept out of Papeete, could appear as the first tangible sign of the weakening and withdrawal of France.[40]

In the event, however, little eventuated. TRAPAS was dissolved in 1951, and Air France took over service to Nouméa; Pan Am discontinued its stops in New Caledonia. The EFO remained without regular air service, although occasionally planes stopped at Bora-Bora; in any case, no airport was constructed in Tahiti until the end of the 1950s. In the decade after the war, therefore, the French Pacific entered the age of airplanes but without particular glory.

Major social as well as economic changes took place after the end of the war.[41] Such questions as the labour supply and potential migration to the French Pacific continued to be of concern. One proposal was to send French orphans to New Caledonia after the war. An article in the Nouméa press argued in favour of the plan, claiming that orphans could assure the survival of the European population in the territory. However, the government strongly rejected this proposal.[42] By contrast, efforts to attract other European migrants and to recruit contract labourers had greater success.[43]

Social changes resulted from post-war legislation. The most important act was the repeal of the *code de l'indigénat* in 1946. The *indigénat*, adopted in the late nineteenth century, was a series of laws aimed at controlling and regulating the native population of New Caledonia. Melanesians were largely restricted to designated reservations and allowed to work or travel outside them only with special permission. A chief was appointed by the French government to regulate the affairs of the tribe according to customary law. The chief was responsible, among other duties, for collecting a head tax from Melanesians. The tribe could be held collectively responsible for various wrongdoings, and the government could punish it with fines or sequestration of goods. Furthermore, under the *indigénat*, administrative personnel could arrest and punish 'natives' for a large number of infractions without resort to a judge and trial – these transgressions included such acts as refusal to render service, negligence of hygiene and failure to pay tax. The code also required Melanesians to provide service for public works projects.[44]

The *code de l'indigénat* was the object of great resentment among Melanesians and great criticism from anti-colonialists, who likened it to a kind of slavery. Since Melanesians were not French citizens, and only a very small number had the right to vote, they had no recourse from abuses of a code which they regarded as unjust. The repeal of the *indigénat* released them from labour conscription and gave them freedom to move about the territory and change jobs at will; it also removed the arbitrary controls and punishments to which they had been subjected. Coupled with the provisions of the 1946 constitution which made Melanesians French citizens – although, paradoxically, not all were given the vote – it amounted to a liberation of the Melanesians.

At the same time laws ended labour contracts for recruited workers in New Caledonia, most of whom came from the Dutch East Indies or French Indochina. They had previously been prohibited from changing employment or acquiring property, and their movements around the territory and possibilities for remaining in New Caledonia after the expiration of their contracts were limited. Now Asians were given civil rights, which encouraged many of them to leave their old jobs in the mines. A large number became traders and opened shops either in Nouméa or the *brousse*. Colonists were less than enthusiastic about this development, as they feared competition from the merchants and a scarcity of labourers. Since the 1890s, the mines (and some plantations) had replied on cheap, quasi-servile labour provided by Asians, and the changes underlined the increased significance of labour as a post-war issue. The emancipation of contract labourers also made it possible for some to leave the territory, and many Vietnamese and Javanese were repatriated. Others, as well as many of the Indonesians, were now allowed to settle permanently in New Caledonia and acquire French citizenship, adding to the territory's ethnic diversity (and causing some resentment among Melanesians).

In the EFO, the situation was different from that in New Caledonia. The subjects of King Pomaré, over whose realm France had declared a protectorate in 1842, became French citizens with the annexation of those domains in 1881. But some of the outer islands maintained separate law codes – or, in some cases, rather ill-defined mixtures of French and customary law – and their inhabitants remained French subjects rather than citizens. The French law code was applied in most of the EFO in 1887, but provisions were retained for various special arrangements, notably for collective landholding (*indivision*) and inalienable property rights. At the end of the Second World War, French law was extended throughout the EFO, granting citizenship to many Polynesians who had not previously been entitled to it. The Chinese remained an exception since only with difficulty could they acquire French citizenship or full political and civil rights. For none of the residents of the French islands did the acquisition of a new legal status bring political power, wealth or social well-being.

CONCLUSION

In 1946, the French 'Empire' became the 'French Union'; 'colonies' became 'overseas territories', the Minister for Colonies became the Minister for Overseas France. The change was semantic, even euphemistic. But it reflected a recasting of the relationship between France and its overseas domains. The old regulations abolished in the 1940s, such as the *code de l'indigénat* and regulations on contract labour, were never reestablished, and many of the new arrangements have endured, including the nomenclature of the 'TOMs' and representation in the

French parliament, as well as such agencies as the FIDES. Technological and economic change which became apparent in the 1940s, particularly the use of the airplane, were permanent innovations.

Another inheritance from that period was the general shape of French international policy: the desire to assure a presence for France in the Pacific, ward off undue foreign influence, guard against dangers from separatist sentiment within and 'contagion' from without, and undertake economic and social development both for their own sake and in order to accomplish other objectives. These aims differed little from the goals of pre-war and even nineteenth century policy. Furthermore, many of the ideas underlying colonial policy persisted, including an ethnocentric and often romanticised view of 'natives'. The state of underdevelopment of the French territories, so often noticed by commentators in the 1940s and 1950s, combined with the anomalies of a colonial system which had become increasingly anachronistic, posed the question of whether the new policies would be able to effect the modernisation of the territories. Soon challenges which even the more foresightful of observers did not foresee rocked the carefully reconstructed edifice of post-war 'colonialism'.

3 The Economic History of the French Territories

THE COLONIAL ECONOMIES

Before the arrival of the French, the economies of New Caledonia, French Polynesia and Wallis and Futuna had begun to undergo economic change. Trading vessels, including a few French ships, exchanged textiles, metal instruments, alcohol, weapons and other goods for island produce. Melanesians and Polynesians sold sandalwood and trepang for the Chinese market and copra for European factories. Passing ships replenished their larders with tropical fruits and vegetables, and islanders acquired no less exotic manufactured goods. Regular trade routes and markets were established by the early 1800s – Tahiti exported pork to Australia and oranges to California. Trade was generally beneficial; foreign merchants made profits, islanders acquired new goods; and certain chiefs, in addition, used their relationships with foreign merchants to enhance their political positions. Overseas investors and policy-makers hoped for a windfall from trade in the Pacific basin, and they saw the islands as convenient refuelling points between the Americas, Australasia and Asia.[1]

With the establishment of protectorates and the annexation of islands, Europeans showed eagerness to develop local resources, maximise returns and compete successfully with their commercial rivals. The French initially hoped to establish plantation economies in the South Pacific, much as they had done in earlier centuries in the Antilles and Indian Ocean. New Caledonia, in particular, seemed fertile ground for prosperous farms managed by European settlers. In the second half of the nineteenth century, Frenchmen in New Caledonia planted coffee, rice, sugar and cacao, and began livestock-raising as well. They faced many obstacles. Few colonists had training in farming, especially in tropical conditions. Capital was in short supply, even if grants of land ensured that properties were available for settlers' use. The domestic market remained small, and export markets were distant. Competition loomed large – after all, most tropical crops grew in France's other colonies in Africa, Indochina and the Caribbean as well as in Oceania. Labour was hard to procure; agriculturalists and pastoralists found Melanesians unreliable workers and had to import other islanders or Asians or, for a time, hire workers from the penal establishments. Despite great hopes, New Caledonia did not become a thriving plantation colony during the first century of French rule.

The situation was similar in the EFO. Small and mountainous islands did not provide promising terrains for cash-cropping, and Polynesians, much like Melanesians, seemed more interested in farming taro or collecting breadfruit and coconuts than in working as hired labourers on European plantations. Foreigners tried to harvest a variety of crops, but generally with even less success than in New Caledonia. A Scot who established cotton plantations in Tahiti in the 1860s was a rare exception. Worked by recruited Chinese labourers, the Tahitian cottonfields created a small-scale economic boom which, however, lasted only so long as the Civil War and its aftermath in the United States restricted supplies of American cotton on the world market. Other plantation crops that were tried in Tahiti, especially vanilla, had brief phases of success but never became profitable enough to sustain numerous settlers.

Elsewhere in the French Pacific, copra formed the main agricultural product of interest to Europeans. In Wallis and Futuna, the Loyalty Islands and the New Hebrides, copra was the only significant export commodity in the late 1800s and early 1900s. France was the largest European importer of copra, destined for the soap factories of Marseille, and the South Pacific islands represented the major source of this dried coconut meat. Islanders harvested coconuts from stands of trees which grew wild on the islands or, increasingly, which were planted by settlers or missionaries.

Minerals also interested Europeans. Soon after the French takeover of New Caledonia, miners found deposits of chromium, cobalt, gold and other minerals on the Grande Terre. In the 1860s, prospectors discovered nickel, the product which became the economic mainstay of the territory. New Caledonia possesses one of the world's largest reserves of nickel, and by the last decades of the nineteenth century, it became the world's major source of nickel ore. Nickel, a precious alloy in the making of hardened steel used for such products as ships and armaments, found increasing demand in Europe; in New Caledonia, France held title to an important strategic mineral as well as a profitable sales item. The Société le Nickel, established in New Caledonia, was the largest French enterprise in the South Pacific. Many smaller but still flourishing mining companies controlled by the inaccurately named *petits mineurs* assured the wealth of their owners and created an export-oriented economy for New Caledonia. Yet the mining economy was never immune to the downturns of trade cycles, difficulties in company organisation and problems in securing labour.

In French Polynesia, miners discovered phosphate on the island of Makatéa; mined from 1908 to 1966, it represented the major export of the colony until the mines were exhausted. Elsewhere in the French Pacific there were no deposits of minerals other than sulphur in the New Hebrides. Although not exploited until the mid-twentieth century, these mines also came to be a useful resource for the French in Oceania.

Not suprisingly, the French colonies did not develop manufacturing sectors; even clothing and furniture were imported from the *métropole.* The tertiary economy, by contrast, had great reason to expand simply in order to handle imports and exports. Some settlers opened small shops in towns or travelled the countryside selling their wares. After the failure of the cotton plantations, almost all the Chinese in Polynesia became shop-keepers in Papeete, in rural districts or on remote islands. Many Asians in New Caledonia similarly became merchants, a position which often caused them to be resented by other residents.

Two French shipping lines regularly served New Caledonia, the Messageries Maritimes and Ballande; both also traded in Australia. The Messageries Maritimes received subsidies from the French government for its postal route to New Caledonia. Ballande operated inter-island steamers and sold goods directly to settlers and islanders. Neither company called at Papeete or other French Polynesian ports; despite lobbying by colonialists, neither agreed to extend its services east of Nouméa. The only regular international shipping runs to French Polynesia were on American and New Zealand lines; and not until the 1920s did a French company regularly call at Papeete. The major trader in French Polynesia until the First World War was a

Hamburg company, the Société Commerciale de l'Océanie, commonly known by the name of its founder, a German of French Huguenot ancestry, Godeffroy. The New Hebrides and Wallis were served by somewhat episodic French shipping, although French traders competed against other companies, notably the Australian Burns Philp line. Nevertheless, a number of French settlers earned their living, sometimes well, by working for French or foreign shippers.

Another economic activity was banking. The number of long-lived banks were few and trading companies supplied the major financial services in the colonies. Only in the first decade of the twentieth century did a large bank open in New Caledonia and French Polynesia, the Banque de l'Indochine. It enjoyed a monopoly on note issue and was the only full-service bank in the colonies, but the profits it gained there were well under ten per cent of its total worldwide earnings – a statistic which itself reveals the minor role played by the Pacific islands in France's economic empire.

The French stakes in the economies of the South Pacific in the century after 1842, therefore, were limited. Although certain metropolitan companies, such as Ballande, the Messageries Maritimes and the Banque de l'Indochine, were present in Oceania, the major domain for their activities lay elsewhere. Only the Société le Nickel and the Compagnie Française des Phosphates de l'Océanie, which operated the Makatéa mines, were international class companies based in the French South Pacific. Even so, the Société le Nickel was controlled by Rothschild investment interests in France. The Société Française des Nouvelles-Hébrides, which held nominal title to huge tracts of land in the Anglo-French condominium and was the major exporter of its copra, dominated the economy of the New Hebrides but played only a small role on a world scale. The South Pacific colonies, like many others, supplied raw materials sold for the profit of small local elites and a handful of metropolitan interests. Yet with their size and isolation they could hardly be expected to compete with France's larger holdings in Indochina, Africa or Madagascar.

It is doubtful whether the Pacific colonies made much of a profit for France, although both agricultural and mineral exports provided income to the *métropole* and the companies which exploited these resources. Some metropolitan investors earned money from their business in Oceania, and a few of the French in the Pacific – the owners of mines in New Caledonia, the proprietors of large plantations or livestock ranches, traders in Papeete and Nouméa – did well from their activities. Many French settlers, however, lived modest, if not downright poor lives, including liberated prisoners and 'poor whites' in New Caledonia, beachcombers in the Polynesian islands and small-time traders unable to compete with larger trading companies or enterprising Chinese merchants. A number of the French existed on their earnings as itinerant workmen, manual labourers or sellers of alcohol to the 'natives' of the islands. The colonial oligarchy in the French islands was small indeed, and such islands as New Caledonia were uncommon in the colonial world in seeing the emergence of a real European underclass. The earnings and standards of living of the poorer Europeans differed little from those of their Melanesian and Polynesian neighbours. By the early twentieth century, the economies of the French Pacific showed the co-existence of capitalist export production of copra and ore, managed by metropolitan and local elites, and an economy of agricultural subsistence and episodic trading which was the lot of the indigenous populations. Between these two groups came the poorer Europeans and the Asian migrants who formed a largely disenfranchised and far from wealthy stratum in the colonies.

The Second World War disrupted, but did not reorient, the economies of the French territories. In the late 1940s and 1950s, the economic situation returned to more 'normal' times. Nickel and phosphate were shipped out, foodstuffs and manufactured goods shipped in. The companies which existed before the war survived, and gradually a few other French companies, such as the airlines, set up shop in the Pacific. The 1950s showed little economic dynamism in Oceania, various government initiatives to revitalise local economies withstanding. Economic activity increased largely in tune with modest rises in population.

By contrast, the 1960s witnessed veritable economic revolutions in New Caledonia (and, by extension, but in a much more limited way, in Wallis and Futuna) and French Polynesia. A nickel boom in New Caledonia and the establishment of the French nuclear testing centre in French Polynesia effected the biggest long-term shocks on the Oceanic economies since the arrival of the Europeans and the accompanying revolutions of trade and mining. In addition, such activities as tourism and the expansion of government employment, as well as more concerted efforts to promote island development, changed the economies of the French islands. By the 1970s, they enjoyed the highest standards of living of any islands in the South Pacific, although critics pointed out that this was the result of the creation of 'artificial' economies totally dependent on France.

ECONOMIC REVOLUTION IN POLYNESIA

Mining

The major economic activity in French Polynesia until the mid-1960s was phosphate mining on the island of Makatéa. In 1908, the Compagnie Française des Phosphates de l'Océanie began operations on this small Tuamotu island. In 1950, at the height of mining, Makatéa produced almost 275 000 tons of phosphate; sales fluctuated over the next fifteen years until the exhaustion of the deposits forced the closure of the mines in 1966. The phosphate exported by the CFPO amounted to a quarter of the total exports of the territory in the 1950s and 1960s. Its main destination was the Japanese market, but Australia and New Zealand were also major purchasers; throughout the life of the mine, the Makatéa phosphate competed successfully with ore from such other South Pacific sources as Nauru and Ocean Island (Banaba). The impact of mining on Makatéa and French Polynesia was immense. The salaries paid by the CFPO accounted for no less than a quarter of total earnings paid in the private sector in the territory and 12–14 per cent of all salaries in French Polynesia. The CFPO employed almost four thousand people. It was the major importer into French Polynesia and built a considerable infrastructure of roadways, loading docks, processing warehouses, housing and administrative offices in Makatéa, ran boats and undertook other commercial ventures. The CFPO, in addition, paid a variety of taxes to the French Polynesian government, including land taxes, business license fees and import and export duties; in the 1960s the phosphate company's taxes provided a quarter of the total territorial budget of French Polynesia. The

CFPO then represented a capital of 750 million CFP, easily making it the biggest company in French Polynesia. Before 1958 it was controlled by the Unilever group, in collaboration with the Anglo-French Phosphate Corporation, but in that year control passed to a French financial institution, the Compagnie Financière de Suez.

In exports, salaries and taxes the CFPO was a big business in a small territory. But its influence reached far beyond a simple monetary accounting. Particularly significant was its recruitment of labour. The population of Makatéa itself was too small (and considered by the company too unreliable) for the needs of the mines, so, from the beginning, the CFPO looked elsewhere for workers. Other Polynesians from the French islands, notably Manihiki, left the employers disappointed, so in the early decades of the twentieth century they recruited Japanese, Indochinese and Chinese, as well as residents of the New Zealand colony of the Cook Islands. The Japanese left during the Second World War, and most of the Vietnamese were repatriated after the war. Their places were largely filled by French Polynesians, despite earlier opposition to using local labour. In 1962, of 2675 Polynesians working for the phosphate concession on Makatéa itself, 15 per cent came from Tahiti, 40 per cent from the Leeward group of the Society Islands and 40 per cent from the Austral archipelago; most were recruited on yearly contracts and worked as unskilled miners or more specialised artisans. The remainder of the work force, including 300 Asians (mostly Chinese), 80 Europeans and a handful of Cook islanders, generally held the more skilled positions; the upper levels, unsurprisingly, were staffed by Europeans, usually Frenchmen from the *métropole* temporarily posted to Makatéa.

The majority of the Polynesians were young men, usually unmarried. Work in the Makatéa mines was for many their first contact with wage labour, and they used their salaries to provide for their daily needs and to acquire consumer goods – motorbikes were a much sought after souvenir of a sojourn on Makatéa. They worked in hard conditions, came down with various diseases and, despite limitations on the sale of fermented drink, sometimes suffered from alcoholism. However, they continued to practise their Christian religions (Catholic or Protestant), joined sporting clubs and had access to a company-sponsored library; the CFPO prided itself on making recreational and religious activities available to the workers. They also listened to Radio Tahiti which was beamed to Makatéa. A number gained training as mechanics or learned other trades. This vocational institution, the salaries workers earned, the goods they purchased, and the experience of 'Western' work had great sociological and cultural effects on the Polynesians; difficult to discern in a precise fashion, these effects certainly survived the end of labour contracts and the closure of the mines.[2]

The CEP

The changes wrought by mining were significant enough in an economy which had previously relied largely on farming and fishing. But an even more dramatic development was the setting up in the territory of the Centre d'Expérimentation du Pacifique (CEP), the French nuclear testing facility, and the auxiliary activities of the Commission à l'Energie Atomique (CEA).[3]

With the independence of Algeria, France had to transfer its nuclear testing station from the Sahara, and in 1962 President de Gaulle announced that it would be moved to French Polynesia. Work on the site started the following year, and the first explosive device was tested in 1966. The building of the test site on the atolls of Mururoa and Fangataufa, as well as a base on Hao and administration buildings in Tahiti, created an immense demand for labour and goods in French Polynesia. Two million cubic metres of soil and rock were displaced, a hundred thousand cubic metres of concrete poured and two kilometres of quays, three aerodromes and twenty-five hectares of buildings constructed on Mururoa and Fangataufa. Just building an airport on Hao necessitated uprooting over 7000 coconut trees, displacing 880 000 cubic metres of coral, laying 100 000 tons of bitumen and putting in place 4000 tons of steel; the creation of a port involved moving another 50 000 cubic metres of coral. In 1966, on Hao alone 2650 workers were stationed – 1920 military personnel, 280 European civilians and 450 Polynesian civilians. In Tahiti, a new port was constructed. Accompanying these developments came a whole military infrastructure: a military camp at Arue, a military airbase at Fa'a'a, staff headquarters at

Pirae, and various housing, medical and recreational facilities for the troops needed to carry out the nuclear tests.[4]

Although technical and administrative expertise for the construction of the facilities came from expatriate Europeans, French Polynesians provided much of the labour. The government recruited workers from around the territory for the construction sites, and it paid attractive wages for what were generally six-month employment contracts. Polynesians welcomed such work, especially since the Makatéa phosphate mines were then winding down operations and closed in the same year that nuclear experiments began. Yet the CEP was not just a replacement for Makatéa's mines; it brought into the wage economy a larger group of Polynesians than had previously been touched by mining.[5] Polynesians, who saw the chance to make quick money either by working for the CEP or in other European concerns, flocked to Papeete and the testing stations in the Tuamotus, abandoning plantations and villages and distancing themselves from traditional sources of income and ways of living.

The effects of the CEP and CEA activities did not terminate with the construction of the test sites: the CEP remained the major economic activity and the major employer in French Polynesia. The number of employees attached to the CEP rose from 4000 in 1964 to 7000 in 1965 and 13 000 in 1966; the CEP workforce dropped to 8000 in 1967 but grew again to 15 000 in 1968. It has since varied according to the frequency and importance of particular nuclear tests. Possibilities for work attracted many *métropolitains* in addition to Polynesians; the number of Europeans in the territory increased from 2500 in 1962 to 5500 three years later. Demand for auxiliary services connected with the CEP and the spending of CEP workers helped increase both public and private sector jobs – the number of salaried workers in the private sector grew from 8850 to 26 000 during the 1960s.

The impact of wage labour was particularly significant for ethnic Polynesians. By 1966 and 1967, the CEP employed some 2000 to 2500 islanders, which represented between one-sixth and one-seventh of the total male population in the labour force. In some islands, the proportion was much higher; 40 per cent of the men of Bora-Bora, for instance, worked for the CEP. Similar to the workers in the Makatéa mines earlier, two-thirds of the Polynesian CEP workers were unmarried, and more than two-thirds were between the ages of fourteen and thirty. They came to work on the CEP sites from around French Polynesia, including several hundred from the remote Marquesas and Austral islands. Paid around 40 000 CFP per three months of work, and provided with food and lodging, they accumulated previously unknown savings which could be spent on various purchases. (In 1965 alone, fifty motorbikes arrived on the tiny island of Bora-Bora with returning CEP workers.) Having developed a taste for salaries, and having been exposed to city life in Papeete, many showed reluctance to return to remote villages and subsistence livelihoods.[6]

Evaluating the precise role of the CEP/CEA in the French Polynesian economy is difficult; much of its expenditure is absorbed in the general expenses of the government and military, a high proportion of the money paid in CEP salaries and purchases returns to France to families of personnel working in the territory or to French commercial suppliers, and the exact extent of economic multiplier effects (in housing, food, consumer purchases and other areas) is almost impossible to gauge. One estimate, however, was that in 1966, expatriate employees of the CEP spent just under 39 million French francs[7] on food and housing and the CEP spent another 67 million francs on its *métropolitain* personnel; local families connected with the CEP accounted for 31.2 million francs of expenditure; the administration spent 30.3 million francs in investment, 44.9 million on various services and 16.4 million on construction and other works.[8] Another estimate suggested that the global expenditures of the CEP/CEA and the French army ranged from 4200 million CFP in 1964 to a high of 12 356 million CFP two years later and 7700 million CFP at the end of the decade; this equalled, respectively, 46 per cent, 76 per cent and 36 per cent of the total Gross Domestic Product (GDP) of French Polynesia. The same calculations also suggested that from 1964 to 1980, CEP/CEA and military expenditures never fell below 18 per cent of the territory's GDP and generally accounted for between a quarter and a third of GDP.[9]

Once the infrastructure for the tests had been put into place, outlays for salaries and construction diminished. When France changed from atmospheric to underground experiments in the mid-1970s, spending further decreased, and some French Polynesians worried about the detrimental effects this could have on the territory's economy. But throughout the 1970s and 1980s, the CEP continued to be the cornerstone of the local economy. An official estimate of the economic role of the CEP, CEA and army put military expenditures in 1985 at 1.5 billion francs. The military and nuclear experimentation organisations spent 607 million francs with local enterprises (for supplies, rents, and so on), as well as 302 million francs (notably import duties) in taxes and other duties; these taxes represented 27 per cent of the receipts of the territory's exchequer in 1985. Salaries of workers recruited in French Polynesia totalled 308 million francs, and 534 million francs were spent locally by military personnel and another 4000 civilians. In short, the total expenditure of the army and CEA represented about 15 per cent of the GDP for 1985, slightly down on the proportion of previous years, but nevertheless of great consequence in the local economy.[10]

The CEP and its activities therefore changed both the structure of employment in French Polynesia and the contours of the local economy. Exports dropped from 1.1 billion CFP in 1960 to 434 million at the end of the decade, partly because of the end of mining, but also because of a downturn in agricultural production and the flight from the primary sector. Meanwhile imports jumped from 1.6 billion CFP in 1960 to 13.6 billion a decade later, reflecting the needs of the testing site, new European residents and their particular consumption patterns and Polynesian workers and their families who were developing a taste for Western, and therefore imported, foodstuffs, clothing and other goods. The state became the major provider of salaries; from 1962 to 1970, salaries paid in French Polynesia doubled, but while the share of salaries provided by the private sector slipped from 60 per cent to 33 per cent, that of the administration grew from 12 per cent to 34 per cent. Public expenditure grew from 29 per cent of the GDP in 1960 to 54 per cent four years after.[11]

In less than a decade, Tahiti had changed from an economy dominated by agriculture, fishing and mining to one in which the tertiary sector held pride of price. From being a region with a modest export of primary products which covered most imports, French Polynesia became a net importer which covered only a small proportion of its purchases by exports. It became, too, a place where the state – and, in particular, one activity – was the major financier, employer, economic regulator and, in general, motor of the economy.

Other Economic Changes

Mining, before 1966, and the CEP, from 1963 onwards, over-shadowed – but, in fact, contributed to – many other economic developments in French Polynesia. Two sectors showed dramatic transformation: growth of tourism (especially on Tahiti, Mooréa and Bora-Bora), and attempts to stimulate agriculture and pastoralism (as on Tubuai and Maiao). Case studies illustrate the extensive impact of such changes in micro-societies, but also the constraints on Western-style development in an economy such as that of French Polynesia.

Large-scale tourism in French Polynesia did not really begin until the early 1960s. Hotels were small, tourist services largely undeveloped and travel difficult. Small planes served the territory only infrequently, and the landing strip on Bora-Bora was the only aerodrome which could handle large international planes. In 1959, a French airline began serving Tahiti with a propeller-driven aircraft which flew from Nouméa to French Polynesia via Fiji. Air travel became easier with the opening of the international airport in the Papeete suburb of Fa'a'a in 1961, and such carriers as Air France, Qantas, Air New Zealand and Lan Chile began regular flights. Concurrently, tourist interest increased. The filming of Metro-Golden-Mayer's 'Mutiny on the Bounty' on Bora-Bora in 1959 had renewed the image of Polynesia as an idyllic destination. The announcement of the transfer of the nuclear testing site to the Pacific also promised more travel to the islands.

The first major hoteliers to take advantage of the situation, however, were American rather than French. In the early 1960s three Americans, later nicknamed the 'Bali Hai Boys', arrived in French Polynesia after abandoning their jobs as a lawyer, salesman and stockbroker. Their first endeavour, to revive a vanilla plantation, failed, so they opened the Bali Hai Hotel on Mooréa, which proved an immediate success. The proprietors proved themselves innovative by organising excursions and other activities for their guests and inventing new sorts of hotel accommodation – neo-Polynesian huts (*farés*) built on stilts directly over the ocean, sometimes with glass floors which allowed tourists to gaze at underwater life. In 1966, the Bali Hai Boys opened a second hotel in Raiatea, followed in 1973 by a hotel in Huahine. These hotels brought tourists to see the Polynesian ruins and sleepy fishing villages of the Leeward Islands, which extended tourism beyond Tahiti and Moaréa.[12]

The government in 1965 set up a Tourist Trade Development Office to promote and define policy on tourism. The next few years saw the building of still more hotels, often owned by international companies, on Tahiti, Moaréa, Bora-Bora and other islands. Some were large Western-style hotels, others bungalow hotels built in the fashion pioneered by the Bali Hai. The number of hotel rooms in Tahiti grew from only 51 in 1960 to almost 1400 in 1973. The number of tourists also leapt upwards, from 1472 in 1959 to 37 299 in 1966 and 77 988 five years later. Most tourists stayed in the territory for only about a week, but they spent enough money to have some impact on French Polynesia. Tourism during the 1960s rarely accounted for more than three per cent of GDP, but at the beginning of the 1970s tourist receipts equalled a third of the value of French Polynesian exports and over seven per cent of imports. In 1971, the tourist trade directly or indirectly employed 2500 people in the territory, roughly six per cent of the working population. Many of the hotel staff were local Polynesians, although higher-level executives were generally *demis* or French expatriates. Such employment, like that in mines or in CEP-related activities, hastened the move of Tahitians from rural to urban areas and from the primary to the tertiary sector. This symbolised one of the paradoxes of tourist development: in a locale renowned for exoticism and natural luxuriance, tourists wanted both the joys of a paradise free from worry and stress and, at the same time, the comforts of urban living. The infrastructure of the islands, and the lives of their people, were thus modernised, a transformation which helped assure comforts for visitors (and many in the local population) but increasingly put an end to the tranquillity, isolation and exoticism which first lured tourists to Polynesia. Visitors consequently vaunted the beauty of Tahiti but bemoaned its high prices, traffic jams and rampant consumerism.

The island of Mooréa provides a particular example of changes brought by tourism. Mooréa, the closest island to Tahiti and its international airport, was in an excellent position to take advantage of tourism. Before the 1960s, Mooréa's productive economy was based entirely on agriculture, centred on the growing of foodstuffs for the local population plus some copra, vanilla and coffee farmed as cash crops; these were sold in Papeete to earn money for building materials, tinned food and clothing. A crisis in the vanilla industry in the early 1960s, caused by plant disease and soil exhaustion, attacked one pillar of Mooréa's cash economy; copra production continued temporarily, only to decline later in the decade. Plantations were abandoned, and some proprietors left Mooréa. Increasingly islanders took jobs in Papeete and moved from agricultural to tertiary employment; the most popular local alternative was a position in the growing tourism industry or related service sector jobs. Before the 1960s, only several small, family-run hotels existed in Mooréa, but in that decade other, larger hotels opened, including a Club Méditerranée and the Bali Hai. Local people found jobs constructing hotel buildings or working in the hotels; still others earned their living transporting tourists around the island, producing handicrafts for sale, performing in folkloric shows or working in auxiliary activities. In one district with a major hotel, tourist activity directly or indirectly accounted for two-thirds of the population's wage labour. The old isolation of Mooréa came to an end as regular boat services connected it to Tahiti; in 1968, with the construction of a landing strip, the two islands were linked by airplane. The other side of the coin was the degradation of Mooréa's environment through the levelling of land and the proliferation of litter. There appeared a marked contrast between that area of the island where tourist activities grouped, the north coast, and the remainder of the island. The island and its workforce became a part of the 'modern' economy but dependent on the strategies of tour-operators and hotel chains.[13]

With the growth of tertiary employment connected with the CEP and CEA, tourism and the expanding bureaucracy, agricultural activity plummeted in French Polynesia in the 1950s and 1960s. Imported foodstuffs replaced local goods (even in the diet of the Polynesians), the proportion of the GDP created by agriculture dropped and old staples of production seemed in danger of extinction. Faced with these problems, the administration made efforts to stimulate agricultural production, targeting growing urban demand for farm products.

One notable initiative occurred on an island close to Tahiti, Maiao. In the early twentieth century, this tiny island exported copra harvested by an Englishman who controlled most of the land. He lost his holdings in 1935 and an agricultural co-operative was set up, partly to avoid the problem of dividing the planter's land among the many claimants to his estate. Neither the co-operative nor the production of copra showed particular success in the next fifteen years. In the 1950s, greater demand for copra and for fish for the Tahiti market encouraged island entrepreneurs to increase sales. Technical progress also helped: in 1957 the island acquired a shortwave radio, permitting traders to alert the local population to their visits; the following year, the territorial administration banded coconut trees with metal rings, which limited the destruction caused by rats. Then at the beginning of the 1960s, tourism in Tahiti created a market for pandanus leaves, used as thatch for the roofs of neo-Polynesian bungalows. Sales of both pandanus and copra grew, and trading vessels came to the island more frequently. Yet islanders remained dissatisfied with the conditions of trade – boats continued to call irregularly, and the traders, who paid a low price for copra, reaped most of the profits. A solution was found when the co-operative successfully applied to the government for money to buy a boat of its own. The new vessel allowed easier access to Tahiti for passengers and crops, and fishermen sold their catch for four or five times as much when they marketed it directly in Papeete as when they relied on intermediaries. During the first full year that the co-operative used its own boat (1964), earnings from cash crops doubled by comparison with past totals; per capita income on the island trebled in three years. The Maiao experiment provided the example of a successful agricultural co-operative, and showed how a direct link with a market, stimulated by government subsidy, could effect a major change in a small economy. Certainly demand for pandanus, copra and fish in Papeete was limited, and few islands were so advantageously close to Papeete as Maiao, but this particular island had found a way to maximise its resources.[14]

Another example of economic innovation and island spe-
cialisation was the Tuamotu island of Tubuai. In Tubuai, as in
many other Polynesian islands, land was traditionally owned to
some extent collectively, a situation which many planners and
agricultural economists considered a bar to modernisation;
however, the case of Tubuai showed that such land tenure
could underpin economic development. The soil of Tubuai was
not particularly promising for the planting of cash crops, but in
the 1960s, intervention by the government, along with greater
demands for European foodstuffs, provided the stimulus necessary for agricultural revival. Local farmers planted tomatoes,
lettuce, beans and other Western crops: almost all the produce
was exported to Tahiti. Tubuai was also the only island in
French Polynesia to produce potatoes, and in the 1970s government and private business initiatives targeted potatoes as an
appropriate specialty for Tubuai. A local entrepreneur in government employment extended his plantings of potatoes in
1977; although not initially an overwhelming success, the gains
were significant enough to encourage other farmers to convert
their fields. By 1985, 180 of 230 households on Tubuai earned
their income from potato-farming, an income which in 1981
reached the high level for French Polynesia of $US4500 annu-
ally for each household. Forty-nine hectares under cultivation
produced three-quarters of a million kilos of potatoes. Tubuai
farmers faced competition from Chinese share-croppers in Tahiti and, until the government subsidised a trading boat for the
island, suffered from problems of transport. But their earnings
provided money for consumer durables, and the potato-plant-
ing project allowed them to preserve collective land tenure: the
island population itself distributed short-term use of land to
those who were interested in cash-cropping.[15]

Maiao and Tubuai were perhaps exceptions in the economic
history of French Polynesia. Despite government efforts, agriculture did not prove dynamic in the territory. Islands such as
the Marquesas were too distant or, like the Tuamotus, too
infertile to take advantage of markets in Papeete. Yet, by contrast, imported food was easily available and relatively afford-
able. Urban tertiary jobs continued to exercise more attraction
than agricultural labour. Other initiatives at island development, therefore, focused again on mining or tourism.

For instance, in 1978, a French entrepreneur named Jean Bréaud expressed interest in reviving phosphate-mining, this time from the undersea deposits next to the atoll of Mataiva. Bréaud formed a company in which he held a quarter of the shares; the rest of the capital was fairly evenly divided among the French mining and chemicals company Pechiney, the Canadian mining company Comincon and the American Union Oil. The company offered to pay mining rights to the territorial government to extract a million tons of phosphate annually. The local and metropolitan governments welcomed the initiative, although the 174 inhabitants of Mataiva worried about pollution of the lagoon and the killing of the fish which formed their basic source of food. The company extracted only nine hundred tons of phosphate for analysis in the early 1980s before a series of cyclones buffeted the island, destroying most houses and coconut plantations in 1982 and 1983.[16] The idea of mining phosphate in Mataiva has continued to be mooted, and prospectors predict that deposits are large and would be extremely profitable. In late 1990, the French Polynesian government announced that mining would finally go ahead. But local residents again protested, demanding a larger share of the profits.

Another, rather novel, approach to development was the plan to sell Tupai island to a consortium of Japanese interested in developing a large tourist complex for visitors from their country. In this case, the holiday spot would be developed almost solely by and for foreign interests, and the effects on the French Polynesian economy remained unclear. The precedent for the sale of an island does exist – in the 1960s Marlon Brando bought the small atoll of Tetiaroa, where he maintains a house and provides a few rooms for fee-paying tourists – but the Japanese overture had not yet been accepted or rejected by late 1991. In any case, Japanese business has become increasingly involved with French Polynesia through the acquisition of hotels which are already operating and the purchase of land for future resorts.

THE ECONOMY OF FRENCH POLYNESIA IN THE 1980S

The economy of French Polynesia in the 1980s showed the

successes and failures of various efforts to stimulate it and displayed characteristics of both development and underdevelopment.[17] The per capita GDP was higher than that of other island states of the South Pacific, even including New Zealand, and significantly greater than the GDP of the micro-states of the region; it was, in fact, not far below the per capita GDP of the *métropole*. The structure of the economy and labour force was distinctly post-industrial, as seventy per cent of gross domestic product came from commerce and other tertiary activities. Yet the economy of French Polynesia was turned firmly towards the exterior – exports covered only about a fifth of imports. Regional development among the various archipelagos was unevenly distributed, and differentials in salary had become established between the European, Chinese, *demi* and Polynesian populations and between Tahitians and residents of outer islands.

Production of agricultural products destined for export had not ceased in French Polynesia. Sales of copra increased worldwide during the 1980s, although the Philippines and Indonesia cornered most of the market. Production in French Polynesia declined steadily because of the decreasing fertility of the soil, ageing of coconut plantations and lack of replanting, conversion of land to different uses and the further movement of labour from plantations into the bureaucracy or tourist activities. The effects of tropical storms and overseas competition hurt copra production as well. Only in the remote Tuamotus and Marquesas, where there were virtually no alternative income-earning opportunities, did plantations expand, and the marketing of a new brand of copra-based suntan lotion developed in Tahiti (*monoï*) accounted for some sales. The territorial government was obliged to guarantee copra prices and subsidise the coconut oil refining plant in Tahiti (of which it was the majority shareholder).

Other agricultural commodities fared little better. In 1983, local authorities launched a new plan for vanilla production. For vanilla, as for copra, world competition was a barrier to growth since Madagascar produced four-fifths of the world's supply of vanilla and stockpiled reserves equivalent to two years' sales. Nevertheless, some Tahitian vanilla was marketed in Europe and the United States. Local planters also had hopes for the sale of exotic tropical flowers (anthurium, *tiaré* and *opuhi*), and in 1988 they formed a syndicate to commercialise flowers, particularly on the Japanese market. Competition from Hawaii, distance from markets and simple market saturation limited opportunities for expansion. Other tropical crops had declined in volume; local production sometimes did not even satisfy French Polynesian demand (as was the case with coffee, fruits and vegetables). When production was large enough to permit market sales, the lack of better networks for commercialisation, high prices and consumer preference for imported goods limited sales.

Livestock-raising also continued to decline in French Polynesia, just as it had done since the 1960s, because of lack of interest in pastoralism, the predominance of imports and the lure of jobs in the service sector. Milk production by local dairy farmers covered only a quarter of local consumption, although hog-raising provided for over four-fifths of Polynesian demand for pork products.

The ocean around French Polynesia has provided a variety of maritime products. Fish and other seafood have remained bases for the local Polynesian diets, particularly in the outer islands, where artisanal fishing has usually achieved self-sufficiency and permitted local sales. Some three hundred fishermen practised coastal fishing in the 1980s, and there was some commercial fishing. Large-scale fishing was handled exclusively by Japanese and South Korean enterprises through annual contracts signed with the territorial government. In the mid-1980s, the Japanese were enthusiastic about such accords, and local authorities hoped to establish long lasting partnerships for sales, technical assistance and other benefits. But, disappointed at the lack of greater Japanese commercial co-operation, the French did not renew the Japanese contracts in 1988; those accords will probably be revived in the future with hopes for greater French sales on the Japanese market. South Korean vessels have continued to fish the waters of French Polynesia with licences from the French authorities.

Few other maritime resources were developed in French Polynesia with the exception of pearls in the Tuamotu archipelago. In the nineteenth century, pearls and mother-of-pearl had been harvested in French Polynesia. Harvests of mother-of-pearl, used especially for the production of buttons, fluctuated between 300 and 650 tons per annum in the late 1800s and early 1900s; in the record year of 1924, the colony produced 1200 tons. The invention of the plastic button in 1957 dealt a hard blow to the mother-of-pearl market, although some demand remained for the production of luxury buttons and handicrafts. The market for pearls, meanwhile, steadily increased. Previously pearls had been obtained by divers, the famous 'pearl-fishers' whose job was arduous and dangerous, but in the 1960s, the French government maritime research organisation (CNEXO) began to experiment with pearl-farms and artificial breeding-pools. An experimental pearl-farm opened on the island of Rangiroa in 1967 and on Manihi the following year. By 1980, thirteen co-operatives farmed pearl-bearing oysters on ten different islands, all located in the Tuamotu chain. The pearls which were harvested were more numerous and of better quality than those gathered by diving, and the artificial breeding-pools also had the advantage of preserving natural stocks from depletion. Twelve thousand pearls from French Polynesia were sold in 1981, and pearls replaced copra as the major export of the territory. Buyers, especially in the major markets of Europe, Japan and Hong Kong, were especially attracted to Polynesia's black pearls, which fetched as much as double the price of the white pearls of Japan or the yellow pearls of Australia. Pearls therefore represented a major export-earner for French Polynesia; in addition, the pearl industry provided several hundred jobs for largely Polynesian employees and became the commercial speciality of the Tuamotu islands.[18]

The secondary sector of the economy contributed relatively little to French Polynesia's GDP or employment, although activities spanned part of the spectrum – construction, brewing, food-processing, printing, and so on. Enterprises were usually small, and all aimed purely at satisfying local demand rather than export. Most industrial materials continued to be imported from overseas, usually from France. Efforts to create import-substitution industries for manufactured goods were not particularly successful – even many of the tourist souvenirs, postcards and printed fabrics (*paréos*) sold to visitors were produced outside the territory in countries where wages were markedly lower than in French Polynesia.

Tourism remained a growth industry in Tahiti in the 1980s; in the middle of the decade, 122 000 tourists visited the island, and the number steadily increased. More air links with foreign countries – including France, the United States, New Zealand, Australia, Japan and Chile – allowed tourists to fly to French Polynesia directly, although some visitors still arrived by private yacht or on cruise vessels. French people came to the territory, either to visit family members or on official business; the largest number of tourists came from the United States. Tourism suffered the effects of international economic misfortune; the number of visitors from North America, for example, dropped by a tenth after the stock market slump of 1987. The number of French tourists also dropped, a decline linked both to changing fads in holiday destinations and to smaller numbers of people visiting family members employed in CEP and CEA activities, the workforce of which was itself decreasing. By contrast, the number of Japanese tourists increased by a quarter at the end of the decade, thanks to the inauguration of flights from Papeete to Tokyo; Italian, German and British tourists also increased in number, partly because of a new campaign of tourist promotion in those countries. Tahiti was a prestige holiday destination, and one authoritative travel magazine ranked Bora-Bora as the most enticing island in the whole of Polynesia in terms of scenery, beaches and facilities.[19] But the distance, cost, and lack of charter flights – by comparison with the West Indies, Africa and the Indian Ocean – put Polynesia out of reach of many holiday travellers.

In the 1980s, as in the previous decade, the basis of the French Polynesian economy was metropolitan transfers, linked primarily to the administration and public services of the territory and to the presence of the CEP and CEA. The commercial deficit of the territory in 1988 was evaluated at 53 billion CFP, most of which was covered by metropolitan transfers. In 1986, metropolitan government transfers amounted to 94 per cent of the value of imports into French Polynesia. Exports totalled 8112 million CFP in 1988 while metropolitan transfers (in 1986) amounted to 87.5 billion CFP. Such statistics make clear the degree of reliance of French Polynesia on the *métropole*.

Generalisations about French Polynesia, of course, mask differences among archipelagos and, as well, concentrate on the global picture rather than examining particular sectors and specific economic activities. This inevitably reinforces the image of commercial torpor and economic dependence. Microeconomic studies, however, reveal that certain activities are relatively thriving and, in their business structure and the composition of their workforce, play an important social role in the territory.

One example of such an activity is the 'trucks' of Tahiti, public transport vehicles which ply the streets of Papeete and connect rural districts of the island to the capital. The trucks – the English word is used in both French and Tahitian – are chassis of standard trucks transformed by local artisans to accommodate passengers: parallel benches are installed on the truck-bed, and a roof protects passengers from sun and rain. With bright colours and often with blaring music, the trucks are a well-known feature of Tahiti. They travel along prescribed routes but according to only vague schedules; passengers are picked up and set down both at designated stops and, through the goodwill of the drivers, at other points. In the late 1970s, there were three hundred trucks (the number is limited by law) serving some two hundred routes. Fares are set and prices are very low.

Most passengers who use the trucks are ethnic Polynesians or those with lower incomes (or those too young to have driving licences). Many use the trucks to go to work or to go shopping; 17 000 persons arrive or leave from the marketplace in Papeete, the truck terminus, each day. Children are among the most frequent users of the trucks, which they take to go to school. The proprietors of the trucks are generally ethnic Polynesians. The typical owner of a truck licence is a man around forty years of age – although women account for a quarter of the truck-owner-operators; most are the sons (or daughters) of farmers or fishermen and themselves have only a primary school education. There is a considerable waiting-list to acquire a truck licence, although frequent turnover as well. The drivers, if they are not proprietors of the vehicles, rent their trucks, and profits and expenses are shared between owners and operators. Drivers, on average, work ten hours a day for five-and-a-half days per week. Their income usually equals the minimum wage in Tahiti. Regulations on ownership which limit each truck licence owner to three vehicles ensure that no monopolies are created. Approximately two hundred families, or 1500 persons, live entirely or in part from the truck business. Trucks thus form an important source of employment and earnings and are a type of economic activity available to small-scale private entrepreneurs in French Polynesia.[20]

The case of the trucks of Tahiti illustrates a level of economic activity different from that of international big business. That of the Marquesas islands shows the disparities in development between bustling Papeete and a remote archipelago. At the end of the 1980s, 7358 inhabitants lived in the six islands of the Marquesas, and an estimated 7000 Marquesans lived in Tahiti. The distance of the Marquesas from Tahiti, 1500 km, was the major obstacle to greater development. Several ships served the archipelago – a combined passenger-freight vessel called at the islands every three weeks, while a schooner came twice a month to collect copra from the islands. A regular air service connected the island of Nuku-Hiva to Tahiti twice a week, and an eighteen-seat Twin Otter served another three islands from Nuku-Hiva. The cost of fares, however, was extremely high. The infrastructure of the islands was considered generally satisfactory: the islands enjoyed electricity, automatic telephones, television and running water. Most of the valleys had infirmaries and there was a modern hospital in Nuku-Hiva, although problems of health care arose in some districts. Local children received their primary education in the Marquesas but had to travel to Tahiti to complete secondary studies. Vocational training existed in the islands, but there were no tertiary institutions there. According to the Institut d'Emission d'Outre-Mer, the principal characteristic of the economy of the Marquesas lay in the 'pluri-activity' of its inhabitants. Agriculture, fishing and artisanal jobs complemented tertiary employment provided by public works projects, notably construction. Further income was provided by sales of copra (around 3000 tons annually). The *service militaire adapté*, mandatory national service inaugurated in 1989 and usually performed in public works projects, provided further jobs. A small livestock ranch and a refrigeration warehouse for fish completed the economic activities, but the size of the market and lack of marketing networks limited sales. The local population had resisted the construction of hotels in the islands, although a few tourists arrived on cruise ships and on excursions organised by resorts or travel agencies in Tahiti.[21]

The same sort of 'pluri-activity', coupled with the major phenomenon of expatriation to Tahiti, marked many of the other islands in French Polynesia. Such a case highlights the duality which has existed between the micro-economies of smaller islands and the burgeoning tertiary economy, based on French government transfers, of Papeete and its suburbs. The situation also points to the paradox of French Polynesia's economy, where geographical, sectoral and even ethnic enclaves of development (and the prosperity it has engendered) exist in the midst of underdevelopment, traditional economic activity and more modest standards of living. Yet everywhere in the territory economic development – schemes for exploiting natural resources, investment and employment – depends directly or indirectly on the largesse of France.

THE ECONOMY OF NEW CALEDONIA

Nickel

The economy of New Caledonia since the 1860s has revolved around nickel. A period of increased production in the 1950s and early 1960s led to an unparalleled nickel boom at the end of the 1960s. A downturn and stagnation followed in the early 1970s; after a brief revival there was a crisis in the early and mid-1980s. More recently, the industry has again revived. This cycle of booms and busts illustrates the volatility of the nickel market and the relative fragility of an economy largely dependent on one resource. Given the importance of nickel in the territory – mining and treatment of ore have provided the biggest source of employment, and nickel ore has consistently accounted for over 90 per cent of New Caledonia's exports since the Second World War – the cycles of nickel sales have patterned the global evolution of the New Caledonian economy.

Nickel is needed for making stainless steel used in chemical, petrochemical and agro-alimentary industries, as well as special types of steel and superalloys used for the construction of machine utensils, trucks and agricultural machinery and aircraft engines. It is also used in high-tech industries, including the construction of nuclear reactors, coal-treatment plants, gas turbines, desalination plants and electronics. Lastly, many currencies use nickel or nickel alloy coins. The technological changes taking place in the 'third industrial revolution' of electronics and high-tech industries, transport and the processing of raw materials have all increased demand for nickel. New Caledonia has one of the world's largest estimated reserves of the mineral, approximately 60 million tons (of total worldwide reserves of 240 million tons); the content in pure nickel of New Caledonian ore is higher than that of the ore found in many other places. Despite competition from other producers, notably Indonesia, Cuba, the Soviet Union and Canada, New Caledonia was in an excellent position to profit from the expanded demand of the post-1945 period. In the Société le Nickel (SLN), New Caledonia produced an enterprise capable of mining, processing and marketing nickel ore in international markets; four other mining companies also export nickel. The major market for exports is Japan. Nickel is mined in New Caledonia in the centre and east of the Grande Terre with major mines located near Thio, Kouaoua and Poro, and smaller mines near Népoui, Voh, Poum and Koumac. The Nouméa suburb of Doniambo is the location of the only smelter in the territory, a facility owned by SLN.

In the 1950s, rising world demand, fuelled in particular by the Korean War, provided the incentive for modernisation of New Caledonia's mining industry. New mines opened, the metropolitan and territorial administration granted concessions for prospecting and production, and the nickel industry built a large hydroelectric dam at Yaté. Despite some difficulties in finding labour after the end of the contract system under which Indochinese and Indonesians had worked in the mines, and the subsequent repatriation of many of the Vietnamese in the 1950s, the number of SLN's employees doubled in the decade after 1954 (to reach three thousand workers). The company's output of nickel ore more than quadrupled (from 6000 tons to 26 000 tons), and its share of the non-Communist world's nickel production rose from 10 to 18 per cent.[22] In 1961, SLN was the fourth largest nickel company in the Western world.

Slow-downs in production and exports occurred in 1958 and

1962, linked largely to general recession and market saturation, but the nickel industry grew dramatically later in the 1960s. Previous records of production and sales were surpassed in the second half of the decade because of rapidly expanding demand linked to the Vietnam War. By 1971, New Caledonia's production of nickel reached an all-time high, and most was exported at unusually high prices; the territory was at the time the world's second largest nickel producer. This expansion of production and export constituted an economic revolution in New Caledonia.

In the last years of the 1960s, New Caledonia's total exports increased by 60 per cent and its imports by 90 per cent – exports had quadrupled over the last decade. The number of wage-earners increased by two and a half times from 1969 to 1974; and new workers included many Melanesians, who had not previously been employed as wage-labourers, as well as migrants from France, French Polynesia and Wallis and Futuna. Wages grew sixfold during the same period, and high salaries provided a great attraction to workers from both France and elsewhere in the French Pacific. In 1969 alone, almost 3000 people migrated to New Caledonia, followed by 5700 the following year and 4400 in 1971. The per capita GDP of New Caledonia doubled from 1960 to the end of the decade. The multiplier effects of such growth were felt throughout the economy, especially in sectors like construction. Social change, more rapid urbanisation, the incorporation of marginalised groups in the industrial economy and a surge of consumerism accompanied economic development.

In the mid-1970s, the New Caledonian economy suffered stagnation, marked particularly by a crisis in nickel production linked to the world energy crisis, the recession in the Western world and the winding-down of the Vietnam War, all of which diminished demand for nickel. Production of nickel, almost six million tons in 1976, slipped to just over three million tons two years later and had only recovered to just over four million tons in 1979; exports failed to grow and actually dropped in 1978. Per capita GDP remained persistently below the 1972 peak for the remainder of the decade. The crisis wrought its social effects as well: emigration exceeded immigration every year after 1971; in both 1976 and 1978, for example, on balance almost two thousand people left the territory. Purchases of consumer goods, even foodstuffs, dropped significantly. A report issued by the Chamber of Commerce of Nouméa spoke of New Caledonia as a country 'economically in hibernation'.[23]

Nickel revived in the last years of the 1970s, partly because of contracts which assured New Caledonian suppliers half the Japanese market for a period of three years, partly because of strikes in Canada which limited the export potential of New Caledonia's major competitor. But another downturn occurred in the early 1980s. Total production in 1983 and 1984 was less than half that of 1980; the real value of nickel ore exports also fell to less than half that of 1970. The labour force contracted with the closure of some mines and dismissal of many workers: almost 500 workers lost their jobs in one year alone, and the working week was reduced as an economy measure.[24] Not until the end of the 1980s did another revival of nickel mining occur, but by that time the economic crisis had created dramatic effects in political and social life in New Caledonia.

The primacy of nickel in New Caledonia meant that private enterprise and government authorities took a particularly strong interest in the mining sector. Nickel production in New Caledonia has been variously affected by political decisions, international competition and specific policies. In 1969, for instance, the Billotte Law, passed by the French legislature, reserved ultimate decision-making on mining policy to Paris, effectively removing nickel from the brief of the territorial government. This measure demonstrated the determination of Paris to retain control of New Caledonia's strategic resource, particularly in the face of interest expressed by foreign companies, notably the International Nickel Company (INCO), in buying into the industry. Overseas mining companies had been allowed to prospect in New Caledonia, and the INCO had set up a joint venture with non-SLN mining interests in the territory. The tightening of control and restrictions on foreign activities carried out after 1969 reinforced the role of France in New Caledonia. It also meant that foreign concerns such as INCO were only marginally successful at breaking into New Caledonian mining and reducing the role of SLN and the *petits mineurs* in the territorial economy.

Recent decades have seen the restructuring of the mining industry in New Caledonia and more especially of the SLN company. SLN owns title to two-thirds of the nickel concessions in the territory; it is the largest exporter and enjoys a monopoly on nickel-refining. SLN is as well the largest employer in New Caledonia, with a workforce that peaked at over four thousand in New Caledonia, plus several hundred employees in a smelter in Le Havre and offices in Paris. The company was founded in 1880 by John Higginson, but a decade later was reorganised with capital from the Rothschild Bank. In 1965, the Rothschild interests continued to control over 10 per cent of the company's stock. In 1974, when the mining boom had slumped, two French metropolitan companies, Imétal and the public corporation Elf-Aquitaine, acquired the majority interest in SLN. A further change occurred in 1983, in the wake of the French Socialist government's efforts to obtain greater control of major private companies. The government-controlled Enterprise de Recherches et d'Activités Pétrolières (ERAP) acquired 70 per cent of the stock of SLN, leaving Imétal and Elf-Aquitaine each with 15 per cent. SLN now passed into state control, with all New Caledonian operations under the direct control of the Paris headquarters. Two years later, however, the New Caledonian mines and smelter were transferred to a wholly-owned subsidiary of SLN domiciled in Nouméa rather than in Paris. The new company kept the name SLN, while the parent company took the name ERAMET-SLN. This arrangement, it was rumoured, was undertaken to preserve the interests of the company in case of eventual independence for New Caledonia; in parallel, SLN began a more active effort to recruit and train Melanesian managers.

SLN has remained the major nickel-producing company in New Caledonia, but the *petits mineurs* have continued to be a force in the local economy. The *petits mineurs*, private entrepreneurs who held mining concessions, were numerous in the late nineteenth and early twentieth centuries, but the depression of the 1930s and the growth of SLN reduced their numbers. Those who survived often worked in tandem with SLN, selling the ore from their mines to the nickel giant. They were also obliged to use the Doniambo smelter owned by SLN to refine their ore. Some of the *petits mineurs* have commercial activities which extend far beyond mining. One of the most prominent *petits mineurs*, the Lafleur family, is an economic and commercial dynasty – the late head of the family, Henri Lafleur, and then his son, Jacques, have been long-serving *députés* representing

New Caledonia in the French parliament. Jacques Lafleur headed the anti-independence political movement in the 1980s, then was a signatory of the Matignon Accord in 1988. Two years later, Lafleur sold his Société Minière du Sud-Pacifique, perhaps the largest of the *petit mineur* concerns, to the Melanesian-controlled and pro-independence Nord province. French government money financed the purchase, and Lafleur ceded his interest at substantially less than market value. Critics of Lafleur pointed to the large profits he had nonetheless made on the transaction, but his supporters underlined the symbolic nature of a sale which transferred a significant share of mining activity away from European control and into Melanesian hands.

Other Economic Activities

The only other mineral mined in New Caledonia in significant quantities since 1945 has been chrome. During the Korean War, New Caledonia supplied a quarter of the world's chrome, largely from mines in Tiébaghi. The mines closed in 1964 because of lack of demand and the rush to nickel mining, but reopened in 1981 under the control of a consortium called COFRAMINE (which is financed by the French bank Paribas and the International Nickel Company), and New Caledonia now supplies around 4 per cent of the world's chrome.

The slow-down in nickel mining in the 1970s prompted local authorities to target alternative, or at least complementary, areas of economic development, particularly agriculture and tourism. New Caledonia's hotels, though few in number, did good business during the nickel boom as migrants, technicians and business people passed through the territory. No real effort had yet been made to develop the tourist potential of the Grande Terre or the outlying islands. In the 1970s improvements to the Nouméa airport, the start of regular air service in jumbo jets to Australia, New Zealand and France, the building of new hotels and the setting up of a tourist board aided the growth of tourism. For example, Club Méditerranée, a French company known for its comprehensive package holidays in tropical resorts, refurbished an old hotel in Nouméa (the Chateau Royal, built by UTA Airlines in 1966) and opened a Club Med in 1979. The Club employed over three hundred persons, mostly local residents (with the exception of the business managers, who came from France, and the '*gentils organisateurs*', the recreation leaders recruited from around the world). With over seven hundred rooms, Club Med attracted tourists from Australia, New Zealand, and increasingly, Japan. Another major tourist development, likewise located on the Anse Vata beach on the outskirts of Nouméa, was Le Surf hotel, built with capital provided by the mining magnate Jacques Lafleur in collaboration with a Japanese investor. Such enterprises bore fruit as the number of tourists rose from 30 000 in 1975 to 92 000 in 1984. The subsequent political troubles in New Caledonia seriously hurt the tourist industry and the number of visitors dropped dramaticly to 51 000 in 1985. Several projects for new tourist accommodation were abandoned and resorts under construction (for instance, a Club Med on the Isle of Pines) were attacked and destroyed by *indépendantistes*. The hotel industry survived only because thousands of French *gendarmes* and soldiers sent to New Caledonia were billeted in hotels. After hostilities ceased in 1988, tourism revived, although it had still not recovered to former levels by the end of the decade. New proposals were then advanced – the construction of a resort complex catering for Japanese visitors, a second Club Med which would include both on-shore facilities and a large sailing-ship and Melanesian hostels (*gîtes*) in the countryside and the Loyalty Islands.

Efforts to stimulate agriculture in the 1970s were intended to decrease New Caledonia's reliance on imports, develop sources of export revenue, promote Melanesian farming and provide jobs in the wake of the downturn in mining. In 1975, the government set up an organisation for the development of the interior of the Grande Terre and the Loyalty Islands (FADIL). There followed a major development plan, the Plan Dijoud, in 1979, and the establishment of a land reform agency to resolve property disputes. The government also sponsored several particular initiatives aimed at Melanesian farmers. The most important, begun in 1978, was 'Opération Café'. Coffee had been cultivated in New Caledonia since the nineteenth century but largely disappeared during the nickel boom. The authorities envisaged revitalising coffee production, planting 500–2000 hectares in coffee bushes and employing as many as a thousand, mostly Melanesian, workers; work on coffee plantations would provide labourers with a basic income and New Caledonia with a new source of exports. Production increased from 309 tons in 1978 to a modest 664 tons the following year, but then dropped and was barely higher than the 1978 level four years later. New Caledonia had to import coffee from elsewhere in the Pacific (mainly Vanuatu) to obtain the beans re-exported for sale as 'Café des Iles' or 'Café Mélanésien'. Economists blamed competition for the problems, while sociologists blamed the lack of greater success, or outright failure, of 'Opération Café' on misguided technocratic objectives. They charged that the plan for intensive coffee production on relatively large holdings (ideally, three hectares) for solely commercial purposes was incompatible with Melanesian ambitions and attitudes towards work. They argued furthermore that the real intention behind the plan had been less to promote the socio-economic incorporation of Melanesians into the commercial life of New Caledonia than to earn money for exporters.[25] Whatever the reasons for its lack of success, the government in 1991 officially terminated the costly 'Opération Café', admitting its objectives had not been achieved.

Another example of efforts made in the primary sector were programmes undertaken in the 1970s for reafforestation of the Tango plateau on the Grande Terre and part of the Isle of Pines. The intention was more to provide wage-labour for Melanesians than to create a source of exports, but again the initiative was largely unsuccessful. Critics argued that in choosing to plant imported pine trees rather than the native *niaouli* gums, planners had started off badly; lack of consultation with local chiefs, attention to the sociological and psychological dimensions of Melanesian participation in wage-labour and a rigidly technocratic outlook doomed the project to economic failure.[26] The project was also a social failure since it did not reach its goal of integrating larger numbers of Melanesians into the wage economy.

THE NEW CALEDONIAN ECONOMY IN THE 1980S

At the end of the 1980s, despite problems with tourism and agriculture, the economy of New Caledonia looked healthier than it had in several years. The reason, of course, was nickel. From 1987 to 1988, production of nickel grew by a fifth and exports increased by more than a quarter; export earnings from nickel in 1988 were double those of the previous year and higher than in the boom of the early 1970s. Thanks almost entirely to these exports, New Caledonia in 1989 covered the cost of its imports by its exports. Given rising prices for nickel exports, this seemed a new nickel boom.

Other economic activities fared less well in the late 1980s, reinforcing the central role of one commodity in New Caledonia's economy. Production of chrome declined from 1986 to 1988, and exports stagnated in volume although they increased somewhat in value. Harvests of coffee also stagnated, and commercial production and export of copra declined from nominal values in 1987 and 1988 to nil in 1989. New Caledonian production of foodstuffs, including meat, fruit and vegetables, failed to cover local demand. Production of timber in 1988 was only between one-third and one half of what it had been in the previous four or five years. Industrial activity remained confined to goods produced for local consumption, either by individuals or businesses, such as beer, machine oil, copra, soap, cement, oxygen and acetylene. The only area of industrial activity to expand was construction, connected to profits from nickel and renewed business confidence which promoted speculation. The number of construction permits issued in New Caledonia per year doubled from 1984 to 1988, even if the number of finished buildings did not keep pace. Tourism began to recover from the crisis of the mid-1980s, and in 1988 the number of tourists grew to 60 500. The largest number (15 000) came from Japan, followed by visitors from France and Australia. Tourist promotion campaigns – such as special one-week packages and 'weekend in Nouméa' deals advertised in Australia – lured back some of the tourists who had stayed away in the mid-1980s. In 1988, approximately 1600 New Caledonians worked in the tourist industry, which made it one of the major commercial activities in the territory. However, the administration accounted for the largest number of jobs in the territory in 1988; almost ten thousand New Caledonians worked for public and semi-public services, compared to 6000 in commercial activities, 4400 in building and a similar number in other industries, whereas only 2000 were in agriculture and 1000 in mining. The irony is obvious; while nickel mining accounted for the most profit and exports in New Caledonia, the administration, by nature tertiary and non-productive, employed the most workers.

At the same time New Caledonia's economy was characterised by great disparities between regions and ethnic groups. The majority of business and administrative activity was concentrated in Nouméa, while most mining took place on the east coast and pastoral activities were confined to the west coast. The interior of the Grande Terre, and, particularly the Loyalty Islands, remained undeveloped. Almost all of the higher-status and higher-paying jobs belonged to Europeans; of the owners of businesses with more than four employees in 1989, for instance, only four were Melanesians compared to 156 Europeans; twice as many Europeans as Melanesians worked in the public service; 231 Europeans, but not a single Melanesian, were in the liberal professions (lawyers, doctors, and so on); almost all secondary school teachers and scientific researchers were European.

The material comforts of New Caledonian housing revealed geographical disparities which often overlapped with ethnic ones; almost all Nouméa residences, but only two-thirds of those in the countryside of the Grande Terre and less than a tenth in the Loyalty Islands, had running water; 93 per cent of houses in Nouméa had indoor toilets, 53 per cent elsewhere in the Grande Terre, 8 per cent in the Loyalties. The average Melanesian household disposed of approximately 893 000 CFP in monetary and non-monetary earnings in 1988, compared with 2 276 000 for a European household.[27] In short, whether the New Caledonian economy was in a period of expansion or contraction, not all New Caledonians benefited equally. The volatile nature of nickel sales, moreover, meant that even for the fortunate, times of plenty could come quickly to an end.

THE ECONOMY OF WALLIS AND FUTUNA

In the late 1940s and 1950s, after the disruption of the war and the American 'occupation', Wallisians and Futunans returned to a way of life that had changed little since the establishment of the Catholic missionary presence on the islands over a century before.[28] Agriculture, the main activity, provided most foodstuffs for the local population; the main foods remained fish, taro, yams and other tropical products. Some copra continued to be exported, but the coconut plantations suffered from the ageing of trees and failure to replant; infestations of rhinoceros beetle had already devastated the stands of coconut trees in the 1930s. The ships that arrived at Mata-Uta, the only town on the islands, bought copra, sold European goods such as sugar and coffee, and handled passenger traffic. However, ships came to Wallis only once a month in the 1950s and 1960s, and air services, in a tiny plane which flew from Nouméa to Nadi (Fiji), then on to Wallis, were just as infrequent. French control of the islands had little economic impact. Not until 1961 did the islands officially become a *territoire d'outre-mer* of the French Republic; until then, only a Resident and one *gendarme* represented the French administration. The European population on the islands consisted mainly of Marist missionaries, who exercised a strong influence over the customary chiefs and took charge of education. They have continued to be responsible for the public schools in Wallis and Futuna, a situation unique in France and its territories.

In the 1960s, the situation began to change. The number of Europeans grew from only a dozen in the immediate post-war period to around two hundred by the late 1960s, as the administration expanded. A hospital and schools were constructed and the airport runway was sealed in 1970. Ninety per cent of the active population still worked in agriculture in the 1970s, but around 1000–1200 Wallisians and Futunans found salaried jobs, over half of them in the public service. Western comforts arrived, including electricity and running water, radio and telephones and, by the late 1980s, television. The number of automobiles and motorcycles in the islands soared from only 4 in 1964 to 1725 in 1982; one in five Wallisians and Futunans had either an automobile or a motorcycle. The Indosuez Bank opened a branch in the territory in the 1970s, the first bank in the islands, and 1500 Wallisians and Futunans established accounts.

With all the change, however, Wallis and Futuna hardly became bustling Western societies. In 1982, the commercial sector in Mata-Uta consisted of two small groceries, a hardware store, two automobile-dealers and one garage, a butchery and two clothing stores. The two hotels in Wallis jointly provided merely a dozen rooms, and there was no hotel in Futuna. Some thirty tiny bar-restaurants, and one discotheque, provided venues for contemporary entertainment, although the major social gathering remained Sunday morning mass at the cathedral in Mata-Uta. Concrete houses had slowly replaced the old style *falés*, constructed of wood and pandanus fibre, but many residents had both sorts of houses; some modern dwellings remained uncompleted because of lack of funds. Fewer than 6 per cent of residences had indoor toilets, and only 14 per cent had refrigerators. Europeans, in fact, occupied many of the more 'modern' houses. The telephone directory listed around 150 subscribers.

The Wallisian economy, however, was only superficially the 'traditional' economy associated with the South Pacific. Though most residents raised their own foodstuffs, they also bought imported products (such as meat flown in from New Caledonia). Salaries provided by the administration to its employees – high wages increased by various auxiliary benefits – had helped to monetarise the economy further. Family allocations and other social service payments added to incomes. Some Wallisian and Futunan men enrolled for military service, either in New Caledonia or in France; other Wallisians and Futunans won government scholarships to finish secondary education or undertake university studies outside the territory. Most importantly, Wallisians and Futunans found work outside the islands.

Migration from Wallis and Futuna to New Caledonia (and, to a lesser extent, to the New Hebrides) began immediately after the Second World War. In the early 1950s, migration became more regular and migrants more numerous – 106 islanders departed in 1952, 247 in 1954. Some worked on the hydroelectric dam in Yaté, New Caledonia, a project begun in 1951; more often they found jobs in mines. In the 1960s, the mining boom attracted increasing numbers of Wallisians and Futunans; by 1976, 9600 lived in New Caledonia. By this date the migrant population of Wallis and Futuna in New Caledonia exceeded the number of residents in Wallis and Futuna. The first migrants were young men, but later women and children followed. They migrated not so much from pressure on natural resources in Wallis and Futuna, where population densities are among the lowest in the South Pacific, but because of the possibilities of earning wages, often very attractive ones, in New Caledonia. For many, the transition was difficult, work hard and housing and living conditions poor. But faced with the lack of opportunities in Wallis and Futuna, they preferred trying their luck in New Caledonia. The remittances they sent back to Wallis and Futuna constituted a major component of the territory's economy; from 1970 to 1977, remittances ranged from 98.8 million CFP to 167.7 million CFP annually. By comparison, Wallis and Futuna's exports, even a decade later, totalled only 2.75 million CFP.

Wallis and Futuna's economy had become totally dependent on the possibilities of wage employment in New Caledonia and the assurance of direct metropolitan transfers to the islands. These two factors largely explained the lack of an independence movement in the islands and the general opposition to independence for New Caledonia among Wallisians and Futunans living there.

From the 1950s onwards, the French government episodicly tried various efforts to stimulate the Wallisian and Futunan economy. It first initiated the planting of coffee, cocoa and pepper, as well as the regeneration of coconut plantations, but with few successes; efforts to diversify production of tropical products for export were abandoned. In 1979, the Secretary of State for the DOM-TOMs, Paul Dijoud, announced a twenty-year plan for decreasing Wallis's economic dependency, but the results were just as slender. The only achievements, in fact, were in government employment and the amelioration of the economic infrastructure of the islands. Since only a quarter of the land area of Wallis and Futuna is arable, and the islands lack any natural resources other than labour, obstacles to development seemed insurmountable. Government aid for the building of fishing vessels, the development of apiculture and the expansion of pork-, beef- and chicken-raising scored some results but hardly led to an economic transformation. In 1985 the president of the territorial assembly charged that the policy of developing local agriculture and fishing had produced no results since 1961.[29] Four years later, the French prime minister visited the islands, lamented their 'isolation and dependency', and called for a new 'policy of development and solidarity'. Once again, government had to be the instigator, and the proposal for employing an additional two hundred workers in community projects simply underlined the economic role of the administration.[30]

The paradox of Wallis and Futuna – other than the simple situation of 'total dependence' on France which the islands epitomised[31] – was that economically France earned no profits from the islands. As a report issued by the New Caledonian Chamber of Commerce's centre for economic studies bluntly put it: 'The archipelago of Wallis, and indeed the whole of this territory, presents no economic interest for France. Wallis [and Futuna] will obviously never be a land of settlement [from overseas]; it has no resources of primary products, energy or agricultural products which can be commercialised; it does not offer a market for French products'.[32] Only with the development of maritime resources, an unsure project, would Wallis and Futuna be of economic significance. France, in sum, was economically crucial to Wallis and Futuna, while Wallis and Futuna remained commercially negligible (even burdensome) to France.

THE ECONOMIES OF FRANCE AND THE PACIFIC

The case of Wallis and Futuna points to a particular question concerning overseas territories: to what extent does the 'mother country' profit from continued relations with these islands? With Wallis and Futuna, the answer is clear, but for the other two Pacific TOMs, the answer is more nuanced. One measure of profit is the proportion of imports and exports exchanged with the *métropole* by comparison with sales to and purchases from other countries. In the case of French Polynesia, just over 53 per cent of the territory's imports came from France in 1988, a proportion not unlike that of previous years; this amounted to 46 691 million CFP in purchases. The other countries of the EC, taken together, came in second place (11.5 per cent), followed by the United States (11.3 per cent), Australia (6.3 per cent), New Zealand (5 per cent) and Japan (4.4 per cent). France, the EC and Japan provided the bulk of manufactured goods, while New Zealand and, to a lesser extent, Australia and the United States, supplied foodstuffs. As for French Polynesian exports, France in the 1980s purchased between one-third and two-thirds of Tahiti's products (3037 million CFP out of 8112 million CFP in 1988). The second market for Tahiti's products was the United States (1537 million CFP in 1988), and the remainder of sales went to Japan, other countries of the EC, New Caledonia and other destinations. In general, France accounted for about half of French Polynesia's trade. A French shipping line, the Compagnie Générale Maritime (the former Messageries Maritimes) was the leading cargo carrier for traffic between Tahiti and Europe, taking over a third of tonnage handled; the runners-up were a Polish line (28 per cent) and a South Korean company (11 per cent). The largest number of tourists in 1988 came to Tahiti from the United States (66 132) but France accounted for the second largest group (41 587). Banking was in the hands of several institutions headquartered in Papeete (the Banque de Tahiti, Banque de Polynésie, Banque Paribas and Banque Socrédi); all of them had larger capital bases than the major French metropolitan bank in the territory, the Banque Indosuez.[33] It is impossible to determine how much of the profits made in French Polynesia ultimately ended up in French hands, or to estimate exactly the division of profits between local and metropolitan companies in French Polynesia. The low level of exports from French Polynesia also put the amount of trade garnered by the French into perspective; France got the lion's share, but it was all the same a meagre ration. All things considered, French Polynesia takes far more money from France than it returns (or perhaps can return).

In the case of New Caledonia, France in 1988 furnished 48 per cent of the territory's imports, followed very distantly by the other countries of the EC (16 per cent) and Australia (10 per cent).[34] Although export sales did not cover the cost of imports in most years during the 1980s, in 1988 and 1989 they did so. A simple equation of imports and exports does not cover the salaries paid to both New Caledonians and *métropolitains* in the territory and the increased investments poured into New Caledonia by French governments in the 1980s. It is therefore impossible to put a numerical figure on the 'cost' of New Caledonia – perhaps a pointless exercise, even if it could be done – but it seems likely that New Caledonia comes far closer to 'paying its way' than either French Polynesia or, certainly, Wallis and Futuna. This does not mean, however, that the territory furnishes huge profits either to specific French companies or to the national accounts ledger as a whole. Of course, nickel is a key resource for France; in 1966, President de Gaulle stated that France must retain control of mining in New Caledonia 'in order to preserve French independence in the world economic system'.[35] This suggested an economic value held by the territory because of New Caledonia's endowment in the strategic resource of nickel which went beyond a simple balance-sheet accounting of profits and losses.

More recently political figures have not maintained that claim. France could probably just as easily procure nickel from Canada or other friendly suppliers as from New Caledonia. Certainly SLN is a big business, but it ranks far from the top in the hierarchy of top French companies; it employs only several hundred people in the *métropole*. In other economic areas, the sale of the Indosuez Bank's interests in French Polynesia and New Caledonia to an Australian bank and the closure of its branch in Wallis indicate that one bank at least did not consider Pacific operations essential.

The implication is that the *métropole* economically has more effect on overseas territories than they have on the *métropole*. Furthermore, the French state is the pivot of the economies of the three TOMs of the Pacific. It is the major employer, the primary source of finance, the agency for planning and development, the provider of social security and the regulator of prices and customs duties. The transferral of metropolitan capital, through investment, subsidies, social welfare payments and salaries, provides an economic lifeline for the territories. If New Caledonia's nickel 'pays for' that territory's imports, French Polynesia and Wallis and Futuna have no such resource capable of righting their balance of trade; in bad years, as was often the case in the 1970s and 1980s, when the nickel market slumped, New Caledonia, as well as the other Pacific territories, became dependent on the state. Estimates of French expenditure on French Polynesia currently total about $55 million per month, a large sum for a territory of fewer than 200 000 people. French officials in the 1980s clearly hinted that such French largesse was dependent on loyalty; if the territories became independent, they could not count on such levels of French aid as they previously enjoyed, although it would be unlikely for the purse-strings to be cut entirely. *Indépendantistes* in French Polynesia have been concerned about the vacuum in the economy which would be left by the departure of the CEP and CEA, and few have any real alternatives to government expenditure to support the economy. Pro-independence groups in New Caledonia see the state as the only actor with the means – and the responsibility – to rectify disparities among ethnic groups, diversify the economy and develop peripheral regions. They call on such agencies as FIDES and the land reform office to effect changes in the New Caledonian economy primarily to the benefit of disadvantaged Melanesians.

Paradoxically, the state is even more involved in the economies of the Pacific territories at present than at any time since 1945 or, indeed, during the colonial period before the Second World War. The economic revolutions of the 1960s, then the crises of the following decades, the growth of a consumer society and the very wealth that has been based on high salaries, family allowances and the other benefits of a 'colonial' presence and an 'artificial' economy have implicated the French state in the economies of its territories in Oceania more than it ever was at the time of the traders, settlers, and colonial administrators. The peculiar combination of underdevelopment and development characteristic of the French Pacific territories underlines the dual role of the *métropole* in their economic future.

CONCLUSION

Drawing conclusions about the economies of the French Pacific territories, it is easy to slip into simplistic charges. Certainly the territories' high GDP, high standards of living and consumer comforts depend largely on metropolitan transfers, subsidies and the controversial activities of the CEP and CEA. Yet few island states are totally independent from 'artificial economies' created by international aid and migrant remittances; examples in the South Pacific are the rule rather than the exception. Therefore, accusations about the 'artificiality' of the French Pacific economies do not constitute a very profound analysis. Obstacles to economic development – small local markets, distant foreign markets, international competition, limited natural resources – would hinder economic growth no matter what political status the territories had. Despite the number of plans and proposals put forward by the various governments, it is unrealistic to suppose that French Polynesia or Wallis and Futuna could become productive economies able to cover all their needs with their own exports and services, or that the residents themselves would be willing to forgo the wages, social security benefits and consumer goods to which they have become accustomed in the past several decades. Economic dependency might eventually be reduced, but it is unlikely that it will end.

By comparison with other economies of the South Pacific, the French territories do rather well; some South Pacific countries have begun to sell passports, seek contributions to an international trust fund or offer to stock toxic wastes to provide their financial wherewithal, and most depend on international aid donors (or patrons such as Australia and New Zealand) to make ends meet. The advantage of French Polynesia, Wallis and Futuna and New Caledonia is to have a wealthy patron, and the political ties between these territories and France create a moral imperative for French aid. The French government is not unaware of this fact. The historical irony is that colonies were once conquered with the hope of finding treasure; in the contemporary world, both territories which maintain official, legal ties with mother countries and small independent nations rely on developed powers (or international agencies) for the aid which keeps them alive.

4 The Populations and Societies of the French Pacific

Some 350 000 people live in the French *territoires d'outre-mer* of New Caledonia, Wallis and Futuna and French Polynesia. Except for foreigners who reside there temporarily or permanently, all are fully-fledged French citizens. Unlike many other overseas territories of 'colonial' powers, there exists no second-class citizenship for inhabitants of the French DOM-TOMs. The French of the Pacific enjoy all the rights of their compatriots born in Paris or Lyon, including the right of migration and abode in France. They also share many of the obligations, even if in some cases they are exempt from income tax or national service. In principle, the French of the *outre-mer* are equal before the law, regardless of skin colour, ethnic origin, place of residence or beliefs.

The century and a half of French presence in the South Pacific, following half a century of previous cultural contacts between the islanders and Europeans, has created a multi-ethnic population in New Caledonia and French Polynesia (although to a much lesser extent in Wallis and Futuna). Even before European arrival, much intermingling took place between different 'tribes' and island groups in Oceania: migrants from Polynesia settled the Loyalty Islands off the coast of New Caledonia; Tonga had regular contact with Wallis, and Samoa with Futuna. Beachcombers, traders and other settlers added their influence and intermarried (or produced children) with the local population. This blood and cultural mix, or *métissage*, was so prominent in Tahiti that it may be the central characteristic of the post-contact social history of that island.[1] Even before the French arrived in Tahiti, the realms of Pomaré were dominated by a mixed Anglo-Polynesian elite created through the intermarriage of English settlers and Polynesian nobles. The migration of Europeans to New Caledonia dramatically changed its demographic structure, reducing native Melanesians to a minority in their own country. In both New

117

Caledonia and French Polynesia, Europeans imported contract labourers to work mines and plantations, primarily Chinese in Tahiti, Japanese, Indonesians and Vietnamese in New Caledonia. Meanwhile, further waves of Europeans arrived in the islands, including transported convicts sent to New Caledonia in the late 1800s, then free migrants recruited at the turn of the century. More recently, migrants were attracted to the French islands during the nickel boom in New Caledonia and the economic transformation wrought by nuclear testing in French Polynesia in the 1960s. But Oceanians also migrated from one island to another; Loyalty Islanders, then French Polynesians and Wallisians and Futunans moved in large numbers to New Caledonia. Others migrated to the islands as well; the most recent census counts ninety different nationalities represented in New Caledonia.

The presence of such diverse groups, and above all the co-existence of islanders and Europeans, has ignited conflict in New Caledonia, while in Tahiti generalised *métissage* has contributed to a certain harmony (albeit an occasionally and ominously troubled one). In New Caledonia, Melanesian revolts in 1878 and 1917 were directed largely against European settlers, the dispossession of Melanesian landholders and other incursions of European society. The struggle for a 'Kanak' independence in New Caledonia in the 1980s placed political confrontation in the context of ethnic dispute. In short, demographic changes have produced political, economic and cultural consequences. The populations of the French Pacific have also witnessed changes common elsewhere, foremost among them urbanisation. Population growth has not solely resulted from migration but also from rapid natural increase. Economic development has moved populations from employment in the primary or secondary sector to the tertiary sector. Higher levels of education and training have altered skills, while secularisation, the diffusion of consumer goods and the effects of the mass media have reduced the isolation of both islanders and Europeans, once considered both literally and figuratively '*au bout du monde*'.

TABLE 1   *Population of French Pacific Territories*

	New Caledonia	French Polynesia	Wallis and Futuna
1935/6	54 700	44 044	6542
1946	62 700	55 734	–
1951	66 400	–	8771
1961/2	86 519	84 551	8325
1969	100 570	–	8546
1971	–	119 168	–
1976	133 230	137 382	9192
1983	145 370	166 753	12 408
1989	164 173	–	–

SOURCES: John Connell, *Migration, Employment and Development in the South Pacific Country Report No. 21 Wallis and Futuna* (Nouméa, 1983); John Connell, *Migration, Employment and Development in the South Pacific Country Report No. 5 French Polynesia* (Nouméa, 1985); John Connell, *Migration, Employment and Development in the South Pacific Country Report No. 10 New Caledonia* (Nouméa, 1985); INSEE, *Images de la Population de la Nouvelle-Calédonie. Principaux résultats du recensement 1989* (Paris, 1989).

TABLE 2   *Population of greater Nouméa and greater Papeete*

	Nouméa	Papeete
1946	–	12 417
1956	22 235	23 233
1967/9	50 488	44 311
1976/7	74 335	77 481
1983	85 098	93 294
1989	97 581	–

SOURCES: John Connell, *Migration, Employment and Development in the South Pacific Country Report No. 21 Wallis and Futuna* (Nouméa, 1983); John Connell, *Migration, Employment and Development in the South Pacific Country Report No. 5 French Polynesia* (Nouméa, 1985); John Connell, *Migration, Employment and Development in the South Pacific Country Report No. 10 New Caledonia* (Nouméa, 1985); INSEE, *Images de la Population de la Nouvelle-Calédonie. Principaux résultats du recensement 1989* (Paris, 1989).

TABLE 3 Population of New Caledonia by ethnic group

	1946	%	1956	%	1969	%	1976	%	1983	%	1989	%
Melanesians	31 000	49	34 970	51	47 300	47	55 598	42	61 870	44	73 598	44
Europeans	18 500	30	25 160	37	36 900	36	50 757	38	53 974	36	55 085	34
Other Pacific islanders			2017	3	9586	10	17 012	13	18 955	12	20 619	13
Asians			6334	9	6250	6	7054	5	7700	6	8 294	5
Others	13 200	21	–	–	800	1	2812	2	2868	2	6577	4
Total	62 700	–	68 481	–	100 836	–	133 233	–	145 367	–	164 173	–

SOURCES: John Connell, New Caledonia or Kanaky? The Political History of a French Colony (Canberra, 1987); INSEE, Images de la Population de la Nouvelle-Calédonie, Principaux résultats du recensement 1989 (Paris, 1989).

DEMOGRAPHIC CHANGE IN THE PACIFIC

The basic characteristic of demographic change in the French Pacific territories since the Second World War has been population growth (Table 1).[2] In forty-two years the population of New Caledonia grew two and a half times over, while that of French Polynesia more than tripled and that of Wallis and Futuna grew by half. Growth, however, was not equally spread throughout the period. In New Caledonia, the population hardly grew at all until the late 1950s, then registered high growth rates until the 1970s; the highest rates, over 4 per cent per annum, came in the early 1970s; subsequently the rates fell but not to the low level of the early 1950s. French Polynesia, differently from New Caledonia, saw a substantial increase in population in the decade immediately after the Second World War, then a slow-down in the late 1950s. Growth increased dramatically to reach 5 per cent per annum in the late 1960s at the peak of immigration. A slow-down which followed, when the growth rate halved, was broken by another spurt of growth in the early 1980s. Finally, Wallis and Futuna lost population in the 1950s, then grew at the tiniest of rates until the mid-1970s; since the early 1980s, growth has been steady, despite continued emigration.

Economic changes, and the resultant migrations, largely account for the variations in population growth. The demographic booms in New Caledonia and French Polynesia coincided with the expansion of the nickel industry and the installation of the CEP, respectively. Lack of growth in Wallis helped engender emigration to New Caledonia before and during the nickel boom, followed by the return of a small proportion of migrants and reduced emigration when boom turned to bust. A small part of the population variation can be connected to very specific incidents: in the case of New Caledonia, repatriation of Indonesian and Vietnamese contract labourers in the 1950s, immigration of some French settlers (and a few New Hebrideans and others) after the independence of Vanuatu in 1980, and emigration of an uncertain number of New Caledonians during the political troubles of the mid-1980s.

The distribution of population growth inside the TOMs has varied from one region to another. In French Polynesia, from the mid-1940s to the mid-1980s, the Windward Islands (in the

Society Islands) registered the greatest population growth (342 per cent), followed by the Marquesas (119 per cent); there was much less of an increase in the Tuamotus (61 per cent) and the Leeward Islands (53 per cent); the Gambiers lost a substantial proportion (–17 per cent) of their population. Distance and isolation explain some of the decline in remote archipelagos like the Gambiers, and the presence of Tahiti, especially the expansion of Papeete, accounts for the upward fluctuation in the Windward Islands. Similarly, some remote communes of New Caledonia, as well as the Loyalty Islands, grew less rapidly (or even lost population) by comparison with the southern region of the Grande Terre, and particularly the capital of Nouméa. Even in Wallis and Futuna, the only administrative and commercial centre, Mata-Utu, grew more rapidly than other districts.

Urbanisation has been especially evident in the French territories (Table 2). From 1956 to 1989, the population of Nouméa tripled. In French Polynesia the agglomeration of Papeete grew from 12 417 in 1946 to 93 294 in 1983, and at the latter date the city accounted for more than half the territory's population. In both cases, small cities became real metropolises, and often the outlying suburbs witnessed the highest population growth of all – communes such as Mont-Dore and Dumbéa on the outskirts of Nouméa, Fa'a'a and Pirae near Papeete. Urban population growth principally followed from the migration of residents both from overseas and from the areas outside the capitals.

The arrival of overseas immigrants perturbed the demographic structures of the French Pacific. *Métropolitains* came in large numbers to New Caledonia and, to a lesser degree, French Polynesia in the 1960s and 1970s (Table 3). Many were on contracts and only remained for several years, but others stayed for longer terms. In the seven years after 1965, for instance, 15 000 migrants (*métropolitains, pieds-noirs*, Tahitians and others) arrived in New Caledonia; it was at this time that Europeans and other ethnic groups came to outnumber Melanesians. In 1983, 33 817 New Caledonians, almost a third of the territory's total population, had been born outside the islands: 20 725 of 53 974 Europeans, 3119 of 5570 Tahitians and 5126 of 12 174 Wallisians were born elsewhere than New Caledonia. In French Polynesia, also in 1983, 86 per cent of the population was born in the territory, compared with 11 per cent in the *métropole* or other DOM-TOMs: the arrival of non-islanders had not 'drowned' the native population in the same way as in New Caledonia. (Wallis and Futuna, marked by emigration, counted only a handful of foreigners and *métropolitains.*)

COMPONENTS OF THE POPULATION:

Europeans and Asians

Only Wallis and Futuna retain a largely indigenous population, although there are significant ethnic and linguistic differences between the people of Wallis and Futuna. The small number of non-islanders, several hundred at most, are French administrative personnel, clerics or Europeans married to islanders. Elsewhere in the French Pacific, however, the population is heterogeneous. In French Polynesia, two specific groups can be distinguished, the Chinese and the *métropolitain* immigrants (in addition to just over a thousand residents who are not French-born). The remainder of the population is composed of those of Polynesian ancestry, ranging from almost 'pure' Polynesians – probably there are no longer any absolutely 'pure' Polynesians – and the *demis*, those of mixed Polynesian and European or Chinese origin.

Figures on the ethnic breakdown of the French Polynesian population are vague, but one estimate is that 84 per cent of the population is formed of Polynesians or *métis* of largely Polynesian extraction; 11 per cent of Europeans or mixed-blood residents who classify themselves as Europeans; and just over 4 per cent of Chinese or Chinese *métis*. Polynesians thus form the vast bulk of the territory's population; their proportion is even greater in the outer islands and areas of less European settlement.[3] Almost two centuries of *métissage* can be seen in the mixture of surnames; next to 'French' names are such Anglo-Saxon family names as Brander, Salmon, Sanford and Bambridge, and a past president of the Tahitian government, a *demi*, bears the distinctly Russian name of Léontieff.

Europeans in French Polynesia mainly live in Tahiti and occupy white-collar positions in the public or private sectors. Some are the descendants of migrants of the 1800s or early 1900s, but most are relatively recent arrivals. Many bureaucrats live in the territory for only three years, the normal term of a posting. They benefit from distinct financial advantages: a salary bonus paid because of their overseas posting and various other benefits boost their wages by at least 40 per cent (and sometimes by 100 per cent) by comparison with those holding similar positions in the *métropole* ; in addition, there is no personal income tax in Tahiti. Such advantages are only partially offset by the extremely high cost of living in French Polynesia. Other Europeans include soldiers and administrators who have stayed on after retirement, long-term residents (often working in business) and those who have been attracted by the lure of the islands. In principle, any French citizen could move to Tahiti, although he or she is required to show an outward transport ticket and must wait for several years before buying property or obtaining a licence to operate a business; these restrictions, however, can fairly easily be circumvented. Non-French migrants must obtain government permission to settle in Tahiti, not a simple matter to arrange, and tourists (except for those from the European Community, Switzerland and the United States) must have a visa. Since most Europeans in Tahiti are transient residents there is no entrenched group of 'whites' (such as the *Békés* of the French West Indies or Réunion) or any large permanently expatriate population.

The most prominent component of the population in French Polynesia are the *demis* ('halves'), those of mixed ancestry. The *métissage* of the population has reduced substantial physical and cultural differences between Polynesians and non-Polynesians. Those in the Tahitian *demi* elite pride themselves on their Oceanic parentage and understanding of the Tahitian language, although in former times they emphasised their European heritage. Most of the important political and commercial figures of the territory have both Polynesian and European or Chinese ancestors. The president of the Polynesian government during much of the 1980s, Gaston Flosse, was a prime example: one side of his family tree is Polynesian, the other French and American.

The Chinese of Tahiti originally arrived as recruited labourers for cotton plantations in the 1860s; the failure of the plantations a decade later left them without employment, and the government barred them from acquiring land.[4] The Chinese generally became traders; a large number of shopkeepers in

Tahiti, and almost all in the outer islands, are Chinese. The Chinese also grew vanilla and worked as market gardeners; Chinese entrepreneurs came, too, to control the pearl-fishing industry of the Tuamotus. Several waves of migration by Chinese swelled their numbers, although they remain only a small minority of French Polynesia's population. The Chinese suffered from periodic campaigns which accused them of dishonest business practices, unfair competition with French merchants, clannishness and lack of integration into local society and such vices as opium-smoking. The Chinese were indeed successful businessmen, establishing trading partnerships on the basis of kinship or friendship networks; labour for their shops or other enterprises was supplied largely by family members. The Chinese founded various associations for mutual aid and for political activities, one of the most important of which was a branch of the anti-Communist Kuo-min-tang party. Most of the Tahitian Chinese claimed citizenship of China or, after 1949, the Republic of China. Business links and political sympathies, added to the fact that four-fifths of the Chinese in French Polynesia spoke Hakka, reinforced their communitarian bonds.

There was a certain complicity between the Chinese and other populations – Europeans or Polynesians often lent their name to Chinese who wanted to set up companies or secure use of land, and intermarriage between Chinese and Polynesians was fairly common. The Chinese learned French, and most converted to Catholicism. But they remained second class citizens until 1964, when the Chinese were collectively granted full French citizenship. The Chinese welcomed this, since most had significant interests in Tahiti and no longer hoped to return to Taiwan or mainland China.

The population of New Caledonia is even more cosmopolitan than that of French Polynesia. Europeans in New Caledonia, presently about four-tenths of the territory's total population, divide into recent arrivals and short-term residents, the *métropolitains*, and the settlers. The latter are known as Caldoches, although many of them consider the term disparaging. They are the descendants of various waves of migrants who arrived in New Caledonia after the French takeover in 1853. In the nineteenth and early twentieth century, voluntary migrants to New Caledonia were few, despite government efforts to populate the island with Europeans. However, thousands of convicts and political prisoners, including rebels from the Paris Commune of 1871, were transported to the colony from the 1860s to the 1890s. Most of the Communards were repatriated, but large numbers of the convicts stayed, either because they were required to live in the colony after the expiration of their sentences or because they desired to remain in Oceania.

The majority of colonists in New Caledonia came from modest backgrounds in France. Those who settled in the countryside became pastoralists or small farmers on the plains along the west coast of the Grande Terre. Poverty, isolation, lack of education and hardship were their lot until well into the twentieth century, a situation aggravated by occasional confrontations with their Melanesian neighbours. Other Caldoches became small shopkeepers in the countryside, often specialising in the sale of alcohol to Melanesians, while others worked in mines. The Caldoches of Nouméa enjoyed greater prosperity as the commercial and political elite of the colony. Mineowners, shippers and administrators amassed capital and social prestige, although dreams of great fortunes were seldom transformed into reality. The Nouméa elite spearheaded economic development and reaped its rewards; they maintained a sometimes strained relationship with the French government, from which they demanded both large subsidies and a degree of political autonomy.[5]

By the middle of the twentieth century there were Caldoches who could trace their lineage in New Caledonia back over several generations and who held substantial commercial and political stakes in the territory. Families grown wealthy through the trade which they monopolised during the Second World War joined the old landowners and mineowners to form the upper echelon of New Caledonian society. The *broussards*, those who lived in the countryside, evolved little, and observers in the 1940s and 1950s still regularly commented on their rather modest situations.

The nickel boom of the 1960s brought new prosperity to the Caldoches, especially the Nouméa elite. As agriculture declined, the world of the *broussards* was endangered. Some moved into mining or migrated to the city; others had no successors to their farms when they became old and died; still other families clung to their farms and stations in the countryside. However, new Frenchmen arrived in New Caledonia, attracted by high salaries, good working conditions, the lure of the South Pacific and the general expansion of the economy in the 1960s and 1970s. The independence of other French colonies, especially Algeria, prompted migration to New Caledonia, often seen as a bastion of overseas France; the number of *pieds-noirs* who moved to New Caledonia from North Africa after 1962 was perhaps as high as six thousand, although this is probably much too high an estimate. Paris encouraged migration – a now famous (or infamous) letter from then Prime Minister Pierre Messmer in 1972 vaunted New Caledonia as one of the few overseas outposts which France might still consider a suitable place of settlement for its nationals. The government intended to stimulate further economic development but perhaps, too, to ensure that the Melanesian population, just then organising into a more militant political movement, remained a docile group, if not an outright demographic minority. The arrival of *métropolitains*, often perceived as mere profit-seekers, at first created resentment among Caldoches as well as Melanesians. Opposition to growing Melanesian nationalism eventually created new solidarities among the Nouméa notables, the *broussards* and the new migrants from the *métropole*. When the nickel boom ended in the mid-1970s, migration to New Caledonia slowed considerably, and the political troubles of the 1980s dissuaded new arrivals. By the 1980s, in fact, a number of Caldoches had begun to emigrate. Some *broussards*, feeling unsafe in the countryside, threatened by Melanesians or suffering economic adversity, migrated to Nouméa. Meanwhile, some from Nouméa – the number has been put at around a thousand – exported their capital and sometimes families to the east coast of Australia.

Europeans continue to form a large segment of New Caledonia's population and are its dominant political and economic group. The short-term *métropolitain* residents have a culture little different from that of the 'mother-country', but the Caldoches claim a particular identity and culture of their own. Their reference points are the geography and climate of New Caledonia rather than (or in addition to) those of France; many also have links with Australia. The Caldoches have often thought of themselves as pioneers in the South Pacific, as indeed their ancestors were, battling against natural obstacles and unsympathetic foreigners and islanders. Much of their past – the convict heritage, the history of mistreatment of Melanesians, the very poverty of many of the European New Caledonians – has been neglected or hidden. Somewhat ironically, the Caldoches share similarities with the Melanesians, since both have been (in different ways) so affected by European colonialism. Furthermore, the Caldoches often display hostility to *métropolitains,* who garner the best job appointments in New Caledonia and whose attitude to the long-term settlers is frequently condescending.[6] The attachment of Caldoches to New Caledonia – many have never been to France – makes them comparable to the *pieds-noirs* of Algeria. Protective of their interests, most have been ardent opponents of Melanesian independence. However, the spectrum of political beliefs in the Caldoche community is wide.

New Caledonia also has an Asian population. The first Asians, who arrived in the late 1800s as recruited workers in the nickel mines, included Vietnamese, Indonesians and Japanese. The French expelled the Japanese after the entry of Japan into the Second World War, although a few Japanese families remained in the territory. The strict rules under which the Vietnamese and Indonesians worked forbade them to change jobs or residence and otherwise kept them in an indentured state. During the Second World War, many took employment with the American forces, and the Americans put pressure on the French government to end restrictions on the Asians.[7] In 1946, the Asians were emancipated; the shortage of labour at the time meant that jobs were available, although the minework that they had previously done was not an attractive option. Many Vietnamese returned to Asia in the 1950s, both before and after the defeat of the French at Dienbienphu and the withdrawal of France from Indochina. The New Caledonian administration, suspecting the Vietnamese of sympathies with Ho Chi Minh and afraid of the spread of nationalism to the South Pacific, encouraged their departure. Several thousand elected to remain in New Caledonia. Most are shopkeepers, both in Nouméa and the *brousse* ; many have intermarried with other ethnic groups, taken French citizenship and converted to Christian religions. The Indonesians, recruited under the authority of the Dutch colonial government in the East Indies, also stayed in New Caledonia in significant numbers, and some new Javanese workers were recruited in the late 1940s after the independence of Indonesia. The Indonesians work in the nickel mines or are market gardeners or shopkeepers; many, although not all, have become French citizens, but are still Muslims. The Vietnamese and Indonesians in New Caledonia generally vote with the conservative political party and are suspicious of any political evolution which might endanger their continued residence in the territory.

The final group of arrivals in New Caledonia have been islanders from French Polynesia and Wallis and Futuna. Constrained by limited employment opportunities in their home islands (particularly Wallis and Futuna and the outer islands of French Polynesia), they were attracted to New Caledonia by the nickel boom. So many came that communities of Polynesians, complete with their own social institutions (such as Catholic and Protestant parishes) grew up in Nouméa. More Wallisians and Futunans now live in New Caledonia than in Wallis and Futuna, and migrant remittances form an important pillar of the Wallisian and Futunan economy. Polynesians in New Caledonia are primarily urban and work in semi-skilled or unskilled jobs. Wallisians and Futunans form a kind of urban sub-proletariat in Nouméa. Like the Asians, they have also generally opposed Melanesian independence, fearful for their future in New Caledonia and faced with lack of jobs in French Polynesia and Wallis and Futuna.[8]

The demographic structure of New Caledonia has decided political implications. Colonisation has brought together Europeans, Asians and Polynesians in a territory where the original Melanesian residents suffered land spoliation and economic and political marginalisation. The charter of the Front de Libération Nationale Kanak et Socialiste (FLNKS) speaks of the 'victims of history' which it promises would have a place in an independent Kanaky, but migrants – from the descendants of convicts forcibly shipped to the Pacific to Asians and Polynesians recruited when labour was needed – all claim to have earned a place in the territory and to have been brought in largely by forces outside their control. They, too, see themselves as victims of history. *Métropolitain* migrants claim that if Melanesians are fully-fledged French citizens, with the right of abode in France, so other Frenchmen should enjoy the right to live in New Caledonia. The Caldoches are fond of pointing out that New Caledonia has been part of France longer than such cities as Nice and that they have an inherited and inalienable right to their Pacific patrimony. Such claims speak of political intent but also point to the situations which colonial history has produced in societies of settlement, where various ethnic groups argue for their own legitimacy.

New Caledonia and French Polynesia represent contrasting examples of settlement: in Tahiti, the importance of cultural and demographic *métissage* moulds social relations, whereas in New Caledonia the separation of ethnic groups – the absence of a 'Creole' population or culture[9] – patterns society. The case of Wallis and Futuna, which has no large exogenous community but where most of the native population now lives overseas, is different yet again. In each case, outside forces have established new political systems, developed the economy and imported the French language and culture that is now omnipresent in the islands. Outsiders have been responsible for the economic and political marginalisation of the islander populations – even the poorer Caldoches and contract labourers from Asia acquired land which had before belonged to islanders or took jobs for which the 'natives' were not considered fit. It is also the presence of the 'foreigners' (including the long-term residents of New Caledonia), both individually and collectively, which is most often the object of controversy.

In the period of expansion, from the time of French takeover of the islands until the mid-twentieth century, the aims of colonialists were to populate overseas territories with Europeans, recruit labour where it was needed and to make certain that indigenous populations were pacified and could suitably be either kept 'out of the way' of colonists or appropriately integrated into European economies and converted to European culture. The emphasis was on the settlers, their succcesses and failures, their needs and rights, their grievances and loyalty. Such concern has not disappeared, but increasingly since the 1940s attention has shifted towards the indigenous populations of the island Pacific. The government has been forced to address new demands by Melanesians and Polynesians, at first gradually then with greater urgency, as islanders increasingly came onto the political stage.

Polynesians and Melanesians

The original inhabitants of the French Pacific territories are Melanesian and Polynesian islanders.[10] They developed systems of production and exchange, political organisation and beliefs and traditions long before the arrival of the Europeans; such institutions and customs were often misunderstood, romanticised or denigrated by Europeans.[11] The history of European relations with the Oceanic islands is one of 'culture contact', and often confrontation, between these native systems and those of foreigners. Foreigners imposed their own languages, administration, economy and beliefs. Yet the impact was not fatal, and Melanesian and Polynesian social, political, economic and cultural structures survived, even if in transmuted form.[12] The history of the French Pacific under imperial control was one of the subjugation of native peoples, as well as their continuing resistance, in various forms, to European domination. That situation has continued, *mutatis mutandis*, since 1945.

Among elements of pre-contact islander culture which felt the greatest effects of the European presence were attitudes to and use of land, political authority, cosmology and economic relations. Land, in the Melanesian and Polynesian world-view, was not simply a material necessity for raising crops and a place for habitation but the basic source of identity. Islanders drew their sense of tribal or clan unity and geographical settlement from their belonging to particular areas of land which possessed ancestral meaning. In the pantheistic religions of Oceania, land held sacred value. Appropriation and use of land depended on ancestral rights and agreement by chiefs and members of the clan; islanders had no equivalent to the European notion of outright land ownership. Europeans dispossessed islanders of much of their land and, therefore, of a crucial feature of their identity. In French Polynesia, settlers and traders bought land from islanders, often for nominal payments; the imposition of the French civil code in Tahiti in the 1880s made possible the acquisition and exchange of properties in, for islanders, non-traditional and foreign ways.[13] In the New Hebrides, foreigners similarly took land, eventually holding nominal title to half of all land in the archipelago. The French in New Caledonia's Grande Terre even more dramatically dispossessed islanders of their holdings. Laws passed in the nineteenth century allowed the state to confiscate, then sell, vast tracts of land to colonists or delegate them to government use. Melanesians were confined to native *réserves* which totalled only one-tenth of the land area of the Grande Terre, concentrated in mountainous and less fertile regions of the island.[14] Only Wallis and Futuna, which attracted few settlers, and the Loyalty Islands, maintained as Melanesian *réserves* , escaped spoliation.

Their land taken, Melanesians and Polynesians were marginalised from the mainstream European economy in the colonies. In both major territories, islanders were used as labourers (sometimes under coercion) or domestic servants. In Polynesia, they also found work as pearl-fishers, while in New Caledonia they were employed in nickel mines. Most islanders, particularly in the New Caledonian *brousse* and the outer islands of French Polynesia, remained subsistence farmers, raising traditional crops such as taro. However, the islanders developed needs which only imported commodities could satisfy: Western foodstuffs, clothing, metals and alcohol. In this way, they became increasingly dependent on the European economy. Furthermore, the colonial power forced islanders to pay a head-tax, the *capitation,* which obliged them to donate their labour or to earn the money to pay their taxes in cash or kind. The islanders' ambiguous role in the capitalist economy of the territories was still further affected by the import of Asians. Access to positions of economic power was lacking, except to a certain extent for the Tahitian *demis,* able to play on the double register of a European and Polynesian heritage. In short, the arrival of the Europeans disrupted the islanders' subsistence economic system, but they were only incompletely assimilated into the market economy which replaced it.

French law and administration also transformed the life of islanders. The state consolidated political power in its hands, and even European colonists often chafed under the authority of distant ministers. Islanders had little if any power, except that which they could attempt to exercise by rebellion (which was unsuccessful)[15] or by manoeuvring between various European factions, such as between Protestants and Catholics or between administrators and colonists. (In such negotiations the islanders displayed great skill and enjoyed a certain success.) French authorities incorporated only a small number of 'natives' into the political process, usually islander notables selected as district chiefs and charged with collecting taxes, for which they received a commission. Otherwise, islanders were kept outside the political process. Polynesians of the Society Islands nevertheless became French subjects with the annexation of the chain in 1880. To become a fully-fledged citizen, it was necessary for a subject to be born and domiciled in the colony, have attained the age of twenty-one, be able to read and write French, be of good character, prove his devotion to French interests and show that he had adequate means of existence. (Those few indigenes who had been decorated with the Legion of Honour or the Médaille Militaire or who had performed signal services for France or the colony could be exempted from the requirement to know French.) The Melanesians of New Caledonia did not have French citizenship and in the early twentieth century could acquire it only by having rendered great service to the 'mother country' (as in the First World War) or having earned diplomas or other vocational qualifications or through marriage to a French citizen.[16] There were few Melanesians who met the requirements.

Lack of citizenship deprived islanders of political rights and made them subject to differing law codes. From 1887, the whole corpus of French law was applicable to the indigenes of the former realm of King Pomaré, although a specific indigenous law code was promulgated for the Leeward Islands in 1898 and for remote Rurutu and Rimatara two years later. These regulations maintained traditional islander customs and allowed the appointment of native judges, but required that French officials supervise and approve their decisions. In New Caledonia, French law left the indigenes to their own devices for the resolution of tribal conflicts but gave the Nouméa tribunal authority to judge and sentence Melanesians for offences against European law. In addition, the French imposed a *code de l'indigénat* in New Caledonia in 1887. The *code de l'indigénat* was a special disciplinary code applicable to all Melanesians (and other islanders in the colony) who were not French citizens, and allowed administrative officials to levy fines, sequester property or intern offenders, without a trial or other judicial process, for a variety of offences. Among these were littering, cutting down trees, selling certain products, vagabondage, lack of hygiene, disobedience of public authorities and insubordination.[17] This quintessentially colonial code provided the means by which Melanesians were arbitarily maintained in an inferior position, and it was not repealed until the end of the Second World War.

Religion, land acquisition, economic activities and political relations were not the only ways European presence disoriented island life. European diseases, including syphilis and alcoholism, in some regions caused significant depopulation. Quarrels between various clans or tribes sometimes intensified as they took sides for or against the colonisers or converted to one or another foreign religion. The arbitrary appointment of certain islanders as administrative chiefs upset traditional hierarchies of power and authority. Settlers and soldiers seduced, or sometimes kidnapped and raped, islander women.

Islanders were not powerless to resist European encroachments, nor were they without strategies of collaboration with foreigners. In fact, island culture proved remarkably resilient and adaptive. The impact of European conquest did not totally destroy Oceanic traditions and institutions for the simple reason that Melanesian and Polynesian cultures blended many of their pre-contact customs with new foreign influences. The result was often a 'syncretism' of the two forces. Islanders adopted Christianity but preserved some old beliefs and values, grafting Christian ideas and practices onto non-Christian beliefs; if Christian priests prohibited dances and songs, hymns substituted for them as forms of culture and entertainment. Traditional social relations, such as the primacy of the chiefs, ritual gift-exchange and *coutume* (custom), persisted; now, however, European cloth, tobacco and banknotes entered the network of customary exchange. Old notables sometimes became French-appointed heads of districts or assumed positions of authority as deacons in the Protestant church. A compromise eventuated between the pre-contact, traditional system and the imported European one. A 'new tradition' emerged which lasted from the first arrival of the Europeans through the age of the colonial consolidation in the early twentieth century and the reconstruction of the colonial order after the Second World War. Only in the 1960s, with the nickel boom in New Caledonia and nuclear testing in French Polynesia, did this 'new tradition' give way to a third stage in the socio-cultural history of the islanders, marked by increased wage employment, consumerism, growing secularisation and political activism. Such changes in the last three decades represent the imposition (or adoption) of traditions and attitudes which originate outside the islands yet which have often been fairly easily integrated into island life.[18]

The complex relationship between the French and the islanders took place along a number of channels, among the most important of which were religion, language, education and employment, and urbanisation. Each, initially foreign, provided a basis for a 'new tradition' among the islanders as they adopted and adapted Western institutions. The speed of the process increased markedly in the period after 1945.

RELIGION

One of the most important institutions in the French Pacific territories has been Christianity. Protestant missionaries first arrived in Tahiti from England in the 1790s, fifty years before the French takeover, and a quarrel between Catholic and Protestant missionaries provided the opportunity for France to declare a protectorate over Tahiti. Marist priests converted almost all the inhabitants of Wallis and Futuna in the 1830s and extended their influence throughout central Oceania – in the nineteenth century, 'French' and 'Catholic' were practically synonymous in the South Pacific thanks to the activities of Catholic religious orders. Marist interests in New Caledonia preceded the French flag-raising by a decade. Protestant pastors and Catholic priests competed for the souls of Melanesians in New Caledonia and the New Hebrides. By the 1920s or 1930s, almost all Melanesians and Polynesians in the French colonies (with the exception of still numerous 'pagans' in the New Hebrides) had become at least nominal Christians. The missionaries indoctrinated the islanders, but also served as teachers, medical practitioners, traders and political counsellors. Coming into closer and more regular contact with them than did other Europeans, missionaries were both agents of colonialism and intermediaries between islanders and other Europeans. This ambiguous position provoked opposition from anti-clerical administrators and colonialists who charged that missionaries hindered labour recruitment and their acquisition of property, as well as from free-thinkers and critics of colonialism, who judged that the evangelists had robbed islanders of their own culture and forcibly imprinted foreign mores and beliefs on them.[19]

The islanders themselves reacted to Christianity in a complex fashion. Many avidly adopted the exotic beliefs and ceremonies of the Christian religion and willingly submitted to the authority of the missionaries. For others, conversion remained limited to formalistic observance and public obedience; pre-Christian behaviour and beliefs survived, often concealed from missionaries. Most islanders probably opted for a sort of religious syncretism, in which Oceanic and Christian cosmologies blended or overlaid each other in an original if unorthodox way.[20] The churches had a significant impact on the socialisation of islanders to European life and contributed to the formation of indigenous elites of church leaders and teachers. Many Polynesian and Melanesian leaders were educated in church schools, and a large number were deacons or priests.

In addition to Roman Catholicism, French Protestantism and, in the New Hebrides, Anglicanism and Presbyterianism, other Christian denominations gained converts, notably Mormonism, imported into French Polynesia from the United States. Several non-Christian religions also attracted followers in the French Pacific, including Islam among Indonesians and descendants of Arabs in New Caledonia, and Oriental religions among a few of French Polynesia's Chinese.[21] There is a small Jewish community in Papeete. Various mystic cults have a few followers, mainly among Europeans. The number of agnostics or atheists has probably grown in past decades, but most islanders profess some Christian creed, even if they are not assiduous practitioners of their religions.

The importance of religion can be illustrated by Wallis and Futuna, where the population is totally Catholic, and religious practice is regular. The Marists exercised virtual theocratic power in Wallis and Futuna for a century after the arrival of the first missionaries in the 1830s.[22] In the 1940s a law code approved by both priests and the 'kings' of Wallis and Futuna, and tolerated by the French government, still fined islanders for absence from church, disrespect for the clergy and non-Christian behaviour.[23] Priests served as official interpreters and, if no French Resident were present in the territory, were the acting French representatives. The missionaries kept a dozen or so adolescents as domestic servants in their own residence, and housed larger numbers of children and adolescents in a dormitory under their direct control and supervision. These institutions did not disappear in Wallis until around 1960 and only later in Futuna, despite charges that priests abused the young people for free labour. In the mid-1980s, missionaries still gathered together young people for communal evening activities or to sleep in dormitories in Hihifo. Older residents of Wallis and Futuna continued to treat clergy with great deference in the 1950s and 1960s, sometimes kneeling and signing themselves with the cross when a priest passed. Attendance at mass assured respectability in Wallisian and Futunan villages, and islanders presented food, gifts and tithes to their spiritual fathers. The Catholic mock-Gothic cathedral is the most imposing building in Mata-Uta, and islanders donated money and voluntary labour to construct a large basilica in Futuna. The church, dedicated to Pierre Chanel, a Catholic missionary killed by islanders in the 1800s and canonised in 1954, is the largest church in the South Pacific. Numerous other Catholic churches, often constructed of coral, dot the islands of Wallis and Futuna. Most priests and other religious, including the bishop of Wallis and Futuna, are indigenous islanders; a religious vocation represents an avenue of social mobility, although the privileges and relative wealth of the clergy can spark envy. The Wallisian and Futunan migrants to New Caledonia are among the most active and faithful of Catholics there; Wallisian priests minister to them and promote solidarity among the community, for which the church has been the chief cultural and social rallying-point.[24]

In French Polynesia, Catholicism dominates in the Marquesas archipelago, as well as the Gambiers and eastern and central Tuamotus, while Protestantism prevails in the Society and Austral islands. A third of Polynesians profess loyalty to Catholicism, compared to two-thirds who are Protestant. (Until very recently, Polynesians played a smaller role in the Catholic church than in the Protestant Church. In 1960, there were only four locally-born priests, compared with sixty European *curés*.) Non-Catholic Christianity is split among a number of denominations. Seventh

Day Adventists, Mormons and a break-away Mormon sect known as the Sanitos count a large number of members, although most Polynesians belong to the Eglise Evangélique (the Calvinist-oriented French Reform Church). Most pastors are Polynesian or *demis* and conduct services in Tahitian (or other dialects of Polynesian). Even in secularised and Westernised Papeete, Sunday morning church services are major social events drawing capacity congregations to the impressive Protestant church on the Boulevard Pomaré. French Polynesians who move to New Caledonia, like Wallisians, take their religion with them; both Protestant and Catholic Tahitian parishes in Nouméa minister to the expatriates.[25]

In New Caledonia, only one thousand Europeans are Protestants, but the Melanesian population is almost equally divided between Protestants and Catholics. Melanesian Protestants are in turn split between those who belong to the Eglise Evangélique and the Eglise Evangélique Libre, a denomination which broke away from the main reformed church in the 1950s under the influence of Raymond Charlemagne, a *métropolitain* pastor active in Melanesian political organisations. Relieved of his duties by Protestant officials in Paris, Charlemagne remained in New Caledonia and organised an independent church which won substantial Melanesian support. As in French Polynesia, the clergy of the Protestant churches is overwhelmingly Melanesian – all but two out of the eighty pastors in the early 1980s. By contrast, only five of sixty-one Catholic priests were Melanesian. The Catholic bishops in both Nouméa and Papeete in the early 1980s were European Frenchmen.[26] Although the role of all churches has diminished with de-Christianisation and secularisation (especially among the young), in New Caledonia and in French Polynesia, although to a lesser extent in Wallis and Futuna, religion retains considerable influence.

Deeply rooted traditions, the combination of social and institutional roles played by Christianity and genuine belief all account for the continued importance of religion. The role of missionaries in studying Oceanic cultures[27] and the status of priests as intellectual and cultural figures[28] highlight the power of the church. The political role of the churches, or at least strong links between islander political figures and their respective denominations, has been evident. In French Polynesia, Pouvanaa a Oopa, the most important Polynesian politician of the 1950s and 1960s and advocate of autonomy for the territory, was a prominent Protestant layman and punctuated his speeches with Biblical references. In New Caledonia, the two organisations which embodied the first expressions of Melanesian political sentiment in the post-war period were organised by Catholic priests and Protestant pastors. Later Melanesian leaders almost all came from a religious background. The head of the independence movement in New Caledonia, Jean-Marie Tjibaou, was a former Catholic priest. (The Catholic seminary in New Caledonia was considered by the hierarchy as such a potential hotbed of rebellion that it was closed in 1970.) In the New Hebrides, the major political leaders in the 1970s were an Anglican minister and a Catholic priest, heads of the largely Anglophone and Francophone parties.

The churches have taken stands on issues of concern to islanders.[29] The Catholic churches of New Caledonia and French Polynesia have been hesitant to support autonomist or independence movements, although they have spoken out against discrimination, economic inequalities, violence and social problems. Catholic leaders argue that it is not the role of the church to meddle in politics and call for amicable and co-operative solutions to the territories' problems. Nevertheless, certain individual clergymen, and the influential and activist Catholic Justice and Peace Commission, have spoken out strongly in favour of Melanesian and Polynesian rights.[30] The Protestant churches have been more vocal and more radical. Since 1982 the Eglise Evangélique in Tahiti has demanded that French nuclear tests be ended, and since 1986 it has called for the restoration of traditional Polynesian land rights.[31] In New Caledonia, the Protestant churches expressed increasing concern with the situation of Melanesians during the 1970s and, in 1978, the central synod of the Eglise Evangélique unanimously declared itself in favour of independence. In the 1980s, while condemning violence it supported electoral boycotts and other protest measures taken by the independence movement. Such positions have provoked hostility from those opposed to independence; but the reticence of churches to be more outspoken has also sparked criticism.[32]

Religious organisations outside the French TOMs have taken positions on political issues in Oceania as well. In particular, the Pacific Council of Churches, an ecumenical organisation of

Protestant denominations, and the Catholic Episcopal Conference of the South Pacific, in 1976 and 1981 respectively, called for the independence of New Caledonia. The Pacific Council of Churches supported the move to re-list New Caledonia on the United Nations register of non-decolonised territories, and it condemned further immigration to the territory. The Council provided grants for the New Caledonian church to fund its activities and otherwise directly and indirectly supported the independence and anti-nuclear movements.[33] Protestant churches in Australia and New Zealand, especially the Uniting Church of Australia, supported the New Caledonian independence movement through donations, publications and office space for representatives of the movement.[34] Churches both inside and outside the French territories, therefore, have become increasingly politicised; religious institutions and leaders have distanced themselves from, or turned against, the colonial powers which they originally served. Churches, and the Christian religion in general, have been the crucible for islander activism and remain powerful social forces among Melanesians and Polynesians.

LANGUAGE

Another point of intersection between islanders and the French has been language. Just as language forms a primary element of cultural identity, so changes in use of language – disappearance of one or more languages, imposition of a foreign tongue, incorporation of words – serve as barometers of cultural evolution. Colonisation of the islands of Oceania brought different foreign languages to local populations. Most of the Oceanic languages, however, have survived and have even witnessed a revival in recent years. The various native languages of French Polynesia display differences of vocabulary and pronunciation but are largely mutually comprehensible; although they were not originally written languages, by the early nineteenth century missionaries had compiled glossaries, usages were becoming standardised and the Polynesian elite wrote their own languages as well as English or French. Bibles and translations of other books into Tahitian followed. Colonial administrators used French for official communications, although decrees concerning the islander population were published in Tahitian. Protestant pastors conducted services in Polynesian languages (except in Papeete, where French was also used), while Catholics used Latin and French. State and religious schools taught in French, and authorities did little to encourage preservation and use of Polynesian languages. The mixed-blood *demis* used French (or English in the period before the French takeover), while those outside the élite had limited knowledge of French, particularly in the outer islands. Polynesians adopted numerous French words and expressions; likewise, Tahitian words entered the French of the Pacific. But no real pidgin emerged as, for example, occurred in the New Hebrides. The Chinese immigrants, for their part, retained their native language amongst themselves.[35]

In the 1960s not all of the population of French Polynesia was fluent in French. Almost all Europeans in the territory could read and write French; only three-quarters of *demis*, half the Chinese and fewer than a third of the Polynesians could do so. Although Polynesians did not consider French a 'foreign' language, use of it was restricted to official occasions and communications with non-Polynesians. This incomplete knowledge and use of French indicated the limitations of an education system in which almost all school age pupils were regularly enrolled but which was not fully successful in teaching French. The decades since the 1960s have seen concentrated efforts, and greater success, at inculcating knowledge of French. But there has also been a revival of Polynesian languages. The *demi* élite began to contest the official monopoly of French and promote greater bilingualism. Under the terms of a 1984 law, Tahitian is now used alongside French in official documents. There is a small, but growing, body of literary works in Tahitian.[36] Rejection of French did not accompany this interest in Tahitian, but French Polynesia has not yet attained real bilingualism; many islanders have not fully mastered French, nor have all the French (and particularly *métropolitains*) in the territory acquired knowledge of Tahitian.[37]

The Melanesians of New Caledonia have over thirty different languages. As many as nine thousand speak Dehu (the language of Lifou), and 5000 speak Ajië (in the Houaïlou region), but some other languages are used by 1500 or fewer people; several are threatened with extinction, although others have expanded because of the high birthrates among the Melanesian population. No native language can claim to be a 'national' language in New Caledonia. Melanesians often speak several languages and understand those of neighbouring regions, but they must use French to communicate with distant compatriots. There is no pidgin in New Caledonia, and Melanesians speak a more or less standard French. (The French of New Caledonia, however, displays several peculiarities of vocabulary, notably the assimilation of Australian words.[38])

One survey in the early 1980s tested understanding of French in Melanesian tribes. Residents of rural areas understood approximately half of a selected French text; those under thirty years old understood more than their elders, and differences between tribes also appeared, partly relating to their degree of isolation. Melanesians preferred using their own languages for daily life, inside the family and for discussions relating to 'custom' and Oceanic traditions. They used French for work and for communication with outsiders and other Melanesians whose language they did not understand. Those with a higher socio-economic position or who lived in Nouméa used French more often and more easily than those in the countryside. As in Polynesia, Protestant churches used the vernacular, while Catholic services were held mostly in French. Most Melanesians felt a knowledge of French to be useful and desirable, yet they maintained a certain ambivalence about the language of the 'colonisers'.[39] They were committed to the preservation of their vernaculars.

In both French Polynesia and New Caledonia, therefore, more than a century of French control has been unsuccessful in entirely replacing native languages with French or in creating French literacy among the whole islander population. Polynesian and Melanesian languages, even in a reduced position, have survived to become elements of a new cultural and national identity. Neither group of languages, however, has completely made the transition from a spoken to a written language, and there exists but a small body of modern literature (as opposed to the recording of traditional legends) in island languages. Both New Caledonia and French Polynesia, as both independentists and anti-independentists agree, will remain a province of Francophonie.[40] The fact that many islanders are at home in both French and Oceanic languages suggests a receptivity to cultural assimilation and ease in juggling different cultures.

EDUCATION

Next to churches, schools were the European institutions to have had the most effect on Melanesians and Polynesians; the two are sometimes linked. Missionaries were the first teachers, and church schools remain important adjuncts to the state education system in the French Pacific. Church schools in New Caledonia, for example, enrol just over half of all Melanesian students; in Nouméa, Catholic schools teach twice as many Melanesians and three times as many Wallisians as public schools. Ever since their installation in the colonies, the churches have considered education part of the evangelisation of native peoples, and the French state likewise viewed education as a force for assimilation. Yet access to education, and the training which allowed social mobility, has remained restricted and unequal in the TOMs. The schools, just as the churches, have served as training grounds for contestatory indigenous élites; their role has become a subject for debate in the Oceanic territories.[41]

French metropolitan laws concerning universal and obligatory primary education (dating from the 1880s) and constraints placed on the role of religious congregations in education (connected with the separation of church and state in 1905) were not applied in the Pacific colonies. Paris made efforts to establish public schools with lay teachers, but much teaching continued to be done by missionaries. Only after the Second World War did the state allocate large sums of money for the school system and establish larger numbers of schools in rural districts and on outer islands. The private Catholic schools in New Caledonia, as well as in French Polynesia, still receive large subsidies, while the Marists enjoy a monopoly on primary education in Wallis and Futuna. By the 1950s most children in the Pacific territories (both islanders and other ethnic groups) had access to at least primary education in religious or lay schools, and almost the entirety of the primary school-aged population in the French Pacific has since been enrolled. Not until the

1950s, however, was secondary education available to most Melanesians, and there are only two secondary schools which cater for Melanesian students.[42]

In principle, the curriculum offered in New Caledonia conforms to French metropolitan standards and, until recently, Paris made few attempts to adapt courses and pedagogical methods to the particular situations of the South Pacific. As in France education has been highly structured, classical in orientation and directed at success in competitive examinations. Most Polynesians and Melanesians, at best, have aspired to and obtained only a '*certificat d'études primaries*' (CEP) awarded at age eleven. Those who continued their studies received a school leaving certificate (the BEPC), and at a higher level, the *baccalauréat*, which gave access to tertiary education. The numbers of islanders who progressed this far was small; the first Melanesian *bachelier* passed his examinations in 1962, and the first to earn a university degree graduated in the early 1970s.

Disparities between ethnic groups are obvious. In New Caledonia in the early 1980s, 15 per cent of Melanesians were illiterate, while only 3 per cent of Caldoches could neither read nor write. Of the total population, 39 per cent of Europeans possessed a diploma higher than the CEP, compared to just over 4 per cent of Melanesians. (By comparison, 24 per cent of Vietnamese, 10 per cent of Tahitians, 8 per cent of Indonesians and under 5 per cent of Wallisians and Futunans in the territory had such qualifications.[43]) Inequality of education was connected with ethnicity but also with place of residence and socioeconomic background. Children who lived in Nouméa and those whose parents were themselves more highly educated or held higher-level professional jobs stood a better chance of attending school and succeeding at their studies than did others. Since most Melanesians lived in rural areas and most were agriculturalists or non-workers, their children suffered multiple disadvantages. Students did not entirely overcome these obstacles even if they persevered in their studies: the gap between the proportion of European and Melanesian students who obtained a BEPC, already significant, widened dramatically at the level of the *baccalauréat*. Of 100 Melanesian primary school students, only two candidates attempted the *baccalauréat* examinations each year, and only one was successful; for 100 European students, twenty-two sat for the examination and seventeen passed it. Critics say that such results prove the failure of the French education system to live up to its own goals of equal education, despite the steadily increasing enrolment of recent decades.[44] The result has been severe under-representation of Melanesians at higher socio-professional levels.

In spite of handicaps, a certain number of Melanesians have continued their studies to university level. Until the recent establishment of a French university in the Pacific, with campuses in Nouméa and Papeete, they were obliged to enrol in metropolitan universities. Priests often trained at the Catholic universities in Lyon or Paris, while others studied at the French state universities. While they were at university some students came into contact with new social or political theories which influenced their subsequent activities in the Pacific. For instance, Jean-Marie Tjibaou studied ethnology in Paris and explored Melanesian philosophy in his writings. Apollinaire Anova-Ataba's book on the 1878 rebellion originated as his Master's thesis. Nidoish Naisseline, now the leader of the political party Libération Kanake Socialiste, studied in Paris in the late 1960s and was influenced by the ideas of the New Left and the demonstrations of May 1968; on his return to the Pacific he established a radical Melanesian party. Others have used their education to obtain positions in the administration, although they do not necessarily adopt anti-independence positions as a result.

Dissatisfaction with 'colonial' education grew with political agitation in the 1980s. Melanesian groups demanded the establishment of an alternative system or substantial modifications to the French state syllabus. In 1985, at the height of the New Caledonian 'troubles', the main independence party organised a boycott of French schools and set up '*écoles populaires kanak*' (EPK). The EPK, grouping together volunteer students and teachers, attempted to introduce an indigenous type of education. Melanesian languages replaced French for instruction, and French was taught as a second, foreign language. Teaching emphasised practical skills, stressed Melanesian traditions and oral literature, and promoted the use of natural resources – the canteens of the EPK served local food rather than imported tinned goods. EPKs sprouted up around the Melanesian regions of New Caledonia and became a vital element in politicisation of the population and the efforts of pro-independence activists. Yet with a lack of funding and staffing, they were unable to compete with the state and church schools. Some parents also worried about the quality of teaching the schools dispensed. Most of the experimental schools have disappeared.[45]

In French Polynesia there are also connections between education and ethnicity. Less than one per cent of Europeans and just over one per cent of *demis* were illiterate in 1977, compared to 2.7 per cent of Polynesians. A quarter of the Europeans, half the *demis* and three-quarters of the Polynesians had no school certificate or diploma; by contrast, almost three-quarters of the Europeans, around half of the *demis* and less than a quarter of the Polynesians held a CEP or higher certificate. Nevertheless, the Polynesians have improved their levels of education in recent decades; the number with a CEP or higher certificate doubled between 1962 and 1977.[46]

A central issue in education in French Polynesia has been the question of language. Lack of true bilingualism and difficulties in adapting to instruction in both French and Tahitian created obstacles for school children. Many Polynesians spoke an islander language at home – Tahitian, one of the two varieties of Marquesan, Rurutu, Puamotu or Mangarevan. Yet until 1975 Polynesian was banned in state schools. In 1980, however, the government gave official recognition to Tahitian as a school subject, and two years later it became a necessary subject for the award of a CEP. A 1984 law reinforced this provision, stating that the 'Tahitian language is an obligatory subject to be taught during normal school hours in kindergartens and primary schools'. Such measures have improved the status of Tahitian and introduced non-islander children to an Oceanic language. But it has not solved the problem of children in Polynesia lagging behind in their studies. In the 1980s, by the time they reached middle school, between 13 per cent and 74 per cent of children in French Polynesia (depending on the archipelago) were obliged to repeat a class, compared to 13 per cent in the *métropole*. Schools in central Papeete had the best success rates, while those further away did much less well. There was also a problem with the level of teacher training; half the elementary teachers in French Polynesia in the mid-1980s held only a *brevet élémentaire* (a relatively low-level teacher's certificate), and only

40 per cent had a *baccalauréat*.[47]

In French Polynesia, as in New Caledonia, the education system was making efforts by the 1980s to incorporate islander language and culture into the curriculum. Advances had been made since the Second World War, and particularly since the 1960s, in providing education to all residents of the territories, particularly to the Melanesians and Polynesians, who had previously been neglected by schools. Yet the level of teaching was still less than what was considered desirable, and disparities in success rates were linked largely (although not exclusively) to ethnic background and language. The schools, an important medium for the entry of islanders into European life, had not entirely fulfilled their mission.

These situations have had repercussions in other areas of society. Melanesians and ethnic Polynesians have been underrepresented in jobs which demand more advanced education. They have also been over-represented among the jobless and among delinquents. In the case of New Caledonia, Melanesians accounted for 47 per cent of juvenile delinquents in 1987, compared to 26 per cent who were Europeans, a further 26 per cent who were Polynesians and fewer than one per cent who were of Indonesian or Vietnamese background. Approximately 70 per cent of all crimes in New Caledonia were committed in the metropolitan area of Nouméa, with the greatest frequency in the Melanesian suburbs of Tindu, Montravel and the Vallée du Tir. Half of all crimes were thefts or attacks on property. The underprivileged and unschooled, Melanesians (and Polynesians), were among those most apt to be arrested for petty crime. Lack of training, unemployment, ghetto housing conditions and 'lack of adaptation through incomprehension, marginalisation and sometimes even exclusion' characterised many such youth in the territory.[48]

ECONOMY AND SOCIETY

Economic developments have played their role in the transformation of islanders' lives. In the century after French takeover, islanders worked episodically as mine workers or manual labourers, and little effort was made to encourage them to undertake independent commercial activities.[49] With the economic developments of the post-Second World War period, islanders became more thoroughly integrated in the European economy although still as (usually lowly) wage labourers. The expanding bureaucracy mandated by the new political statutes and development efforts provided some employment. Tourism gave jobs in hotels, airports and other parts of the service industry. The nickel boom in New Caledonia and nuclear testing in French Polynesia attracted many Melanesians and Polynesians to new jobs (and produced, as well, the labour migration from Tahiti and from Wallis and Futuna to New Caledonia). New projects for economic stimulation and diversification such as market gardening, pearl fishing and coffee plantations, also had effects on the islander work force.[50]

Regular employment provided salaries, access to consumer goods and avenues for social advancement; conversely, lack of training and prejudice created obstacles to social mobility. Wage employment contributed to migration and urbanisation as increasing numbers of islanders moved from their villages or outer islands to Nouméa or Papeete. Different types of housing, social relations, patterns of consumption and attitudes confronted them in the cities, and islanders were sometimes divorced from the context of rural life and traditional society. At its best, this allowed a freedom of movement, work and thought perhaps inaccessible in their former environment. At its worst, it led to alienation, misery and material poverty – as evidenced in the emergence of slums in Papeete and ghettoisation of Melanesians in public housing in Nouméa. Islanders had to face all of the problems of contemporary urban life and, at the same time, balance the demands of the city and wage labour with their traditional responsibilities of membership in a family or a more extended social group. For some, the balancing act was relatively easy, but for others the difficulties led to crime, prostitution and increased use of drugs and alcohol.

The effects of urbanisation and employment in a capitalist economy were not entirely different for islanders and others in 'modernising' societies, but the process was aggravated by the great cultural divide between islanders and Europeans, and by the domination of the islanders by a 'foreign' élite which held the reins of political and economic power. Particularly in New Caledonia, where there existed no *métis* class as an intermediary between Europeans and islanders, the native population continued to suffer the after-effects of colonialism even with the political changes of the period after 1940.[51] Some of the changes, including economic fluctuation, heightened their ambiguous position in society. Previously ignored and excluded, Melanesians now became a potential work force, the object of social programmes and development strategies, and clients for political factions. The city provided the venues for these developments – in Nouméa, for example, the nickel-smelting plant at Dumbéa, the housing complexes of Montravel, the *lycées* and other educational institutions, the political forums of the 'Haussariat' and territorial assembly and the sociability of the Place des Cocotiers[52] – and the crucible for the transformation.

The islanders have been the group most affected by economic change. Few live in economic autarky, and all now have access to various social security payments. The public service is the largest employer in the territories; many who are not in the active population – the infirm, pensioners and the unemployed – receive benefits from the state. Since the Second World War, almost all Melanesians and Polynesians (even in Wallis and Futuna) have thus been incorporated, to a greater or lesser degree, into the market economy through wage labour, consumer habits and social security. There has also emerged an islander élite, those who have jobs in the public service, educational institutions and the church. It is they who have the education which opens up such job possibilities, and with their high salaries, they are the prime beneficiaries of economic change. Such men and women represent the political and cultural élite among the islanders as well. Side by side with them live larger groups of islanders who have received fewer rewards of economic growth. They are even more vulnerable than the élite to recessions or crises which create unemployment or, conversely, development programmes which offer new training, positions or promotions. Just as islanders over the past century have been ineluctably and probably irreversibly brought into the fold of Christian churches, enrolled in Western schools and taught foreign languages and other subjects, so they have been drawn into Western economies. This metamorphosis has impinged on old cultures and attitudes, but economic and social developments – combined with the impact of political evolution – have formed the context for the renewal of interest in traditional cultures and the forging of new identities.

ISLANDER CULTURE AND IDENTITY

Despite colonisation, attempts to modify or destroy Oceanic culture and the transformations effected by Christianity, foreign political administration and economic change, the Melanesians and Polynesians of the French Pacific retain and proclaim a separate identity, one based on their pre-contact civilisation but which incorporates elements of French religion, politics, economics and culture. Recent years have seen attempts at reviving local cultures and developing a sense of 'nationalism' based on indigenous traditions. Particularly in New Caledonia, pro-independence writers and political activists have criticised the depreciation of island customs and the alienation created by foreign colonisation. Jean-Marie Tjibaou and others emphasised the importance of land to Melanesian identity as a prime element in their struggle for political rights.[53] Leaders have promoted island communitarianism and mutual aid as an alternative to the capitalist economy, as well as consensual resolution of conflict as an adjunct to Western parliamentary processes. They resurrect figures from Melanesian history as prototypes of resistance to colonialism and heroes in their political struggle; Ataï, chief of the 1878 rebels in New Caledonia, has become a folk hero and symbol of Kanak liberation, now joined by more recent martyrs, such as Eloi Machoro, Yeiwéné Yeiwéné and Tjibaou. Use of Melanesian languages, efforts to revive and preserve art, dance and music and the recording of oral literature all serve to revitalise islander identity and create a sense of nationalism. With these efforts, islanders have recovered part of a culture of which they had been largely dispossessed and have tried to rescue it from folklorisation or extinction.

Europeans long considered Melanesian art a paradigm of 'primitive' culture; sculptures, jewellery, money and clothing were acquired by private collectors or museums around the world. Melanesian skeletons were shipped to ethnographic museums overseas, and even the head of Ataï rests in a Paris museum. Melanesians themselves began to abandon their cultures. Not until 1975, with the Festival Mélanésia 2000, organised by Jean-Marie Tjibaou, did Melanesian culture again attract general interest. The festival was a shock for both Melanesians and Europeans, who for the first time came into contact with languages and cultures previously considered retrograde. The festival marked a first step in a Melanesian cultural renaissance, and many of the organisers of the 1975 event became political leaders in the Kanak independence movement. Meanwhile, Melanesian art objects were being preserved and displayed at the New Caledonia territorial museum built in 1971; a century had passed since the first proposal for a museum of Melanesian 'artifacts' was advanced in 1863.[54]

By the early 1980s, other institutions had begun to promote Melanesian culture, including a museum and cultural centre established by Tjibaou in his municipality of Hienghène and an Office Scientifique et Culturel Kanak in Nouméa. Individuals, notably the poet Déwé Gorodey, began publishing works both reflecting traditional Melanesian culture and voicing current political grievances;[55] the writings of Tjibaou also formed an important literature on Melanesian culture. A publishing company and bookshop, Edipop, were opened to make available information supportive of Melanesians. Groups of musicians combined traditional Melanesian music with modern rock; the best known group has been Yata – the name is Ataï spelled backwards – which sings in Melanesian languages.[56] A small but growing number of painters and sculptors have returned to or been inspired by traditional designs.[57] Efforts also continue to preserve and display the older Melanesian cultural patrimony; a major exhibition, 'De Jade et de Nacre', shown in Nouméa and Paris in 1990 marked the greatest grouping of Melanesian art to date.[58] Fifteen years after Tjibaou's Festival Mélanésia 2000, it symbolised a new step in an evolving cultural identity and wider public recognition of that culture.

Similarly, in French Polynesia islanders have revalued their ancestral culture.[59] The recovery of islander culture, and efforts at articulating new identities, chart the evolution of French Polynesia. As in New Caledonia, old cultural forms were largely devalued or folklorised until the 1960s. In 1965 a proposal was made to establish an Académie Tahitienne, seen by the chief French administrator in Tahiti, Governor Sicurani, as a means of promoting the complementarity of Polynesian and French cultures. But the way the project was outlined in 1967, when the government formally considered the idea, was resolutely assimilationist, as it foreshadowed an institution which would promote various cultures, but be mainly interested in translations and have as its primary activity an annual literary prize awarded on the anniversary of the French annexation of Tahiti. The proposal was not popular in this form, and was subsequently redesigned. When the Académie Tahitienne opened in 1973, it was centred more specifically on Polynesian culture. The Academy's major accomplishment has been a new dictionary of Tahitian, published in 1985. In 1980 the Centre Polynésien des Sciences Humaines (Te Ana Vaha Rau) was established to promote the study of archaeology and Oceanic traditions; the Centre was also given charge of the Museum of Tahiti and the Islands, which had been inaugurated in 1977. Other official organisations such as the Office Territorial d'Action Culturelle followed.[60]

Alongside these government-sponsored institutions, and the ideology of recognition but also of cultural fusion which they represented, there emerged more contestatory cultural activity. This emphasises Polynesian traditions and has been intentionally *passéiste* in its search for Polynesian cultural identity in distinction to (and generally in opposition to) imported values and forms.[61] The promoters of this 'Maohi' identity seek to demarcate themselves from the *demis* and Europeans (*popaa*) and promote a unitary and purified Polynesian identity. The name 'Maohi' – the Tahitian equivalent of 'Maori' – is preferred, in fact, to 'Tahitian' or 'Polynesian'. The major writer on Maohi culture, Duro Raapoto, evokes Maohi spirits and sacred sites, defends the use of island languages in preference to French and voices a strident critique of the French administration and contemporary Polynesian society. He writes about the mythic homeland of Polynesians (*havaii*) and alludes to Polynesian temples (*marae*) and the importance of land and customs. Raapoto's theoretical writings constitute cultural manifestos, and the poems of Raapoto and Rui a Mapuhi are examples of the neo-Polynesian art he espouses.[62]

There has also been new Tahitian theatre and film,[63] a renewal of Polynesian music and dance and a cross-fertilisation with popular music. For instance, the dance company of Coco Hotahota began as a folklore troupe in the mid-1960s but then incorporated more authentic references to kava, pearl-diving, *marae* offerings and taboos into their performances. By the 1980s Coca Hotahota's performances included dances with props like tin cans, Walkmen and jeans and such scenes as the enact-ment of a birth. Although his material has been controversial, Hotahota is considered the most innovative promoter of Maohi culture.[64] Lastly, there has been a renewed interest in tradi-tional Tahitian body-art. Tahitian men (and some women) customarily had their arms, legs, chests and backs covered in intricate tattoos which served as decoration and indication of status. Missionaries and other Europeans (except for sailors) regarded the long and painful process of tattooing as barbarous and attempted to eradicate the practice. Tattooing had all but disappeared among Polynesians until the 1980s, when it again became popular. Samoan and Hawaiian tattoo artists arrived in Tahiti to teach their methods, and the territorial cultural office in 1983 held a tattoo fair. Tattooing is a fad but also a sign of Polynesian cultural revival.[65]

It was only, therefore, in the 1970s and, particularly, in the 1980s that Polynesians and Melanesians began to recover a number of old cultural traditions, that they began to explore new media (such as Western-style painting, rock music and experimental dance) and that official recognition of these ef-forts occurred. The goal was to convince both islanders and Europeans of the persistence and vibrancy of the islands' cul-tures, an effort to establish their legitimacy and authenticity in the face of efforts to denigrate them or even deny their exist-ence. Opposition was sometimes acute, especially at moments of political tension. For example, the conservative French newsweekly *Le Figaro Magazine* grudgingly wrote on the tenth anniversary of Tjibaou's Festival Mélanésia 2000 in 1985: 'Tjibaou, thanks to the complicity of a few leftist ethnologists searching for thesis topics, indeed succeeded in convincing [the public] that there exists a Kanak culture'.[66]

Problems arose in establishing a new cultural identity, par-ticularly one based on ceremonies and rituals which seemed rather archaic in the era of television and compact discs. Many islanders themselves have been and are estranged from their culture and have had to learn and relearn it consciously. As a Melanesian in New Caledonia explained: 'The young people have schools now, but they have forgotten Kanak culture. The young are like the balls of bulls, which swing between their legs. With the elders, they say they have European learning and customs, and with the whites, that they have Kanak custom. But they really know nothing about the Europeans, and they know nothing of the tribe'.[67] Some islanders wanted to accept only certain parts of ancestral culture, considering other practices outdated, while others favoured a more wholesale recovery of traditional culture. A study of young Melanesians in New Caledonia in the early 1980s showed that if nine-tenths respected the authority of traditional tribal chiefs, only two-thirds thought authority in general should reside with the elders for the simple reason of their age. Three-quarters believed in the communitarianism of traditional society, and particularly in the right of the individual to use or appropriate the belongings of others, but more than two-thirds thought that customary marriage (with arranged partners) was no longer acceptable, and half thought similarly of the traditional dominance of men over women in Melanesian society. Attitudes towards such institutions as chieftainship depended partly on urban or rural background, level of education and socio-economic status.[68]

Another problem was whether Melanesian and Polynesian culture applied only to those of particular ethnic backgrounds or whether others in the territories could share these identities. The question of whether it was possible for inhabitants of the contemporary world to return to the traditional ways of life advocated by some of the more radical proponents of island culture also appeared. Lastly, there was the issue of conflict between the various cultures of the islanders – pre-contact customs, the 'new tradition' of Christianity, the still newer demands of modern political and economic activity and the appeal of a secular, consumer-oriented culture. Still other sirens also called – from the fringe Pentecostal religions to the cults of drugs and delinquency. If cultural options had multiplied, so had the pressures to adopt or reject particular patterns and beliefs. By the 1970s and 1980s, culture had become a pivot for politics.

ISLAND WOMEN IN THE FRENCH PACIFIC

One group which has particularly experienced economic, political and cultural change in the French Pacific islands has been Polynesian and Melanesian women. The status of women in traditional Oceanic societies, through hardly the same as that of men, was far from absolute oppression. In Melanesia, the mother passed the spirit of the clan and family (the totem) to a child, and a child's maternal uncles played an influential role in his or her life. Women did not hold chiefly positions in New Caledonia, but women, particularly elders, exercised some power in local communities. In Melanesia, as in Polynesia, particular domains – housekeeping, certain kinds of artisanal and most agricultural activities – were reserved to women. In Tahiti, women were generally free to contract whatever sexual or romantic liaisons (often multiple ones) they preferred.

The developments of the nineteenth century often touched the lives of women. Missionaries made a concerted though not always successful effort to eradicate what they considered promiscuity. They persuaded women to wear demure dresses of patterned calico, which hid their arms, legs and breasts; these 'Mother Hubbards' as English pastors called them, although the French name of *robes mission* ('mission dresses') is more appropriate, became the standard apparel for island women in Melanesia, though not in Polynesia. Missionaries also dispensed education to island girls, and young Polynesian women probably achieved greater literacy and numeracy than men. The church provided a new avenue of social mobility for the numerous women who joined religious orders, although, of course, they could not be ordained Catholic priests. (Nor did women become Protestant pastors or deacons.) Women remain pillars of the church in Oceania; hymn-singing and prayer groups have been special areas for women's activities.

In recent decades, economic changes have provided new job opportunities for women, usually in the tertiary sector. The number of women in paid employment is still significantly smaller than their proportion of the population, their salaries lower and their jobs located further down the managerial hierarchies. But women have increasingly entered the salaried workforce in the public service, the tourist industry and such other service enterprises as restaurants and cafés. The arrival of tourists has provided a demand for handicrafts, especially in Polynesia, where women make *leis* (flower garlands), *tapa* (fabric made from bark) and *tifaifai* (quilts) for sale to visitors – the nightly gathering of women artisans in *farés* along the Boulevard Pomaré in Papeete is evidence of feminine sociability and the commercial value of artisan work. In the back streets of

Papeete are located the brothels where other Tahitian women earn a living, catering for the soldiers and other men who seek their services.[69]

Many Polynesian women have married European men, although intermarriage is less common in New Caledonia. (Fewer Oceanic men have wed European women.) The tradition of inter-ethnic marriage dates from the first period of island contact with foreigners. No social censure is attached to such unions, which may even be preferred to marriage to islanders of lower status. Children of mixed marriages in Tahiti grow up as *demis* and are in a privileged social position in the community. In New Caledonia, by contrast, children of inter-ethnic couples are generally reared as either Europeans or Melanesians and, in the absence of a *demi* or Creole class, culturally and politically integrate into the group in which they have lived.

Rural women in French Oceania have continued to exhibit traditional aspirations; in Polynesia, a rural woman's agenda remains dominated by the search for a male companion and the desire to have children rather than by the search for a job. Many young and urbanised women are little interested in traditional activities and desire to resemble European women as much as possible. Younger women in Nouméa, for example, seldom wear the old mission dresses. The women of Wallis and Futuna, just as those of New Caledonia, are less 'modern' than their counterparts in urban Tahiti, but the spread of consumer goods, artificial contraception and new job possibilities have also altered their lives.

Women have not played a large role in politics in the French territories, although French women have enjoyed the vote in Polynesia since the end of the Second World War (and, in New Caledonia, since the extension of the suffrage to all indigenes in the late 1950s). In French Polynesia, politics has continued to be regarded as a male preserve, despite the presence of a small number of women in the Territorial Assembly. In New Caledonia, women have appeared more visibly in the independence movement. One of the five groups which originally composed the FLNKS was the ephemeral Groupe des Femmes en Lutte. Women have been active in the newspaper *Bwenando* and in the *écoles populaires kanakes* . One of the best known Melanesian cultural figures is the poet Déwé Gorodey, and the widow of Jean-Marie Tjibaou, Marie-Claude, is president of the

Kanak Cultural Institute. Women in the French Pacific, as else-where in the world, have increasingly been under pressure to fulfil their traditional duties as wives and mothers and, at the same time, excel at schooling and professional life. Women have been expected to be the guardians of tradition (whether the tradition of the pre-contact period or that of Christianity) and yet adapt to the contemporary world with its possibilities for employment and political activities but also with its different mores and behaviours. Women, in short, embody in a particu-larly clear way the ambiguities of islander identity.

5 Politics in the French Pacific, 1945–1980

Politics in the Pacific territories since the Second World War has been formed by a mixture of, and often clash between, policies emanating from the central administration in Paris and the actions of various groups in the islands themselves. The often conflictual relationship between the metropolitan government and its representatives in the territories, on the one hand, and local interest groups, individuals and parties, on the other, persisted past the formal end of the colonial era in 1946. Several new features overlay this traditional antagonism, however, notably the formation of political parties and the enfranchisement and politicisation of indigenous islanders. The result was a heightened demand for greater autonomy in New Caledonia and French Polynesia and, ultimately, calls for outright independence. The reformist, conciliatory politics of the 1940s changed into a campaign against the French state in Tahiti in the 1950s, and in the 1980s New Caledonia witnessed a violent struggle for independence; however, cycles of confrontation always alternated with ones of compromise. During these decades, proposals for *départementalisation* (and thus greater integration of the territories into the French Republic), autonomy, 'independence-in-association' and a more radical ethnically-based independence were all broached, political leaders were exiled, imprisoned and assassinated, and charges of treason, collaboration with colonial oppressors and interference by outside powers were proffered. Such developments took place against the background of independence movements in France's larger colonies in the 1950s and 1960s which forced Paris to relinquish most of its empire, then an effort to preserve the remnants of the overseas domains which remained under its control. Yet independence for the Pacific islands hardly seemed possible in the 1940s and almost half a century later, after a brief period of optimism amongst its supporters, especially in New Caledonia, it had not occurred.

158

TRAITS OF POLITICAL LIFE IN THE PACIFIC TOMS

Political life in New Caledonia and French Polynesia, as well as in Wallis and Futuna and the New Hebrides, since 1945 has displayed many of the characteristics of politics in Europe: the setting up of representative institutions, the formation of parties, regular elections, the emergence of political leaders and their attempts to marshall support, battles for power and influence. For the Pacific, many of these were new developments of the post-war period. The French territories of Oceania showed particular traits as well, some of which were common to France's other *départements et territoires d'outre-mer*.[1] Most important is the fact that officials in Paris mould the shape of politics in the overseas territories: the French parliament legislates law codes, establishes institutions and decides on the franchise; the President of the Republic appoints many local officials, especially the chief administrator; Paris retains control of defence, law and order, foreign policy, currency, education and immigration. The French state can grant, or withdraw, powers and privileges from local officials; the degree of autonomy exercised by territorial governments, therefore, depends on the goodwill of the *métropole*. When it deems such action necessary, the French state can assume direct and near total control in the overseas territories.

The exact division of power between the central and territorial governments has varied considerably since 1945, but in every case the authorities in Paris have determined the power-sharing arrangements. With the constitution of the Fourth Republic in 1946, Paris conceded elected representation to the overseas territories through the setting up of local assemblies and provisions for the nomination of *députés* and senators to the French parliament.[2] The local assemblies had strictly limited powers, however, and were more consultative than legislative bodies. A decade later, the *loi-cadre* Defferre gave the territories wider powers; councils of government were created as executives of the territorial assemblies, particular portfolios were assigned to designated ministers, the authority of the governor was reduced. Only two years after the Defferre reforms, in 1958, the Fifth Republic's constitution abolished these powers, and the brief experiment with devolved authority came to an end. The power-sharing arrangement between state and territory in the case of French Polynesia then favoured the central authorities until 1977, when Paris adopted a statute which again allowed a greater degree of local autonomy; in 1984, yet another statute assured French Polynesia a larger measure of self-government than had otherwise been witnessed by local authorities anywhere in the French Republic.[3] In New Caledonia, the local assembly and its executive did not gain substantial power until the beginning of the 1980s, then the troubles of the next years led Paris alternately to assume almost complete administrative control and experiment with various plans to devolve authority onto various local congresses, provincial assemblies and other organs. As for Wallis and Futuna, the administrative structures set in place when those islands officially became a *territoire d'outre-mer* in 1961 have altered little and allow for a unique division of power among the French-appointed chief administrator, an elected assembly and customary chiefs (the 'kings'). Throughout the three territories, Paris has also occasionally altered the form of municipal or regional government, for instance, by creating *communes* in French Polynesia and carving out 'regions' or 'provinces' in New Caledonia.

The primacy of the central government (and its representatives) over local authorities in territorial affairs relates both to the administrative centralism which is a hallmark of French government and to the colonial past of the overseas possessions. Despite several efforts to decentralise administration, France has remained a country in which power emanates from the centre; not until a concerted programme of decentralisation in the early 1980s did local government authorities, even in the *métropole* , acquire substantial power. France ruled its colonies directly in the period before 1945 (and, in some areas, until their independence); French colonial theory had little notion of the self-government or 'responsible government' which Britain allowed its dominions of white settlement (although generally not its non-settler colonies). By contrast, after 1946, France allowed its colonies to elect representatives to both houses of the French legislature; such delegates enjoyed all the rights and privileges of other *députés* and senators and some served as ministers or secretaries of state in the central government. Such a level of representation was unusual in the 'colonial' world of the time and unknown in the British empire.[4] In the 1940s, France's policy of allowing the overseas *départements* and territories to elect delegates to parliament was, in fact, considered an extremely progressive and enlightened view of the relationship between *métropole* and colonies.[5] But such a move was also part and parcel of the long-standing French colonial idea of the 'assimilation' or 'association' of non-European peoples into the political and cultural life of France, an integration which would logically earn them representation. These ideas took institutional form in the establishment of a French Union in 1946 and a Community in 1958, short-lived French equivalents, *mutatis mutandis* , of the British Commonwealth. The two aspects of the political links between France and its territories, administrative centralisation but also direct representation, therefore represented a not illogical complementarity in French ideology, even if, in practice, it always resulted in the *métropole* having the upper hand over the TOMs.

A second development in the political life of the French Pacific after the Second World War was the enfranchisement of all French nationals. Under the 1946 constitution, all nationals became citizens although not all were given the right to vote, at least in New Caledonia. In French Polynesia, the residents of the realms of Queen Pomaré which had been annexed by the French in the nineteenth century already enjoyed the suffrage, but those in several outer archipelagos could not vote until the institution of the Fourth Republic. In New Caledonia, only a few Melanesians were able to cast a ballot, generally those who worked for the French administration, who demonstrated their competence in the French language or who were decorated war veterans. The French enfranchised a much larger number of Melanesians in 1951, bringing the number of islander voters almost to the same level as that of European settlers. Not until 1957, however, was the suffrage extended to all indigenes in the islands. Furthermore, at the end of the Second World War, Frenchwomen won the vote, which substantially increased the electorate, and women in the Pacific territories were given the vote at the same time as men. Finally, in the 1960s, it became easier for the large Chinese population in Tahiti to acquire French citizenship and the right to vote, and the Chinese soon made their presence felt in local political life. But migrants to the territories, so long as they were French citizens, also had the right to vote – the *métropolitains* who were attracted to New Caledonia by the nickel boom and to French Polynesia by nuclear testing, just as the Wallisians, Futunans and French Polynesians who migrated to New Caledonia could vote in local and national elections in their new places of residence after only a short delay. These changes, especially the enfranchisement of the Melanesians in New Caledonia, brought new groups into the electorate, allowed new concerns to be voiced in public debate and encouraged the formation of political groups representing the island populations or their interests.

A particular point of resentment among Melanesians in New Caledonia was the possibility for *métropolitains* and other migrants to vote in elections, and help determine the future status of the territory, even when they were posted to the South Pacific only on short contracts and had no vested interests or long-standing connections with New Caledonia; in response, Paris restricted the electorate for a referendum in 1988 to those who had resided in the territory for more than three years and limited the electorate for another referendum scheduled for 1998 to those who had been registered voters in 1988 or their descendants. Such restrictions did not satisfy those in the independence movement who argued that only those of Melanesian parentage or those who had proved their commitment to the country through active support for independence should be allowed to vote; to their opponents, by contrast, any restriction on the right to vote contravened the principle of universal suffrage guaranteed by the French constitution. The simple inclusion or exclusion of particular groups in the electorate by the French government was thus fraught with political repercussions.

Of utmost importance in these changes was the extension of the vote to the 'native' populations. Combined with other developments, including the end of the *code de l'indigénat* , rising levels of education and the emergence of an islander élite, increasing wage employment and urbanisation, this had a dramatic effect both on the lives of Melanesians and Polynesians and on the political evolution of the French territories. Before the 1950s, the only access to political expression available to Melanesians in New Caledonia was through extra-parliamentary channels, and those strategies were seldom employed and generally unsuccessful. In French Polynesia, the *demis* dominated politics, and those *ta'ata Tahiti*[6] who had the right to vote seldom participated in political life.

The entry of islanders into modern political life began immediately at the end of the Second World War with the formation in both New Caledonia and French Polynesia of committees which voiced the grievances of the Melanesian and Polynesian populations. Islanders henceforth played a major role in the two political movements which dominated the territories in the 1950s. In French Polynesia, the *ta'ata Tahiti* found a leader in Pouvanaa a Oopa and provided the base of support for his political party, while in New Caledonia the Union Calédonienne sought support among Melanesians. In later decades, more exclusively ethnic parties came into being, especially in New Caledonia, and the 1980s saw demands for a specifically 'Kanak' independence for New Caledonia and for a diminution in the economic and political power of those not of Polynesian heritage in Tahiti. Wallisians and Futunans in New Caledonia also set up their own ethnically-based political party. In a broad sense the politicisation of islander populations was also evident in the growth of the media, union activity, a cultural revival and the continued use of extra-parliamentary actions ranging from petitions and lobbying to blockades and electoral boycotts; in French Polynesia and, particularly, in New Caledonia, violence seemed to be embedded in the political process in the 1980s. But islanders were not all opponents of French authority in the islands; the main conservative parties of French Polynesia and New Caledonia included prominent islander spokesmen, some of whom were elected to both local offices and the French parliament. Conservative, anti-independence parties began to pay more attention to islander issues; the fact that all political parties in French Polynesia now bear Polynesian names illustrates an effort to 'indigenise' political life.[7]

Another characteristic of politics in the Pacific TOMs since the 1950s has been the emergence of formal political parties. In the pre-war period, political groupings were informal associations of individuals loosely grouped around a leader, a special interest or an élite; even the highly organised political parties which played a large role in the *métropole*, such as the socialists and communists, were unsuccessful in implanting themselves in the Pacific territories. From the 1950s, however, the situation changed, as the Rassemblement Démocratique des Peuples Tahitiens (RDPT), Pouvanaa a Oopa's movement, and its rival, the Union Tahitienne, in French Polynesia and the Union Calédonienne (UC) in New Caledonia became strong political forces dominated by charismatic leaders and well-articulated ideologies. These parties subsequently fragmented, and politics in both territories in the 1960s and 1970s saw the establishment, and often rapid demise, of a multiplicity of political parties. The baffling evolution of party politics in the two territories indicated the abandonment of the consensual policies which the UC embodied in New Caledonia, as well as the militant tendencies of the RDPT in French Polynesia. But the proliferation of political groups also showed the adoption of new programmes, the influence of outside ideologies (notably, the impact of the 'New Left' and of ethnic and regional nationalism), the rise to prominence of popular leaders, and the possibilities of shifting alliances in local and national politics. Not until the 1980s did the various groups in New Caledonia coalesce into two major groupings, one party which opposed independence for the territory and a coalition – sometimes torn by internecine strife – which promoted independence; even so, other parties remained active. In French Polynesia, even that degree of unification had not occurred except in temporary, and changing, accords among different politicians and their supporters.

The permutations in party politics proved that many factors played a role in political processes in the French territories in addition to the usual contests for power between movements. Individual leaders have loomed particularly large in Pacific politics; Pouvanaa in Tahiti in the 1950s and Jean-Marie Tjibaou in New Caledonia in the 1980s were rallying-points for their supporters and targets for their opponents. They dominated their respective parties, and both of their movements had difficulty maintaining their unity and momentum after Pouvanaa and Tjibaou were removed from political life. In a more general sense, allegiance to particular parties has depended at least partly on 'non-political' factors; in New Caledonia, for instance, the major party in the pro-independence coalition, the UC, has been dominated by those from a Catholic background, while Protestant Melanesians have formed the majority in several other parties. There has also been a generational split in some groups between founding fathers and younger, sometimes more radical followers. Monopolies in the print and electronic media have constrained political debate – New Caledonia has only one daily newspaper, which has always espoused a strongly anti-independence viewpoint, and the two newspapers in Tahiti are owned by the same company and express the same opinions. Until the 1980s there were only official, government-controlled radio and television stations in the territories. Much of the content of radio and television programmes, in any case, is directly imported from France, and locally produced programmes seldom venture onto the delicate terrain of politics.

The French state has retained, and regularly used, its powers to limit political action. Pouvanaa and the leader of the UC in the 1950s, Maurice Lenormand, were both arrested on what were probably spurious or trumped-up charges and removed from their legislative seats; Pouvanaa was deported to France for a decade. French administrators until the 1960s had the right to dismiss public servants who engaged too openly in politics and even to banish them from the territories. Charges of the government denying access to the media to politicians whose views it did not accept, harassing dissidents and limiting their campaigning were often sounded, and there were, as well, outright accusations of election-fixing and voting fraud engineered by officials. It was claimed that particular individuals or parties often bought votes or coerced residents into supporting them.[8] Such charges are difficult to prove, but also to disprove.

Because of these idiosyncracies, political life in the Pacific TOMs since the 1950s has not always obeyed the 'rules' that have obtained in some other places, and contestatory movements have at times (and avowedly) adopted the strategies of national liberation fronts. Disruption of political campaigns, occupation of assembly buildings, and the taking of hostages have been rationalised as legitimate reactions to a colonial system. From the other side of the barricades, French officials have often justified heavy-handed tactics as a necessary action against 'terrorists' and 'subversives' or simply as legitimate moves against those who wish to foment political turmoil. The arguments and justifications perhaps say as much about political developments as do the actual actions taken. While the French Pacific territories have not experienced civil war, guerrilla struggles or the sort of political violence which took place in

Indochina in the decade after 1945 or in Algeria in the 1950s, their political life has still been marked by a struggle between the central administration and local governments, between 'loyalists' and '*indépendantistes*' and between different ethnic groups and political factions, clashes that have not been dissimilar to colonial struggles at other times and in different places.

THE POST-WAR POLITICAL AWAKENING

The years immediately after the war saw the emergence of new forces and the voicing of new political demands in the French islands; indeed, political activism had begun during the war years. For instance, the first political actions of the Polynesian who dominated politics in Tahiti during the 1950s and 1960s, Pouvanaa a Oopa, took place in 1942. Pouvanaa, a Polynesian artisan who had not previously taken part in politics, rode his bicycle around Papeete collecting signatures on a petition. The demands it listed were hardly revolutionary and showed a mixture of everyday concerns, political goals and moral considerations: prohibition on sales of alcohol, the setting up of a *conseil général*, more equitable rationing of petrol and cloth, expulsion from the administration of supporters of the Vichy regime and 'false Gaullists'. For his efforts, Pouvanaa was arrested and incarcerated on several occasions during the war. In 1945, Pouvanaa was a candidate at legislative elections, but he received only a handful of votes. The following year he set up the 'Comité Pouvanaa' which metamorphosed into the leading political party in the territory.[9] In New Caledonia, a 'group of volunteers' wrote to the Minister of Overseas France in 1946 outlining various grievances, including the forced labour that Melanesians were required to provide, the lower wages paid to Melanesians by comparison with Europeans ('We would like to be paid according to our work not according to the colour of our skin'), the salaries given to tribal chiefs ('a form of slave trade') and the appointment of chiefs rather than their election by islanders and the lack of education and medical care.[10] The same year the minister received a copy of a 'Cahier des revendications indigènes au grand Parti Communiste Français' which demanded the 'abolition of slavery – the abolition of the [*code de l'*] *indigénat*'. Citizenship rights must be extended to all indigenes, and freedom of speech, publication and assembly must be guaranteed; Melanesians should be represented on the *conseil général*, and forced labour and the *capitation* (head-tax) must be abolished.[11] The connection with the Communist Party came from the presence in New Caledonia of two Communist activists, Florian Paladino and Jeanne Tunica y Casas, who promoted the party among both Melanesians and Vietnamese contract labourers.[12] A more moderate, and longer-lasting, political effort was the formation of two committees sponsored by the Protestant and Catholic churches; they aimed to group together Melanesians and keep them from temptation by the Communist ideology circulating in the territory. The Catholic Union des Indigènes Calédoniens Amis de la Liberté dans l'Ordre (UICALO), established in 1946, began its manifesto with a condemnation of Communist propaganda and went on to demand the end of forced labour, prohibition of alcohol sales in tribes, guarantees of the inviolability of the *réserves*, more equitable taxation and the establishment of a special legal statute for islanders.[13] The Protestants established a parallel organisation, the Association des Indigènes Calédoniens et Loyaltiens Français (AICLF), which had similar goals. These organisations were the breeding-ground for a generation of political leaders.

It was significant that these political actions in both French Polynesia and in New Caledonia were mounted by the islander populations or those who identified themselves with Melanesians and Polynesians. The organisations set up in the mid-1940s marked the first time that islanders had become directly involved in politics since the insurrections of the nineteenth century (and the revolt of 1917 in New Caledonia). The effects of the Second World War and a century of French rule had combined to stir up islander feeling and now it found a parliamentary channel for expression. Religion also played an important role; both New Caledonian associations of Melanesians were established by clergymen and recruited members among students and ex-students at parochial schools, while in French Polynesia, Pouvanaa and his supporters were staunch Protestants. Yet another crucial aspect to these political movements was that they did not seek autonomy for their territories, let alone independence. One of the letters sent to the French Minister of Overseas Affairs in 1946 affirmed: 'We want to remain under the banner of the French Republic, and we reject autonomy for our country'. The manifesto of the UICALO used the same metaphor of the French Tricolour being a guarantor of liberty and equality and concluded with a statement of assimilation that had a decidedly colonialist ring: 'We want greater liberty in order to have greater justice in the respect of our rights without prejudice to our duties. Thereby we are certain of evolving more rapidly towards true civilisation and of making a greater contribution to the happiness of all [New] Caledonians, all Frenchmen and all humans. *Vive la Calédonie! Vive la France!'* In French Polynesia, the Comité Pouvanaa, responding to a request for clarification of its aims from the French administration, explained that it was 'in favour of a complete and freely conceded adhesion to the French Union'.[14] Such sentiments comforted the French authorities, who at this time saw some of the new organisations as bastions against communism and anti-colonialism. The sorts of requests made in the various petitions, at least those drawn up by the reformist groups in New Caledonia – Pouvanaa's movement in French Polynesia was viewed with greater suspicion – were not incompatible with the institutional provisions of the Fourth Republic.

Events in Tahiti in the late 1940s showed that political activism could take a form different from the simple presentation of petitions or the establishment of indigenous organisations under the aegis of churches. In 1947 the ship *Ville d'Amiens* arrived in Papeete bearing several newly-appointed officials; a large group of residents massed around the quay, held demonstrations and kept the officials from disembarking on the grounds that their posts could have been filled by local candidates rather than by *métropolitains*; they saw the arrival of the Frenchmen as evidence of continuing French colonialism. The incident shocked French authorities because of the widespread support the protests attracted; the acquittal of several men arrested in the affair, including Pouvanaa, seemed an affront to the administration. The governor sent a telegram to Paris saying that the acquittal might 'give courage to the agitators in their efforts and they will not miss an opportunity to create new incidents'. The head of military forces in the territory worried that it would henceforth be impossible to count on the loyalty of even the Tahitian police in the case of troubles. The chief of the naval staff in Tahiti added that the 'autonomist and racist movement directed by . . . Pouvanaa, with the more or less avowed support of several Europeans' had been at the base of the troubles. Pouvanaa and his associates had lent their support to the demonstrations, which were led by his deputy, Jean-Baptiste Céran-Jérusalémy. Some officials thought the *Ville d'Amiens* incident was indicative of greater dangers facing France in the islands: the director of political affairs at the Ministère de la France d'Outre-Mer commented in 1948: 'For over a year, our Etablissements Français d'Océanie have been prey to a political malaise which is so grave that we must not hide the fact that the very sovereignty of France has been endangered by demonstrations like those of June 1947'. The Minister of Overseas France sent a note to the prime minister charging that the Pouvanaa movement 'in reality, if not according to the official affirmations of its promoters, is trying to eliminate Frenchmen from Tahiti and to detach Tahiti from France'. Another official thought that the demonstrations, combined with the upheavals in Wallis and Futuna the previous year, would not augur well for the French in the Pacific.[15]

After the 1947 demonstrations, Paris sent Inspector-General Lassalle-Séré to Polynesia to investigate the political situation of the territory.[16] He reported that Tahiti had always been characterised by sudden episodes of political agitation due to individuals or local concerns. Furthermore, the war years had been difficult in the colony: a *ralliement* which was not easily achieved, economic hardships and the presence of the American troops. Trade unions had been organised and 'public opinion began to be agitated, influenced by the upheavals of the postwar and by independence movements which eventuated here and there' – presumably a reference to French Indochina and Algeria. Elections in Tahiti had provided a favourable climate for the expression of dissent. The report also pointed to the 'deficiency or incoherence of repression' which had followed the incidents, the inefficiency of the local administration, a lack of information and government propaganda activity and poor relations between the administration and the assembly in Papeete. Lassalle-Séré's report contained specific critiques of Governor Maestracci for his lenient attitude towards Pouvanaa and Céran-Jérusalémy;[17] some local Europeans were accused of casting their lot with the rebels. However, Lassalle-Séré did not think that problems in Tahiti were strictly 'political' in nature.

One other area of difficulty was commerce; in requiring Tahiti to sell its primary export, copra, to France since the war, although France was not willing to advance hard currency or to buy other products in return, 'the *métropole* had reconstituted the *pacte colonial*, even in aggravated form'. A second problem was the bureaucracy, criticism of which Lassalle-Séré said was unanimous among the demonstrators, who castigated the 'mediocrity' of certain administrators, the low level of local recruitment of personnel, the complexity of administrative procedures and the defective organisation of the French services. Next, there was the issue of information and the need for France to win the hearts of the Polynesians; in a perceptive historical analysis, Lassalle-Séré noted: 'This population, foreign to our civilisation, only a century ago had its own chiefs and its king, its sorcerers and customs. It has kept its language and is now showing a tendency to rediscover a past which often seems a mirror of imaginary felicity. If we do not want it to fall under the influences which are acting against French influence, in favour of an autonomy which would then have every chance of becoming total, we must orient public opinion, act on minds, penetrate them in the way that a drop of water ends up by piercing a rock, by the indefatigable daily action of an office of information and propaganda using all the techniques of the press, radio, films and books. In short, we must make this country, so far from France, live a French life'.[18] But Lassalle-Séré also had his finger on the pulse of daily life in Papeete and was aware of the sociological aspect of politics: 'The mass, indifferent but sensitive to every influence, follows leaders or orders which come from the city. In the city, the least rumours are spread, carried about, and are the object of often passionate discussion, serving as arguments to some and carefully taken note of by others whom they can serve during a rebellion. And it is these facts, these discussions, which help to create a political atmosphere'.[19]

The implication in Lassalle-Séré's report, the most thorough single analysis of political life in the Pacific territories by French authorities in the late 1940s, was the need for vigilance against rebellion, the spreading of autonomist sentiments and the sorts of economic and social grievances which could fuel disenchantment with French rule. Movements such as those of Pouvanaa, and the demonstrations promoted by Céran-Jérusalémy, could be the thin end of the wedge which eventually could cause chaos in the French islands. Underlying the report was the idea that France must incorporate local figures – Europeans and indigenes from the élite – into decision-making but must be ever ready to do battle with rebels. The possibility of self-government or autonomy was not even discussed, and the Polynesian masses were still considered a malleable force incapable of a political activity much more sophisticated than obeying the calls of agitators and trouble-makers.

The political developments of the 1940s in New Caledonia and, particularly, in Tahiti, showed new ideological currents entering the isolated world of Oceania, including calls for liberal and parliamentary reform, 'autonomism', a kind of ethnic nationalism, even the 'spectre of communism', all in the context of changes taking place elsewhere in the French empire. In few of the documents of the period is independence yet mentioned by either officials or dissidents. By the end of the 1940s the first phase of post-war politics, experiments with different strategies of protest but the maintenance of 'colonial' ideas among all groups, had come to an end. The 1950s then saw the maturing of these grievances, personalities and committees into different forms. After only a decade independence would be a real issue in French Polynesia.

POUVANAA AND POLITICS IN FRENCH POLYNESIA

Much of political life in French Polynesia in the 1950s revolved around Pouvanaa a Oopa and the movement he created. Born in 1895 in Huahiné to a family of traditional farmers and fishermen, Pouvanaa arrived in Papeete as a youth. He enlisted in the army during the First World War and served in battle in Europe, for which he was decorated. On his return to Tahiti, Pouvanaa worked as a carpenter. He did not become involved in political activities until the 1940s, with the *ralliement* to General de Gaulle. In 1947 the setting up of the Comité Pouvanaa grouped his friends and supporters into a quasi-political party. Pouvanaa failed to win a legislative election immediately after the war, but he secured a seat in the representative assembly in 1949. Two years later, Pouvanaa became French Polynesia's *député* in the French parliament, a post he retained for the next decade. Meanwhile, the Comité Pouvanaa merged with a union of returned servicemen to form the Rassemblement Démocratique des Peuples Tahitiens (RDPT), which fielded candidates in territorial elections as well as in the election for a *député* from Tahiti to the National Assembly.[20]

Pouvanaa was a charismatic figure who drew his support from the Polynesian masses rather than from the *demis* , Europeans or Tahiti's Chinese. Although of mixed Polynesian and Danish ancestry, Pouvanaa portrayed himself as the voice of the *ta'ata Tahiti* who had been exploited by both settlers and the colonial government. He stirred crowds with his considerable oratorical skills, always speaking Tahitian and punctuating his speeches with Biblical quotations and religious allusions. According to his biographer, Pouvanaa was a 'figurehead, something like the "prophet" of Semitic societies, a catalyser and often even an inventor'; Pouvanaa compared himself to David fighting the Goliath of the colonial administration: 'I am a humble man like David who takes Jesus Christ as his only guide and saviour'.[21] His themes were simple: Polynesian nationalism, an attack on money and profiteers and commitment to the Protestant religion. As his 1949 political programme stated: 'Our islands have remained in the claws of a handful of profiteers, the masters of colonisation, such as the Compagnie Française des Phosphates [de l'Océanie] and the group of exporters which are draining away all wealth to the detriment of the population and, in particular, of the producers. These colonial masters have never ceased to benefit from the support and the protection of the colonial rulers in France and an omnipotent administration which continues to direct the affairs of the territory. The most basic liberties are denied. . . . Racial and social inequalities remain. . . . Ignorance remains common among our population. Hygienic and social conditions are in a primitive state because no one wants to find money where it could be available. Our "kids" lack milk, yet the shops are running over with alcohol to the great profit of business.' Pouvanaa demanded reduction of the 'scandalous super-profits' of businessmen, trimming of the bureaucracy, encouragement of agricultural production (especially of consumer crops), protection of Tahitian land against spoliation, the institution of a progressive income tax, the improvement of maritime and air connections, and the teaching of Tahitian in schools.

Pouvanaa's platforms, in 1949 and afterwards, always contained a list of grievances and suggestions for substantial political and economic changes. He was also an active member of trade unions and helped set up agricultural co-operatives. But Pouvanaa's real force came from his populism rather than from particular aspects of a political programme; he aimed to strike an emotional chord among Polynesians and to attack the government and the élite of French Polynesia. Underlying Pouvanaa's message was his deeply held Christian faith, which he claimed inspired him to combat injustices and fight for the improvement of the life of his fellow countrymen. He was revered by his supporters as a national leader, known by both defenders and critics as the *Metua*, or leader. He promoted 'Polynesianity' against the centralising and assimilating tendencies of the French state and French culture; for instance, the RDPT used as its emblem the red-white-red tricolour which had been the flag of the Pomarés before France took control of Tahiti. He defended the 'little man' against the economic and political power-brokers and islanders against foreigners – Pouvanaa was particularly suspicious of the Chinese who dominated much of the territory's commercial acitivites. The underprivileged and the ethnic Polynesian, to him, were one and the same.

The basic tactic of Pouvanaa and the RDPT in the 1950s was to organise supporters into over one hundred sections of his party. The RDPT counted between eight and ten thousand registered members, a larger number than in any other party in French Polynesia. Discussions in the party sections concentrated on daily problems faced by the local population, such as food, jobs, education and health, rather than politics. Elders dominated such debates, and women were largely absent from the movement. Most members lived in villages or the outer islands of the territory. They came largely from modest backgrounds, and the RDPT was hesitant to allow wealthier people, public servants or teachers into their midst, regarding them as paid employees or perhaps agents of the French administration. Pouvanaa's chief lieutenant, Céran-Jérusalémy, was a trade union organiser, although most of the party faithful were engaged in agriculture or fishing. Protestant deacons figured prominently among party officials. Many of the individuals who dominated Polynesian politics even after Pouvanaa's removal were initiated into public life through the RDPT at this time.[22]

Pouvanaa and his colleagues took part in the debates of the Territorial Assembly on a regular basis, sometimes using provocative tactics. For instance, in 1957, Pouvanaa insisted on making his opening speech as dean of the Territorial Assembly in Tahitian rather than French; the governor interrupted him when he did so. A lively debate ensued about the proper language to be used for assembly debates, which revealed many of the issues of contention between the RDPT and the administration.[23] Pouvanaa was by no means adverse to public confrontation, either in the assembly chamber or in the streets. His skill lay in mobilising sentiments and electors rather than in working out technocratic reforms or patiently wading through parliamentary minutiae. (In fact, during his ten years as Tahiti's representative in Paris, Pouvanaa never took the floor in the Chambre des Députés.)

Pouvanaa and his movement provoked a strong reaction from French officials. A 1951 report from the governor to the Minister for Overseas France acknowledged that Pouvanaa was a 'brilliant orator in the Tahitian language' but otherwise had little good to say about him and his party. The governor felt that it was 'advised and supported by communist representatives' and that 'the most active members of the RDPT are extremists'.[24] The governor told Paris that 'despite his mediocrity, Pouvanaa is now unbeatable because of the speed [his movement] has acquired, the support provided by his numerous committees and, even more, by the lack of cohesion of the opposition'.[25] The public meetings and other activities taking place in Tahiti were 'premeditated demonstrations which issue from the intrigues which the RDPT has been pursuing . . . under the cover of Christian syndicalism'.[26] Another official stated that the RDPT was 'a party of indigenes inspired by suspect ideas and directed by men of very limited intelligence'.[27] The authorities' estimation of Pouvanaa's associates was less than complimentary; in a private letter, the governor said that Céran-Jérusalémy was 'a young man of twenty-six years, already the father of five children whom he has abandoned, and the very epitome of the ambitious type, devoured by envy and an inferiority complex. Under his mask he shows all the ugliness of his soul'.[28]

Faced with the growing strength of the Pouvanaa movement, government officials discussed various ways to limit his influence. French agents infiltrated the RDPT and reported on its activities; Pouvanaa was kept under surveillance when he visited France.[29] Efforts were made to woo away some of his supporters; in 1954, for instance, the governor dined with Céran-Jérusalémy and reported to Paris that the union organiser 'is divided between his desire to appear moderate . . . and his fear of the voters. I believe that there is a chance to *embourgeoiser* him'.[30] If other parties could not select a convincing opponent to Pouvanaa, then there existed 'a possibility, indeed a necessity, of multiple candidacies, each of which addresses itself to a different social milieu and different friendship networks' to try to cut into Pouvanaa's vote totals.[31] In general, the governor must make local politicians aware that their powers were strictly limited and that they must not act outside the narrowly enumerated list of prerogatives contained in their brief.[32] By the late 1950s, the government had gone further in its campaign and was denying Pouvanaa access to the radio and official transport throughout the territory.[33]

The ultimate goal of Pouvanaa's movement was never entirely clear. In the 1940s, his committee had affirmed to the governor that they desired a peaceful evolution of the territory in the framework of the French Union; there was no talk of independence, although calls for administrative autonomy were regularly sounded. In 1953, Pouvanaa seemed to favour closer integration of French Polynesia to the *métropole* through *départementalisation* . In that year, Pouvanaa stated that 'if we do not become a *département* , we will no longer be French. It is by becoming a *département* that we can get rid of the governors, administrators and companies which eat up your, the people's, money, you who are burdened with taxes to pay those who, instead of respecting the laws of the republic, act like monarchs'.[34] This position was similar to the argument of various other politicians in the French overseas territories, who felt that only *départementalisation* could end the arbitrary powers of 'colonial' officials, such as the governor, and allow local citizens more control over their own affairs. Yet Pouvanaa was already suspected of being in favour of independence,[35] even if over a decade later he stated privately that he still preferred *départementalisation*.[36] In 1956, the *loi-cadre* Defferre gave greater autonomy to French territories, and Pouvanaa, now at the height of his power, benefited from the move and welcomed it.

Two years later, however, citizens of overseas France were called upon to make a radical choice about their future. On his return to power in 1958, during the Algerian war, de Gaulle organised a ballot in the French territories on the new constitution of the Fifth Republic, foreshadowing a choice between future independence or continued affiliation with France. Conflict between Pouvanaa and the French authorities, and between the different political forces in French Polynesia, thus came to a head in 1958, both because of the vote and because of Pouvanaa's proposal for an income tax. A graduated tax on income in Tahiti, where no such impost existed, had always been dear to the heart of Pouvanaa and other reformers, but such a tax was hotly opposed by the local élite. Pouvanaa's proposal in 1958 for an income tax provided an occasion for opponents to vilify him, although Pouvanaa with a certain wiliness managed to put much of the onus for the unpopular proposal onto his deputy and now rival Céran-Jérusalémy. The incident showed that the RDPT was not entirely united, but also indicated that Pouvanaa indeed had a social programme, albeit a somewhat vague one, in addition to his political goals, whatever they might be. In short, he looked even more dangerous than his critics had previously feared. The ballot on the future of the territory seemed crucial. Pouvanaa, almost alone among major political figures in the French overseas territories, campaigned for a rejection of the new constitution.[37] Paris made it clear that France would wish luck to any territory opting for independence, but that any territory which chose that path could hope for neither material nor moral aid from France. Faced with such an ultimatum, and a particularly vitriolic campaign in Tahiti,[38] the French Polynesian electorate rejected Pouvanaa's position. The election also marked the final break between Pouvanaa and Céran-Jérusalémy, who had favoured the new constitution and the statute of a TOM for French Polynesia.

The referendum took place on 28 September 1958; a few days later, the Conseil du Gouvernement, the executive of the Territorial Assembly headed by Pouvanaa, was suspended and the privileges Pouvanaa had enjoyed in this capacity, such as an official automobile, were withdrawn. On 10 October, various political meetings were held in Papeete; Pouvanaa spoke to one group allegedly saying that 'the city of Jerusalem will be destroyed and I will rebuild it in three days'. That evening a large fire, thought to be a case of arson, broke out in Papeete. The next day police arrested Pouvanaa and searched his house, where they found an assortment of five guns, munitions, some knives and twenty Molotov cocktails. On 19 October 1959, after a year of investigation, the trial of Pouvanaa and fourteen of his associates opened in Papeete; they were accused of arson, attempted theft, illegal possession of arms and attempted murder. The testimony at the trial was contradictory, with some saying that Pouvanaa had instructed his followers to burn Papeete and others rejecting this claim. When Pouvanaa himself was asked whether he had done so, he replied enigmatically: 'I said something like that, but I was referring to the Bible which says . . . "The fire to which I am referring is the evil fire which continues to burn in the heart of the government"'. After only three days of hearings, Pouvanaa was convicted and condemned to eight years of imprisonment; he was also forbidden to reside in French Polynesia for fifteen years. A higher court rejected an appeal, and in March 1960 Pouvanaa was sent to France to serve his sentence; he returned to Tahiti only in 1969, after a presidential pardon.[39]

Despite the conviction of Pouvanaa, doubts lingered about his responsibility for the fires and other crimes of which he was accused. Public officials certainly found the Polynesian leader and his movement dangerous and the government had sought to oppose the RDPT since its inception. Pouvanaa's stand on the 1958 referendum was one of the most radical in the whole of overseas France and came at the moment when de Gaulle was attempting to recast the relationship between the *métropole* and France's possessions, establish the Fifth Republic and solve the Algerian problem, which had divided France almost to the point of civil war. Pouvanaa was a thorn in the side of France, and his movement spelled upheaval in a small and distant territory; Paris needed to devote its attention to more urgent matters in Europe and Africa. That the government used the 1958 incident to hush Pouvanaa is not surprising, although the opposition to his party since the early 1950s and the strength of reaction to it in 1958 indicated the general French attitude towards indigenous politics, contestatory movements and the ideology of autonomy.

The *dénouement* of the Pouvanaa affair came in 1963, when the French government dissolved the RDPT on the basis of a 1936 law which allowed such action against political parties or other associations which 'aim to commit an offence against the integrity of the national territory or to attack by force the republican form of government'.[40] By 1962, Paris had decided to establish a nuclear testing facility in French Polynesia, an action loudly opposed by some members of the RDPT. Furthermore, eight of the twenty-one members of the executive committee of the party now openly favoured independence for French Polynesia, and ten more supported some change in the territory's statute. In fact, a congress of the RDPT was already planned to discuss the question of independence when the dissolution orders were issued. The connection between France's need for a testing centre, opposition to further erosion in the overseas territories – by this time, Algeria and France's colonies in black Africa had all become independent – and the dissolution of the RDPT could hardly have been coincidental.

Pouvanaa's return to Papeete in 1969 was a postscript to the events of earlier years. A campaign in favour of his rehabilitation had been active since 1959, and Pouvanaa was finally pardoned; however, his conviction was never reviewed nor overturned. Pouvanaa came back to Tahiti as an elder statesman and hero, but by the late 1960s his movement had fragmented, and Pouvanaa was physically and intellectually incapable of putting it together again. Nevertheless, he was soon elected to a seat in the French Senate and continued to play a role in local politics. Pouvanaa more clearly than ever before proclaimed his support for independence. He explained his position:

For me, internal autonomy is now outmoded. Henceforth I will struggle for independence. It is not with a light heart that I have come to this conclusion . . . . Ten years ago, I was the man that the holders of power most detested for having spoken the word autonomy. Ten years later I am beginning again with independence . . . . But see, internal autonomy has become something that is respectable, and it will be the same with independence . . . . I am convinced that one day, very soon even, [French] Polynesia will be independent

.... The system under which we live is a legacy of colonialism and I am persuaded that more than ever we can assure a better future for our children under another system. Independence will doubtless be hard during the first years, but once that stage is passed we will leave something enduring and sure.

Pouvanaa further said that French Polynesia would be able to draw on its maritime resources and on the interest in investment expressed by overseas companies in order to develop a strong economy. Independence would lead to better social conditions. After all, he added, the 'French government took on the responsibility for this territory and what has it done? There exist a class of proprietors and a great majority of people who have nothing'. Walking through the car parks and seeing the large automobiles of the wealthy gave an indication of the social conditions of the territory, Pouvanaa said. Certainly the élite might have something to fear from eventual independence, but the others 'have no fear of independence. They have nothing to lose and everything to gain. For them, independence will hold the hope for a more equitable and just division of wealth'. Independence must be achieved through a peaceful referendum, however; Pouvanaa concluded on a conciliatory note: 'It is not a crime to desire independence but an ideal. I want to say to you again that independence does not signify a complete rupture with France'.[41] Somewhat ironically, it was in the year of Pouvanaa's death, in 1977, that Paris accorded a new statute to French Polynesia which gave a larger measure of autonomy to the territory as well as official recognition to the Tahitian language: goals towards which Pouvanaa had aimed since the 1940s.

The career of Pouvanaa embodied many of the themes in the political evolution of the French Pacific territories from the 1940s to the 1970s. Proposals for redress of various specific grievances, particularly those of the islander population, matured into demands for administrative autonomy. The French government alternately conceded to some such demands, as in the constitution of 1946 and the *loi-cadre* of 1956, then opposed movements of contestation and, as in 1958, limited or rescinded the autonomy previously given. Meanwhile, the demands of those opposed to French authority changed from calls for autonomy to calls for independence. Pouvanaa himself was very much a figure of the 1950s with a rhetoric based on Christian ideals and a moral rather than a technocratic approach to politics. His personal efforts largely held his movement together, and the faction-fighting and personal rivalries which had been latent during the 1950s came into the open in the 1960s. Yet, in any case, the French state possessed the means to control such opposition, as shown in the trial of Pouvanaa in 1959 and the dissolution of the RDPT in 1963. It should be added, however, that although Pouvanaa's party garnered the majority of votes in French Polynesia, it by no means enjoyed unanimous support among the population, and the French state could always rely on a substantial number of Polynesians who disagreed with Pouvanaa and who supported rival parties. This collaboration between the state and certain groups in the territory, in opposition to the ideology and the personal power of Pouvanaa, was also a cause of the lack of greater success of his movement in attaining its ultimate goals. But gradually some of those very aims were incorporated into the projects of his opponents; the erection in the 1980s of a monument to Pouvanaa outside the Territorial Assembly in Papeete, now dominated by politicians who were both his rivals and who are yet heirs of his ideas, symbolised his importance in the political history of French Polynesia.

THE UNION CALÉDONIENNE AND POLITICS IN NEW CALEDONIA

At the same time as the Pouvanaa movement emerged in French Polynesia, a new political force came into being in New Caledonia. In New Caledonia, however, a different political situation prevailed largely because Melanesians were denied universal suffrage until the late 1950s and because the territory had a large settler population eager to safeguard its advantages and perhaps even more suspicious of islander demands than were the French in French Polynesia. Melanesians still lived in rural areas or in tribal *réserves*, and few were Europeanised; there was no class of politically active *métis* comparable to the *demis* of French Polynesia. Among islanders, Melanesian customs and traditions remained strong, and the indigenous population kept alive the memory of the unsuccessful revolts of 1878 and 1917. Yet, in a constitutional situation similar to that of French Polynesia, the structures of government were those dictated by Paris, and the degree of autonomy varied during the 1950s and 1960s. Furthermore, in both territories, the role of religion in politics was strong, and most of the Melanesian political leaders emerged from a religious background; the Protestant and Catholic schools and seminaries were the incubators of the islander political élite. The dislocations of the Second World War had led to the formation of new political associations, and new ideologies circulated through the country; these developments helped politicise Melanesians.

The major legislative development which altered politics in New Caledonia was a 1951 law which increased the number of Melanesian voters from 1144 to 8700. The law, adopted by the French parliament, was designed for the African colonies, where there were few European residents, rather than for a 'settler colony' such as New Caledonia, but the statute was also applicable in the Pacific. The number of Melanesian voters after the enactment of the law was not far removed from the number of European voters, who totalled 10 888. This partial enfranchisement of the islander population created the possibility for a new political movement to recruit supporters, and the new electorate would not necessarily be favourable to the settler interests embodied in the existing parties. The change in the franchise showed how clearly the extent of the suffrage and demographic conditions could pre-determine election results in New Caledonia.[42]

Dissident political interest crystallised in the early 1950s in the Union Calédonienne (UC). Among those active in its foundation were the pastor who had organised the AICLF, the head of the territory's agricultural service and an ethnologist. Several Melanesians took part, notably Roch Pidjot, traditional chief of the La Conception tribe and leader of the Catholic UICALO. The French administration, which saw in the movement a useful counterweight to the possible spread of more radical ideas, supported its creation.[43] Maurice Lenormand served as head of the movement.[44] A *métropolitain*, Lenormand migrated to New Caledonia to work as a pharmacist, but he also had business interests in coffee plantations and nickel mines in New Caledonia and investments in the New Hebrides.

Lenormand married a Melanesian woman from the island of Lifou. The natural constituency for the UC lay in the newly enfranchised Melanesians, the *petits blancs* and others of modest means who felt at odds with the mining and commercial magnates who dominated other political parties in the territory. It promoted co-operation between the ethnic groups in New Caledonia under the slogan of 'Two colours, but one people'. The programme of the party targeted their concerns, and its first platforms highlighted economic and social issues. The party called for the promotion of Melanesian interests and the end of racial discrimination, the breaking-up of large estates and the monopolies exercised by such companies as the Banque de l'Indochine, provisions for family allowances, holiday pay, minimum wages and sickness benefits, the opening of vocational training centres and a labour office, the construction of public housing complexes, increased access to public schools for Melanesians, the creation of new municipalities and improvement in the economic infrastructure of the territory.[45] The party, in the early 1950s, did not demand autonomy, let alone independence, for New Caledonia; Lenormand stated forthrightly: 'New Caledonia and its dependencies are and will remain French by the irrevocable and permanent wish of its inhabitants'.[46]

In 1951, Lenormand won election as *député* for New Caledonia in the French parliament, a position he held until the beginning of 1964. By the middle of the 1950s, the UC held New Caledonia's seats in both houses of the French legislature and, as well, formed a majority in the New Caledonian territorial assembly. Under the *loi-cadre* of 1956, local assemblymen were given increased power; an islander became the vice-president of the assembly – the governor was the titular president – and other islanders held local ministerial portfolios. This represented the first time in the South Pacific colonies of any country that Melanesians had become ministers.[47] At this time the French territories of Oceania enjoyed a greater degree of 'self-government' than any other 'colonies' in the region (despite French centralisation), and islanders in the French TOMs were playing a larger political role than anywhere else in Oceania.

Arrayed against Lenormand and the UC were various conservative groups, whose names and coalitions shifted during the years. The dominant figures were a wealthy *petit mineur*, Henri

Lafleur, who later became a French senator, and Roger Laroque, associated with the trading company Ballande, who for thirty years served as mayor of Nouméa. Most were Europeans from the capital city of New Caledonia, but their political philosophies differed, and real unity was difficult to achieve in the 1950s in the face of the UC's strong position. In 1958, the return to power of de Gaulle bolstered the fortunes of his supporters in New Caledonia, most of whom opposed the UC. The constitution of the Fifth Republic diminished the power of the UC-dominated territorial assembly. Lenormand, unlike his counterpart in French Polynesia, Pouvanaa, campaigned in favour of a 'yes' vote to approve the new constitution, and that result was easily achieved. The administration nevertheless remained suspicious of Lenormand and his supporters, and in 1958 the governor dissolved the territorial assembly. The next few years saw greater problems for the UC, as some of its earlier supporters moved away from Lenormand, whom they regarded as increasingly autocratic. Yet even with lessened support, he was regularly re-elected *député* .

Matters came to a head in 1962, when Lenormand was again successful in his campaign for re-election. In that year, the Société le Nickel asked the French government for a major tax exemption, a proposal which the UC, which still held a majority in the territorial assembly, did not favour. A bomb exploded in the assembly's building, followed by another explosion in the headquarters of the UC, whereupon the governor banned political meetings and arrested three suspects. All were members of the UC, including Lenormand. Two of them confessed to having planted the bomb at the UC headquarters with, they said, the consent of Lenormand, in an effort to frame the Gaullist politicians in the territory, presumably by making them look responsible for the act. The accused were convicted; Lenormand was given a one-year suspended gaol sentence and deprived of his civil rights for five years; early in 1964, the French government removed him from his post as *député* because of the conviction. Roch Pidjot, a fellow member of the UC, succeeded Lenormand (and held the seat until 1986).

The events in New Caledonia seemed to telescope into a shorter period of time what had happened in French Polynesia in 1958 and 1963, although the UC, unlike the RDPT, was not dissolved. The parallels were obvious to contemporaries and

later observers. Lenormand, like Pouvanaa, protested his inno-
cence, and critics argued that the charges laid against him, if at
all true, were trumped up to eliminate him from political life
because of his opinions and because of more urgent French
concerns in the South Pacific. These developments occurred
not only against the backdrop of the accession of Algeria to
independence and the transferral of the nuclear testing site to
French Polynesia, but also just at the beginning of a nickel
boom in New Caledonia from which France hoped to reap
large profits. The year 1962, perhaps coincidentally, was also
the date of independence of the first South Pacific island country, Western Samoa.

After his removal from office, Lenormand played a reduced
role in local politics. But the UC did not disband and actually
increased the number of seats it held in the territorial assembly
after 1962. However, the powers of the assembly remained
restricted; the Jacquinot law of 1962 and the Billotte law of 1967
further reduced the powers of the New Caledonian government council and in particular increased Paris's control over
the territorial budget. The UC continued to press for greater
attention to social and economic problems in New Caledonia,
and especially for the improvement in living standards and
greater possibilities of participation in public life for the
Melanesians. It did not yet favour independence: late in the
1960s, the UC called for 'a statute of self-government to
implement decolonisation in New Caledonia' rather than
secession or sovereignty.[48] Even such a relatively measured goal
did not win approval in Paris. In 1968, a combined delegation
of politicians from New Caledonia's UC and the parties in
French Polynesia which were the successors to the RDPT
travelled to Paris to discuss the future of the Pacific territories
with the Minister for Overseas France, who simply refused to
receive them. Pidjot then affirmed: 'The demand for autonomy
by the Polynesians and ourselves is due to our disgust with the
ill-will and stupidity of a colonial administration attached to a
mandarinate which dates from the age of sailing ships and
kerosene lamps. The Polynesians, like the Melanesians, feel
immensely frustrated . . . . Neither of us wants independence,
which is too often illusory . . . but a new contractual relationship
that will give us full internal autonomy'.[49]

Since the early 1950s the goals of the UC had changed little, although the political context of relations between the *métropole* and its overseas territories had altered greatly through decolonisation of most of France's possessions. Different ideological currents were now also in circulation; the year of the Pacific delegation's unsuccessful mission to France was also that of the student rebellion in Paris, protest against de Gaulle's government in particular and against the tenets of Western politics and economics in general. The ideas of the 'New Left' would soon be imported into France's territories in Oceania. Other changes were also occurring in New Caledonia. The nickel boom led to the immigration of numerous *métropolitains*, which disrupted the delicate population balance between islanders and non-Oceanic ethnic groups. Melanesians increasingly worked as wage labourers and were becoming more urbanised. Meanwhile, some supporters of the UC became disenchanted with its reformist leaders and gradualistic programme. The late 1960s and 1970s, therefore, marked a new period in the political history of New Caledonia, just as in French Polynesia.

POLITICAL FRAGMENTATION AND RADICALISATION

The UC was held together both by the multi-racial constituency which supported it and by the disarray of its opposition in New Caledonia, just as the Pouvanaa movement was kept together by the magnetism of its founder. After the forced withdrawal of Pouvanaa from local politics, their parties underwent substantial changes. At the same time, there emerged different, and competing, opposition movements, often inspired by more radical ideologies, which sometimes contained calls for outright independence for New Caledonia and French Polynesia. As a reaction, the conservative, anti-independence forces regrouped. Meanwhile, the French government maintained its position that the TOMs should enjoy only very limited self-government. Not until the late 1970s, during the presidency of the non-Gaullist Valéry Giscard d'Estaing, did policy become more flexible – during Giscard's presidency the French territories of Djibouti and the Comoros Islands, as well as the Franco-British condominium of the New Hebrides, gained independence. Also during his term of office, a new statute with provisions for greater autonomy for French Polynesia was enacted in 1977. However, in neither French Polynesia nor in New Caledonia was Giscard's reformist policy sufficient to undercut opposition to French rule or to prevent the emergence of groups demanding independence for France's remaining 'colonies'.

In French Polynesia, the cohesion and dynamism of the RDPT in the 1950s turned into fragmentation and compromise by the 1960s, and scission affected the conservative movement as well as the nationalist party. In 1962, the Union Démocratique Tahitienne which, in varying forms had served as a rallying-point for conservatives since 1956, split in two, although one branch soon disappeared; the surviving party, which renamed itself the Union Tahitienne in 1971 and the Tahoeraa Huiraatira in 1977, both led by Gaston Flosse, has survived as the main conservative group among a plethora of parties in Tahiti. The RDPT also split into two parties in 1962, the culmination of a long personal struggle between Pouvanaa and his associates against his younger adversary and erstwhile supporter Céran-Jérusalémy. Céran-Jérusalémy's party was dissolved by the government the following year, at the same time as the RDPT, but he reconstituted it on the platform of 'independence in association with France' for French Polynesia. Several ex-members of the RDPT created a new party in 1965; at the same time, yet another party, also formed of ex-RDPT supporters, came into being and pronounced itself in favour of the accession of French Polynesia to internal autonomy.[50]

Differences of opinion in opposition politics in Tahiti were less important than clashes of personality and the ambitions of two Polynesians who considered themselves the heirs of Pouvanaa. John French Teariki (1914–1983) was a Protestant land-owner and shipper, originally from Rimatara, who in 1953 was elected to the territorial assembly on the RDPT list. In 1961, he was elected *député* of French Polynesia, to fill the seat of Pouvanaa's son, Marcel a Oopa, who had been elected after his father's removal from office but who had died in an accident. Teariki's party, the Pupu Here Ai'a Te Nuna'a Ia Ora, throughout the 1960s campaigned on the basis of demands for a retrial of Pouvanaa, autonomy for the territory and opposition to French nuclear testing. Teariki himself became a particularly controversial figure when he personally confronted de Gaulle over French nuclear testing during a visit by the French president to Tahiti.[51] Teariki remained an ardent anti-Gaullist and supported the candidate of the left for the French presidency in 1965, François Mitterrand. The other dominant opposition politician was Francis Ariioehau Sanford, who was born in Papeete in 1912. From a more modest background than Teariki, although like him of mixed Polynesian and European ancestry, Sanford was by profession a primary-school teacher. He was among the first group to rally to de Gaulle and the Free French in 1940, when he was an administrator in the Gambier archipelago. During the war, he served as liaison officer between the French administration and the American troops on Bora-Bora, for which he was awarded the Medal of Freedom by the United States government. After the war, Sanford returned to teaching, but in 1963 he became chief of staff to the governor of French Polynesia, a post he held until his retirement five years later. Despite his appointment as a civil servant, Sanford became involved in political activities, first among Tahiti's Gaullists and then on his own. He won election as mayor of the Papeete suburb of Fa'a'a and, in 1965, founded a centrist party, the Te E'a Api no Polynesia. Sanford was critical of the French administration but, unlike Teariki, spoke little about the nuclear testing facility; in 1967, he defeated Teariki in a campaign for the French parliament, partly (although somewhat paradoxically) with the support of the French administration, which considered him a less undesirable representative than Teariki. Afterwards, however, Teariki and Sanford united their supporters in a Front Uni pour l'Autonomie Interne, allied in their calls for autonomy and opposition to French nuclear testing; in fact, Teariki became Sanford's parliamentary *suppléant*.[52] Teariki remained the more vocal opponent of nuclear testing, but even Sanford in 1975 signed a petition, together with Pouvanaa, then a senator, stating that 'if France pursues its nuclear experiments, we will ask, through the intermediary of the United Nations, that a referendum on independence be carried out in French Polynesia'. After the cessation of atmospheric testing, Sanford muted his criticism, and he withdrew from politics in 1977, pronouncing himself satisfied with the new autonomy statute adopted that year. Teariki then replaced Sanford as *député*.[53]

In addition to the conservative Union Tahitienne-Tahoeraa Huiraatira of Flosse and the rival parties, then coalition, of Teariki and Sanford, French Polynesia in the 1970s saw the emergence of numerous other parties – between 1976 and 1980 some ten new parties appeared (although some were but short-lived). Notable among these were parties with the declared aim of independence for French Polynesia. One of the smaller such parties, the Te Ta'ata Tahiti Tiama was founded in 1976 by Pouvanaa's nephew, Charlie Ching, who was subsequently arrested for acts of terrorism in Tahiti. A second pro-independence party was the Front de Libération de la Polynésie, set up in 1977 by Oscar Temaru. A customs official and longtime mayor of Fa'a'a, Temaru was an ardent opponent of nuclear testing, an advocate of closer links between indigenous peoples of the South Pacific, and a promoter of immediate and unconditional independence for French Polynesia. His rhetoric combined elements of Protestant Christianity, electoral populism and ecological awareness. The third, and most moderate, of the pro-independence parties was the Ia Mana Te Nuna'a, created in 1976 by Jacqui Drollet, a marine biologist and son of a prominent RDPT politician of the 1950s. Ia Mana promoted sovereignty for French Polynesia but argued that independence must be prepared through efforts at economic self-sufficiency, planning and the transition to democratic socialism.[54]

The pro-independence parties garnered only a small portion of the votes cast in French Polynesian elections (generally less than 15 per cent), so throughout the 1970s, and indeed afterwards, the anti-independence parties held power. However, most of those parties, including Flosse's Tahoeraa Huiraatira, had by now enthusiastically embraced pro-autonomy stands and campaigned in favour of increased local control over the administration, budgets and social and cultural issues; this reversed the position of conservative groups of earlier decades, which had often feared that autonomy might be a prelude to independence. Now most of the mainstream parties saw it more as a substitute for independence, guaranteeing the territory the level of French subsidies which underpinned a largely unproductive economy based on metropolitan transfers. With this ideological consensus, elections revolved around personal allegiances and faction-fighting between those who held office and those eager to displace them.

As French Polynesia moved towards a certain ideological consensus in the 1970s, New Caledonia displayed greater political fragmentation.[55] Over a dozen new political parties were established in the territory in the 1970s, some of which were only ephemeral formations or coalitions welded together for particular elections. Others were minuscule groups brought together in support of an individual or a cause. But, in general, the main feature of New Caledonian politics was the increasing importance of ethnicity as an issue in party loyalty. By the mid-1970s most of the Europeans (and other non-islanders) had abandoned the UC, which consequently became a predominantly Melanesian party. Some Melanesians also left the UC, which they considered insufficiently radical. In 1970, for instance, a Melanesian politician named Yann Céléné Urégei broke away from the UC to form the Union Multiraciale de Nouvelle-Calédonie (renamed, in a more militant fashion, the Front Uni de Libération Kanak or FULK in 1977); Urégei's party at first called for autonomy for New Caledonia but, in 1975, it became the first party officially to demand independence for the territory. In 1974, two Melanesians expelled from Urégei's movement formed the Union Progressiste Multiraciale (which, significantly, substituted 'Mélanésienne' for 'Multiraciale' in its name in 1977); it favoured independence but preferred a more gradual evolution of New Caledonian politics with greater attention to the advancement of Melanesians inside the existing society. Two years later, the Parti Socialiste Calédonien was formed with the aims of autonomy and socialism but without calling for independence for New Caledonia. Also joining the ranks of new political parties in the 1970s was the Mouvement Libéral Calédonien, formed in 1971 by yet another ex-UC member (and future mayor of Nouméa), which opposed independence but wanted decentralisation of administration. Another European settler, a former member of the UC as well, who charged that the UC had betrayed its old multi-ethnic goals, formed a moderate Union Nouvelle Calédonienne in 1977. In 1976 was formed the Parti de Libération Kanak, or Palika, a pro-independence party which espoused vigorously anti-colonial and revolutionary ideals. At least three other opposition parties formed, and the 'pro-French' parties underwent fraction and fusion before achieving a certain unity in a conservative and anti-independence Rassemblement pour la

Calédonie in 1977; it, too, underwent a name change to become the Rassemblement pour la Calédonie dans la République (RPCR).

The differences in ideology among the various parties were not the only reason for their disunity; many, after all, had emerged from the UC. The parties often had different clienteles. The UC continued to draw most of it support from Melanesians who lived on the Grande Terre and from Catholics. FULK drew much of its support, by contrast, from Protestant Melanesians in the Loyalty Islands, especially Maré, Urégei's home. Palika was also largely Protestant, but its *militants* were generally younger and more concerned with cultural and ideological issues than members of other parties. Several groups tried to rally Europeans who were disenchanted with both the UC and the conservative parties; their leaders were generally European, although the head of the Union Nouvelle-Calédonienne, Jean-Pierre Aïfa, was of Arab descent. Powerful personalities also served as magnets for their supporters and helped shape parties. The conservative, anti-independence movement, for example, continued to be dominated by the long-time mayor of Nouméa, Roger Laroque, Henri Lafleur and his son Jacques. Roch Pidjot served as the elder statesman of the UC, whose leadership fell to a younger generation of Melanesian politicians (including Tjibaou, Machoro and Burck, as well as the European Pierre Declerq – three of whom were assassinated in political violence in the 1980s).

The major developments in the political history of New Caledonia in the 1970s were a revaluation of Melanesian cultural identity and renewal of islander land claims combined with the first demands for independence from French rule. Already at the end of the 1960s, several small political groups had begun taking a more radical stand on the issue of independence, such as the Foulards Rouges led by the hereditary chieftain of the island of Maré, Nidoish Naisseline, who had himself been influenced by the new ideologies and strategies he witnessed while a university student in Paris in 1968.[56] In 1975, Yann Céléné Urégei, at that time head of the territorial assembly in New Caledonia, made the first major call for Melanesian (or Kanak) independence for New Caledonia. In a speech to the assembly, he argued: 'We demand Kanak independence as the logical end to the policy of colonial exploitation led by the

French government. We have rejected integration, and only Kanak independence will acknowledge the existence and cultural identity of the Kanak people. . . . We say NO to the French government, YES to Kanak independence, YES to Free New Caledonia'.[57] The same year a Comité de Coordination pour l'Indépendence Kanake was created and organised a petition demanding a referendum on independence; the signatories included the *député* (Pidjot), the president of the assembly (Urégei) and six other members of the assembly. Two years later, the UC marked a clarification of its position in a statement which said that 'autonomy is a stage which should in principle lead the inhabitants of New Caledonia to independence . . . which should allow the Kanaks . . . the first inhabitants [of the country] . . . to assume all of their rights'.[58] In elections to the territorial assembly later that year, thirteen autonomists and *indépendantistes* won seats compared to nineteen members who supported French control (and three others with less clearly defined positions). The remainder of the decade saw marches and demonstrations, strikes and hunger strikes and the arrests of several Melanesian activists. In 1979, the leader of the UC, Tjibaou, proclaimed that New Caledonia should seek to become independent the following year and participated in the creation of a Front Indépendantiste; the coalition won fourteen seats in the assembly (compared to fifteen seats for the pro-French RPCR, and seven seats for a centrist party).[59] New Caledonia was now divided into opposing camps, almost equal in strength, on the single issue of independence; ethnic origin, to a significant degree, correlated with political sentiment.

The reasons for this evolution are multiple. The ideologies of national liberation and anti-colonialism had taken root, with some delay, in New Caledonia and were espoused by such militants as Urégei and Naisseline. There was a new sense of Melanesian identity, promoted through the cultural festival organised by Tjibaou in 1975, which had been a public affirmation of Melanesian dignity.[60] A younger generation of Melanesian leaders had come to the fore; many were university-trained, had served in government or had professional careers and were articulate advocates for their causes. Tjibaou, for instance, was a former Catholic priest, who had studied theology and ethnology in France; he was mayor of Hienghène and head of the

Melanesian cultural centre. Machoro was a school teacher; Tjibaou and Urégei, at various times, held the highest elected office in New Caledonia as heads of the territorial assembly. Furthermore, the end of the nickel boom in New Caledonia had burst the bubble of economic growth and prosperity, a process in which Melanesians did not always share but which had brought to the territory thousands of European and Polynesian migrants and distorted the demographic balance among ethnic groups. The increasing unity of the conservative groups under the banner of Lafleur's RPCR led to an increasingly militant anti-independence position among Caldoches and other non-islanders, as well as among Wallisians and Futunans in New Caledonia.

Conditions outside New Caledonia also provided a context for the political evolution of the territory. A number of dependent territories in the South Pacific became independent in the 1970s, including the Australian colony of Papua New Guinea and the British colonies of Fiji, the Solomon Islands and the Gilbert and Ellice Islands; the New Hebrides also headed towards independence in 1980. During the 1970s France withdrew from two of its remaining overseas possessions, the Comoros Islands and Djibouti.[61] The government of Giscard d'Estaing seemed anxious to discuss the future of the territories, and his Secretary of State for the *Départements et Territoires d'Outre-Mer* , Paul Dijoud, put together a comprehensive plan for their economic and social development. Such reformism did not necessarily satisfy local demands, however, and was contested in the *métropole* by leftist parties, such as the Socialists and the Communists, who were sympathetic to Melanesian grievances (and whose political fortunes were rising in France in the late 1970s). Calls for independence in the 1970s represented the maturation of a political struggle which had progressed since the organisation of the UC in the 1950s (and, indeed, had its antecedents in earlier Melanesian resistance to French control). The formation of new movements bearing such names as 'independence fronts' in the 1970s was a manifestation of goals which coincided with greater politicisation of Melanesians who, by all accounts, remained second-class citizens in New Caledonia. Thirty years after the abolition of the *indigénat* and twenty years after the granting of universal suffrage, Melanesians had clearly not been able to achieve economic or political parity with Europeans in New Caledonia.

TOWARDS POLITICAL CONFRONTATION

France's attitude towards its overseas possessions changed from denial of the very possibility of self-government at the Brazzaville conference in 1944 to acceptance of total independence for the Indochinese colonies in 1954, the black African possessions in 1960 and Algeria two years later, and several other territories in the 1970s. During this same period, the demands of contestatory politicians in the Pacific territories had evolved from affirmations of total loyalty by such groups as the UICALO and the AICLF in New Caledonia and the Comité Pouvanaa in French Polynesia in the 1940s, through demands for autonomy in both territories in the 1950s and 1960s, to calls for independence in French Polynesia from the 1960s and in New Caledonia from the mid-1970s. There was, thus, a metamorphosis of ideology at both a national and local level. By the end of the 1970s, pro-independence groups were in a stronger position than ever before in New Caledonia, and the same was true, with reservations, of those groups which *explicitly* demanded independence in French Polynesia.[62] In neither territory, however, did such groups form a majority of the electorate, nor did the metropolitan government cast a benevolent eye on pro-independence activities.

The history of political life in the territories since the 1950s saw the establishment, scission, fusion and disappearance of various parties. Divisions among them were not always clearly drawn and were based on local loyalties and personal considerations as well as on ideological stances. In any case, French Polynesia and New Caledonia had established a vibrant, if often confusing, political life, in which universal suffrage, regular elections to territorial assemblies as well as to the French parliament, and extraparliamentary politics were the norm. The French state was hardly an impartial observer of the political process in the territories. Paris, after all, set the rules by which politics were played and, as the reaction against Pouvanaa and Lenormand clearly indicated, could and did interfere when it felt such action was warranted. It was also obvious that France gave national priorities pride of place above local ones; the safeguarding of a French stake in the South Pacific, which included the possibility for carrying out nuclear experiments, was crucial.

By the end of the 1970s a polarisation of politics in the French Pacific territories had occurred. Despite earlier disunity, the 'pro-French' forces had come together in the Tahoeraa Huiraatira in French Polynesia and the Rassemblement pour la Calédonie dans la République in New Caledonia, both of which were linked with the neo-Gaullist political party in the *métropole*. Voters in both territories could cast their ballots for avowedly pro-independence parties, either the Front Indépendantiste in New Caledonia or one of several independence movements in French Polynesia. In New Caledonia, political polarisation was in the process of becoming ethnic polarisation as well, since almost all European residents, as well as most of the Polynesian and Asian residents, supported the RPCR, and a large majority (although by no means all) of the Melanesians gave their endorsement to the Front Indépendantiste. Because of the racial and cultural *métissage* of French Polynesia, by contrast, ethnic lines were not so sharply evident; many political leaders, no matter what their ideologies, were *demis*, even if the pro-independence parties made a special effort to appeal to ethnic Polynesians or Maohi (who, not coincidentally, were generally the socially least privileged group in the population).

In some ways, politics in the French Pacific did not fit into the usual schema of parties and allegiances. Divisions between the 'élite' and the 'masses' (or 'working classes') were blurred; in New Caledonia, for instance, the RPCR included both the mining magnates and big businessmen of Nouméa and migrants from French Polynesia and Wallis and Futuna who formed an under-class in the territory, alongside urban Melanesians.[63] The divisions of 'left' and 'right' also did not really obtain, particularly in French Polynesia, where elections usually represented contests between various individuals and factions for control of power, what the French term *politique politicienne* . The pro-independence parties might bear such muscular names as the 'liberation front' of the Kanaks or the Polynesians, but island traditions, respect for the authority of elders, deference of women to men, communitarianism and deeply-held Christian beliefs, permeated even the most radical parties. (In both

French Polynesia and New Caledonia, most party leaders were practising Catholic or Protestant believers, many party congresses opened with prayers and the emblems of some groups – such as Temaru's independence movement – included a Christian cross.) The revival of Maohi customs and the affirmation of Kanak identity by independence movements combined, sometimes rather uneasily, with a rhetoric of anti-imperialism, socialism and militancy.

At the close of the 1970s, France's Pacific territories were in different situations. Wallis and Futuna seemed barely touched by political currents which had affected other regions and showed no signs of even an embryonic independence movement. In French Polynesia the statute of 1977 had provided an increased measure of self-government but had not silenced either those who demanded a greater degree of autonomy or those who aimed at independence. In New Caledonia the pro- and anti-independence movements faced each other off with increasing belligerency. Meanwhile, the condominium of the New Hebrides moved gradually towards independence, even though the French were at best resigned to that process. The French territories, therefore, displayed a spectrum of political alternatives available to 'colonies' at the time. The following decade became a flashpan in which new and more adamant demands would be voiced, reactions to those demands experimented with and choices made.

6 From the New Hebrides to Vanuatu

One of the oddest arrangements in the colonial Pacific was the joint Franco–British 'Condominium' of the New Hebrides.[1] In the nineteenth century, no European country took possession of the New Hebrides archipelago, although a small number of settlers established themselves as traders and planters. Among them was John Higginson, who had developed nickel mining in New Caledonia, then took a great interest in the New Hebrides. Higginson became a French citizen and founded the Compagnie Calédonienne des Nouvelles-Hébrides, later renamed the Société Française des Nouvelles-Hébrides (SFNH), which purchased large tracts of land in the islands and lobbied for French take-over. However, Australians, who were also attracted to the New Hebrides, pressured England not to allow the French to do so. Meanwhile, French Catholic missionaries and Anglo-Australian Presbyterians competed to convert the New Hebrideans. Outright takeover by either Britain or France became difficult, and proposals for a division of the archipelago satisfied no one.

In 1906 France and Britain came to an arrangement for a 'Condominium' over the islands. The New Hebrides would be a colony of neither France nor Britain but a sphere of 'joint influence'. Both countries maintained resident commissioners in Port Vila and district officers in the main islands. The Union Jack and the French Tricolour both flew over the New Hebrides, French and English were the official languages, the French franc and the British pound (and later the Australian dollar and the French Pacific franc) served as legal tender. The French in the islands came under the jurisdiction of the French law code and French administration, while Britons came under the British system. Foreigners resident in the islands ('optants') were required to choose to come under the authority of either the French or the British. The Melanesians were ruled jointly by the French and British authorities but could not claim the citizenship of either administering power and enjoyed almost no rights. Registration of land claims, and adjudications of disputes, were handled by a Joint Court comprised of a French and a British judge and presided over by a judge appointed by the king of Spain.[2]

With very few changes, the Condominium endured until the independence of the New Hebrides, under the name of Vanuatu, in 1980. Yet the Condominium was never popular. The French in the New Hebrides, their supporters in New Caledonia – who regarded the New Hebrides as a geographical and economic appendage of New Caledonia – and other promoters of French interests in Oceania campaigned for full French sovereignty. Suggestions for an exchange of colonial territories between the British and French, French purchase of British interests or a simple cession of the island group to France met with no success, largely because of opposition from Australia.[3] Melanesians increasingly resented a two-headed administration which gave them few benefits; the New Hebrides was for them 'a doubly oppressed colony' and the 'Condominium' really a 'Pandemonium'.[4] Because no alternative had been accepted to the arrangement – and, perhaps more importantly, because the Condominium allowed the various interests present in the New Hebrides a wide field of manoeuvre and imposed relatively few restrictions – the unwieldy binational administration endured.

The co-habitation of the French and British in the New Hebrides led to occasional clashes between colonial bureaucrats. After the 1930s the Spanish government did not appoint a presiding judge in the Joint Court; when the remaining French and British judges agreed on a case, their verdict was applied, but when they disagreed, the case was dismissed. French and British bureaucrats ostensibly were punctilious in making certain each side had equal representation, treatment and status; in reality, they engaged in regular oneupmanship. For example, at the celebration of the fiftieth anniversary of the Condominium, in 1956, the visiting French High Commissioner of the Pacific was miffed to discover that British officials had brought along a message from the Queen and had not so informed the French, who had only obtained a greeting from the Minister of Colonies; in return, the French High Commissioner made a point of not telling his British counterpart of his intention to award the Légion d'Honneur to several residents until just before the ceremony.[5] Dual administration also caused practical problems: when the first automobile arrived in the New Hebrides, no one knew whether it should drive on the right hand side of the road, as in France, or on the left, as in England. Bureaucrats decided to consult the customs archives to see if the first two-wheeled vehicle imported into the Condominium was of French or British origin; it turned out to be a Peugeot bicycle, so traffic in the New Hebrides kept to the right.[6] Such problems were normally solved in a congenial manner, and the French and British officials maintained a gentlemanly relationship in the New Hebrides.[7]

The French Resident Commissioner presided over a growing French community. The first French citizens to settle in the archipelago came from New Caledonia, but they were joined by others who migrated directly from France or moved from elsewhere in the French empire. Few had a particularly privileged background; some had been artisans or soldiers before their move to the colonies, and most became small-scale planters or traders. They generally found spouses among their compatriots in the Condominium or in New Caledonia; a few married Melanesians.[8]

The background of one Frenchman in the New Hebrides illustrates this profile. His father arrived in the islands at the beginning of the century after serving in the French Navy. A *culterreux* ('clod-hopper'), in his son's words, the migrant purchased a coconut plantation on the northern island of Espiritu Santo, then sold his holding in order to move to New Caledonia for the education of his seven children. He returned to the New Hebrides, again to work as a planter, during the Depression, and ultimately owned stands of 14 000 coconut trees in the south of the island group. He sold the copra to French companies. His son married a Frenchwoman from the New Hebrides and inherited the plantation. The son has lived almost all his life in the territory; he did not set foot in France until 1958. He now lives in retirement in Port Vila.[9]

Thanks to such planters the French amassed greater economic interests than did the English in the New Hebrides. French settlers numbered twice as many as English colonists in the early twentieth century. Before the Second World War, France took nine-tenths of the New Hebrides' exports and provided two-thirds of its imports. The SFNH claimed nominal title to roughly half the land in the islands. In 1940 title to only

20 per cent of the land in the New Hebrides was officially registered, of which only 3 per cent was held by British citizens or optants – most of whom were Australian – versus 12 per cent which belonged to French citizens or optants. (Individual Melanesian owners and reserves, as well as property held by the two colonial administrations, accounted for the remainder.) Most of the European land, including the French properties, lay in the more fertile coastal parts of the larger islands, Efate, Malakula and Santo. French companies such as Ballande and the Comptoirs Français des Nouvelles-Hébrides dominated trade with strong competition from the Australian Burns Philp Company. (Indeed, Burns Philp set up a French subsidiary, known colloquially as 'B.P. Français', in an effort to cut further into its rival's profits.) Australian Presbyterian and Anglican clergymen also competed with French Marist priests. In general Anglo-Australian interests were commercial and religious, while the French ones were those of settlement and agriculture. The French ambition was to make the New Hebrides thrive as a *colonie de peuplement* in the South Pacific.[10]

The planters' main commercial activity was the production of copra, a labour-intensive but simple activity which demanded little equipment or capital and for which a market existed in Marseille. A major problem was lack of labour, since planters considered Melanesians unreliable and lethargic workers. The decline in the islander population, consequent on the arrival of European diseases, in any case reduced the local labour force. The solution was to recruit labour from French Indochina; the first convoy landed in Port Vila in 1921 and by 1940 some 21 915 Vietnamese had arrived in the New Hebrides. The Vietnamese, mostly men, worked under contract for several years before returning home, although some elected to stay on in the New Hebrides. With the new labour, plantations of coconut trees, as well as coffee and cocoa, increased rapidly. The decade of the 1920s was the golden age for the planters, and the dream of a settler colony seemed on the verge of realisation. The Depression of the 1930s quickly put paid to this optimism: prices dropped, settlers became heavily indebted, and the French government had to negotiate loans to save the colony.[11]

A territory barely recovered from the Depression then felt the effects of the Second World War. The New Hebrides' French administrator, Sautot, was one of the first colonial officials to rally to General de Gaulle in 1940, inspired by his own political views, but also by pressure from the British administration.[12] The *ralliement* cut off the market for New Hebrides copra in Marseille, as well as the supply of labour from Indochina. The problem of defence also arose, and the joint administration organised a small New Hebrides Defence Force of Europeans and Melanesians. (One of the main activities of the militia was to round up and send to Saigon those who continued to support the Vichy government.) The islands suffered little damage during the war, although the Japanese did bombard Santo.[13]

The most dramatic effect of the war was the presence of several hundred thousand American soldiers in the New Hebrides from 1942 to 1945. Their impact was phenomenal in islands which had seen relatively small numbers of European planters, traders and missionaries and which were little developed. On Santo, the Americans constructed a huge aviation and supply camp, including three bomber airfields, two fighter airstrips, a Navy yard, over fifty kilometres of roads, six wharves, and a dry dock. At any one time, over one hundred ships anchored off the coast of Santo, and 100 000 men were permanently stationed on the island. The GIs brought the cinema to the New Hebrides, installed a telephone system, electricity and running water, and built offices and tennis courts.[14] The French administrator of Santo described the change:

> Imagine Santo with thirty or so plantations scattered along fifty kilometres of coastline. No roads, little administration, no social life. In the space of several months this region was transformed into an entrenched army camp with workshops – I would almost say factories – next to an aerodrome and, on the horizon, the largest floating dock in the world.[15]

Some ten thousand New Hebrideans, about a quarter of the population, worked for the Americans as stevedores, labourers or domestic servants. Less legitimate activities also flourished, such as the sale of black-market alcohol – including the notorious 'Torpedo Juice', a mixture of Coca-Cola and torpedo motor-fuel. Islanders and settlers generally welcomed the Americans. One resident recalled: 'The Americans invaded and took over the whole country – fortunately, because otherwise I don't know what would have happened to us.' He particularly credited the Americans with cleaning up swampland and eradicating malaria.[16] There were, however, occasional clashes between the foreign soldiers and the local populations, and some criticism of their use of Melanesian labour.[17]

Such was the largesse displayed by US soldiers that subsequently 'cargo cults' emerged among the Melanesians. The nativistic John Frum cult on Tanna created a millennial vision of the arrival of a saviour bringing riches and freedom – a fantasy directly linked to the presence of the American army and its great provisions and money.[18] The planters, meanwhile, experienced a boom during the war years, providing foodstuffs for trade with the Americans; a few became rich, and all sought ways to maintain the economic momentum after the war. When the Americans left the New Hebrides, some of their materials were bought up by colonists in the New Hebrides or New Caledonia. But much of it was simply thrown into the ocean; 'Million Dollar Point' marked an ocean graveyard for jeeps, machines and other supplies which the Americans junked rather than risking post-war sales, an ironic conclusion to several years of foreign occupation.[19]

THE NEW HEBRIDES IN THE 1940s AND 1950s

After the end of the Second World War, the colonial governments took stock of the situation in the New Hebrides. In 1949, the British reported that the current population was 45 000 Melanesians plus 320 British citizens (and 76 other British optants), 875 French citizens (plus 25 optants) and 1758 French protected persons (mostly Indochinese labourers and their families). The economy was still based on tropical agriculture. Forestry and commercial fishing remained undeveloped and there were no native crafts of market importance. Only traces of minerals had been discovered. A quarter of the land was contained in inalienable native reserves, a quarter covered in dense bush or forests; the other half was divided between livestock stations and plantations. Only sixty ships had called at New Hebrides ports over the past year to purchase the copra that formed the major export. Settlers lived in simple conditions: there was no water or sewerage system in most places, houses were wooden dwellings with corrugated iron roofs and tanks for the storage of rain water. The Condominium counted only three French and two British doctors, twelve French and six British nurses. Crime rates were fairly low, although six Europeans were at that time imprisoned for illegal sale of alcohol, one for contempt of court and one for assault.[20]

A more detailed French report from the same years concentrated on the problems of the archipelago. The author, sent by Paris to audit the SFNH, began with a discussion of the company which dominated the New Hebrides. The 'great sacrifices' which the French state had made to sustain the SFNH, he said, had aimed at 'the goal of safeguarding important landholdings which are considered French and to which the future of the New Hebrides seems linked'; the company, in fact, had 'been established, on the request of the state, to serve as a screen for French seizure of the archipelago'. Despite the company's difficulties, it needed to be supported since no other agency, notably the French administration, was sufficiently capable of maintaining control of French interests. The colonial bureaucracy, the report continued, had to administer a small but determined settler population, among whom 'everybody is a relative or an ally. . . . An administrative official is ill-equipped against the temptations of demagoguery and the snares of family relationships'. Settlers formed a veritable mafia: seven brothers and sisters filled the major posts in the French bureaucracy; among local appointees, three-quarters appeared related by marriage. A further problem was the legal ambiguity of the French position and land-titles: certain tribes, perhaps supported by Protestant missionaries, could challenge French claims. The French population of the New Hebrides was also 'fragile', living astride ruinous failures and a few successes. The exploitation of French-owned land had declined in the previous fifteen years since the Depression, and a quarter of all plantations had been abandoned. ('This is a measure of the vanity of the courageous efforts of these pioneers and the fruitlessness of French financial sacrifices'.) New migrants were few and the cutting-off of links between the South Pacific and France during the war 'accentuated instinctive segregation in a very particular insular milieu'. The few young migrants who did arrive 'come up against the prejudices and the egoism of those already established – their beginnings are difficult and take place in an atmosphere of hostility almost inconceivable in a country so deprived of new blood'. *Métissage* was on the increase; of 875 'French nationals' registered with the authorities in 1948, more than a third had at least a quarter Melanesian blood.

Economically, the Condominium was hardly a prize for the French, the 1948 report continued: 'France bears the cost of the New Hebrides economy by buying for a high price copra of dubious quality'. France bought almost 300 million CFP of copra in 1948, compared to 12 million CFP bought by Australia, the second largest market. Yet Australia sold four times as much (by value) to the Condominium as did France, and even US exports to the New Hebrides exceeded those of France.

The report lamented the lack of Francophile sentiments among the indigenes. The New Hebridean Melanesian population, 'a retarded vestige of the Neolithic [age] . . . no matter how amorphous and primitive it can be, tempted as it might be to return to a xenophobic neo-paganism, for a casual observer is obedient to the English'. Nine out of every ten natives, when asked who the 'capman' of the archipelago was, designated the British Resident Commissioner. The reason was simply that

> native policy, no matter how rough and rudimentary it be, is an English thing . . . This monopoly has often existed because we devote our modest means to the administration of our egocentric and turbulent compatriots, assimilating their interests to those of our flag. The indigenes, surrounded by 'teachers' and Presbyterian 'schools', call upon the missionaries and the arbitration of the English representatives. Meanwhile, our obstinate defence of our nationals and their economic and landholding interests has often led us to forget the existence of the [native] New Hebrideans, other than their value as labour. So long as they exist, their point of view cannot be considered negligible for the future of these islands . . . . One might wonder whether their British suzerain, by abandoning plantations and land, has not very simply won over the New Hebrideans.

The report concluded that the Condominium would probably continue to exist; but if 'this fragile edifice based on compromise' lasted, it would be because of the innate conservatism of the British, 'in the face of Australian appetites', and 'these particularistic immunities which make [the New Hebrides] for both capital and men a "country of refuge" on this planet. To the extent that this stillborn system of government has proved itself perfectly inoperative, it has increased its chances of enduring'.[21]

In short, even by South Pacific standards, the New Hebrides seemed a remote, under-developed and unpromising outpost of the French empire. Primitive tribesmen, a small but obstinate settler community and a flaccid French administration combined with the slightly more energetic English presence to mean that the French stakes in the archipelago were insecure and that the indigenes could hardly be counted upon to support the French cause. The New Hebrides seemed quintessentially colonial. As one Frenchman observed in the mid–1950s: 'Nouméa may well be provincial, but Port Vila is frankly colonial. Here one really lives in the bush, and so one must never forget to take quinine and to have a siesta. If, in Nouméa, what is familiar is nearby to what is exotic, Port Vila is the very essence of a colony'. The pictureque image of the capital – 'near the port and around the shops stroll many barefoot indigenes, muscular Kanaks, native girls clothed in strange dresses with splashes of colour, Tonkinese women in silk pyjamas and white hats, a frangipani tree dropping its flowers on the ground, a mango tree offering its fruits to passers-by' – truly bespoke colonialism.[22]

The French government realised that it was not in a sure position, despite the predominance of French settlers and landholdings. Yet it took a decade and a half after the end of the war before Paris decided to buttress its power and influence *vis-à-vis* the British administration and the Melanesian population. As late as 1962, a newly-arrived French Resident Commissioner noticed that in the New Hebrides, 'We looked like poor relations in comparison with the British, who were well set up with good boats [and other materials] and a vast political and logistic support network in the form of missions spread throughout the archipelago'. He recommended that the French 're-establish a political equilibrium [of the French and British] in the indigenous population'; to do so, it was necessary to teach them French, 'to win the battle of Francophonie'. The Minister of Overseas Territories had instructed the official to 'disseminate quality French education in order to produce local élites, to collaborate in this sense with our Catholic and Protestant missionaries, to create new schools and to organise, through information, active propaganda [for French support]'.[23] That such orders were necessary indicated the neglect from which the New Hebrides had continued to suffer in the years since the 1940s. During this time, however, a series of changes had very slowly begun to take place which ultimately led to a successful challenge to the colonial presence in the New Hebrides.

ECONOMIC DEVELOPMENT

Production of copra grew in volume and value in the 1940s and 1950s. Increasingly it was produced by Melanesians rather than by European planters – already in the early 1950s Melanesians produced over half the islands' copra. The main problem for European planters remained labour.[24] The war in Indochina threatened the supply of Vietnamese workers, most of whom supported the nationalists fighting for the independence of their homeland. In 1953, about 1500 Vietnamese, the majority of those in the New Hebrides, were repatriated to Indochina and most of the remaining Indochinese workers returned home in 1963.

To replace the Vietnamese, planters recruited small numbers of Tahitians and Wallisians, although one European brought in two dozen workers from Italy. The numbers of labourers remained insufficient for settlers to extend coconut production. Furthermore, the mid–1950s saw the end of the Korean War boom, which had temporarily boosted demand. Then in 1959, a hurricane destroyed many stands of coconuts. More generally, by the late 1950s, the palms planted by settlers earlier in the century had grown old. The French Resident wrote in 1960 that the future of the settlers looked bleak: 'Accustomed to Indochinese labour, then to the profits which their various dealings with the American forces had given them, and finally to the boom created by the Korean War, the New Hebrides colonists in general are having difficulty adapting to the new economic conjuncture'.[25] In that year, settler agriculture amounted to ten British and ninety French plantations, mostly small or medium-sized holdings employing fewer than a hundred workers each; few of the plantations flourished.

A possible solution for planters was diversification. Already in the 1950s some tried to grow and market cocoa and coffee, but competition from overseas suppliers and the lack of workers kept sales relatively low. A more promising alternative was livestock-raising, especially with growing demand for meat in New Hebrides towns, and many planters converted to livestock production. They grazed animals under coconut trees or cleared land for pasture; some 4000 hectares were put into service in the 1960s. Extension of grazing land meant a move inland from coastal holdings, and exploitation of land to which Europeans held nominal title but which they had never used. This push into the 'black bush' or 'dark bush', as the hinterland was called, provoked opposition from traditional Melanesian owners. Opposition was especially strong on Santo, the main centre of French settlement (other than Efate); half of the new cattle ranches were located on Santo, where the activities of a French livestock-raising firm, the Compagnie d'Elevage du Pacifique, were concentrated. Despite Melanesian resistance, European pastoralists increased their herds from 45 000 head in 1960 to 100 000 a decade later. Livestock-raising formed a new source of modest profits. The ranchers were unable to carve out a real niche for their beef on the international market, partly because of potential buyers' concerns about health and hygiene, although the arrival of a veterinary surgeon in 1963 made some exports possible.[26]

Other developments changed the economy of the Condominium as well, although benefits to both Europeans and Melanesians were marginal. In 1958, on Santo, Japanese businessmen opened a plant to process the fish caught by Japanese vessels in the South Pacific. Gradually, fish replaced copra as the New Hebrides' major export. However, the fishermen, except for a few Koreans, were all Japanese, and the freezing plant employed only fifty New Hebrideans. Europeans found greater profits, at least for a short time, in New Hebridean manganese. The Compagnie Française des Phosphates d'Océanie opened a manganese mine in Efate in 1961. The mine functioned for six years, closed for two years, reopened in 1970, then closed permanently in 1979. Neither the deposits in the New Hebrides, nor world demand, made manganese a long-term source of profit for Europeans nor of employment for Melanesians. Similarly, a timber concession on one of the southern islands of the New Hebrides, granted to a French company in 1969, produced little long-lasting economic growth.[27] A small tourist industry began in the New Hebrides in the 1960s, primarily to serve visitors from New Caledonia and Australia. Several tourist complexes were constructed, notably a Japanese-owned resort, and international air connections were improved. Yet the lack of a more developed infrastructure limited revenues and employment in the tourist industry.

The economic boom in neighbouring New Caledonia in the 1960s, by contrast, created a great demand for workers, and New Hebrideans responded. From the mid–1960s onwards, New Caledonian companies hired New Hebrideans as miners, general labourers or, particularly, construction workers. In 1968, 400 New Hebridean Melanesians worked in New Caledonia; by 1971, between 3000 and 3500. The salaries they earned, as much as $350 per month, represented four or five times the wages they could have expected in the New Hebrides. The migrants were able to save much of the money, which they brought back to the New Hebrides at the conclusion of three- to six-month work contracts. Some 2.5 million dollars entered the New Hebrides in this way in 1971 alone. Remittances from workers in New Caledonia became, after fish and copra, the third most important income-earner in the New Hebrides. With the end of the economic boom in New Caledonia in the 1970s, most New Hebrideans returned home.[28] The only remaining alternatives to working for settlers in the New Hebrides or New Caledonia was to sell their agricultural products to traders or the cooperatives which the French and British had set up in the 1960s.

The administering powers of the Condominium at this time began to pour large sums of money into the territory. Overall government spending by France and Britain grew from $7 million to $14 million from 1968 to 1972, then rose by more than 26 per cent annually from 1972 to 1976. An evident need for better schooling and medical care, and an improved economic infrastructure, as well as competition between the two imperial powers, provoked the increased spending. Trying to win favour with the Melanesians, France and Britain vied with each other to provide funding and undertake new projects. Most of the money was targeted to the major towns of Port Vila on Efate and Luganville on Santo and was invested in services such as medical care, education and communications.[29]

The French outspent the British during these years. The French budget in the New Hebrides grew from just under 600 million New Hebrides francs (FNH) in 1971 to 1.6 billion five years later, while British expenditure increased from 245 million in 1975 to 582 million in 1976. From 1961 to 1973, the French Caisse Centrale de Coopération Economique lent some 442 million FNH to finance public works, agricultural development and hotels. France became the main source of capital for the New Hebrides, since customs receipts, the major source of income for the Condominium, equalled only a third of the money France spent in the mid-1970s.[30]

Officials were determined to invest in the territory, despite the manifest absence of great returns, and foreign investors were also attracted. Land speculation began in the late 1960s with buyers from New Caledonia and especially from the United States. The most notorious was a businessman from Hawaii, Eugene Peacock. He first visited the New Hebrides in 1966, then the following year he bought a plantation called Hog Harbour on Santo, for which he paid $86 000 in the name of a subsidiary of a Hong Kong firm. He settled in the New Hebrides as a permanent resident and over the next three years increased his holdings on Santo and Efate. Peacock announced plans to develop farming, subdivide his land and bring 350 American families to Hog Harbour (now renamed Lokalee). By 1969, he had indeed subdivided his properties into 1450 lots of five acres each, which he had sold for a total of between $4.5 and $5 million to overseas investors. He targeted purchasers in Hawaii and Hong Kong, but particularly American soldiers serving in Vietnam. His advertisements in army newspapers promised soldiers a share in a tropical paradise, where they could become property-owners after their tours of duty, perhaps with a Vietnamese war bride who might be unwelcome in the United States. The speculators' financial wherewithal was shady, their legal claims to land uncertain, and their advertising misleading. In short, they were involved in a great swindle which ultimately frightened Condominium authorities. The British especially were alarmed at the prospect of an influx of migrants demanding services and antagonising the local population. Legislation in the New Hebrides in 1971 which instituted new tax regulations and prohibited the registration of land subdivisions, terminated the project. Most of those who had 'bought' properties lost their money, but Peacock remained involved in New Hebrides affairs.[31]

A more straightforward project to promote development and provide a refuge for speculators was the creation of a tax haven in the New Hebrides. The British, perhaps already foreshadowing their disengagement from the New Hebrides and hoping that the Condominium would do more to pay its own way, proposed in the late 1960s to introduce an income tax in the islands. The French authorities objected since their citizens would have been the major tax-payers; many foreigners in the New Hebrides had become French 'optants' since they viewed French commercial regulations as more lenient than those of the British. The alternative to an income tax was for Britain to allow the registration of foreign companies in the New Hebrides. By 1972, some five hundred companies had taken up the option. Most had only a small office or just a postal address in the New Hebrides, a nominal presence which assured them tax-free status. Some $150 million a year passed through the Condominium by the mid-1970s, making it the most important 'financial paradise' in Oceania.[32] Apart from a minor building boom, benefits to the New Hebridean population were minimal.

The New Hebrides in the last decade of Franco-British rule succeeded in becoming a more diversified economy, but one dependent on exterior sources of capital and markets; it provided profits largely for foreigners, as well as modest incomes for a small group of settlers. Yet in the mid-1970s the French Resident Commissioner himself admitted that the economic situation 'is not brilliant'. Copra production was at a new low: 'The threshold of profit-making has been reached, and if the price were to fall even slightly lower, it would no longer be worthwhile even to harvest copra'. Pastoralism was faring better, but world prices were low for livestock as well. The world recession and the distance of the archipelago from world markets were great obstacles. Neither buyers nor investors were flocking to the New Hebrides: 'We are at the end of the line', concluded the French Resident, M. Gauger.[33] Only a handful of

French and British companies had stakes in the Condominium. Business remained highly concentrated. Excluding the export of fish and manganese, 97 per cent of all foreign export was in the hands of only five companies, none locally owned. The copra trade, for instance, was controlled by the Australian Burns Philp Company, plus two French companies, the Comptoirs Français des Nouvelles-Hébrides (a subsidiary of Ballande in New Caledonia) and the Maison Barrau (also headquartered in New Caledonia).[34] These companies had difficulties in marketing,[35] but along with the SFNH, the Messageries Maritimes shipping firm and the Banque de l'Indochine represented a closely linked nexus of French commercial interests in the New Hebrides. The continuation of the Condominium and French political involvement in the New Hebrides provided a safeguard for their interests. The activities of foreign speculators, British desire to decolonise and emerging Melanesian nationalism upset the status quo in the 1970s.

LAND, MELANESIANS AND NATIONALISM

For those who dreamed of a successful European settler colony in the New Hebrides, land was the key to the installation of migrants and the setting up of plantations. For the New Hebridean islanders, just as for other Melanesians, land was more than an economic commodity. Land embodied their identity and held a cultural and spiritual value. In Melanesian society, land could not be permanently alienated, although custom and negotiation provided for the distribution and use of property. The European and Oceanic conceptions of land rights were difficult to reconcile, and the Joint Court set up by the Condominium authorities to register land claims not surprisingly favoured the European view. New Hebrideans had no recourse to protest the alienation of their land, and the rules of the court even put the burden on Melanesians of proving European claims invalid.[36]

Frustration with European land takeovers mounted after the Second World War, especially when in 1951, the Joint Court confirmed the SFNH's title to a 20 000 hectare tract in Luganville. The SFNH held legally recognised titles to some 60 000 hectares in the mid–1970s, French settlers owned a further 50 000 hectares, other French companies 45 000 hectares and the French state 22 000 hectares; British holdings amounted to some 35 000 hectares.[37] Accepting foreign ownership was already difficult for Melanesians, but the expanded use of the land in the late 1950s and 1960s brought home the point of Melanesian dispossession. The move of planters into the 'black bush' to create pasture for their livestock was rendered particularly invasive by the use of bulldozers and heavy machinery and the speed with which they cleared land.

Resentment against appropriation of land combined with opposition to the lack of rights given to Melanesians. A law code adopted by the French and British in 1927 and revised in 1962 prescribed capital punishment for murder and various fines and periods of imprisonment for crimes against persons or property, but also for such infractions as sorcery, cruelty towards animals and 'unnatural' sexual acts. Certain provisions attempted to take account of Melanesian customs (notably as concerned incest), but the law code sought to impose European order on the native population. A special administrative regulation also allowed authorities to put under house arrest 'any indigene whom they consider to be in a state of rebellion against the government of the Condominium or dangerous to peace and public order in the New Hebrides'. Some regulations attempted to preserve the Melanesians against excessive European encroachments; the government, for instance, established reserves of land and could forbid the sale of land that officials considered vital to Melanesians' livelihood. Authorities also set minimum ages at which Melanesians could marry – eighteen for men, sixteen for women – and required parents to support their offspring, including illegitimate children. Still other regulations aimed at improving health and hygiene. Until 1963, the sale of alcohol to islanders was illegal, although the interdiction was often flouted. Laws adopted by the Condominium government in 1940 and 1951 required that beds must be installed in houses and that latrines be constructed and used; the authorities could require islanders to demolish or clean insalubrious dwellings; they could also oblige a 'native' to undergo medical treatment.[38]

These rules and regulations aimed to keep 'natives' pacified and to make them 'civilised' rather than to develop Melanesian society. Even later development plans, insofar as there were any, targeted settlers rather than islanders. Apart from an Advisory Council, neither group had any sort of political representation until Local Councils were set up in the late 1950s, and in any case, they were only consultative bodies. There resulted a vague but growing disaffection with the colonisers rather than a Western-style politicisation in the first two decades after the Second World War. Yet the very nature of European-Melanesian relations – episodic contact, under-administration, and marginalisation except for the recruitment of labour – reinforced traditional Melanesian customs and attachment to land.[39] This made the increased incursions on land in the 1960s particularly offensive. Such actions sparked the first reactions among Melanesians; the lack of clear divisions between religious, political and economic authority in Melanesian tradition accounted for the syncretic nature of early protest movements.

Protests began in Santo, where many of the SFNH's holdings and other ranches lay. In the early 1960s, Melanesians led by Buluk, a local chief, occupied foreign-held property and pulled down fences and boundary markers. Buluk then joined forces with Jimmy Stephens, who would become a key Melanesian leader. The illegitimate son of a planter father, himself of mixed British and Tongan stock, and a Banks Island mother, Stephens had worked for the Americans as an adolescent during the war, then took a variety of odd jobs. An imposing figure with a patriarchal beard and considerable oratorical talent, Stephens soon attracted a cult following. In 1964, along with Buluk, he organised the Nagriamel movement. The name, a combination of the names of two local plants, one of which was used ritually to designate certain areas as taboo, symbolised Nagriamel's ideological base in traditional Melanesian 'custom' and its opposition to European takeovers of land.[40] In 1967, Stephens and Buluk occupied two thousand acres at Vanafo, Santo, which led to a brief period of imprisonment for them. But Vanafo became a self-proclaimed autonomous community of Melanesians aiming to put into practice Stephens' utopian and anti-European schemes. In the late 1960s and early 1970s Nagriamel recruited numerous supporters and Stephens consolidated his authority as spokesman for disaffected Melanesians on Santo and as guardian of 'custom'.

Nagriamel marked the beginnings of Melanesian nationalism in the New Hebrides, but in the 1970s nationalist sentiments were also channelled into political organisations. In 1971, to protest against Peacock's land purchases and subdivisions, Melanesians founded the New Hebrides Cultural Association. Clergymen, teachers and civil servants formed the majority of its members, who were largely Anglophone and Protestant; their leader was an Anglican priest, Walter Lini. The organisation called for an end to land spoliation, but it gradually became the spearhead for those who demanded the abolition of the Condominium administration. Renamed the New Hebrides National Party, then the Vanuaaku Party (VAP) – taking the name from a local word meaning 'land' – it became the major political party in the islands.

In opposition, and also in 1971, French settlers, some urban Melanesians and *métis* and Francophone Catholics set up a rival Union des Populations des Nouvelles-Hébrides (UPNH). There emerged other Francophone organisations, especially the gradualist Union des Communautés des Nouvelles-Hébrides (UCNH), the Mouvement Autonomiste des Nouvelles-Hébrides (MANH), which enjoyed support from the Nagriamel movement on Santo, and the Tan-Union, which was linked to the John Frum cult on Tanna.[41] These parties, and several smaller organisations, which grouped loosely together as the *Modérés*, favoured the continuation of the Condominium at least for the immediate future. The *Modérés* in general represented a heterodox coalition of French-educated and French-speaking Melanesians, Catholics and members of smaller Protestant denominations, French settlers and *métis* New Hebrideans. All were concerned about the Anglophone, Presbyterian-Anglican and increasingly pro-independence orientation of the VAP. The best known leaders of the *Modérés* were a French-educated Catholic priest, Gérard Leymang and a lawyer, Vincent Boulékoné.[42]

Corresponding to the new ideologies and parties was a change in the attitude of one of the administering powers in the Condominium. Since the late 1960s, Britain had been intent on withdrawing from its overseas territories and, in general, pulling back from 'east of Aden'. By the 1970s, London was speedily granting independence to most of its remaining island possessions. In the South Pacific, Fiji became independent in 1970, and the Solomon, Gilbert and Ellice islands followed later in the decade. Britain was interested in winding up the New Hebrides Condominium as well. France, however, was not obviously interested in withdrawing, especially because of the proximity of New Caledonia and stirrings of autonomist movements there, as well as the interests of French planters and companies in the New Hebrides. Visiting the islands in 1972, the French prime minister, Pierre Messmer, stated that Paris considered any major change in the Condominium statute premature. What the French thought in private may have been different. One highly-placed British official has suggested that by the end of the 1960s, some French authorities, or at least the then French Resident Commissioner, Jacques Mouradian, were convinced that independence was inevitable for the New Hebrides. However, Mouradian thought that independence would only occur within a decade or so hence. At that moment, the French considered the islanders still too primitive for any significant degree of constitutional advance.[43]

Nevertheless, in 1974 the French Minister for the DOM-TOMs, Olivier Stirn, met with his British counterpart, Joan Lestor, and approved a new agreement for the New Hebrides which foreshadowed the setting-up of a Representative Assembly in 1975 and the creation of new local government councils. More powers were to be granted to the Assembly than had been given to the old Advisory Council and attempts were supposed to be made to combine British and French administrative services where possible. Paris and London also considered the possibility of giving New Hebrideans a new legal status, perhaps making them dual nationals of France and Britain. The two governments had already appointed a Condominium Land Tenure Adviser to advise on land reform within the framework of the 1914 Protocol. Lastly, Stirn and Lestor drew up an economic and social development plan for the New Hebrides.[44] In 1974 neither Condominium authority publicly mentioned independence for the islands; the agreements signed that year represented a compromise between British wishes to quit the territory and the French desire to remain. The plan was also an attempt to defuse criticism of the Condominium from the Melanesian nationalist movement.

The VAP was now becoming more militant in its demands for independence, and Walter Lini made a trip to the United Nations to call for an end to the Condominium. Combined with the VAP's insistence that an independent New Hebrides would be an English-speaking state, Lini's ideological stance, widely perceived as leftist or radical, increased the fears of the VAP's opponents. The main organisation of French settlers sent a letter to the French government asking that, no matter what the political future of the New Hebrides might hold, they be guaranteed French citizenship and rights to property, as well as the safeguarding of their possessions; they also wanted to be certain that French education would continue to be provided.[45] The *Modérés*, led by Leymang, Vincent Boulékoné and Maxime Carlot, also insisted on the maintenance of French culture and the rights of French nationals. Regional parties, such as Tan Union, expressed discontent at possible domination of the future government by politicians in Efate.

The population was largely divided between two broad political movements and polarised between different ideologies. Various levels of political interest and ideology overlay each other. Economic and social changes had wrought their effects. For instance, Port Vila and Luganville had become large towns, and most of the population increase came from young Melanesians or *métis*. The *métis* of mixed French and Melanesian parentage, the product of unions between plantation owners and women employees, had the right to French citizenship, provided their fathers legally recognised them, unlike the full-blooded Melanesians.[46] Many consequently showed interest in assimilating into European society and chose to support the Francophone parties. With the dramatic increase in French and British spending on education since the 1960s, especially by the French, there was a growing group of educated Melanesians, divided between Francophones and Anglophones. Many were active in the various churches which themselves were relatively politicised; both major Melanesian leaders were clergymen.

The first direct elections in the New Hebrides were held in 1975 to select members of the municipal councils in Port Vila and Luganville (Santo), as well as to choose members of the new Representative Assembly. The results showed the degree of political differences. The UCNH won 18 seats on the Vila council, compared to 6 for the VAP, while on Santo the MANH/Nagriamel alliance won 15 seats versus only 1 for the VAP. In the Assembly elections, the VAP won 17 seats, the UCNH 10, MANH/Nagriamel 2; other members of the assembly were 3 representatives of the Melanesian agricultural co-operatives, 6 members of the European-dominated Chamber of Commerce and 4 elected tribal chiefs.[47]

The Representative Assembly first met in 1976, by which time troubles had broken out on Tanna and Santo. Tanna was home of the John Frum movement as well as the site of opposition to the Presbyterian missionaries who had tried to impose a strict code of conduct on islanders in the early twentieth century ('Tanna law') and who were now seen as leaders of the VAP. A number of Tannese rallied to a Frenchman named Antoine Fornelli. A Corsican who had been a French soldier in Indochina, Fornelli arrived in the New Hebrides in 1973 and bought property there. He established good contacts with the Melanesians in Tanna and in the year of his arrival organised the Union des Travailleurs Autochthones on the island; this evolved into the 'Four Corner' movement, an alliance of custom chiefs and Fornelli. (In a parallel action, other Tannese gathered around an Australian trader, Bob Paul.) In 1974, Fornelli declared the birth of the Nation of Tanna, complete with flag ('that of union, peace and "custom"', he claimed) and Fornelli as head of state. He informed the French and British Resident Commissioners of his action, but to no avail. His secessionist movement petered out for lack of recognition, and Fornelli was expelled to New Caledonia, one of a number of rebel Frenchmen who took politics into their own hands in the New Hebrides.[48]

On Santo, Jimmy Stephens' Nagriamel movement, started in opposition to European landholding, now moved towards *rapprochement* with the settlers in opposition to the VAP, which Stephens considered opposed to 'custom'. The French had initially been suspicious of Stephens, but 'by 1975 Nagriamel had come to be considered by the French Administration as a key component of the network of conservatively-minded and French-influenced political groups, also including John Frum on Tanna, which, it was hoped, would constitute a bulwark against domination of the New Hebrides by the National Party'.[49] Stephens had also been involved in an American scheme promoted by Eugene Peacock. He reappeared on Santo in the mid-1970s in the company of a New Caledonian businessman, Henri Leconte, and another American called Michael Oliver. Oliver was the prime mover of an American libertarian group, the Phoenix Foundation. Campaigning against communism and collectivism, he set himself the task of creating a haven for free enterprise. In 1972, Oliver and the Phoenix Foundation had tried to create a new country, the Republic of Minerva, by raising a flag over a partially-submerged and uninhabited coral reef in the territorial waters of Tonga; they planned to build an artificial island republic to embody their principles, but Tongan authorities quickly staunched their efforts. The foundation then attempted to establish a new country on one of the Bahamas islands, but this project also came to nought. Now they turned their attention to Santo and donated money and material to Stephens, whom they attempted to convince of the benefits of a tax-haven and free-enterprise economy. With backing from French settlers and the Phoenix Foundation, Stephens proclaimed the independence of Santo in 1975. The declaration went unrecognised, but the Vanafo headquarters of Stephens continued to serve as a rallying-point for dissent.[50]

Hostility to the Condominium and the VAP was not silenced on Santo or Tanna, and the New Hebrides' political élite remained divided between supporters of the VAP and the *Modérés*. The Condominium authorities tried to muster support from New Hebrideans while ostensibly the British and French cooperated with each other. The French minister of the DOM-TOMs, Paul Dijoud, visited the New Hebrides in 1978 to promote new development efforts and said that France would continue to aid the New Hebrides if it became independent. French authorities, however, were less than enthusiastic about that eventuality, especially if the new state promised to be dominated by the Anglophone and Protestant VAP.

Party politics continued in earnest in the New Hebrides. In 1977, the VAP adopted a more militantly pro-independence platform and boycotted new elections for the Representative Assembly. The same year the French and British agreed to the naming of an executive government, headed by a chief minister, George Kauakau, and the following year foreshadowed a referendum on independence in 1980. The *Modéré* Leymang briefly headed a unity government in 1978–9 but the VAP won two-thirds of the seats in the Representative Assembly in elections at the end of 1979. Lini, of the VAP, became chief minister. Negotiations between Lini's largely autonomous government and the French and British authorities began. The opposition *Modérés* were excluded from official discussions but continued to promote their cause both in the New Hebrides and in France. Tensions ran high, especially on the question of language. Lini announced that his government would not guarantee French education unless Paris were willing to pay for it after independence; Boulékoné, an opposition leader, charged that 'the prime minister refuses to see and admit that in this country there are Melanesians who speak and think in French' and said the VAP was creating apartheid by favouring appointment of Anglophones to public service posts. Boulékoné said that the VAP was 'inebriated' by its recent electoral victory and the New Hebrides was witnessing 'the birth of a "Melanesian colonialism" which is making the same mistakes that we reproach the administering powers with doing. Added to a pronounced nepotism this does not settle anything. This Melanesian colonialism is trying to perpetuate British colonialism, thanks to which the VAP was able to win the elections'.[51]

Nevertheless talks between Lini and the Condominium authorities resulted in a constitution signed in 1979. The constitution guaranteed the rights of the Francophones (by making French, English and the local pidgin, Bislama, official languages) and planned the setting-up of regional councils. These were designed to preserve certain powers for local governments but did not satisfy the *Modérés'* wish for a more devolved, federalist government. The French remained unenthusiastic about the arrangements (which included a radical overhaul of land tenure, with the reversion of all land, including registered titles, to customary ownership) but acquiesced to them. The Condominium representatives and the New Hebrides assembly decided on 30 July 1980 as the date of independence for the new nation to be called Vanuatu – although the name itself, close to that of the Vanuaaku Party, dissatisfied the *Modérés*. The VAP, the British and the French had now ostensibly agreed to decolonisation, but the *Modérés* disagreed with the very name of the country, the form of its government and the domination of the VAP. There was to be more trouble before the Condominium ended and the new state was born.

TANNA, SANTO AND VANUATU

The dissent which troubled the last months of the Condominium again centred on the islands of Santo and Tanna.[52] In Tanna, the John Frum movement continued to challenge the VAP and provide support for the opposition *Modérés*. Tension heightened with the return to the island of Fornelli, the Frenchman who had earlier tried to declare himself ruler of Tanna. The situation deteriorated in 1979 with the move towards independence and reached secessionist proportions the next year. On 1 January 1980, an alliance of custom leaders (including some from the John Frum cult) and supporters of the *Modérés* proclaimed the 'Nation TAFEA', composed of Tanna and the other southern islands of Anatom, Futuna, Erromango and Aniwa. Their manifesto announced that 'in order to separate from the New Hebrides government directed by the Vanuaaku Party, the five islands are forming a nation, on the basis of Custom and with the aid of the governments of the following countries [*sic*]: France, Nouméa, Paris, Corsica, America'. (The reference to Corsica pointed to Fornelli's background, that to America recalled the orientation of John Frum.) The main argument of the TAFEA movement was that 'custom' had been corrupted by Protestant missionaries and the VAP; a missive from the organising committee to the Resident Commissioners stated in December 1979:

> This letter has been written in the name of the custom chiefs and the inhabitants of the island of Tanna, in order to inform the two of you, the officials of France and Great Britain . . . that henceforth Custom rejects the system of the Condominium and that it no longer recognises the current government of the New Hebrides [i.e., that of Lini] . . . . In times past, Custom alone reigned in our land and on our island of Tanna. Then Presbyterian missionaries arrived and, in their wake, the agents of the Condominium government. All of them lied to us because they were going to work with Custom, and they worked against it.[53]

The leader of the Tanna revolt was Alexis Yolou, a young French-educated politician who found support among both the 'custom' rebels and the pro-French dissidents, whom he skilfully welded together. They directed their anger at the opposing coalition of the VAP, the Presbyterians and the British. Yolou told a meeting in Tanna in January 1980:

> This is what we have seen: the English have used the 'Vanuaaku' and now it has won. All that the English cherished is in the process of being realised, that is, to chase the French out of the New Hebrides . . . . We have heard it said that Walter Lini has already asked Paris to recall M. Robert [the French Resident Commissioner] because he gave too much help to the *Modérés*. [But] who aided the 'Vanuaaku Parti'? Did not the English aid it?[54]

Yolou's rebellion continued through the first half of 1980, but collapsed in June when he was killed. Yolou's opponents said his death occurred during a general riot in Tanna, while his defenders argued that he was assassinated by VAP supporters. The actual culprit remains unknown, but his death – as well as the unwillingness of both the French and the British to support the secession of Tanna – brought the rebellion to an end.

The revolt in Santo likewise mobilised defenders of custom, in this case, Nagriamel, the *Modérés*, and Francophones, but support also came from the numerous French settlers on the island, the French administration itself and American libertarians connected with the Phoenix Foundation.[55] This motley assortment shared few interests except opposition to the VAP and the plan for independence which concentrated political and economic power in the hands of the VAP leaders whom they regarded as anti-French, leftist and bent on a centralised state.

Jimmy Stephens' supporters in the Nagriamel movement lived in a state of quasi-segregation in Vanafo as independence approached. In early 1980, Stephens proclaimed the secession of Santo and the establishment of the 'Republic of Vemarana' with Stephens himself as president. Lini's government and the Condominium authorities not surprisingly refused to accept the move, but Stephens held out. The flag of Vemarana was raised, and passports and coins emblazoned with the republic's emblem arrived from the United States through the good graces of Michael Oliver and the Phoenix Foundation, which also drew up a constitution for the free-enterprise, multi-ethnic republic. Despite requests from Lini, as chief minister, the Condominium authorities refused to send troops to suppress the revolt. Meanwhile, several Frenchmen from Nouméa arrived in Luganville to give aid to the new government, which by now had appointed a cabinet and was broadcasting from a radio station. At the end of May, the situation turned violent with an attack on the 'British Paddock', the neighbourhood just outside Luganville inhabited by members of the British Administration based in Northern District. Several hostages were taken and shops looted. Still no action was taken by Port Vila, and the Vemarana government soldiered on with encouragement from its diverse supporters.

In July, Lini again asked for action by France and Britain, and the South Pacific Forum – a conference of independent Oceanic nations which supported the VAP and the independence of the New Hebrides – called for the rebellion to be crushed. Finally, France and Britain agreed to dispatch a force of several hundred soldiers to Santo. The day before their arrival, the French Resident Commissioner, Robert, flew to Santo to tell the gathered secessionists that the Franco-British forces were being deployed to stop a 'massacre' of the Santo supporters of Vemarana by foreign troops, a reference to Papua New Guinean soldiers who had landed in Port Vila for the New Hebrides independence ceremonies; he added that the Condominium would be restored and maintained on the island of Santo until satisfactory arrangements had been worked out, and that the interests of Santo would be safeguarded. In the over-heated atmosphere, when asked whether the Santo rebels were similar to the Free French supporters of 1940, Robert answered: 'It's like that. Exactly like in '40. But still – I don't imagine that I'm de Gaulle'.[56] He asked the rebels to welcome the soldiers and cooperate with them.

The Franco-British troops arrived on schedule and indeed received a warm welcome from the local population. The Vemarana flag continued to fly over Santo seven days later as the Republic of Vanuatu was proclaimed throughout the archipelago. The Condominium had now come to an end, although French and British troops remained in Santo until the middle of August. They were then replaced by a military force of three hundred men from Papua New Guinea, commanded by Australian officers and transported in Australian military jets. The Papua New Guinea forces pulled down the Vemarana flags and attacked Jimmy Stephens' camp, killing his son and arresting Stephens. In the days that followed, over a hundred other Santo men were arrested, most French residents fled (with the aid of the new French ambassador in Port Vila), and the secession came to an end. Later Vanuatu expelled a number of other Frenchmen or forbade them to live in the country. Melanesians who supported the secessionist movement were brought to trial, and the court sentenced Stephens to fourteen years imprisonment; he was released only in 1991.

The attempted secession on Tanna, and even more that on Santo, inspired great polemics. The most fervent critics of French policy, at the time and afterwards, saw the rebellions as French-supported and engineered plots. They argued that France was trying to stop, or at least postpone, the independence of Vanuatu, to bring about the secession of islands which could be retained as bases of French economic, political and cultural interests, or, at the very least, to assure a loosely organised, federalist state in which autonomous islands such as Santo would be hospitable to French settlers and influence.[57] Defenders of the French position rejected such arguments, and the French attorney who represented Stephens and the other rebels at their trial even accused the French of having abandoned those who supported them in Santo, leaving them to the mercies of the VAP politicians and the Papua New Guinean troops.[58] Another French observer strongly criticised the French for doing too little to support the forces opposed to independence.[59]

Other commentators[60] have pointed to the odd alliance of French settlers, 'custom' chiefs and others (notably the Francophones, Catholics and members of minority Protestant churches) who allied in opposition to the VAP. Layers of opposition melded together in the revolts: traditional opposition to Presbyterian authority in Tanna and to the domination of the VAP by Protestant clerics, political quarrels among the various parties in the New Hebrides vying for control of the newly independent state, and traditional regional and island interests afraid of being swallowed up in Vanuatu. To these conflicts were joined the activities of the agents of the Phoenix Foundation, French planters trying to preserve their land and livelihoods against a government which had already announced that once independence arrived only Melanesians would be able to own property in Vanuatu, *métis* whose social and political position was ambiguous, and speculators from New Caledonia.

The role of the French state, and French authorities in the New Hebrides, is difficult to judge. Most controversial was the role of the French Resident in the New Hebrides at the time of independence and thus the Frenchman directly 'in charge' during the secessions. Robert's visit to Santo, and his speech to the supporters of Vemarana, certainly encouraged (and perhaps misled) them. A longtime French inhabitant of the New Hebrides has suggested that Robert's action 'did not calm the situation' there and added that his effort was 'shabby' and 'stupid'.[61] Some have conjectured that Robert acted largely on his own initiative; a somewhat rustic man, a former boxer, he was also thought to be strong-willed. Others, however, have argued that his actions, including attempts to forestall independence and promote secession, were carried out on orders from Paris.[62]

Critics think that the French refusal to send in troops to quell the insurrection in Santo in the early days of the revolt implied their complicity. For their part the British were reluctant to send troops on their own. The French always publicly affirmed that independence would arrive on schedule, as it did. In a more long-range view, the French had aided such groups as Nagriamel, and some of the leaders of the rebellion, such as Yolou in Tanna, had French education and connections. Up until the moment when independence seemed inevitable, it appears that France attempted to retain support among Melanesians and used certain individuals and groups for that purpose, providing them with enough support to keep their often unrealistic hopes alive. No evidence exists, however, that the rebellions were remote-controlled from Paris, Nouméa or the French Residency in Port Vila; there is no proof of a conspiracy. A difference must be made between the efforts of particular Frenchmen, acting separately or together, and official government policy. A former French Resident in the New Hebrides has concluded: 'The attitude of the French Government concerning independence, in delaying and in dragging its feet, followed that of the rest of the territories of the Empire.

It is unfortunate that it finished badly. In any case, the French Government counted for nothing in the secession movement in Santo, which in part can be attributed to the managers of large farm properties in the north of the archipelago'.[63] That, of course, is a personal opinion.

Individual Frenchmen undoubtedly used the means at their disposal, and allied with whatever partners they could find, to forestall an independence that went against their wishes or to salvage as much as they could from that independence.

FRENCH POLICY IN THE CONDOMINIUM

Paris's policy in the New Hebrides since the 1800s had been to encourage settlement by colonists and to foster links between the New Hebrides and New Caledonia. It sought as well to prohibit British annexation of the archipelago and to limit the activities of British and Australian traders, missionaries and settlers. The French government used the intermediary of Higginson's SFNH and other companies such as the Banque de l'Indochine. Conversely, Higginson was anxious to use his French citizenship and his promotion of French interests in the island chain to justify, perhaps to hide, his profit-making. Public and private interests, therefore, mixed together in the French presence in the New Hebrides in the colonial era just as at the moment of decolonisation.[64]

Despite the failure of attempts to constitute a large colony of prosperous planters, what productive and export activity that existed in the agricultural sector was largely due to French settlers. French officials were naturally enough intent on safeguarding the livelihood of their compatriots. In a more general sense France wanted to protect its citizens and subjects in the Condominium. In the 1970s, some 3500 residents[65] enjoyed French citizenship or had opted for French-protected status. Most foreigners chose to join ranks with the French because they were considered more lenient concerning immigration, work, and use of Melanesian labour. French solicitude for its settlers and optants earned their loyalty – and sometimes excited the envy of other residents. According to Pierre Anthonioz, a former French Resident Commissioner:

'One can even say that the "mother hen" role of the Republic towards its nationals – the introduction of Vietnamese labour, indemnisation for [damages caused by] cyclones, subsidies during economic crises, etc. – encouraged English colonists to ask for French citizenship'.[66] French citizens and optants could claim French protection and play on French national pride. Like Higginson, they put themselves forward as representatives of French national interest. According to a French administrator, Yves Geslin: 'A settler who applied for a permit to recruit [labour] never failed to add a word about the necessity of maintaining French agriculture at an honourable level'. In a later period, just as at the time of the foundation of the SFNH, 'national interests and private interests more or less mingled'.[67]

Neither the value of agricultural production nor the number of French nationals in the New Hebrides represented a major stake in France's international policy. But the possible rivalry of Britons and Australians, the interests of New Caledonia's settlers in the archipelago and their feeling that the New Hebrides was an extension of New Caledonia helped justify continued control. Other reasons for the French desire to stay on have been suggested. For example the New Hebrides provided vital labour for New Caledonia in the 1960s.[68] The New Hebrides also might have been thought to provide 'a back-up base and agricultural reservoir' for New Caledonia.[69]

But the major rationale for opposition to independence was probably fear at what effect decolonisation would have on France's other South Pacific territories. A popular approach to international relations in the 1960s and 1970s was the 'domino theory'; generally applied to Southeast Asia, it argued that if Vietnam or another state became Communist, others would inevitably follow. *Mutatis mutandis*, in the South Pacific, independence for the New Hebrides might risk 'setting in motion a chain reaction'.[70] Officials in the British Residency felt that France wanted to keep the New Hebrides as a Condominium for as long as possible

> because there was no French policy at the time for the granting of independence at any foreseeable future point to New Caledonia or even French Polynesia, and we were quite sure that it was the view held by the French High Commissioner

and the French government that if one gave accelerated self-government to . . . the New Hebrides, that would weaken the position of France in New Caledonia and French Polynesia.[71]

From the early 1970s, precisely the time of the emergence of nationalist movements in the New Hebrides and increased British pressure for an evolution towards independence, echoes of Melanesian activism were heard in New Caledonia with the increased militancy of the Union Calédonienne, the first calls for independence and episodes of violence. Paris may well have wished to avoid encouragement to the New Caledonian independence movement from an independent New Hebrides, or even outright interference by a radical government in Port Vila.[72] French political concerns therefore outweighed the influence of the settler lobby in the New Hebrides or any real commercial benefits the Condominium provided France.

French policy in the New Hebrides in the 1960s was based on the assumption of staying put and putting off drastic political change, or immediate independence. The French Resident Commissioner in Port Vila in 1969 summarised the attitude pithily: 'a) The policy of the government: This is quite clear. My instructions from General de Gaulle were: "We stay". b) The policy of the French Residency: Simply to implement those instructions.'[73] In the background, undoubtedly, the French hoped various alternatives for the future of the New Hebrides might be considered. The French Resident Commissioner in the early 1970s, Robert Langlois, still affirmed that 'independence is not the only solution. There may be other forms', although he did not say exactly what these were.[74]

The impetus towards independence came from the Melanesian leaders of the VAP and the British administration. 'The idea that independence was ineluctable came first from the British side, principally under the influence of the missions', according to Anthonioz.[75] Some of the French apparently believed that independence was being promoted almost conspiratorially by officials in London anxious to rid Britain of a small imperial vestige, by Anglican and Presbyterian clergymen in the New Hebrides, Melanesian nationalists, Australians keen to increase Canberra's political and economic influence in the South Pacific and even by a group of 'Oxbridge' bureaucrats who dominated the British Residency in Port Vila.[76] Yet it is unlikely that a real 'conspiracy' existed any more on the British than on the French side.

Nevertheless, during the last two decades of the Condominium, Paris made efforts to shore up its position in the New Hebrides. French strategy, in addition to efforts on behalf of French citizens, took the form of support for Francophone islanders (especially in education) and stalling actions against British decolonisers. Recruiting Melanesian support was the major long-term activity. Few French schools had existed in the New Hebrides before the 1960s; in 1960, French schools enrolled only two thousand pupils, while there were eight thousand in English schools. In the early 1970s, one *lycée* and four French rural schools served the Condominium. Most education was in the hands of the missionaries, although Catholic teachers heretofore received little aid from the French government. The French and British then both stepped up spending on education to win influence and prepare élites for the eventual taking of power. The French established fifteen new state schools (with an enrolment of 1060 pupils) and extended aid to the mission schools. The French schools were often opened near already existing British state schools or Protestant missionary schools as well as in rural areas not served by educational institutions; the French district agents played a large role in securing the agreement of local populations. Yet the British and French attitudes towards islander education differed. The British charged fees (although, at $4 per child per year, these were nominal) and got local residents to donate labour and money for the construction of buildings. The French, by contrast, provided education free of charge, and the state paid for the building of schools and their operating expenses. The English used both vernacular languages and English, and employed New Hebrideans as teachers; the French provided instruction only in French and used largely expatriate teachers (mainly from New Caledonia). French teachers received salaries as much as twice those of British-recruited New Hebridean teachers. The English schools dispensed religious education and taught children agricultural techniques on small plots of land; the French state schools were rigorously secular, and education was more classical and centred on 'book-learning'.[77] The differences represented varying philosophies of education but also different aims. According to George Kalkoa, a Melanesian administrator in the service of the British who later became president of Vanuatu (when he assumed the chiefly appellation Ati George Sokomanu): 'The British are training the New Hebrideans to take on more responsibilities in the administration, but the French seem to concentrate on bringing up our children as little brown Frenchmen'.[78]

The French system was successful in providing high quality education to Melanesians, and by the end of the Condominium period, more New Hebrideans were enrolled in French than in British schools. Several prominent Melanesian politicians were products of the French system, notably Gérard Leymang. Born on the island of Malakula, his parents moved to Port Vila to work for the Catholic mission. After his education there, Leymang attended a seminary in New Caledonia, was ordained a priest in 1962, then studied at the University of Lyon. Leymang and most students, although not all of those who received a French education, supported the *Modérés* opposed to independence.

France and Britain also advanced Melanesians by appointing them to public service posts. But bureaucrats employed by the French received substantially higher salaries than their British counterparts. The French Resident Commissioner explained: 'French officers' salaries are based on metropolitan standard salaries . . . French law governing the conditions of employment for French officials or native officials working in the French Service are governed by one general code, so that in the French administration we can guarantee that a New Hebridean, with the same qualifications, will receive exactly the same salary as an official of metropolitan origin'.[79] In short, Melanesians working for the French not only received better salaries than those working for the British, and the same wages as European employees, but their pay scales were based on those in metropolitan France.[80]

French egalitarianism, which implied that Melanesians under French control received the same salaries, were given the same education and had the same civil status as Europeans, was particularly important for the *métis*, who, in addition, were eligible for citizenship. The British were unwilling to raise the salaries they paid to Melanesians to the French levels, nor could they persuade the French to set up a unified civil service. Such a situation helped promote French clientelism among the Melanesians, but probably excited the envy and hostility of those denied such benefits. Melanesians in the Condominium were aware that they gained various advantages from the rivalry of the two powers for their support and that some islanders had artificially high living standards induced by the 'welfare dependency' and 'benevolent paternalism' of the 1960s and 1970s.[81]

In private, the French were straightforward about the goals they hoped to accomplish. Mouradian, French Resident Commissioner in the late 1960s, wrote in a confidential report that the aim was to win support among the Melanesians, and he considered that the French effort was encountering some success: 'We are here to stay but . . . we now matter enough in the eyes of the people for them to want us to stay'. He continued: 'A further illustration of the impact of our efforts [in addition to support of investors] has been the material advantage of the French presence for the New Hebrideans. The highest salaries have been those paid by the French. . . . A knowledge of French is no longer merely access to the language of the "mastas": it is also and above all the key to the best-paid jobs'. Speaking of 'our need to concentrate on our new clientele of New Hebrideans undergoing Gallicisation by way of education', he recommended a vigilant attitude towards Francophone administrators: 'They should be supported, even if that involves a degree of prejudice in their favour, because they represent our participation in the Joint Administration at the executive levels. If they are supported, they will support our efforts'.[82]

French authorities realised that the unwieldy Condominium structure could work to their advantage, since it hindered British efforts to proceed more rapidly to independence. The British had advocated independence since 1965, Mouradian pointed out, and the British Residency 'still retains the political initiative and has been able to force us to play the independence game'. Yet 'in order to implant ourselves, the French Residency has not allowed unified structures to be created which could undermine our influence. It has refused to agree to the integration of the police forces, to the unification of laws and legal procedures, and above all to the extension of local councils and their integration'. Furthermore, 'We already have our education service, we have a divide between the two medical services, and we have deliberately rejected plans . . . for a joint hospital'.

The French could also stall political developments. The Condominium authorities had set up an Advisory Council in 1957, composed of both Melanesians and Europeans. In the 1960s, there was agitation from the British and Melanesians for the 'Adco' to be transformed into a Representative Assembly and in 1975 this was done. Yet, according to Mouradian, writing in 1969, 'Where political institutions are concerned, we have applied the brakes to the accelerating democratisation of the Advisory Council favoured by our partners'. France insisted that several members be elected from the French settler-dominated Chamber of Commerce and avoided universal suffrage for Melanesians. In the 1960s, when local councils were established, the French refused to let unitary councils be set up for larger islands, ostensibly because of the difficulty of communication between villages on larger islands, but in reality for fear that larger councils would amass power and allow islanders to exert undue pressure. Only the smallest islands, such as Anatom, with a population of a few hundred, had island-wide councils. In general, local councils were set up under British pressure, and the French provided minimal co-operation.[83]

The French also confronted land claims. Some land held by the French state was returned to Melanesian owners. In 1973, the French state purchased roughly half of the land held by the SFNH; much of this property, together with some other land owned by the French government, was ceded to New Hebrideans. (The share of land held by the SFNH and the French state fell from 30 per cent of the total area of the New Hebrides to just over 6 per cent.)[84] The French, however, resisted British attempts to set up a land commission to examine the question of property rights. Mouradian argued that he had dealt with claims individually to minimise confrontation and reduce support for those favouring large-scale land returns. Mouradian's successor, Robert Langlois, added: 'The French Residency tries to settle disputes case by case, sparing at the same time the interest and peace of mind of our nationals, as well as the aspirations of the natives it appears advisable to satisfy'.[85] The French district agents, just as their British counterparts, could gain advantages by arbitrating land disputes between Melanesians. Such disputes often dragged on for years, and aggrieved parties could play one district agent off against another. This underlined the dual nature of the Condominium administration, the importance of the land issue, and the possibility of jockeying for influence and gain by the French, British and Melanesians.[86]

The French, Mouradian admitted, looked favourably on approaches by investors from New Caledonia, as well as those of American speculators. 'I have supported the establishment here of American landowners whose presence means that we are no longer the only ones under attack', wrote Mouradian. The Resident Commissioner candidly reported: 'It is in a favourable context that the American phenomenon appears. . . . Briefly, if these investments extricate the SFNH from the ownership of their 70 000 hectares which are a burden . . . it would be a good thing. But evidently this new pressure became a risk through the substantial means at the Americans' disposal'. Mouradian also thought in 1969 that the purchases would be 'an opportunity on the one hand for allowing those French settlers who no longer have the wherewithal to develop their estates to sell them advantageously, and on the other hand for having others, not only Frenchmen, confronted by the natives, should they insist on using the land ownership question politically'.[87]

Land indeed became a critical issue, but the *rapprochement* between the French and Nagriamel in Santo provided an occasion for a tactical alliance. As early as 1969, Mouradian thought that 'it is preferable to complicate the problem of Santo to our advantage' and so was 'not at all against seeing Jimmy Stephens throw himself into the arms of the New Caledonian millionaire, Leconte'. Two years later, Langlois expressed disapproval of Stephens but recognised his value to the French:

Stephens' behaviour, his costly journeys, his mistresses (who are honoured in the movement's calendar as 'ladies who gave themselves to the cause'!) are giving the slow-thinking Melanesians doubts as to his integrity and the sincerity of his concern for the interests of his half-brothers by race. As for me, I am not in a hurry to see him disappear from the scene, as there is the danger of his being replaced by tougher, more sincere leaders who will not have the same weaknesses of greed, venality and knavery.

Langlois intimated longer-range benefits of Stephens' activities:

> Experience shows that his actions turn the wave of native demands away from the political goals which he could attain and leave the door open for European enterprise, provided that it is comprehensive. In that sense he could unwittingly help us to get through the few years necessary for fixing new frontiers of colonisation and for establishing it in a context of co-operation with the natives.[88]

In the 1970s, however, strategies of support for such unpalatable men as Peacock and Stephens became more difficult. In 1976, the French Resident Commissioner, Gauger, worried about the continued interference of the Americans in Santo. He was also concerned that if the French tried to pry Stephens away from 'his American protection . . . disappointed in his expectations, his sympathy may turn towards the National Party [the future Vanuaaku Party]'. He therefore counselled continued but guarded support for the Nagriamel movement. Now that the possibility of encouraging the parliamentary moderates existed, the French influenced coalition-building between the UCNH and the MANH. The Resident Commissioner also used government funds to provide jobs, undertake public works projects, and cede land in constituencies where the chances of pro-French candidates for election to the Representative Assembly could be improved. Even after the disappointing electoral results of the *Modérés*, Gauger in 1976 still thought that 'the UCNH is our surest and principal ally'.[89]

The confidential reports of the French Resident Commissioners are incomplete, and those from which the preceding quotations are taken became public only by accident. They do indicate, not unsurprisingly, that the French authorities worked with various individuals, movements and parties to buttress their position. However, the British acted little differently; such politicians as Alexis Yolou at the time complained of collusion between the British and the VAP. Furthermore, the French representatives in the New Hebrides might have expressed personal opinions in their reports which did not necessarily mirror official policy in Paris. Administrators, such as Robert in 1980, possibly acted largely on their own initiative.[90] Undoubtedly,

French policy evolved during the 1970s, and from 1977 Paris officially acceded to the plan for New Hebrides independence.

Evidence of French efforts to gain favour among Melanesians by education and employment, and French collaboration with particular individuals and groups to stall independence, should not obscure the fact that many Melanesians were fearful about independence, particularly under the control of the Vanuaaku Party. A third of the population was French-speaking, and a majority of children in the late 1970s studied in French schools, yet until 1979 the VAP proposed an independent state with English as the basic non-indigenous language and little room for French language, culture or education. About 15 per cent of Melanesians were Roman Catholics, and the VAP was dominated by Anglicans and Presbyterians. A new state under VAP leadership would be administratively centred on the island of Efate and islanders elsewhere (particularly those with strong local identities, as in Santo and Tanna) were uncomfortable at the domination by Port Vila. Although the VAP's leaders were neither Marxists nor wild-eyed radicals, many Melanesians regarded them as having leftist leanings and contacts with radical 'liberation groups' outside the country. In sum, enough New Hebrideans had serious reservations about a VAP-administered independence to cast their lot with the French.

If the French used Melanesians to further their own cause, the reverse was true as well. Whether collaborating with the French authorities or with individual Frenchmen, Melanesians skilfully mobilised support for their own concerns. As one chief on Tanna remarked: 'It is believed that we are supporters of Tony [Fornelli], but that's not true: *he* is *our* supporter: by coming to Tanna, he did not intend to promote himself but to promote Custom'[91] – a statement which may be taken at face value or which may indicate the possibility of duplicity. Stephens, far from being a simple-minded tool of foreign interests, showed himself able to manipulate American speculators, French administrators, European settlers and Melanesian defenders of 'custom'. Other politicians could also use their Francophone culture and French connections, as well as a variety of alliances, to advance their personal goals and careers, as the post-independence politics of Vanuatu would prove.

FRANCE AND VANUATU

Whatever the political machinations of the 1960s and 1970s, the French were evidently making concerted efforts to ensure the influence of Paris, French settlers and Francophone islanders in the future. Yet, in maladroitly and tardily attempting to develop support before independence, in seeming to stall the end of the Condominium, and in allowing the French state to be implicated in the Santo rebellion, France did not adequately prepare its post-independence role in Vanuatu. The French government was regarded as an adversary, if not outright villain, by the Vanuaaku Party and the leaders who took power in the new republic. The French and British Resident Commissioners stood side by side as their flags were lowered and the new flag of Vanuatu was raised in July 1980; the protocol that was punctiliously followed masked the compromised position of one of the former administering powers. France could now set itself only three objectives for its links with the new state: to watch over the security and the interests of French citizens in Vanuatu, to assure a strict application of the principle of non-interference in the affairs of a foreign state – that is, that Vanuatu not meddle in New Caledonia – and to promote the future of the Francophone minority.[92]

Relations between France and Vanuatu in the years following independence were unsettled. In 1980, over one hundred French nationals were forbidden to live in Vanuatu by the Lini government, and several dozen were formally deported; the notorious 'green letters' issued by the new government obliged any resident considered *persona non grata* to depart the country immediately. The French ambassador organised the departure of others who elected not to remain. Some 800 Frenchmen left Vanuatu – about 60 for French Guiana, 30 for French Polynesia, 40 for the *métropole* and the rest for New Caledonia. The French government provided funds to them and afterwards indemnified them for their losses.[93] The Vanuatu constitution limited land ownership to Melanesians, although it allowed long-term leases for others; this effectively dispossessed French landholders.[94] Prime Minister Lini, however, called for good relations between Vanuatu and France, and he stated that 'Vanuatu will be able to play a useful role in cementing relations between the French-speaking and English-speaking Pacific island states and territories'.[95] France offered aid to Vanuatu, and the Port Vila government acknowledged that such foreign assistance was necessary for economic development. In return for aid, the French listed a number of conditions: the possibility for dual French-ni-Vanuatu citizenship for French nationals, the establishment of a French consulate at Luganville, permission for a staff of thirty to be employed at the French embassy in Port Vila, authorisation for deported French nationals to return from Nouméa, non-interference by the government of Vanuatu in French internal affairs, and automatic long-term leases to planters whose land had been taken over at independence.[96]

These conditions were not met, but Paris nevertheless provided aid. But within months of independence, a crisis broke out. The French had granted visas to several ni-Vanuatu politicians to attend a meeting with pro-independence Melanesians in New Caledonia in February 1981. At the last moment, the visa of Barak Sope, Secretary-General of the Vanuaaku Party and First Secretary to the Prime Minister, was withdrawn, and he was denied entry into New Caledonia. Two days later, the Vanuatu government declared the French ambassador *persona non grata*; in retaliation, France broke off diplomatic relations with Vanuatu, recalled several French diplomats and aid workers and suspended discussions about future aid. The crisis blew over within a few weeks, partly because of French desire to ensure the functioning of French schools in Vanuatu. An aid agreement was signed at the beginning of March 1981, but a new French ambassador did not arrive until six months later. By that time, the election of François Mitterrand as President of France augured better relations. Vanuatu's ambassador-at-large, none other than Barak Sope, told the French president in June 1982, 'With deeper understanding, co-operation and friendship between our two peoples, France will always be assured that, far away in the South Pacific, Vanuatu is a friend and partner'. Mitterrand answered: 'The difficulties which surrounded your accession to independence and strained the relations between our two countries have been overcome'.[97]

Almost inevitably, minor quarrels erupted between Paris and Port Vila, for instance, conflict over the Matthew and Hunter Islands. These uninhabited volcanic islets lie between Vanuatu and New Caledonia. France had always claimed the islands, and in 1975 bronze plaques were affixed to the rocks affirming

French possession; France also included the islands within the territorial waters of New Caledonia. In 1983, Vanuatu sent a ship to plant the Vanuatu flag on the islands; it was accompanied by chiefs who claimed the disputed islands had traditionally been within their domains. The volcano on Hunter erupted during the visit, forcing the party to leave, although not before it had removed the French plaques. Two weeks later, French paratroopers arrived and built a heliport on Hunter, where they celebrated the 14 July holiday. The two countries by 1992 had not yet negotiated ownership, although the French claim appears legally stronger.

Other disagreements were indicative more of the repercussions of independence and a lingering suspicion about French designs rather than real confrontation. For example, in 1983, the Vanuatu government refused to allow the French ambassador in Port Vila to visit Malakula, noting that 'it is not normal practice for foreign diplomats to make such a visit as they wish rather than at the invitation of people or MPs on the islands'.[98] The government rejected the appointed of a permanent French consular official on Santo, saying that this 'runs the risk of being severely misunderstood by the population' and adding that 'unity and harmony must be restored to Santo'.[99] France proposed several development projects which a Vanuatu official greeted with reservations: 'The French proposals for aid looks [*sic*] too attractive. It has to be thought out very carefully. . . . We have to read between the lines'.[100] The Vanuatu Minister for Home Affairs complained shortly after independence about 'most disturbing reports from ni-Vanuatu living in New Caledonia that some of our people there have been threatened by their employers with loss of jobs. This has apparently occurred in the aftermath of the attainment of Independence by Vanuatu – the motive allegedly being vindictiveness'.[101]

Those who supported the French, and some who were members of the *Modérés*, claimed the VAP government allowed harassment or even torture of their opponents.[102] Leymang accused the VAP of a 'black colonialism' which, according to him, was worse than the white colonialism of the British and French; Vanuatu, by the late 1980s, he added, had become a 'banana republic' which 'has fallen under the stick of the Australians and New Zealanders'. The Francophone minority was being neglected by the government, and the French language was falling into disuse.[103] Internal political problems fuelled such criticism, and the controversy over New Caledonia inflamed passions and created new tensions between France and Vanuatu.

The Vanuaaku Party had established contacts with pro-independence parties in New Caledonia in the late 1970s, and Walter Lini became the major champion of the FLNKS and independence for New Caledonia. In the early 1980s, Lini's government supported the proposal for New Caledonian 'independence in association' with France. The failure of the plan and the hardening of the French position in 1986 and 1987 pushed Vanuatu to a more strident denunciation of French administration of New Caledonia and condemnation of the violence which had resulted in the deaths of prominent pro-independence leaders. Lini took the cause of the pro-independence movement to the United Nations, where the Vanuatu ambassador acted as a spokesman for the FLNKS in the General Assembly and before the Committee of Twenty-Four, which investigates questions of decolonisation; a representative of the FLNKS sat with the Vanuatu delegation in the General Assembly. Similarly, Lini promoted the setting up of the Melanesian Spearhead Group, which brought together the governments of Papua New Guinea, Solomon Islands and Vanuatu to combat the French position. Lini also regularly criticised French nuclear tests at Mururoa, and denounced the sinking of the *Rainbow Warrior* in 1985.[104]

Nevertheless, Vanuatu continued to accept aid from France, although aid was reduced because of Vanuatu's hostile position on New Caledonia. Lini maintained his country's membership in the international Francophone organisation, the Association de Coopération Culturelle et Technique, and he personally attended the summit conference of Francophone nations in Paris in 1986. Soon afterwards, however, relations between Paris and Port Vila worsened. Lini's right-hand man, Barak Sope, padlocked the French embassy in Port Vila, and the French ambassador was expelled from Vanuatu. Lini charged that the French had been interfering in domestic politics in Vanuatu by providing funds and assistance to the coalition of parties which formed the official opposition to his government, the Union des Partis Modérés (UPM), led by the Francophone Melanesians Vincent Boulékoné (a lawyer trained at the University of Bordeaux) and Maxime Carlot (who had been an official in the

French administration under the Condominium). Paris retaliated by suspending aid.[105]

Relations once again improved with the signing of the Matignon Accord on New Caledonia in 1988. At the end of that year domestic politics in Vanuatu sparked an alliance of the Francophone leaders, Boulékoné and Carlot, with their old opponent, Sope. In a move against their stance, Lini had the UPM deputies suspended from the Vanuatu parliament. In co-operation with the President of Vanuatu, Ati George Sokomanu, the rebels then tried to topple Lini, himself weakened by diminishing support and the physical effects of a stroke. The president dismissed Lini and swore in an interim government, including Sope, Carlot and Boulékoné as ministers. Lini then went on the offensive by having Sokomanu and the members of the interim government arrested. He thereby maintained power and proceeded to have the rebels brought to trial. Almost all were convicted of an attempted *coup d'état* and sentenced to varying prison terms; a higher court overturned the verdict in 1989, freeing the prisoners. During the affair, there were occasional, but unproven, hints of French involvement.[106]

Although most of the French planters left the New Hebrides, certain French trading and commercial interests have remained. Between 1000 and 1500 French citizens reside in Vanuatu, although double citizenship is not permitted. The French citizens include a number of elderly planters, as well as Vietnamese and Wallisians who work as shopkeepers or labourers, respectively, and *métis* who retained French citizenship after 1980. In addition, there are 80–100 French aid workers in Vanuatu, mostly on Efate or Santo.[107] The French have given particular aid to research on coconut oils (through the Institut des Huiles et Oléagineux) and to education. Some 40 per cent of Vanuatu's population is now Francophone, and there are French language state schools, supported by funds from Paris, on Efate, Santo, Pentecost, Malakula and Tanna; there are also French Catholic and Protestant schools. (A handful of students receive French scholarships to continue their studies in France.) Most teachers in French-language schools in the early 1980s were French, but their number has dropped both because of the training of ni-Vanuatu staff and because of the sometimes difficult relations between Paris and Port Vila. (In the mid-1980s, when relations were at a nadir, Tunisian teachers largely replaced French instructors in Vanuatu schools.[108]) Vanuatu retains three official languages, all of which are used in official publications and on Radio Vanuatu.

The French presence in Vanuatu remains strong. The French embassy is one of the dominant buildings on Vanuatu's major street, Kumul Highway (previously, the Rue Higginson). There are French cafés and shops with neighbouring Anglo–Australian establishments; Port Vila's two major vendors are still the Australian Burns Philp store and the New Caledonian firm Barrau; the town has an English chemist and a French *pharmacie*. The two main airlines serving the capital are Air Calédonie and Air Vanuatu, the latter owned and operated by an Australian company. Two of the best known figures in Port Vila are a French Wallisian artist, Alois Pilioko – perhaps the most significant of all Oceanic artists – and his colleague, a Franco-Russian designer named Nicholas Michoutouchkine. The heritage of the Condominium, and the cross-currents of the colonial era, have not disappeared from Vanuatu.

7 The Crisis in New Caledonia in the 1980s

Soon after the difficult French withdrawal from Vanuatu, problems increased in New Caledonia. The two developments were not unconnected, as Melanesian nationalists in New Caledonia were buoyed by the successful struggle for independence in the New Hebrides, and the new government in Port Vila encouraged their aspirations; yet the lack of dexterity displayed by Paris in handling the accession of the Condominium to independence, even amounting to outright opposition, gave a clear indication of what France's attitude towards a similar effort in New Caledonia might be. The 1980s witnessed extraordinary confrontations in New Caledonia, marked by hostage-taking, blockades and assassinations which seemed more reminiscent of the colonial wars in Indochina and Algeria in the 1950s than of the 'Pacific way of life' and peaceful cutting of ties between Oceanic colonies and their administering powers in the 1960s and 1970s. Almost a decade of political turmoil ensued before a truce was called and a moratorium on struggles for or against independence was declared.

The events of the 1980s brought upheaval to New Caledonia and became topics of intense debate in France, in the Pacific territories and in other countries. Political parties, ideologues, activists and the media used New Caledonia to wage war against their opponents in France just as the various factions were battling 'on the ground' in New Caledonia. The troubles provided clear reflections of French domestic problems and concerns, revealing the capacity and willingness of French institutions to safeguard perceived national interests and demonstrating the variety of strategies which French authorities, as well as those who contested them, could employ to further their ends.

This chapter will examine in brief the developments of the 1980s in New Caledonia and then turn to the issues and intentions lying behind these events.[1]

THE EVENTS OF THE 1980S

In August 1980, the month after the independence of Vanuatu, the eleventh congress of the Union Calédonienne called for the independence of New Caledonia within two years' time.[2] The French government made no reply, but, in the closing months of the administration of President Giscard d'Estaing pursued its plan for economic development and land reform in the territory. The national elections scheduled for May 1981 indicated that a change in policy might eventuate. If Giscard were re-elected, the status quo would probably continue, whereas if the Socialist Party under the leadership of François Mitterrand came to power, a reorientation of policy might be in the offing. In 1979, the Parti Socialiste (PS) had announced its support of the goals of the Front Indépendantiste, which had also gained the backing of Mitterrand's election allies, the French Communist Party. Although Mitterrand and the Socialists won only thirty-five per cent of the votes cast in New Caledonia, their election bid was successful in the *métropole*, and Mitterrand succeeded Giscard as head of state. In the legislative elections which followed the presidential elections, Jacques Lafleur and Roch Pidjot, representing the anti- and pro-independence movements respectively, were re-elected to New Caledonia's seats in the French National Assembly.

On his first official visit to New Caledonia as the new Secretary of State for the DOM-TOMs, in August 1981, Henri Emmanuelli denounced the colonial character of New Caledonia; during the same month, a delegation from the independence movement won the support of the South Pacific Forum for their goal of sovereignty. But overshadowing these developments was the assassination, on 19 September, of Pierre Declercq, the secretary-general of the Union Calédonienne and president of the Front Indépendantiste group in the Territorial Assembly. A teacher by profession, Declercq was a European who had been a longtime member of the UC. The 'white Kanak', one of the rare Europeans in the territory to cast his lot with the islanders, was despised by opponents of independence; responsibility for his assassination has never been decisively proven, nor those who committed the act brought to justice, but the killing of Declercq was almost certainly political.[3] It served as a warning about the possible escalation of violence and provided another hero for Melanesian *indépendantistes*.

The goals of the UC, in which Eloi Machoro succeeded Declercq as secretary-general, did not change, nor did the assassination ignite an explosion in New Caledonia. The following year was punctuated by congresses of the various, and by now numerous, political parties in New Caledonia; at the meeting of the UC, its executive set 24 September 1982 as the date for a unilateral declaration of independence unless the French government had begun negotiations for a change in New Caledonia's status. The entry into local political life of the Union des Syndicats des Travailleurs Kanak et Exploités (USTKE), whose slogan was 'No Kanak Independence without Socialism, No Socialism without Kanak Independence', further widened the Melanesian struggle in 1982. Attention focused, however, on parliamentary activities. The *indépendantistes* in 1982 agreed upon an alliance with a small centrist party (most of whose members were European New Caledonians), the FNSC, and together they formed a majority in the Territorial Assembly. Jean-Marie Tjibaou, the Melanesian head of the Front Indépendantiste, won election as vice-president of the territorial government – the highest elected office in New Caledonia since the French High Commissioner was *ex officio* president of the Assembly. For the first time, an avowed advocate of independence, supported by both Melanesian and European *conseilleurs du gouvernement*, was now in a favoured position to negotiate with a French administration not unsympathetic to his aims. Reaction was swift, if episodic: a right-wing commando group attacked and briefly occupied the Territorial Assembly, while Jacques Lafleur resigned his position as *député*, although he was soon re-elected in balloting from which Melanesians largely abstained.

In 1983, Paris tried to effect a reconciliation of the different groups by organising a round table meeting of Tjibaou, Lafleur and other prominent political leaders, along with French officials, at Nainville-les-Roches. The communiqué published at the end of the conference was signed by the Front Indépendantiste and the FNSC, but the anti-*indépendantistes*, although they had participated in its formulation, withheld their signatures. The three paragraphs of the declaration set down the principles of the Mitterrand government and, authorities hoped, provided a consensus for action. First, the document expressed the 'shared will of the participants to see the confirmation of the definitive abolition of the colonial state of affairs [*fait colonial*] by the recognition of the equality of Melanesian civilisation and the manifestation of its representativity through *coutume* in institutions which will be set up'. Secondly, and most importantly, the document pronounced a 'recognition of the legitimacy of the Kanak people, the first inhabitants of the territory, seeing in this an innate and active right to independence, the exercise of which must be done in the context of the self-determination foreshadowed by and defined by the Constitution of the French Republic, self-determination which for historical reasons must also be open to the other ethnic groups whose legitimacy is recognised by the representatives of the Kanak people'. Thirdly, the declaration announced the government's intention to grant internal autonomy to New Caledonia as a transitional measure towards an ultimate choice of future status 'including independence'.[4] The *indépendantistes* considered the Nainville-les-Roches agreement at least a symbolic victory, particularly because of the recognition of the historical legitimacy of Melanesian rights in the territory and their right to choose independence; for these very reasons, the RPCR and other anti-independence parties rejected the declaration.

Along with negotiating the Nainville-les-Roches agreement, the government also formulated a new statute for New Caledonia. The Lemoine statute, named after the Secretary of State for the DOM-TOMs who had replaced Emmanuelli, allowed the election of the president of the territorial government by the Territorial Assembly and thus reduced the powers of the French High Commissioner. Lemoine also planned the setting up of six regional councils of Melanesians (to include, as well, representatives of social and economic interest groups) in New Caledonia. The plan fitted into the Mitterrand government's efforts at administrative decentralisation throughout France. The *indépendantistes* opposed the proposal, arguing that it did not address the central issues of decolonisation and the place of Melanesians in New Caledonia and that it would allow power to devolve to an anti-*indépendantiste* majority. The government's reiteration that it saw the autonomy statute as only a transitional measure leading to a later expression of self-determination failed to satisfy the *indépendantistes*.

The second half of 1983 and the early months of the following year saw periodic demonstrations, often coinciding with visits of French ministers, as well as a number of outbursts of violence around New Caledonia. Yet other political forces emerged, including the far right wing Front National set up in 1984, and the Libération Kanak Socialiste, which seceded from the Front Indépendantiste but maintained its pro-independence position. The *indépendantistes* multiplied contacts with potential supporters overseas, including the governments of the Soviet Union, Libya and Cuba; although such links were superficial, they provoked the fury of anti-*indépendantistes* and concern in Paris. Elections for representatives to the European Parliament were held in June 1984; in voting in New Caledonia – which as an overseas territory of France was allowed to take part – Melanesians sympathetic to the *indépendantistes* staged a boycott, and most other Melanesians did not bother to vote for parliamentarians whose work seemed of little immediate relevance to them. Three-quarters of those who did vote cast their ballots for conservative candidates, compared with less than half who voted in that way in the *métropole*, an indication of the increasingly polarised political situation in New Caledonia.[5]

The next elections in New Caledonia, scheduled for November 1984, were for members of the Territorial Assembly. This event provided the occasion for a regrouping of the *indépendantiste* forces. In September the Front de Libération Nationale Kanak et Socialiste (FLNKS) was formed, grouping together the UC, FULK, Palika, UPM, the USTKE and a women's group. The charter of the FLNKS, 'drafted for a limited period: the period of the national liberation struggle, a transition preparing for Kanak socialist independence', outlined the coalition's goals and rationale. It charged that 'the French government is complicit in the colonial process that it perpetuates', that President Mitterrand 'has not kept his promises' and that the Nainville-les-Roches principles 'have not been put into practice'; it rejected the Lemoine statute and criticised 'capitalist and imperialist exploitation . . . in our country for the profit of colonial France and its allies', as well as the French policy of immigration to the territory and French 'judiciary and military provisions to repress the forces working towards Kanak socialist independence'. The charter affirmed the existence of the Kanak people endowed with 'legitimate and inalienable rights' to recognition, dignity and liberty, self-determination and exercise of sovereignty, the return of land and the means to pursue economic development. The charter also affirmed 'the custom of welcoming non-Kanaks' and made an appeal to them: 'They must recognise the sovereignty of the Kanak people and support their liberation struggle and contribute to its success. Only [this] . . . will guarantee their future citizenship in an independent socialist Kanak nation'.[6] The FLNKS also decided to break off official contacts with French authorities, to withdraw from participation in French institutions and to mount an 'active' boycott of the November elections.

The elections in November crystallised political sentiment in New Caledonia and brought the territory to the attention of the French and world media. The vast majority of Melanesians boycotted the voting; 41 of the 107 polling booths, all in Melanesian areas, simply did not open. Activists tried to persuade other Melanesians – sometimes by strong-arm methods, their opponents charged – not to cast ballots, and in an act relayed around the world by newspaper photographs, Eloi Machoro used an axe to smash open a ballot-box; this was considered 'a symbol and substance of the independence struggle and a measure of French humiliation'.[7] Anti-*indépendantistes* characterised the FLNKS as a minority leading a terrorist campaign, especially as the period of the election and the weeks afterwards saw increased Melanesian protest actions. Several captives were taken, roads blockaded, *gendarmeries* occupied and houses burned. The centre of Melanesian resistance was Thio, on the east coast of the Grande Terre; a major mining town, Thio had a largely Melanesian population but a strongly anti-independence European mayor. FLNKS activists blockaded the roads to Thio and other villages on the east coast and virtually sealed off this part of the island from French control. The Kanak flag flew over areas guarded by muscular young *militants*, armed with a variety of weapons, and a FLNKS congress held immediately after the November election set up a 'provisional government' for Kanaky with Tjibaou as president and Machoro as minister for security. The election of Dick Ukeiwé, the Melanesian RPCR senator, as head of a rump Territorial

Assembly consisting only of opponents of independence seemed largely irrelevant.

A month after the election President Mitterrand dispatched a new High Commissioner and personal representative to New Caledonia, Edgard Pisani. A senior administrator, Pisani had once been French Minister of Agriculture and more recently a Commissioner of the European Community, holding the port-folio concerned with relations between Europe and developing regions; with such credentials, and as a close personal associate of Mitterrand, he seemed in a good position to negotiate a solution to the New Caledonian stalemate. His initial overtures to the FLNKS were tentatively welcomed, but the RPCR and Caldoches were hostile to Pisani from the outset. Meanwhile, violence escalated, as Tjibaou's house was bombed and Ukeiwé's house burned. Bloody violence occurred on the night of 5 December 1984, when a group of Europeans and *métis* ambushed sixteen *indépendantistes* on the road from Hienghène, where they had attended an FLNKS meeting, to their own village, Tiendanite. Ten men, including two of Tjibaou's broth-ers, were killed and others seriously injured. Surmounting his personal grief, Tjibaou called for calm and rejected reprisals; those arrested for the killings quickly became heroes for the anti-*indépendantistes*. President Mitterrand offered his condo-lences to the families of the victims, while Caldoches set up a support fund for the imprisoned assassins. Although the FLNKS lifted its barricades in Thio, sporadic violence continued and tensions remained at breaking point, aggravated by extremely polemical newspaper reports and the graffiti which covered New Caledonia's buildings.

In such unpromising circumstances, Pisani drew up and, in January 1985, presented his plan for New Caledonia. Pisani tried to reconcile French national interests with the aims of both Kanaks and Caldoches, but his proposal was generally seen as being partial to the FLNKS since he envisaged inde-pendence for New Caledonia. In Pisani's timetable, a referen-dum on independence would be held in July 1985; if it proved favourable, an option Pisani clearly supported, New Caledonia would sign a treaty of association with France and independ-ence would officially be proclaimed in January 1986. The pro-posal for 'independence-in-association' intended that France would maintain close ties and provide significant aid for a nominally sovereign but multi-racial state. The arrangements for France to hold responsibility for foreign relations and security, and provisions for non-nationals of the new state to live and work there, were intended to reassure Europeans and to maintain France's strategic presence in the territory, while the granting of sovereignty was designed to meet the FLNKS' demand for independence.[8] Perhaps not surprisingly, the Pisani plan failed to satisfy any of the different groups in New Caledonia. The *indépendantistes* were not satisfied with an offer of less than total independence and feared the continued domination of New Caledonia by French neo-colonial or settler interests; the anti-*indépendantistes* were even more vocal in condemning Pisani for what they saw as a sell-out, little less than treason.

Almost immediately after Pisani presented his proposals, another wave of violence afflicted New Caledonia. A European teenager, Yves Tual, was killed by Melanesians, which set off rioting, looting and arson by anti-*indépendantistes* during a night in which Nouméa seemed to have become a battlefield. Just a day later, French policemen ambushed a farmhouse near La Foa, in which Machoro and thirty-five other Melanesians, including another FLNKS leader, Marcel Nonaro, were staying. Machoro and Nonaro were killed in the raid. Some observers testified that the FLNKS leaders were shot by police after they had emerged from the house to bargain with the authorities, while others argued that the police had opened fire in defence when armed Melanesians threatened them. The ambivalence of the authorities was highlighted when it was revealed that the French High Commissioner had approved an order to 'neutralise' Machoro, who was considered the most obdurate and perhaps the most powerful of the *indépendantiste* leaders. Differing reports and interpretations about the event filled the columns of papers in both New Caledonia and France; Pisani declared a state of emergency with a dusk-to-dawn curfew in New Caledonia and military forces in the territory were strengthened. The FLNKS broke off negotiations with French officials, and Pisani's plan was obviously doomed. New Caledonia seemed on the brink of civil war. A surprise visit by President Mitterrand to the territory, during which he met with the FLNKS leadership, only partially restored calm; less than a day after his departure, saboteurs attacked the Thio nickel mines, which had been scheduled to reopen.

Intransigence characterised the positions of the FLNKS and RPCR throughout 1985. The *indépendantistes* proceeded with plans to destabilise New Caledonia and to establish a degree of Melanesian autonomy inside the territory by opening alternative schools and trying to organise alternative systems of agricultural production and marketing. The anti-*indépendantistes*, especially the far right, also remained active, organising demonstrations and setting up a settlers' militia. The French government, meanwhile, designed another plan for New Caledonia, this one taking its name from the French Prime Minister, Laurent Fabius. The Fabius Plan divided New Caledonia into four 'regions', each with its own elected council, the members of which, meeting together, would serve as the congress of the territory. The congress would have little power, and each of the regions was to deal directly with Paris and with the French High Commissioner and administration. The demarcation of the territory, into northern, central and southern regions plus the Loyalty Islands, was controversial since the drawing of the boundaries implied that pro-independence Melanesians would win control of two, and possibly three, districts; this indeed proved to be the case, and only Nouméa and the south was left as a stronghold of the RPCR and Caldoches. The result underlined the separation between the city of Nouméa, where economic and political power was concentrated, and the largely Melanesian *brousse*. But the Fabius Plan at least allowed a degree of local autonomy, and both the RPCR and the FLNKS agreed to participate in the new regional institutions even if neither group expressed enthusiasm about the arrangement. Voting largely followed ethnic lines in the September elections. France now recalled Pisani to Paris, where he was given a titular position as Minister for New Caledonia, and a High Commissioner with a lower profile replaced him in Nouméa.

The months after the 1985 regional elections provided a period of relative calm in New Caledonia although every move by the French administration, the FLNKS or the RPCR sparked intense debate and sometimes more direct political action. Paris poured money into the FLNKS-dominated regions (as well as into Nouméa) for economic development and advancement of Melanesians in the administration, and the Office

Foncier made an effort to buy land from settlers and return the properties to Melanesian clans or the public domain. The RPCR and settlers roundly objected to this policy, and to what they considered the general favouritism accorded the Melanesians by Paris. Some Kanaks felt that the government was making an attempt to buy their support and to develop a third political force as an alternative to the FLNKS and RPCR. The FLNKS' goal never wavered from its aim of eventual independence, nor did the determination of the RPCR to oppose such a development.

Elections to the French National Assembly in March 1986 bore directly on the future of New Caledonia. The Socialist Party and government had been losing support in France and faced a stiff challenge from the conservative RPR and its ally, the UDF. Heading the right-wing alliance was Jacques Chirac, former prime minister under Giscard, mayor of Paris and strong supporter of Jacques Lafleur's RPCR in New Caledonia. The Socialists, although still favourable to Melanesian interests, were in an awkward position as the party in power and could hardly lend direct support to the FLNKS (even if they had wanted to do so). For the first time, New Caledonia became an issue in French elections. Mitterrand and Fabius pointed to the relative smoothness with which the new regional councils were operating and the present lack of violence. Chirac, by contrast, accused the Socialists of bowing to *indépendantistes* and not defending loyalist French citizens in New Caledonia. In the voting, the RPR–UDF coalition won a narrow victory over the Socialists, and Mitterrand was forced to name Chirac as prime minister. (In New Caledonia, the FLNKS boycotted the elections, and a coalition of the RPCR and Front National won almost nine-tenths of the remaining votes cast.) From 1986 to 1988, government in France was exercised with the *cohabitation* of a Socialist president and a neo-Gaullist prime minister; in day-to-day matters Mitterrand usually deferred to Chirac. New Caledonia was in the hands of the Minister for the DOM-TOMs, Bernard Pons, also head of the RPR and a close colleague of Chirac.

Chirac and Pons acted quickly to put electoral promises into effect. The government announced it would hold a referendum in September 1987 on whether New Caledonia should remain a French territory. All residents, even those of only several years' standing, would be eligible to vote. Chirac abolished the Office Foncier, although continuing government purchase of land (some of which, however, was now distributed to settlers) and transformed the Office Culturel Kanak into a more general department of Oceanic cultures. Funds for the regional councils were effectively frozen, and more powers were given to the RPCR-controlled Territorial Congress. The French military presence in New Caledonia was greatly reinforced, and groups of soldiers were sent around the countryside (ostensibly to help in development projects) in a policy of military *nomadisation* which heightened tensions. Chirac and Pons flaunted their support for the RPCR and, on their visits to New Caledonia, pointedly refused to speak of Melanesian grievances or concerns. The government adopted legislation to change the electoral boundaries of the regions; over strong opposition from the FLNKS, the Pons plan divided New Caledonia into three new regions, two of which were likely to be dominated by anti-*indépendantistes*. After a year and a half of uneasy quiet enforced by thousands of French policemen and soldiers in New Caledonia, the referendum was held on schedule in September 1987. The FLNKS boycotted the referendum, and the remaining voters – the participation rate was less than half the territory's total qualified voters – overwhelmingly supported the maintenance of New Caledonia's ties with France; Chirac and Pons claimed a victory, despite the high rate of abstention, and pressed on with formulation of the Pons statute. Voting for the revised regional councils was scheduled for April 1988. The FLNKS labelled the referendum a farce.

Two years of *cohabitation* had not staunched independence fervour among Melanesians – Pons' tactics, in fact, may have increased the determination of the FLNKS. The *indépendantistes* had now garnered support for their cause from various overseas organisations, such as the South Pacific Forum and the United Nations' Committee on Decolonisation, as well as from non-governmental bodies. Only several small parties in France, and a host of private citizens and groups, championed its cause in the *métropole*, and the independence movement could not match its opponents for finance, resources or the support of larger parties. The FLNKS admitted that it neither could nor wanted to mount a guerrilla war against France. Chirac's efforts had created a triumphalist anti-independence RPCR, and the might of the French military was buttressed by private militias of Caldoches and the Wallisians and Futunans they recruited. The French president, obviously frustrated at the policies of his prime minister, kept his distance but did little to mould those policies; the Socialist Party merely campaigned to change direction again if it were returned to office in the parliamentary elections.

Events in New Caledonia reached a new level of violence in 1988. The Chirac government, having already alienated the *indépendantistes* and cast its full support behind the RPCR, set the date for local elections (for the councils of the redrawn regions set up under the Pons plan) for 24 April, the same day as the first round of voting in French presidential elections. The FLNKS viewed this as outright provocation, an attempt to overshadow the New Caledonian question by the national ballot and an effort to use New Caledonia to improve the RPR's election chances in France. The FLNKS had already announced that it would not participate in the elections and had hinted at a more militant type of boycott; however, it had not agreed upon a strategy. The pro-independence *comité de lutte*, or struggle committee, on the Loyalty Island of Ouvéa, a Melanesian *réserve*, decided on direct action, although whether the central administration of the FLNKS was aware, or gave its approval, remains uncertain. On Friday, 22 April, four Kanaks, led by a UC activist, attacked the *gendarmerie* in Fayaoué, a village in the south of Ouvéa. Their intention was to neutralise the *gendarmes* and occupy the premises. A scuffle ensued, and a policeman fired on the Kanaks, wounding one of them – the first blood spilled in the incident belonged to a Melanesian. The fracas escalated; the Kanaks killed three *gendarmes* and took the other twenty-seven hostage. (Subsequently a fourth *gendarme*, who had been wounded, also died.) The hostages were secretly taken to a cave in the north of Ouvéa, at Gossanah, and sequestered there.

The FLNKS, accepting responsibility for the action, said that the hostages would not be released until French military forces were removed from the island, the regional elections scheduled for 24 April were postponed and the President of the Republic named a mediator in the dispute. The Chirac government announced that it would not negotiate, directed the military commander in New Caledonia to take charge of an operation to rescue the hostages and flew several hundred more soldiers to Ouvéa. Meanwhile, the elections took place; the regional elections, boycotted by most Melanesians, produced results favourable to the RPCR in New Caledonia, while in the national elections the PS's vote totals surpassed those of the RPR and the UDF in the *métropole*. By now, wild rumours circulated in New Caledonia and France. An especially potent one, although untrue, held that the *gendarmes* had been killed by axes and hatchets, a rumour which resurrected notions held by some on the extreme right about the savagery of Melanesians. Other rumours spread that the law and order forces in Ouvéa were using strong-arm tactics, if not torture, on Melanesians in attempts to extract information about the hostage-taking. Subsequent testimony indeed reported long interrogations, verbal harassment, physical attacks and the use of electric shocks; one elderly Melanesian died of a heart attack after being questioned.

Some attempts were made to negotiate. The hostage-takers, led by a young Kanak named Alphonse Dianou, agreed to talk with an emissary sent by the military, Captain Legorjus, and the FLNKS proposed one of its members, Frank Wahuzué, as mediator. Later, several religious figures, unsuccessfully, offered their services as arbitrators. Three RPCR politicians volunteered to take the place of the hostages, a proposal which was rejected. The crisis dragged on as the new territorial Congress, with no *indépendantiste* representatives, was duly installed in New Caledonia, and the date for the second round of French parliamentary voting approached. Isolated incidents of violence continued to take place in New Caledonia: two young Melanesians were killed on the Grande Terre, as well as one of those implicated (but never convicted) in the Hienghène massacre. The government in Paris increased pressure, both in terms of military presence and rhetoric. Bernard Pons threatened to outlaw the FLNKS, characterised Dianou as a 'sort of holy fool' and promised to resolve the situation with 'firmness and reason'. President Mitterrand maintained his distance from the hardline positions in the days immediately preceding the second round of voting. Tension remained extremely high, rumours continued to circulate and the outside world was presented with a spectacle of hostages and violence rarely seen in either the South Pacific or France.

On 5 May, French military forces attacked the cave at Gossanah where the hostages were held. 'Operation Victor' lasted all morning and ended with the safe release of the hostages but the deaths of nineteen Kanaks. Military forces had stormed the cave, and gun battles ensued (including the firing of weapons that Legorjus' deputy had smuggled in to the hostages). Chirac and Pons saluted the military 'victory' and congratulated the soldiers involved, yet President Mitterrand expressed his concern about the manner in which the conflict had been resolved, and the FLNKS spoke of a 'colonial butchery'. Later revelations in the press, particularly the investigations of journalists from *Le Monde*, cast great doubt on the official version of events. In particular, conclusive proof was offered that several of the Kanaks who had been killed, including Alphonse Dianou and Wenceslas Lavelloi, had been killed *after* they had surrendered. Testimony from various sources showed that if they had not been summarily executed by French soldiers, at least military personnel had been negligent in their treatment of the wounded Dianou (for example, by removing an intravenous drip from the man's arm, treating him roughly and subjecting him to a particularly arduous evacuation from the cave); in the case of Lavelloi, a Kanak messenger who had brought food to the cave for both the hostage-takers and the hostages, evidence pointed to direct execution after the siege ended. In the second round of voting on 8 May, Mitterrand was re-elected president, and the Socialists also won the parliamentary elections which followed.

The blood-letting at Fayaoué and Gossanah posed great questions for all sides about the strategies employed by pro- and anti-independence groups, the use of New Caledonia for electoral purposes in France, the role of such institutions as the French army in New Caledonia and the responsibilities borne by particular leaders. An independent commission of inquiry, sponsored by French human rights groups and headed by an admiral, was highly critical of the decision of the Chirac government to storm the cave, as well as the hardline and provocative rhetoric of Chirac and Pons and the behaviour of army units on Ouvéa; the commission also faulted the official version of events and even the reports relayed back from Ouvéa at the time and given to Mitterrand. The President of the Republic, it seemed, had given his general approval for rescue of the hostages but on condition that violence be kept to an absolute minimum; he was not involved in planning the action and expressed his grief at the deaths which resulted. The hope of the RPCR leaders to use the hostage-freeing to win votes did not work, as the Chirac government lost office: the strong-armed and avowedly partisan approach followed by Chirac and Pons since 1986 had not ended a cycle of violence, nor had it broken the independence movement or definitively assured that New Caledonia would remain French.

Ironically, the deaths of two dozen Frenchmen and Melanesians, however, opened the way for new efforts at conciliation. The blood-letting in Ouvéa, and the return of the Socialists to government with a new parliamentary majority, shocked the opposing forces in New Caledonia into negotiating an agreement. The Matignon Accord, signed in mid-1988, was worked out between the French prime minister, Michel Rocard, and the leaders of the RPCR and FLNKS, Lafleur and Tjibaou. For the first time in several years, there seemed a broad scope for agreement on short-term and medium-term plans for New Caledonia, and newspapers printed photos of Lafleur and Tjibaou shaking hands and chatting in the French prime minister's office and back in Nouméa, a decidedly different image of New Caledonia after months of unprecedented violence. There was dissension in both the FLNKS and the RPCR about accepting the Accord, as well as criticism from outside, but both leaders persuaded their followers to support the agreement. The French government also organised a referendum, this time held in both New Caledonia and in the *métropole* in October 1988, to ratify the Matignon Accord; in this ballot, only several small political groups staged a boycott, and the plan was overwhelmingly approved. The Matignon Accord remains in force in New Caledonia.

The Matignon Accord and the auxiliary measures known as the Rocard Plan called for direct rule of New Caledonia by the French High Commissioner for one year from 14 July 1988. During this period, a massive injection of finance into the territory targeted development projects, the training of Melanesians for the public service and the rebuilding of the territory's infrastructure. In March 1989, elections were held for new local councils. The old 'regions' – in both the Fabius and Pons version – were replaced by three new 'provinces' in the south, centre and east. The councillors, elected for a six year term, took office in July 1989 and, meeting together, acted as a Territorial Assembly. The provinces enjoy a large measure of autonomy and are able to treat directly with the High Commissioner and officials in Paris. Finally, the Rocard Plan foreshadowed a definitive referendum on the future of New Caledonia, to be held in 1998.

From mid-1988 New Caledonia seemed in the process of recovery, as the economy was stimulated by government investment and by rising prices for nickel; new buildings mushroomed around the island, tourism picked up and Melanesians were increasingly appointed to jobs in the administration. Elections were duly held, and Melanesians won control of the central and northern provinces. Yet one tragic incident marked the history of the territory after the signature of the Matignon Accord, the assassination of Jean-Marie Tjibaou and another prominent FLNKS leader, Yeiwené Yeiwené. In May 1989, on the anniversary of the incident at Gossanah and the death of the Melanesian activists, Tjibaou and Yeiwené went to Ouvéa for a ceremony of commemoration. A Melanesian shot the two leaders dead, despite the presence of security guards and a crowd of onlookers. The assassin, a young FLNKS member who had stated his opposition to the Matignon Accord and who had other differences with the FLNKS leadership, was arrested and convicted of the murders. Tjibaou and Yeiwené's funeral was attended by the French prime minister, most political leaders of New Caledonia (including the head of the RCPR) and thousands of mourners who paid homage to their efforts to build an independence movement and to foster a sense of identity and historical legitimacy among Melanesians. The French government subsequently decided to build a cultural centre in memory of Tjibaou.

Since 1981, the FLNKS had suffered the deaths of all its prominent leaders – including Declerq, Machoro, Tjibaou and Yeiwené. The new head of the FLNKS, Paul Néaoutyne, was the first to come from outside the UC, always the main party in the coalition. Inheriting Tjibaou's mantle as head of the UC was François Burck, a comrade of the assassinated leaders. Both the UC and the FLNKS have maintained their commitment to independence, at least in principle, but the leaders, especially Burck, have since begun to speak about some variation of absolute and total independence and referred to continuing 'interdependence' between France and New Caledonia. The elections to the provincial councils in 1995 and the referendum in 1998 will test the political climate in New Caledonia, but events either in the territory or in France itself could change the political equation.

INTERPRETING THE CRISIS: NAMES AND SYMBOLS

A full understanding of the crisis in New Caledonia in the 1980s would demand a detailed study of political, ideological and sociological issues both in that territory and in France. Furthermore, a more definitive assessment must await the release of various documents and reports, which will not take place for many years. Yet it is possible to make some observations about specific questions, including the problem of names and symbols (and what they represent) in the dispute, the strategies pursued by the different political actors, the role of the French state, and echos of the New Caledonian drama in the *métropole*.

The crisis in New Caledonia in the 1980s, in addition to the very real stakes which it held, also illustrated the use and abuse of polemic. For example, conservative Frenchmen and New Caledonians carefully referred to the island group by its constitutional nomenclature as a *territoire d'outre-mer*, while *indépendantistes* and their sympathisers did not hesitate to use the word 'colony'. Those trying to avoid the issue, to compromise, or simply to be more historically precise sometimes spoke of the 'colonial situation' or the 'colonial inheritance' in New Caledonia, or the 'colonial character' of the territory's society and economy. The emotiveness of 'colony' and 'colonial' meant that the choice of word was loaded with meaning and often intentionally provocative. But at issue, too, was an implicit historical interpretation: whether the inequalities and discrimination of the pre-1946 period had ended with new policies and statutes adopted subsequently, or whether they persisted in spite of such changes, whether New Caledonia was ruled by arbitrary administrators from the *métropole* in collaboration with a local élite, or whether it was a democratic, potentially egalitarian society.

Similarly, labels applied to particular groups in New Caledonia were indicative of the political positions of speakers or writers. Those who opposed independence divided local political forces into 'loyalists', those who wanted the territory to remain attached to France, and 'secessionists'; the pro-independence groups, on the other hand, preferred what on the surface appeared the more neutral terms of *indépendantistes* and anti-*indépendantistes*. 'Secession' had a strongly negative connotation coloured with a tinge of illegality, just as 'loyalism' conjured up images of docility and legality. 'Independence', in the context of a world climate favourable to sovereign states, had a positive connotation for supporters, while sounding dangerous to opponents. Even more strikingly, opponents of Melanesian independence continually referred to the FLNKS and its supporters as only a 'minority' interest. Chirac and other conservatives labelled the FLNKS *militants* 'terrorists', and at least one observer argued on French national television that the FLNKS had recruited its first followers among 'hoodlums, prostitutes and other ne'er-do-wells' in New Caledonia. With the spread of violence, the words 'assassination' and 'massacre' became more common, used to underline the bloodthirstiness of the perpetrators (on both sides) and to inspire an emotional response to deaths and acts of violence. Once again, what was implied were different interpretations of specific events – did Eloi Machoro *die* from an attempt to *neutralise* him that went wrong or was he *killed, assassinated* by policemen? The choice of vocabulary already contained a statement of a political position.

Even the names used for the populations in New Caledonia held implications. During the history of French contacts with New Caledonia, the Melanesians were variously referred to as *Indiens, naturels, natifs, indigènes* and *autochthones*, each word corresponding to a particular political and scientific attitude.[9] The Melanesian population of the territory was more specifically labelled 'Kanak', usually spelled 'Canaque' in French; the word, in Polynesian, simply means 'man'. Melanesians in New Caledonia resented the appellation as derogatory, just as islanders elsewhere in Melanesia disliked the English 'Kanaka' applied to them. Yet by the 1970s, Melanesians had appropriated the term as a label of self-description, thus subverting the derogatory application and finding an Oceanic name more appropriate than the Latinate 'Melanesian'. Some conservatives consequently shied away from the term. Many French writers, including *Le Monde*, continued to use the traditional French spelling of 'Canaque', while the FLNKS and other pro-independence groups adopted 'Kanak'. The use of the 'k' at the beginning and end of the word seemed a slap at French orthography, and the FLNKS practice of leaving the word unvaried from masculine to feminine and from singular to plural violated usual French style. 'Kanaky', used either as a synonym for New Caledonia or as the name for a future independent state, raised the same problems of nomenclature and ideology. Meanwhile, the European populations of New Caledonia were either called 'New Caledonians', making them sound perhaps more legitimate and melding them into the general population of the islands, or 'Caldoches'. The word 'Caldoche', which originated in the 1930s and came into general use by the 1970s, however, struck many of those with European ancestry as offensive, particularly with its ugly '–oche' ending (reminiscent of the derogatory term for Germans, 'Boches'); 'Caldochie', as a description of the European community, was even more highly resented. Terms for other groups – '*métros*' or '*z'oreilles*' for recent European migrants, *niaoulis* for Asian residents, *z'Arabes* and *Viets* for specific ethnic groups[10] – to different ears sounded either acceptable or racist. Commentators on occasion used even stronger rhetoric to discuss ethnicity, of which one example will suffice. A journalist for the conservative Paris daily *Le Figaro* wrote during the tense days of 1985 that the French government was leaving its loyal citizens in New Caledonia 'at the mercy of a handful of savages who are ready for a massacre . . . It is almost as if the Canaques are heating up their cooking pots . . . At the barricades one would have thought one were witnessing a stone-age horror film. All were armed to the teeth, with filthy looks, bloodshot eyes and perhaps a little drunk'.[11] Use of words such as 'savages' and 'stone-age', as well as a reference to imagined cannibalism, intentionally revived eighteenth and nineteenth century fears about Pacific islanders for blatantly emotive and political purposes. This example was not unique, and it was not only the anti-*indépendantistes* whose rhetorical excesses were apparent.

Labels for political parties also carried weight. The name of the Front de Libération Nationale Kanak et Socialiste recalled the 'liberation fronts' which fought for the independence of Vietnam and Algeria; 'Kanak' explicitly promoted the rights of the indigenous population over those of other ethnic groups, and 'socialist', left undefined in the coalition's literature, sounded a militant alternative to the inequalities of capitalism. By contrast the Rassemblement pour la Calédonie dans la République, as the main conservative party was renamed in the 1980s, sounded inclusive rather than exclusive, moderate rather than radical; not coincidentally, the name and initials RPCR were close to those of the party's main supporter in the *métropole*, the Rassemblement pour la République, or RPR, and echoed the various names of neo-Gaullist parties going back to the 1940s. The smaller parties chose names which distinguished them from other groups – the Libération Kanak Socialiste preserved the idea of a new state and economy but without the aggressiveness of the 'Front de' prefix. The Front National used the same title in New Caledonia as in the *métropole*, combining chauvinism with militancy while the Front Calédonien, a party with similar aims but local organisation, adopted a variant name. The pro-independence Union Syndicale des Travailleurs Kanak et Exploités combined the indigenous word 'Kanak' with recognition of the presence of other 'exploited workers' in the syndicalist movement. Like the other components of the FLNKS, it announced its platform in its very name. The Union Calédonienne preserved the centrist, neutral name it had adopted in the 1950s, while the Front Uni de Libération Kanak and Parti de Libération Kanak used terms associated with the political rhetoric and strategy of the New Left in the 1960s. But political organisations were not the only ones with coded names. One of the initiatives of Bernard Pons as Minister of the DOM-TOMs was to replace the Office Culturel Kanak with a new office of 'Oceanic' cultures, depriving it of its Kanak specificity. By contrast, the FLNKS chose Melanesian names for its radio station, Radio Djiido, and its newspaper, *Bwenando*, while the name selected for its alternative schools, the Ecoles Populaires Kanak, sounded both revolutionary and mass-oriented.

Other symbols were potent representations of political stances. A prime example was whether the French Tricolour or the Kanak flag flew over a particular building since a flag is generally considered a recognised emblem of statehood or national identity, particularly in France where local flags are little used. Visits by French dignitaries, surrounded by the pomp and circumstance of official occasions, underlined the might of France, although friendly foreign governments sometimes accorded *indépendantiste* leaders the sorts of ceremonies usually reserved for heads of state. The graffiti which covered New Caledonia's buildings in the 1980s screamed political positions; even the American flag painted on buildings by a number of anti-*indépendantiste* residents indicated their sympathies for the United States and memories of American largesse during the Second World War. T-shirts and badges similarly proclaimed political preference.

HISTORICAL LEGITIMACY

The troubles in New Caledonia raised a number of significant questions about the structure of state and society in the modern world. Some of these pertained more especially to the peculiar 'colonial' situation of New Caledonia, while others reflected more general contexts. One which loomed particularly large was the issue of political legitimacy, which in New Caledonia was directly connected to ethnicity. The basic argument of the *indépendantistes* has been that Melanesians are the original inhabitants of the territory, which gives them the right to sovereignty and an exclusive right to decide the future of the territory. In the past, few observers contested the claim that the Melanesians formed the indigenous population of New Caledonia, yet with the heat of the 1980s, several commentators rejected even this historical fact.[12] Using sometimes disingenuous or historiographically debatable approaches, they emphasised that the Melanesians were themselves migrants to the western Pacific, minimising the chronological fact that this movement of people had occurred several thousand years before the arrival of the Europeans. They also pointed to migrations of Polynesians to the Loyalty Islands of New Caledonia to emphasise the pluri-ethnic make-up of the population. Finally, the observers who rejected the implications of the Melanesian historical ante-cedence in New Caledonia argued that the territory's population had been so mixed by inter-marriage and miscegenation that there remain no real or pure Melanesians. Thus they pointed to the large number of people in the island with both Melanesian and European, or sometimes Asian, ancestry, citing such examples as Tjibaou's Japanese forebear or Burck's Irish grandfather. What they ignored, however, was that there exists no *métis* group in New Caledonia, unlike the case of the *demis* of French Polynesia and the Creoles of the Antilles and Indian Ocean. Individuals in New Caledonia perceive themselves as *either* European or Melanesian, no matter what their skin pigmentation; they are reared in one or other culture, are generally accepted by the community to which they belong and do not form a separate mestizo stratum of society.

Such controversies provided grist for the mill of social scientists, but they also held great political significance. If Melanesians were *not* the original inhabitants of the territory or if they could *not* establish the purity of their genealogy, according to the anti-*indépendantistes*, what claim could they advance to possess the sole right to govern New Caledonia? For the 'loyalists', Melanesians formed only one of a number of ethnic groups which the circumstances of history had brought together, including the French and other Europeans who had settled there, the Japanese, Indonesians, Vietnamese and other islanders who arrived as contract labourers, the Arabs deported there in the 1870s, the Tahitians and Wallisians who migrated during the boom of the 1960s, the *pieds-noirs* who came after the independence of Algeria and the ni-Vanuatu who moved after the independence of the New Hebrides, as well as West Indians and others. For the anti-*indépendantistes*, New Caledonia was therefore a 'melting-pot' (*creuset*) – one of their preferred words – in which no ethnic group should usurp the rights of other communities and claim precedence or authority over them.

This debate on historical antecedence spilled over into racial (and outright racist) rhetoric; charges of racism were hurled by both pro- and anti-independence speakers. But such questions also entered into official documents. For instance, the formulation of the Nainville-les-Roches agreement recognised the inalienable and unique rights of one particular group. The FLNKS referred to the United Nations' view that the indigenous population of a colony alone holds the right to self-determination and that an administering power must not disrupt the ethnic balance in territories under its control through policies of migration. The FLNKS charter claimed in no uncertain terms the sole right of Melanesians to decide their future status, although it admitted that there would be a place in an independent Kanaky for the 'victims of history' from New Caledonia. The meaning of that pregnant phrase was left unclear, but FLNKS leaders referred, for example, to the descendants of convicts who had been transported to New Caledonia. In more general terms, they also acknowledged the rights of long-term residents to have a role in the future of the territory. Some of the FLNKS opponents balked at being labelled 'victims of history', although others countered that, in fact, much of the resident population could be classified as victims, whether of the poverty which had induced migration, contract labour or judicial conviction. Once again, definitions and language were full of social and political import.

The question of the historical legitimacy of a particular ethnic group to a share in decision-making points to a second theoretical issue: how could true democracy be exercised in a territory so battered by the vicissitudes of history as New Caledonia? Political thought and constitutional provisions in France are founded on the idea of universal suffrage with one vote cast by each elector. 'One man, one vote' (modified to take account of female suffrage) did not become the rule in New Caledonia until the late 1950s. But all French citizens in the territory enjoyed the right to vote after only a minimal period of residence (generally, six months); included were those who migrated to New Caledonia in the 1960s and 1970s, as well as public servants and others who intended to live in New Caledonia for only a short period. (Public servants from the *métropole*, for instance, usually held posts for only three years.) This obviously distorted voting to the detriment of both Melanesians and long-term European residents. Anti-*indépendantistes* seldom objected, since recent migrants who were uncertain of their future or cramped by limited prospects in their home islands, notably the Tahitians and Wallisians and Futunans, as well as public servants, generally voted for conservative candidates. The *indépendantistes* roundly rejected the provision of 'one person, one vote', since it was precisely migration to New Caledonia which had reduced them to a minority of the electorate. With the present demographic balance, they pointed out, it would be impossible for pro-independence Melanesians to win a democratic vote, even if they voted unanimously as a bloc, which they did not.

The FLNKS in the mid-1980s proposed that only those of Melanesian origin and those born in New Caledonia of parents themselves born in the territory should be allowed to vote on the islands' future. The suggestion won little support from the French state or the 'Caldoches', much less from more recent migrants. The FLNKS then informally suggested that it would accept an arrangement whereby only one grandparent of a resident needed to have been born in New Caledonia for him or her to enjoy the right to vote; this, similarly, attracted little support. Their opponents continued to maintain the principle of 'one person, one vote'. Paris tried to find a way to extricate itself from a thorny legal and moral problem in which the result of a vote was often determined before the ballot began. The aborted 'independence in association' plan Pisani proposed in 1985 allowed a restriction of the suffrage to those resident in New Caledonia for a minimum of three years. The precedent was the referendum on the independence of the French territory of the Afars and Issas (Djibouti) in the 1970s; this restriction effectively excluded public servants and other temporary residents. Opponents of independence in New Caledonia objected, claiming a denial of civil and constitutional rights to French citizens. The Chirac administration adopted the viewpoint of the anti-*indépendantistes*, and the referendum of 1987 was held on the basis of universal suffrage. The Matignon Accord and the Fabius plan restricted the electorate for the 1988 referendum in a manner similar to that of the Pisani plan and largely froze the electorate for the 1998 referendum: only those registered on the electoral rolls in 1988 or their descendants who reach voting age will be allowed to cast a ballot in 1998. The compromise, seen to preserve the sacrosanct universal suffrage but allowing the exclusion of short-term residents, satisfied both the FLNKS and the RPCR, but extremist parties on both ends of the spectrum rejected the arrangement.

Connected with questions of suffrage was the question of electoral boundaries in New Caledonia. In a territory where the majority of the population (and most of the economic power) is concentrated in Nouméa, and in which the rural areas are divided between a largely Melanesian east coast and Loyalty Islands and a predominantly European west coast, the constitution of electoral districts held much political significance. Under the Fabius plan, New Caledonia was divided into four regions: Nouméa and the Loyalty Islands seemed natural enough divisions, but the partition of the remainder of the Grande Terre was more difficult. Despite the ethnic distribution, and the mountain chain which runs down the centre of the island, there are significant ancestral and social links between the two coasts. Furthermore, much of the mineral-rich land lies on the Melanesian east coast, a stronghold of the *indépendantistes*. Paris opted for a division of the *brousse* into 'north' and 'centre', which upset anti-*indépendantistes* who feared that the 'centre' and its nickel mines would escape their control. In elections according to the Fabius plan, the FLNKS did win control of three regions and gained a majority in the Territorial Assembly. The RPCR subsequently demanded a revision of electoral boundaries, and under the Pons plan the number of regions was reduced to three. This time the Grande Terre was divided transversally, with the Loyalty Islands attached to the eastern district. The obvious intention to reduce FLNKS administrative power was only partially successful since the FLNKS boycotted the voting. Under the Matignon Accord, the boundaries were once again redrawn and New Caledonia partitioned into three 'provinces'; the FLNKS gained control of two of the three. The blatant gerrymandering of electoral districts, and the *prises de position* which the drawing of boundaries implied, showed that the principle of 'one person, one vote' could never be thoroughly democratic in New Caledonia.

THE ROLE OF THE STATE

The role of the French government in redrawing the electoral map and defining the electorate is part and parcel of another major issue in New Caledonia: the overall role of the state. In a country traditionally marked by administrative centralism, economic planning, cultural assimilationism and the overwhelming role of the capital city in public life, the state has seldom been only a minor player in political dramas. The powers of the state have been all the more formidable in a 'colonial' context where certain constraints of the *métropole* are removed and where there exists a greater margin for the state to manoeuvre than 'at home'. However, it has been unclear whether the state should primarily promote *métropolitain* interests, or what are perceived as national interests, take sides in conflicts by supporting one or another party, or act as an impartial arbiter between factions. The Socialist Party and the Mitterrand government were seen to be pro-Melanesian. Especially when Pisani was High-Commissioner, Paris was viewed, from a Melanesian viewpoint, as sympathetic to the islanders' cause although slow-moving and not wholly committed; from an anti-independence perspective, Pisani, Mitterrand and the Socialists were thought absolute partisans of the FLNKS. Yet observers also saw the government trying to create a third, centre force composed of reformists and moderate *indépendantistes*. After 1986, the situation changed dramatically. The RPR in Paris openly and unhesitatingly took sides with the RPCR in New Caledonia, and Pons pursued policies intentionally designed to reduce the influence of the FLNKS and perhaps eliminate the independence movement entirely. This alienated Melanesians, and dialogue between Paris and the *indépendantistes* was interrupted. Paris had abandoned any pretence of trying to reconcile the communities or arbitrate between them. The Chirac government, in short, overtly and unapologetically took sides, more so than the Socialist governments of the early 1980s had ever done. After the elections of 1988, following the violence at Fayaoué and Gossanah, the position of the government once again changed. The Rocard administration, although again seen to be favourable to Melanesian (even *indépendantiste*) interests, steered a fine course between the different factions and with considerable dexterity negotiated the Matignon Accord. The ensuing referendum emphasised the role of the state as arbiter, but the different groups in New Caledonia either feared or hoped, depending on the case, that results of future elections might again swing the pendulum of government action in their favour.

This new stance of the state, perhaps not surprisingly, did not win universal acclaim. Diehards among the anti-*indépendantistes* accused Paris of selling out to secessionists and terrorists and argued that French law, the results of the referendum of 1987 and the constitutional provisions making the President the guarantor of the territorial integrity of France obliged the government to support the 'loyalist' cause. On the other hand, diehard *indépendantistes* accused the government of selling out to the Caldoches. Some even commented that morally the State should have proceeded towards independence and refused to negotiate with the 'settlers'; independence, in this interpretation, was an affair of Melanesians and the authorities in Paris, and the 'colonists' should simply have to accommodate themselves to the decisions taken.

The different responses of the French government demonstrated the arsenal of actions and means it could deploy, including the might of the French army and police force, vast amounts of money which could be made available or be withdrawn, and the power to design and pass legislative acts which succeeded each other rapidly during the 1980s. Some possibilities, in fact, were not used – Paris did not unilaterally grant independence to New Caledonia, as it most certainly could have done, nor did the military and police resort to mass arrests, treason trials or, as Pons supposedly considered, dropping a bomb on the island of Ouvéa when hostages were sequestered. Different governments did however pursue varying strategies. The Giscard administration, with the Dijoud plan, sought to stimulate economic development but skirted political issues and any change in the legal status of the territory. The Mitterrand government, in its early years, addressed the political grievances of the Kanaks and such thorny issues as the land question; this willingness to consider radical changes in the political relationship between New Caledonia and France, including the very possibility of independence, marked a substantially new approach even though it backfired and exacerbated tensions. The strategy of the Chirac government was a militarisation of New Caledonia and an effort to destroy the independence movement. Finally, the policy followed by Rocard from 1988 to 1991 was to engineer a moratorium on political issues, downscale the military presence and inject enormous amounts of money into the territory, aiming at economic development and targeting in particular the Melanesian population.

Both continuities and ruptures in the behaviour of political parties and individuals appeared in these processes. The RPR assumed the mantle of de Gaulle, hailed by most (if not all) as the statesman who was able to effect a peaceful decolonisation of the French domains in black Africa and, also, to grant independence to Algeria after the protracted war there; yet the neo-Gaullists were the prime opponents to any further cessions of territory or grants of independence in the French *outre-mer*. The Socialists, who championed decolonisation, through their flexibility in negotiations concerning New Caledonia, maintained less doctrinal purity, and the plan for 'independence in association' was an obvious compromise. Mitterrand and Rocard spoke about 'decolonisation' *within* the context of the French Republic and stressed the need for economic development and a levelling out of the inequities between various ethnic groups. Yet there was a basic continuity in Mitterrand's attitude towards the colonies (and the ex-colonies), marked by his preference for continued close ties between France and its old possessions and the willingness to provide technical, economic and cultural assistance to them.[13]

In short, when the French state acted in New Caledonia, it was not an impersonal and an objective institution which intervened — indeed only rarely did the government use the resources of the administration to act as an impartial broker – or that political figures, of whatever belief, thought that it should do so. Pro- and anti-independence movements regularly clamoured for government intervention, although to different ends. This lobbying points to the variations in strategy followed by political forces and, as well, to the politicisation of other institutions in New Caledonia during a period of intense strife.

POLITICAL STRATEGIES

The methods used by the pro- and anti-independence parties, as well as the French state, to advance their cause reflected the means at their disposal and the changing circumstances to which they responded. The RPCR, which held power in New Caledonia's Assembly during much of the 1980s and cloaked itself in constitutional legitimacy, could employ official channels in its campaign to keep New Caledonia French. The party enjoyed the membership of many of the wealthiest and most powerful men in New Caledonia, and its leader, Jacques Lafleur, benefited from personal wealth, his political lineage as son of a member of the National Assembly and his own mandate as *député*, connections with the RPR and considerable oratorical skills and tactical acumen. The party, however, was loosely structured until late 1984. At that time, the national RPR decided to make New Caledonia one of the major platforms on which it would combat the PS and its other opponents. The RPR delegated Charles Pasqua, a major figure in the party with a reputation for determined and aggressive politicking, to visit

New Caledonia and revitalise the RPCR. A team of counsellors accompanied Pasqua to Nouméa, and remained there after his departure to reorganise the RPCR and give advice on its finances, propaganda, recruitment and other activities. The RPCR emerged a more militant and better structured party, although some of the 'Caldoche' members felt that they had been shunted to the side by *métropolitain* advisers.

The RPCR utilised the tactics available to all political parties: regular participation in elections, meetings, petitions, lobbying in both Nouméa and Paris and publications. During the period of FLNKS withdrawal from official elected bodies, the RPCR monopolised control of such institutions as the local assembly. The RPCR prominently displayed its Melanesian members, notably Senator Dick Ukeiwé and Maurice Nénou, a *député*, who were New Caledonia's only representatives in the French Parliament after the FLNKS boycotted elections. It gave publicity to its Tahitian, Wallisian and Futunan and Asian members as well and promoted itself as a truly multi-ethnic party. But the RPCR also acted on the borderline of legal politics. Opponents accused it of buying votes among Melanesians by outright gifts of money, promises of preferment in employment and backroom influence; they said that the RPCR had acquiesced to, if not actually participated in, the organisation of militias and violent attacks on *indépendantistes*. The close links between the RPCR and certain local businesses, as well as the local press, provided further possibilities for political manoeuvring.

Other anti-independence parties lacked the institutional and parliamentary base of the RPCR. The Front National and the Front Calédonien were often accused of using primarily illegal tactics. The two groups nominated candidates for local elections, published broadsheets and newsletters and gave frequent interviews to the media, but they were thought to distribute arms, organise ambushes and harass Melanesian and European supporters of Kanak independence as well. So clandestine was their organisation, and so legal the veneer of their public image, however, that prosecutions for such alleged activities did not follow.

The FLNKS used a remarkable array of tactics to bring its message before the territorial, national and international public. A decentralised organisation, the FLNKS adopted a 'party line' but allowed much disagreement among its constitutive groups.

Congresses of each party, and the coalition as a whole, determined policy and the FLNKS organised a 'provisional government' of Kanaky, but much day to day activity remained in the hands of local *comités de lutte* around New Caledonia; these committees also organised actions which they considered appropriate to local situations. The FLNKS issued a charter and adopted the symbols of an independent nation. It designed a flag, a horizontal tricolour of blue, red and green, on which were superimposed a yellow sun and the carved wooden symbol which adorns the top of Melanesian houses. The FLNKS pursued a campaign of propaganda inside and outside New Caledonia through its press office, newspaper, and a radio station. FLNKS leaders made frequent trips overseas, gave press conferences, wrote articles for newspapers and met with supporters. In these efforts the oratorical skill of Tjibaou served to a distinct advantage; the quiet, slow delivery, punctuated with wry smiles, softened the rhetoric; the use of Melanesian stories and folklore, combined with a finely-honed political vocabulary and style, was of great benefit to the *indépendantistes*. Other leaders, particularly Machoro and the often renegade Urégei, also became media personalities. To complement their work, the FLNKS sent emissaries to Australia and New Zealand; although not officially accredited to the host countries, they recruited support and popularised the Kanak cause.

In New Caledonia, the FLNKS made efforts to create alternative institutions for Melanesians. Not altogether successfully, the FLNKS tried to set up agricultural cooperatives; it promoted a return to indigenous farm products to lessen the need for imported European goods. The FLNKS leaders who controlled the North and Centre under the Fabius plan accepted grants and subsidies from Paris and the central government in Nouméa and undertook programmes of economic development; overtures were also made to potential entrepreneurs and foreign investors. Another strategy was the Ecoles Populaires Kanak (EPK), alternative schools to the official French educational system. Such schools, staffed by Melanesian instructors, opened in a number of villages; the curriculum consisted of the usual primary subjects (reading, writing, and so on) but also Melanesian languages and culture, as well as practical skills (such as cultivation and fishing) all imbued with a Melanesian (and *indépendantiste*) perspective.

The independence movement's political strategy metamorphosed during the 1980s. Early in the decade, before the formation of the FLNKS, the *indépendantistes* participated in local government, and Tjibaou, as head of the Front Indépendantiste, served for a year as head of the New Caledonian Territorial Assembly. Later, the FLNKS boycotted elections in 1984, just as it refused to participate in the Pons referendum of 1987. However, it took part in local elections in 1988. And at no time did the FLNKS withdraw from New Caledonian municipal councils. The FLNKS' extraparliamentary strategy extended to peaceful rallies and demonstrations in Nouméa. But it occasionally extended to the occupation of *gendarmeries*, the setting-up of roadblocks (especially in November 1984), harassing of European residents and, in 1988, the hostage-taking at Fayaoué. For supporters, such violence represented a necessary response to the violence of anti-independence groups, continued exploitation and discrimination and the tergiversations of the French government; violence simply confirmed detractors' fears that the FLNKS was a group of terrorists.

The variety of strategies pursued by the FLNKS, rather than indicating a lack of clear ideological or practical logic, showed the ability of a dissident political organisation to marshal its resources and, as well, gave evidence of the frustration the FLNKS felt at not achieving its objectives. The other major pro-independence party, the LKS, used many of the same tactics as the FLNKS, although its resources were far smaller. A major difference was that the LKS generally continued to participate in elections to the Territorial Assembly and the French parliament while the FLNKS boycotted voting. The LKS, openly and behind the scenes, also positioned itself as a legitimate alternative to the FLNKS and welcomed approaches from Paris. The LKS never questioned French institutions in the way the FLNKS did.

There were also international actors in New Caledonia. In particular, the FLNKS and independence groups internationalised their struggle. The FLNKS, for instance, took its cause to the Decolonisation Committee of the United Nations. New Caledonia had been listed on the UN register of countries awaiting decolonisation at the end of the Second World War, but France had successfully asked for it to be removed after the adoption of the constitution of the Fourth Republic. Now the FLNKS, with sponsorship from Australia and Vanuatu, approached the Decolonisation Committee to ask for a relisting of New Caledonia. The UN heard testimony and the committee, formed largely of socialist and third world countries, recommended such a relisting. Over the strident opposition of France and the abstention of many of France's allies and former colonies, the General Assembly adopted the proposition. Paris stated that it would take no notice of the decision, but the FLNKS felt that the United Nations had now legitimated the independence movement. The FLNKS also received a sympathetic hearing from the Movement of Non-Aligned Countries, which adopted a resolution demanding independence for New Caledonia. In the South Pacific, the FLNKS enjoyed warm support from Oceanic nations at the South Pacific Forum. The governments of Australia and New Zealand pronounced themselves favourable to independence, although they expressed hope that a moderate and multi-racial state would emerge. Particular support came from the Melanesian Spearhead Group, an *ad hoc* association of the three independent Melanesian states in Oceania. Outside the region, Yann Céléné Urégei, the leader of FULK, approached Libya for support and led a group of Melanesians to Tripoli; opponents accused Colonel Kaddhafi's government of training them in terror tactics and guerrilla warfare. The FLNKS, placed in an awkward position by Urégei's move, which was not officially approved by the coalition, disavowed connections with Libya and any terrorist apprenticeship. In fact, the Libyan overture rebounded against the FLNKS and showed that the search for international support could backfire. More practically, the FLNKS established contacts with various non-governmental organisations, including teachers' and mineworkers' unions in Australia and independent aid organisations in New Zealand. These provided the FLNKS with funding and equipment (such as radio transmitters and printing presses), gave office space to their delegates in Australia and New Zealand and promoted their cause overseas.

The anti-*indépendantistes* did much less to internationalise their movement and seemed hostile to 'outside interference'. Some Francophone communities in the South Pacific supported their point of view – for instance, the French-language monthly newspaper in Sydney, *Le Courrier Australien,* provided coverage favourable to 'loyalists' in New Caledonia. But the South Pacific in general formed a hostile environment for the anti-independence views in the 1980s, although the French government made efforts to recruit support for its position, especially among small Polynesian states. But changes in the South Pacific in the late 1980s, notably the *coups* in Fiji in 1987, finally created a more favourable climate for the spread of French influence. The more conciliatory French policy adopted in 1988 then substantially improved relations with Australia, New Zealand and island states.

Overseas and in the *métropole*, political movements, governments and non-governmental organisations supported one or another group in New Caledonia – generally, the independence movement – out of genuine ideological solidarity. But there was also hope of scoring points with local clienteles or electorates. For instance, Australia and New Zealand were both interested in winning favour with South Pacific micro-states and voters at home; private groups which promoted the rights of indigenous people, environmental action or leftist causes usually targeted France as a convenient villain in Oceania. Similarly, political parties in France used New Caledonia as a political weapon against their opponents, particularly during elections. The RPR posed as the champion of legality and the rights of loyal Frenchmen, while the RPR's coalition partner, the UDF, tried to demarcate itself by a more flexible approach to New Caledonia and stress on the need for compromise. The Socialists, in opposition, seemed explicitly pro-*indépendantiste*, but when in power the party had to confront the complexities of New Caledonia and the opposition its policies engendered. The Communists, briefly and uncomfortably in an electoral alliance with the Socialists, then in opposition, had the luxury of maintaining a more rigorously anti-imperialist line. At the other end of the spectrum, the Front National uncompromisingly defended the 'loyalist' position, despite the party's campaign against non-European residents of France in the *métropole*.[14] Whether any of the parties actually gained votes because of their stances is doubtful; the results of the 1988 election suggest this was not the case.

The political chequerboard in New Caledonia was not without changing alliances and faction-fighting. In the independence movement, for instance, the LKS left the Front Indépendantiste in the early 1980s, then the radical FULK moved away from the more mainstream groups in the FLNKS at the end of the decade. The Matignon Accord threatened division in both the pro-and anti-independence movements in New Caledonia, although in the *métropole*, the Accord and the referendum which followed rallied a broad base of support. (The RPR, however, expressed strong reservations about the agreement.) In a longer-range view, New Caledonia saw periods of intense fighting between Kanaks and Caldoches, as during the mid-1980s, but also times of alliance and collaboration between the territory's two major ethnic groups, as happened in the early years of the Union Calédonienne and again after the signature of the Matignon Accord.[15] Particular groups could also move out on their own, as when in 1989 the Wallisians and Futunans in New Caledonia, previously considered stalwart supporters of the anti-*indépendantistes*, established their own political party and adopted a more moderate position. Such developments indicated not only a desire by all groups to safeguard their positions and maximise whatever advantages might accrue – or to minimise whatever dangers might result – from the evolution of New Caledonia. They bespoke personal, ideological and clientelistic quarrels within parties and communities. As well, they pointed to the wholesale politicisation of public life which characterised New Caledonia.

THE POLITICISATION OF NEW CALEDONIA

Very few institutions or individuals in New Caledonia escaped being implicated in the political dramas which occurred in the 1980s. Intentionally or by default, they were drawn into the fray and thereby labelled as being 'for' or 'against' independence, when politics polarised and tensions mounted. As the centre of the political spectrum faded away, it became more difficult for institutions and residents to remain (or at least to be considered) neutral.

Extraparliamentary groups became extremely active in New Caledonia. The Catholic and Protestant churches wielded great influence in the Melanesian community, and the major Protestant churches pronounced themselves squarely in favour of independence for New Caledonia. Trade unions, such as the

USTKE, also held influence in the pro-independence movement. The military and police forces acted as a tool of the
administration. The killing of Eloi Machoro by a policeman,
the policy of *nomadisation*, and the assault on the cave at Gossanah
put the forces of law and order at the centre of controversy in
the territory. The Chirac government's decision to use army
troops (rather than police officers or *gendarmes*) in Ouvéa in
1988 was particularly controversial, as military forces are not
usually deployed in France itself, particularly to act against
French citizens. The court system, in principle independent of
politics, often failed to satisfy commentators that investigations
were objective and sentences just. The detention of rebels at
several notorious jails in New Caledonia, according to the independence movement, represented the arbitrary arrest and imprisonment of political dissidents.

The press played a prominent political role. Few argued that
the print or electronic media should be totally 'objective', but
the press in New Caledonia usually abandoned all pretence of
presenting the 'full story'. Radio Djiido and *Bwenando* avowedly
presented the opinion of the FLNKS, and the UC and other
parties issued their own news-sheets. The only daily commercial
newspaper in the territory, *Les Nouvelles Calédoniennes*, was rigorously anti-*indépendantiste* and pro-RPCR, even if not officially
associated with the party. *Les Nouvelles* highlighted the speeches
and actions of the RPCR and often ignored those of the
indépendantistes except when it could castigate their pronouncements as the work of agitators and terrorists; words such as
'martyr' were regularly used for Europeans who had been killed,
almost never for Melanesians. The newspaper covered all of the
social activities of the European community in Nouméa, often
concentrating on human interest stories; however, it did not
even print the schedules of Radio Djiido.[16] Other newspapers
which were ephemerally published in New Caledonia, notably
Combat and *L'Objectif*, were even more extremist and often racist. On the airwaves, Radio Rythme Bleu, operated by the RPCR,
presented a viewpoint sympathetic to its political sponsors. The
French state radio and television, RFO, tried to pursue a middle
course but was not above reflecting the positions of those in
power. Attempts made to establish alternative media were sometimes foiled. One newspaper, *L'Autre Journal*, founded in the
mid-1980s, endeavoured to present a more impartial version of

the news but folded when conservative advertisers boycotted its columns.

Metropolitan newspapers entered the conflict in New Caledonia as well. The authoritative *Le Monde* presented wide coverage of New Caledonia. One of its chief political writers, Jean-Marie Colombani, was born in Nouméa and wrote about the territory in the early 1980s. *Le Monde*'s major reporter on New Caledonia, Alain Rollat, established a reputation as an expert on local affairs. Rollat wrote balanced articles, but his sympathies obviously lay with the Melanesians, which earned him the hatred of Caldoches. The leftist *Libération* also provided thorough, generally pro-Melanesian, coverage of New Caledonia. By contrast, the right-wing *Le Figaro*, especially in the articles of its New Caledonian reporter, Thierry Desjardins, unabashedly supported the RPCR and the anti-*indépend-antistes* and used much the same vocabulary as *Les Nouvelles Calédoniennes*.

If journalists took sides, so did academic specialists. The Société d'Etudes Historiques de la Nouvelle-Calédonie in Nouméa occasionally printed articles on Melanesians in its bulletin, but it showed more interest in the history of the settlers. The society also sponsored the publication of historical works which tended to undermine the Kanak position, for instance, the French translation of an Australian work by Linda Latham ascribing the 1878 Melanesian revolt to inter-tribal hostilities rather than opposition to French colonialism, and a pamphlet which questioned whether Melanesians were indeed the first inhabitants of New Caledonia. On the other side, the Office Culturel Kanak, before it was disbanded, published works which revalued Melanesian history or analysed the discrimination and failed economic development to which Melanesians were subject; among these were the works of the sociologist Jean-Marie Kohler, perhaps the most controversial researcher in New Caledonia.

A *métropolitain* who had worked in Africa and Madagascar before being posted to Nouméa, Kohler worked for the Institut Français de la Recherche Scientifique pour le Développement en Coopération (ORSTOM). In a variety of studies of plans to develop forestry in Melanesian areas, the role of the school and the educational success of Melanesians, the role of the church, and the attitudes of young Melanesians towards *coutume*, Kohler questioned the success of Melanesian integration into New Caledonian society and the motives which underlay French policy. His detractors argued that his approach was too critical, limited in its methodology, and ideologically rigid (he was often accused of being a Marxist). In 1987, Kohler published a long article in *Le Monde Diplomatique*, subsequently issued as a pamphlet, which brought together his research findings into an indictment of French colonialism in New Caledonia. Kohler was harassed for his opinions; he received numerous threats on his life, and in 1985 his yacht was blown up in Nouméa harbour. After the Chirac government appointed a new director of ORSTOM, Kohler was recalled to France, which his supporters said was censorship and an attack on academic investigation.[17]

Kohler was not the only researcher involved in the New Caledonian conflict. Jean Guiart is one of the foremost French authorities on Oceania; he studied under Maurice Leenhardt, and his research on Oceanic cultures since the 1950s had led to numerous published works. Guiart's wife is a Melanesian, and his brother-in-law is the UC political figure Maurice Lenormand. In the 1980s, Guiart published a series of articles increasingly critical of French administration, and in which he called for independence for New Caledonia. In the midst of the violence in 1985, Guiart's Nouméa home was burned by opponents of independence. Guiart, however, persisted in publishing his views. In *La Terre est la sang des morts*, in 1983, Guiart denounced French racism in the history of its relations with the South Pacific islands; in stark terms, Guiart drew an uncompromising portrait of European encroachments on Melanesian land, racist attitudes and episodes of settler terrorism, all of which he juxtaposed with the peacefulness and integrity of traditional Melanesian communities. Guiart also contested interpretations which disagreed with his views; the bulletin of the New Caledonian historical society responded bitterly to his critical review of Linda Latham's book on the 1878 revolt. Later Guiart extended his criticism not only to the French government and Europeans in New Caledonia, but also to Kanaks who had negotiated with their opponents. Guiart, like Kohler, opposed the Matignon Accord of 1988. One of Guiart's *métis* sons, himself also an author, participated actively in the cause of the *indépendantistes*.[18] Another scholar involved in the Melanesian struggle was Alban

Bensa, an ethnologist and professor at the Ecole des Hautes Etudes en Sciences Sociales; he participated in a Melanesian support group in France and during one visit to New Caledonia was asked by French authorities to leave. Alain Saussol, author of a study of the land question in New Caledonia, *L'Héritage*, although not a political activist, was denounced in the bulletin of the Société d'Etudes Historiques.[19] Jean Chesneaux, a historian and political activist, published in both English and French critiques of the French presence in the South Pacific.[20] Not all scholars positioned themselves in the pro-Kanak camp; some academics were seen as favouring the anti-*indépendantiste* cause. But few could keep from being drawn into the conflict and being politically labelled: all research was *engagé*. Researchers sometimes participated in the organisation of support groups, generally in favour of the Kanak cause.[21]

The motives and aims of different groups and individuals are not always easy to discern. Many who took a stand on New Caledonia had personal connections with the territory, and it is not surprising that those who had studied the Melanesians and sometimes spent part of their lives among them should be sympathetic to their cause. Roselène Dousset-Leenhardt (the daughter of Maurice Leenhardt), Jean Guiart (his student), and Guiart's son, for instance, have both sorts of connections. Others who have championed the *indépendantistes* are veterans of earlier anti-imperialist causes, such as Jean Chesneaux, an opponent of French rule in Indochina and Algeria. Some assimilated support for the *indépendantiste* movement into a general leftist, anti-colonial position. It would be unfair to suggest that New Caledonia simply represented a new peg on which to hang their activism and ideologies, but certainly the 'anti-colonialist' struggle in the South Pacific was able to animate and focus more general world-views in France and elsewhere; New Caledonia became a new 'cause' to support. Similarly, support for the anti-independence position came from some who had previously defended *Algérie française* or opposed independence in other French colonies (for instance, Vanuatu). Among them were a number of *pieds-noirs*. Yet it would also be unfair to reduce their opposition to independence to a last-ditch effort to save another French outpost from 'abandonment', or to simple political profiteering. The factors important in the decisions made among supporters of both 'loyalists' and 'secessionists', or *indépendantistes* and anti-*indépendantistes,* relate to both personal stakes and ideological decisions.

In New Caledonia itself, the confrontations of the 1980s produced a level of politicisation that for many was indeed a question of life and death, or at least, a question of the future status of a country they all considered their own. In France, the crisis was an occasion for a national stock-taking and for political jousting. Public life and political debate in the French South Pacific centred on continuing issues – the meaning of liberty, civil rights, economic equality – as well as specific problems or developments. In French history, many events and *affaires* – the Boulanger crisis and the Dreyfus episode, the Popular Front and the Resistance, the wars in Indochina and Algeria – have mobilised opinion and political participation. In the 1980s, although to a lesser degree than in some earlier crises, New Caledonia represented a flashpoint for debate in the *métropole.* Polemics often reduced the situation to a caricature – heroic resisters to French colonialism and exploitation versus racist and rapacious settlers, in one view, defenders of Republican legality against terrorist traitors, on the other. From Paris, the small French territory twenty thousand kilometres away, partly because of its very size and distance, appeared more often as a symbol than as a complex reality.

WRITING ABOUT NEW CALEDONIA

A particular lens through which to see how concern with New Caledonia increased is the publications concerned with the territory which appeared in the 1980s. Newspapers which had previously covered the South Pacific only rarely now sent permanent reporters to Oceania, and groups which supported Kanak independence published newsletters.[22] Journals such as *Esprit* and *Les Temps modernes* published special issues on the conflict. Specialists in French history and politics, who had previously displayed interest in quite different areas, turned their attentions to the French presence in the South Pacific.[23] In addition to scholarly works on New Caledonia, the number of which has never been particularly large in either French or English, several dozen books on New Caledonia, often of a polemical nature and intended to promote particular political points of view, were published during the 1980s. The multiplicity of publications indicated that New Caledonia, albeit only temporarily, had assumed an important role in current affairs; they showed, too, that the crisis was particularly fertile ground for testing various theories, political views or literary styles.

The reading public, for instance, was treated to several fictional accounts of the history and present-day situation in New Caledonia. In 1984, the French actress Marie-France Pisier published a novel based on her childhood years in New Caledonia. *Le Bal du gouverneur* recounted the life of the adolescent daughter of a French administrator of the Fourth Republic and her adventures in the European community of Nouméa. Both the book, and the film made from it, enjoyed popular success in France, although they were less well received in New Caledonia. Three years after *Le Bal du gouverneur*, Jacqueline Sénès published *Terre violente*. Sénès, a Frenchwoman from the *métropole*, had worked for many years as a journalist in New Caledonia and published a history of the territory in a French series about 'daily life' in various societies. Her novel, which chronicles three generations in New Caledonia, tells the story of the granddaughter of Irish migrants to the South Pacific in the nineteenth century; Hélène retains the memory of having seen her grandmother decapitated by Melanesians as she and her husband defended the farm which they had carved out of the bush in the face of the vagaries of climate, tumultuous political events and the 'suspicious regard of the tribes'. In 1990 an author of spy novels, himself once an aid to the Australian prime minister, published *Noumea*, an English-language adventure about an Australian secret service agent who stops Australia being used by gun-runners to send weapons to anti-*indépendantiste* Caldoches; the action, in which the hero 'joins forces with the beautiful if enigmatic Madeleine', takes place in trendy cafés in Sydney and Paris and on various South Pacific islands.[24]

In Australia, there has been a long interest in the South Pacific, seen in the occasional novel, newspaper coverage, and in scholarly works. In the 1980s appeared two general studies of New Caledonia, the works of a geographer and a historian respectively. Martyn Lyons' *The Totem or the Tricolour* took a historical perspective and provided an introduction to the territory just when the crisis was reaching its height. John Connell's *New Caledonia or Kanaky?*, whose title put into high relief what then seemed the possible destinies of the islands, studied the 'political economy of a French colony', putting the problem in the context of development theory and geographical perspectives. A collection of essays on 'nationalism and dependency in New Caledonia' combined the work of French and Australian specialists as well as Melanesian activists.[25]

Meanwhile, Australian newspapers reported on New Caledonian developments in detail. Their coverage was generally sympathetic to the *indépendantistes*, so much so that some French and New Caledonian commentators complained of biased and one-sided journalism.[26] The best known Australian journalist reporting on New Caledonia, Helen Fraser, wrote about the crisis for several newspapers and periodicals and published a Pacific islands newsletter. Fraser also wrote a factual chronicle of events in New Caledonia and a memoir of her experiences there, *Your Flag's Blocking Our Sun.*[27] In this autobiography, Fraser explained her attraction to New Caledonia, the lure of exotic climes to a little girl growing up in Tasmania, her introduction to political ideas and the history of the Pacific while a university student and during her career as a journalist. Fraser revealed how she had been harassed by anti-*indépendantistes* in New Caledonia and told of her support for the FLNKS and occasional involvement in the strife there – a most interesting self-commentary on the role of the journalist and the influence of personal political sensibilities on his or her coverage. Another journalist, David Robie, wrote an account of nationalist struggles in New Caledonia, Fiji and Papua New Guinea whose title, *Blood on Their Banner*, hints at its impassioned nature.[28]

French-language works on New Caledonia took an even more partisan position than their English-language counterparts. The writings of French ethnologists and sociologists who specialised in New Caledonia mirrored their sympathies, although the degree of politicisation of their texts varies.[29] A number of 'instant books' on New Caledonia probably gained wider circulation than arcane scholarly works or politically committed journals. Some were blatantly political tracts whose zeal was matched only by their excessive rhetoric; for example, *Les Heures noires de la Calédonie* claimed to document the 'murderous folly of the FLNKS', and the *Chronique des années de cendres*, published pseudonymously, was a reflexion on the 'confrontation be-tween the will of a population, determined to maintain its liberty through its attachment to France, and the policy of the socialist government . . . an objective ally of the minority *indépendantistes*'. Maurice Delage's privately published '*La France Australe*': *Nouvelle-Calédonie*: '*Ile de Lumière*' was the response of an eighty-five year old former employee of Ballande to 'a few Canaques converted to socialism'.[30] Such tracts had little lasting value except as evidence of the passions unchained by the events of the 1980s.

Other French books published during this period included the memoirs of participants in the events or reports of commis-sions of enquiry.[31] A substantial number were the works of journalists who had covered New Caledonia. Alain Rollat, of *Le Monde*, for example, published a biography of Jean-Marie Tjibaou and, with his colleague Edwy Plenel, an investigation of the Ouvéa tragedy.[32] Another study of the Ouvéa affair, although written in the manner of an adventure story rather than an investigation, was the work of a radio journalist.[33] Two left-wing reporters, Claude Gabriel and Vincent Kermel, published *Nouvelle-Calédonie: La Révolte Kanake*, followed by *Nouvelle-Calédonie: Les Sentiers de l'espoir*, while Thierry Desjardins, a re-porter for *Le Figaro*, published a book with a pragmatic title, *Ils veulent rester Français*; the titles again give a clue as to the con-tent.[34] A more balanced general account of the history of New Caledonia was that of the Agence France Presse correspondent, Antonio Raluy.[35] The list of publications continues.[36]

The content of some works was predictable. For instance, Desjardins' study of New Caledonia provided a wholesale de-nunciation of François Mitterrand and the PS government, Marxists, 'leftist ethnologists, close to the seat of power, who try hard to present Canaque "culture" as one of the most precious patrimonies of universal heritage', the "antikolonialistes" [*sic* – as in 'Kanak' rather than Canaque, the author implies] of Left Bank Paris salons who imagine that New Caledonia is a kolonie [*sic*] like any other', Melanesian leaders such as Tjibaou who 'want to use Canaque pseudo-culture . . . as an alibi-trampoline for their politico-revolutionary ambitions', and so on. In more analytical terms, but still marked by a certain rhetorical style, Gabriel and Kermel spoke of 'colonial domination' and the need for New Caledonia to 'progress on the road to emancipation from foreign domination'.[37] The differences among the various works were ones of quality and documentation, but also of political presuppositions; in the less thoughtful accounts, New Caledonia was but an illustration to a preconceived ideological argument.

CONCLUSION

A lengthier discussion of the various works published on New Caledonia in the 1980s would prove what these examples suggest: the conflict in New Caledonia became a prime occasion not only for a struggle over the future of that territory but for a *prise de position* by *engagé* writers to an extent unparalleled since the time of the Vietnam War of the 1960s (or perhaps the earlier Algerian War). The drama in New Caledonia, in Maurice Satineau's metaphor,[38] was a 'mirror' of metropolitan France, an opportunity to reflect on the role of the army, the government and the administration, to discuss ethnicity and nationalism, to question economic and political inequities and the structure of France itself. As a laboratory for observation, New Caledonia seemed for some the example of what a multi-ethnic and economically developed society should or could be, while for others it was an anachronism of colonialism which showed the world the bad face of France. The Melanesians and European New Caledonians themselves became caught up in this debate as clients of or rebels against various political groups eager to win elections, ideologues keen to promote theories, or administrators happy to develop new 'plans' for the territory.

But what occurred in New Caledonia in the 1980s was a very real struggle between opposing forces for the control of the territory. This represented a challenge to an administering power and the settler community which allied with it by a population which legitimately claimed to be the indigenous inhabitants and to be the victims of political and economic exploitation. The polemics voiced, the strategies deployed and the nuances of the sociocultural structure of New Caledonia could not mask this stark confrontation. Both sides advanced rationales for their struggles, and the French government, alternately as arbitrator and partisan, also had its reasons for policy decisions and programmes. The events in New Caledonia were not a replay of previous colonial conflicts; however, many of the elements of a colonial drama were present. The toll was tragic – more lives were probably lost, more property damaged and more hatred generated than in most other episodes of French decolonisation. Yet France did not leave New Caledonia, and by the late 1980s various protagonists proposed solutions to the problem which lay between the status quo, on the one hand, and independence and total French withdrawal, on the other.

It was clear that the future of New Caledonia would be decided in Paris rather than in Nouméa or the *brousse* – even decolonisation, whether inside or outside the framework of the French Republic, was an act of Paris.[39] Furthermore, it was evident that the independence struggle waged by the Melanesians had not succeeded in achieving the goal of sovereignty first voiced in the early 1970s and which it had systematically pursued through parliamentary and extraparliamentary means since the beginning of the 1980s. Yet a decade of political arguments and great blood-letting had successfully challenged the bases on which New Caledonian life had rested since at least the 1940s and possibly since the first incursion by the Europeans – perceptions of the stagnation of Melanesian culture, the natural political right of Europeans to rule over the islanders, the unquestioned benefits of French overlordship, the necessity for a consensual multi-racial society. In short, the anti-*indépendantistes* were those whose ideas if not their practices had most clearly been disturbed, even if their rivals did not succeed in achieving independence. As the 1980s closed, it was from this position of a compromise of ideologies that discussions could begin on the eventual fate of New Caledonia.

In the early 1990s, the situation in New Caledonia remained stable, although hard-liners among both the *indépendantistes* and anti-*indépendantistes* continued to criticise both the Matignon Accord and lack of greater government action to achieve their objectives, no matter how different they were. There seemed to reign a general consensus, however, that the state and the various parties in New Caledonia should attempt to work out some arrangement for the future before the 1998 vote – a simple choice between approval and rejection of independence would again divide the population and could plunge New Caledonia into renewed turmoil. Suggestions for such a compromise included greater autonomy, as has eventuated in French Polynesia, or a 'free association' compact between France and the territory. It is improbable that the referendum in 1998 will fix the status of the territory once and for all unless France agrees to withdraw entirely, a move which would provoke the wrath of the Caldoches (and, undoubtedly, spark violence) and could set off a political crisis in France. No matter what constitutional situation prevails, debates over the symbols of sovereignty (the name of the country and its flag, for example) as well as major issues such as land rights and the division of economic and political power are likely to endure.

8 French Polynesia and Wallis and Futuna in the 1980s

France's Polynesian territories experienced nowhere near the level of upheaval in New Caledonia during the 1980s.[1] Political developments during the decade displayed a distinct continuity with preceding years, both in the ideologies deployed and in the political personalities who took an active role in public life. Yet both French Polynesia and Wallis and Futuna witnessed several dramatic episodes of political confrontation, as well as underlying socio-economic changes apt to recast political life. In addition, Paris granted French Polynesia a statute of autonomy which gave it a greater control of its own affairs than existed in any other overseas *département* or territory, and announced its intention to review the statute in force in Wallis and Futuna.

FRENCH POLYNESIA: POLITICAL FORCES

French Polynesia seldom made the front pages of French or foreign newspapers in the 1980s, except for the continuing coverage of nuclear tests in Mururoa and the controversy surrounding the experiments, the quarrelling among the numerous political parties in the territory, riots which wreaked havoc in Papeete in 1987, the damage caused by hurricanes which occasionally battered the outer islands (particularly in 1983) and several *affaires* which momentarily captured international attention. One such drama was the 1983 trial of two Frenchmen, and their women accomplices, accused of the murder of Olivier Bréaud, the son of a wealthy Tahiti businessman; reports of the gruesome bashing to death of the victim, and the preceding sexual orgies, allegedly attended by a number of French Polynesian personalities, provided ample material for sensational reporting.[2] Several years later came a more spectacular scandal involving the family of Marlon Brando, who owns an island in the territory. Brando's son was accused, tried and convicted of killing Dag Drollet, the son of a prominent Tahitian politician; Drollet was the boyfriend of the assassin's half-sister, Cheyenne, the daughter of Brando and a Tahitian woman. Although the murder and the trial took place in Los Angeles, the Polynesian connection added exoticism to the tragedy, and there is a possibility of judicial action in Tahiti as well.[3] Yet another tragedy which scored headlines occurred in 1987 in Faaite, an atoll of some two hundred inhabitants in the Tuamotu islands. The highly Christianised population of the island had converted to a charismatic movement in the Catholic church, and one night the believers tortured and burned at the stake six of their fellow islanders whom they thought were possessed by evil spirits; anthropologists interpreted the Faaite massacre in terms of excesses of spiritual fervour and collective psychosis.[4]

Underlying and continuing concerns in French Polynesia provided more problems for political life than such episodes of violence, and political opinion was often divided about such topics. The nuclear question remained of great importance to Tahiti, both because of the exceptional role that the CEP has played in the territory's economy and because of fears about environmental pollution and health hazards. The pro-independence leaders, and various other politicians and parties, have opposed the tests although they have expressed concerns about the effect on the Polynesian economy should the test site be closed. Even politicians who have supported the CEP have based their arguments on the economic benefits it brings to Tahiti rather than on the military justification for the testing. Those who have maintained that the testing should be continued have been increasingly on the defensive in the face of harsh criticism of France's nuclear experiments both within French Polynesia, and, particularly, from outside, but few could suggest economic activities to replace nuclear testing and provide the same levels of investment and employment that presently result from the CEP activities.[5]

Concern about the economic health of Tahiti, or lack of it, was a basic source of political bickering, especially since by the end of the 1980s French Polynesia counted 16 000 unemployed persons, the territory showed a ninety per cent trade deficit, and the government registered ever higher budget deficits (which reached $US73.4 million in 1990).[6] Politicians hurled charges against each other of financial mismanagement, over-spending and outright corruption, but all parties faced the difficulty of outlining plans for reinvigorating the economy of islands endowed with few natural resources other than their beauty and tourist potential; the lack of an income tax – and the unwillingness of any party or government to commit political suicide by instituting such a tax – as well as reliance on metropolitan transfers to finance the high wages, extensive social services and comfortable standard of living to which many Polynesians had become accustomed were also obstacles to development.

A third area for regular debate was the status of French Polynesia in relation to France, a subject of contention common in the DOM-TOMs. Revisions of the statute of administration of French Polynesia in 1946, 1956, 1958 and 1977 had not provided a final solution to the problem of these relations. *Indépendantistes* only garnered fifteen to twenty per cent of votes in French Polynesia, but they pursued their cause with great vigour; several of the minuscule fringe pro-independence groups even attempted acts of violence.[7] At the other end of the spectrum, suggestions that French Polynesia be thoroughly integrated with France through *départementalisation* were also heard. But most discussion revolved around the issue of how much autonomy French Polynesia should enjoy, and by the 1980s all political groups, even those which previously had been wary of self-government, favoured greater autonomy. In fact, Gaston Flosse, the leader of the conservative Tahoera'a Huira'atira, allied to the neo-Gaullist RPR in the *métropole*, in 1980 publicly announced his conversion to support for autonomy, which he had previously feared could lead to independence. Flosse subsequently became the prime exponent of autonomy and the promoter of a new statute, adopted in 1984, which vested unparalleled powers in the head of the Polynesian government. Even after the adoption of the new law, various campaigners pushed either for revision of the act, as did occur in 1990, or for the devolution of greater power onto the territorial government; some suggested that French Polynesia be transformed into an 'associated state' in the framework of a revived French Union.[8] The incessant discussion about constitutional and administrative questions prompted President Mitterrand to declare, during a visit to Tahiti, that it was impossible to revise legislation every five years and that more pressing problems needed attention.[9]

If the questions debated in French Polynesian politics seemed to change little over the decade, the personalities also remained the same. The individual who dominated Tahitian politics more than any other during this period was undoubtedly Flosse. Born in 1931 on the island of Mangaréva, Flosse is of mixed European and Polynesian parentage, proclaims himself proud of both heritages and is equally fluent in French and Tahitian. Flosse was trained as a schoolteacher but became a wealthy businessman with interests in real estate, insurance, shipping and the hotel industry. In 1977, he was elected *député* of the Papeete suburb of Pirae, a post he retains. In the 1970s, he had reorganised the conservative forces of the territory into the Tahoera'a Huira'atira and turned it into a modern political party, tightly organised at the base and professionally run from the centre. Flosse recruited support from a number of other prominent figures in Tahiti, but just as often fell out with them. Politics in the 1980s was largely the chronicle of the shifting configuration of politicians allied with or grouped against Flosse. Among those who played important roles were Alexandre Léontieff, an economist who served as a minister in Flosse's government but who eventually ousted his mentor; Emile Vernaudon, nicknamed the 'sheriff' for his colourful personality, also a businessman; Enrique (or 'Quito') Braun-Ortega, another businessman, and others whose connections with Flosse were both business and political. (Such links were in one case personal as well; Edouard Fritch, Flosse's political ally and *suppléant* in parliamentary elections, is his son-in-law.)

Arrayed against Flosse and his forces were the pro-independence leaders who had come to the fore in the 1970s, Oscar Temaru and Jacqui Drollet. Temaru was elected mayor of the working-class Papeete suburb of Fa'a'a in 1983 and has been the vocal leader of one of the independence parties, the Tavini Huira'atira or Front de Libération de la Polynésie; Temaru also won a seat in the Polynesian Territorial Assembly in 1986. Drollet, a marine biologist, was one of the founders of another independence party, Ia Mana Te Nuna'a, and a member of the Territorial Assembly from 1982 to 1991. Another opponent of Flosse was Jean Juventin, the long-time mayor of Papeete. Others who consider themselves the heirs to Pouvanaa a Oopa and his successors, Francis Sanford and John Teariki, joined the opposition to Flosse, who had defeated Sanford in a national parliamentary election in 1977.

These politicians and their parties marshalled support from the Tahitian élite and from the masses of the population during the 1980s. With more sophisticated means of promoting their views and greater media opportunities – the establishment of several newspapers, albeit short-lived, and the opening of the government controlled airwaves to opposition candidates – popular appeals became easier.[10] The rapid urbanisation of French Polynesia, increasing levels of education and concerns about the future all helped to politicise electors in the territory, while these same socio-economic developments created new problems, such as overcrowding in Papeete, rising unemployment and delinquency, which the parties had to promise to tackle. At the same time, the isolation and fragility of the outer islands in French Polynesia meant that the well-timed visit of a political figure or the dispensing of gifts could be of great import in determining the outcome of an election. For instance, Flosse was both praised and criticised for his trips to the Tuamotus after the cyclones of 1983 and the setting up of a government body charged with disbursing large sums of money for reconstruction of the devastated islands.

All candidates drew on the particular situation of French Polynesia to enhance their electoral possibilities. For example, Oscar Temaru emphasised his identification with the authentically Polynesian, or Maohi, identity which he argued was threatened by foreign migration, French control and the local *demi* élite.[11] By contrast, Flosse, in the eyes both of his supporters and his critics, by the 1980s had become a Tahitian leader, or *metua*, much like Pouvanaa (though of distinctly different views), able and willing to reward his allies and embodying the reputation of Tahiti at home and abroad.[12] But both Temaru and Flosse also sought to bolster their positions with help from outside Tahiti. Flosse served as Jacques Chirac's Secretary of State for the South Pacific from 1986 to 1988, the first islander to hold a French ministerial portfolio. In this capacity, Flosse travelled widely throughout Oceania and developed cordial relations with overseas political leaders, particularly in the Cook Islands and Tonga. His work, generally credited with substantial successes, helped improve France's tarnished reputation in the

South Pacific and also boosted Flosse's personal profile (though not without creating some opposition to him). Temaru, and to a lesser extent Drollet, meanwhile gained international stature through their promotion of independence for French Polynesia. Temaru was a regular visitor to conferences on a nuclear-free and independent Pacific and presented the case for an independent French Polynesia (or 'Maohi Polynesia' as he termed it) to the United Nations committee considering the relisting of the territory on its roster of non-decolonised places.[13] Ia Mana, for its part, was the only Tahitian political party to support the French Socialist Party in the election of 1981, although Emile Vernaudon (at least temporarily) and Alexandre Léontieff established mutually beneficial relations with the PS and French government during the 1980s.

FRENCH POLYNESIA: THE EVENTS OF THE 1980S

A summary chronology cannot do justice to the complex political life of French Polynesia, the connections between politics and economics, the working of party apparatuses and the intervention of the French state, the roles of charismatic leaders and clientelistic governments. What it does reveal is that political battling was, to a great extent – although with the partial exception of the pro-independence groups – a struggle of those in power to maintain their position and of those outside (or on the margins of power) to displace them. Ideological differences, or even great variations in programmes and policies, were less important than their personal and electoral struggle.[14]

The first great political change of the decade occurred in 1982 in elections for the Polynesian Territorial Assembly, when Flosse's party defeated Sanford and his allies. Since the Tahoera'a Huira'atira gained only thirteen of thirty seats in the assembly, Flosse initially tried to form a coalition with an old opponent, John Teariki, with whom Flosse, since his conversion to autonomy two years before, shared similar ideas on self-government. Teariki's followers refused to endorse the agreement, however, but Emile Vernaudon and several of his colleagues shifted camps to give Flosse a majority. Elections to the councils of the *communes* the next year confirmed Flosse's domination in Polynesian politics; although the *indépendantiste* Temaru was elected in Fa'a'a and Juventin maintained his hold in Papeete, the Tahoera'a candidate defeated Teariki for the mayoralty of Mooréa, bringing to an end Teariki's thirty year tenure in the office, and Flosse's party won control of various other municipal councils as well.

The year 1984 was dominated by round-table discussions between French Polynesian politicians and French administrators about the new statute planned for the territory. Flosse, Juventin, Senator Daniel Millaud and other politicians expressed reservations about the provisions offered by Paris but most accepted the agreement, which came into force in September 1984. The statute stated that French Polynesia is an 'overseas territory endowed with internal autonomy in the framework of the [French] Republic'. The French state retains control over a significant number of areas, including external relations, immigration, currency, defence, justice and the police and certain areas of law. However, the other areas of administration are handled by the Territorial Assembly, and six to ten ministers who form the government. In addition, there is a president of the government elected by the Assembly. The French state is represented by a High Commissioner, who heads the bureaucracy of the national government. But the territory's government is responsible for French Polynesia's own bureaucracy, finance, public works, and the day-to-day running of the territory's affairs. The president enjoys the right of consultation with Paris on various matters and for all practical purposes acts as chief of state in French Polynesia. The new statute maintained ultimate French political control over the territory, and the importance of metropolitan financial transfers ensures the budgetary dependency of Tahiti on France. But the legal arrangements of 1984, and such symbols as an official French Polynesian flag, have meant that Tahiti has a degree of self-government unique among the DOM-TOMs.[15]

Under the terms of the 1984 statute, Flosse was now president of the territorial government and head of the council of ministers. The next elections in Polynesia for the European Parliament, which were held in 1984, excited little interest, although Flosse was named to the list of nationwide candidates proposed by the RPR-UDF coalition in France. Basing his campaign on the honour which would accrue to Polynesia if it sent a delegate to Strasbourg – 'Between Flosse and Jospin [the head of the PS list of candidates], choose the Polynesian', read one poster – Flosse won twice as many votes as in the 1982 territorial election. In the event, however, as head of the territorial executive council, Flosse was ineligible to take his seat in the European Parliament and was replaced by another candidate from the RPR-UDF list.

His position was reinforced after his 1984 victory and the promulgation of the new statute for French Polynesia, and Flosse began to forge ties with other Pacific countries and groups. In particular, as the situation in New Caledonia reached boiling point, Flosse became more vocal in his support for the opponents of independence there. He hosted and then signed an agreement for cooperation with the RPCR senator from New Caledonia, Dick Ukeiwé, intending to establish solidarity between French loyalist forces in the Pacific; the French government, however, declared the agreement unconstitutional. Flosse's attention to the anti-*indépendantistes* sparked support for the FLNKS among Tahiti's own *indépendantistes*, notably Temaru.[16]

The legislative elections in France in 1986 also saw elections for the territorial government in French Polynesia. The elections were hard-fought and marked by vociferous allegations hurled at different candidates. For example, newspapers labelled Flosse 'Mr Ten Per Cent', made comparisons between him and Emperor Bokassa or pictured him as a crab whose claws grabbed at money – all in reference to his reputedly shady business dealings and personal wealth. Even with such opposition, Flosse came out ahead in the election. The Tahoera'a Huira'atira counted only 30 000 votes, against 45 000 won by their different opponents, but the anti-Flosse forces were badly divided among seven different parties. The *indépendantistes* had doubled their vote total to twenty per cent but were still a small minority; Juventin and Vernaudon remained critics of and rivals to Flosse but could hardly match his political strength. Forming a coalition, Flosse put together a majority of twenty-four seats in the newly enlarged Territorial Assembly of forty-one seats. The Tahoera'a also won both French Polynesia's seats in the French National Assembly, although Flosse ceded his seat to his *suppléant*. Three days after the election, the new French Prime Minister, Jacques Chirac, named Flosse Secretary of State assigned to South Pacific Affairs. Flosse now attained the pinnacle of his power – president of the government of French Polynesia, Secretary of State in the French national government, mayor of Pirae and the victor in elections both to the French and European parliaments.

Flosse's rivals, including some of his allies, soon mounted an assault on him, and his star began to fall. Labour unrest also compromised his position after strikes by UTA cabin crews, dockworkers and Polynesian workers in Mururoa in the last months of 1986. Their industrial action was economic rather than political – the airline employees claimed their wages were lower than those of employees doing comparable work in France or New Caledonia, the dockers objected to a French shipping company using labour from a rival organisation of stevedores, and the Mururoa workers feared the loss of jobs if a rumour of France abandoning its nuclear testing facility proved true. But the controversy, added to criticism that Flosse was both power-hungry and authoritarian, hurt his reputation. Flosse himself confessed that he was wearing too many political hats for his own good, and on 7 February 1987 resigned as president of the Tahitian government.

Flosse was not replaced by his heir presumptive, Alexandre Léontieff, former vice-president of the Territorial Assembly and a *député* in Paris, but by another lieutenant, Jacques Teuira. Rumours circulated that Flosse feared Léontieff would be less malleable as his replacement than Teuira, but some analysts said Teuira's victory represented the triumph of a more traditional and personalised Tahitian style of politics over the technocratic, moderate approach of Léontieff.[17] Rumours also suggested that officials in Paris, including the Chirac government, were unhappy with Flosse's failure to win greater support in the Pacific for France's position in New Caledonia and had urged him to choose between his presidency and his ministerial portfolio.

The new government did not fare well. In July 1987, there was another strike by dockworkers, then in September a renewed round of protest. Ships' officers, deckhands and engineers went on strike to demand higher pay, followed by dockers, and finally by airport workers.[18] Among those on strike were workers on Mururoa, and a strike declared by dockers in Papeete on 22 October was aimed at solidarity with them. The next day dockers occupied the Motu-Uta port area and blockaded roads leading into and out of Papeete; the government called in troops, who fired tear gas grenades. So began a riot on the night of 26 October. A group of 500–1000 protesters rampaged around Papeete, burning and looting. Eight buildings were gutted, twenty-three shops destroyed and seventy-five others damaged. Twenty persons were injured, and damages were estimated at $A70 million. Over seventy people were arrested in the worst such action ever seen in Tahiti. Claims that Temaru's Front de Libération de la Polynésie was involved in the riots went unsubstantiated, as were allegations that the municipal government of Juventin had turned a blind eye to the participation of city workers in the action. Further criticism was directed at the French High Commissioner, who soon retired, and the president of the government, Teuira.[19]

Partly as an aftermath of the riot, Teuira resigned in December 1987, brought down by charges that he had asked the High Commissioner to call in troops in October and by the defection of several ministers from his majority. The new president was Flosse's ex-protégé, Léontieff, who now headed an unwieldy coalition composed of all of the anti-Flosse members of the Territorial Assembly, including Juventin, Vernaudon, Braun-Ortega and Drollet. (Drollet, head of the *indépendantiste* party Ia Mana, even accepted a ministerial portfolio.) The palace coup had obviously been directed at Flosse and Teuira, seen as his trustworthy lieutenant, and the strange bedfellows of the new political coalition struggled to formulate a programme acceptable to its members. The defeat of the RPR by the PS in the French legislative elections of mid-1988 improved its fortunes, and with the resignation of the Chirac government, Flosse also lost his position as Secretary of State. Seemingly omnipotent only two years before, Flosse was now reduced to being mayor of Pirae. The new French government of Michel Rocard was sympathetic to Léontieff, in part because of its opposition to Flosse. Vernaudon, who defeated Flosse as *député*, responded favourably to the overtures of the Socialists though without formal affiliation with the PS. Léontieff's government, largely with funds provided by Paris, undertook new efforts at economic development and the amelioration of social problems in Tahiti, trying thereby to defuse support for both Flosse and the *indépendantistes* and to confront the economic and social problems besetting the territory. Léontieff had his own problems including lack of agreement among the members of his government and a challenge to the very legality of his ministerial appointments.[20] Nevertheless, he held on to power (and meanwhile defeated his rival Teuira in a mayoral election), and he and his ally Juventin were able to welcome President Mitterrand to French Polynesia in 1990 on a visit to celebrate the centenary of the municipality of Papeete.

Political tensions heightened in preparation for the territorial elections of March 1991. Léontieff contested the election under the banner of his Ti Tiarama party, in union with Juventin, one of a total of fifty-seven party groups and 627 candidates vying for the forty-one seats of French Polynesia's assembly. Support for the president came, somewhat unenthusiastically, from the unwieldy coalition he had put together several years previously, but even some who had agreed to back the incumbent coalition stood on their own tickets. The Tahiti newspapers were filled with the various advertisements and the communiqués of the different parties, and rumours about candidates also circulated. Flosse's advocates charged that the French government had already poured large sums of money into the territory – and had promised to wipe out its large budget deficit – to keep Flosse out of office and to secure the re-election of Léontieff. The incumbents alleged financial improprieties on the part of Flosse and pointed to two impending court cases against him connected to his business and political dealings and which, if successfully prosecuted, could make him ineligible to hold office.

Turnout in the elections was high at 78 per cent, but many of the political parties were unsuccessful at returning even a single member to the Territorial Assembly. The Tahoera'a gained the largest proportion of votes, followed by the Juventin-Léontieff coalition, Temaru's party and that of Vernaudon. The results gave the Tahoera'a eighteen seats, against fourteen for the coalition of Léontieff and Juventin; neither group, therefore, had enough seats to form a majority. Among the *indépendantistes*, Ia Mana lost all three of its seats, while Temaru's FLP increased its seats from two to four. (The total vote for the two pro-independence parties remained stable from 1986 to 1991, at around 14 per cent of all votes cast.) The remainder of the seats were held by Emile Vernaudon and his allies. Vernaudon was then elected speaker of the Assembly, defeating Temaru, the only other candidate. The first attempt to elect a president of the government failed, when the Léontieff-Juventin group and Temaru's followers boycotted the session and no quorum could be achieved. Behind the scenes, negotiations were taking place to put together a majority, with Vernaudon the main politician to woo. Most observers guessed he would ally with Léontieff, both because of his declared sympathy for the Socialists in France and because his previous co-operation with Flosse had been extremely short-lived; but even if Vernaudon's five seats had gone to Léontieff, Te Tiarama would still not have had a majority. The Assembly in that case would have been hung with the deciding votes held by Temaru. In the event, and after vacillation, Vernaudon decided to support Flosse, allowing him to be elected president early in April. Flosse thus made a spectacular comeback from his resignation in 1987 and subsequent decline.

Back in power, Flosse ordered an independent audit of the budget of Léontieff's government and demanded that Paris agree to take over the huge Tahitian debt, just as it had supposedly agreed to do before Léontieff lost office. Flosse implied that were the government not agreeable to his demands, he could be tempted into support for independence. An indication of underlying social problems that would eventually destabilise Flosse's rule came with public demonstrations in July 1991 against Flosse's proposal for new indirect taxes. Protesters blocked west coast roads in Papeete; the High Commissioner sent in gendarmes. Both demonstrators and police suffered minor injuries. Flosse agreed to withdraw his tax proposal and, somewhat oddly, stepped down from his presidency for two weeks to reflect on matters. He then resumed control of the government, but political alliances were soon rearranged as Vernaudon and Flosse split, and Flosse aligned with his long-time rival Jean Juventin.

In a decade of the political life of Tahiti, Flosse had shown himself the only person able to co-ordinate a major political party efficiently and to recruit mass support successfully. The other political groups had largely been able only to ally for or against the Tahoera'a; only the *indépendantistes* had managed to maintain their positions intact, yet Ia Mana seemed a spent force, partly compromised by Drollet's participation in the Léontieff government. The multiplicity of political parties, and the ambitions – and, it was often alleged, corruption – of politicians made it difficult to establish a force able to counterbalance Flosse's party machine. But Flosse had also succeeded in appropriating the autonomist position of his former adversaries and institutionalising a new level of self-government in 1984, thus cutting the ground from underneath many of his opponents. The government in Paris, intent on pursuing a policy of administrative decentralisation but also fearing the sort of destabilisation in Tahiti which had erupted in New Caledonia,[21] had been forced to work with Flosse; that very collaboration had made it more difficult, and ultimately impossible, to unseat Flosse in 1991.

The racial and cultural *métissage* which had taken place in Tahiti in the two centuries after the first contacts with Europeans made the sort of rebellion that New Caledonia experienced in the 1980s unlikely. Political debate in Tahiti revolved around two major issues, independence and Mururoa.[22] But, in reality, daily politics in Tahiti continued to involve more mundane issues, and loyalty among electors seemed to centre on a personal figure or party rather than an ideology (except for the *indépendantistes* and then only to a degree). Yet the underlying social problems, notably unemployment, coupled with inequalities among the territory's population, aggravated by inflated salaries for public servants and the lack of an income tax, threatened to widen cleavages between different groups and to become points of political discontent and possibly conflagration.

WALLIS AND FUTUNA

The shape of politics in Wallis and Futuna has been quite different from that of French Polynesia or New Caledonia.[23] Like other citizens of the French Pacific, inhabitants of Wallis and Futuna enjoy the right to elect a senator and *député* to the French parliament as well as a local assembly, and elections are regularly held; never, however, have they experienced the confrontations and violence which have marked balloting in New Caledonia, nor even the political in-fighting and coalition-building popular in Tahiti. In any case, there has existed in Wallis and Futuna an informal power-sharing collaboration among the traditional chieftains – the 'king' of Wallis and the two 'kings' of Futuna and their councils – the elected representatives in the assembly, and the Administrateur Supérieur and other officials sent from Paris. The traditional chieftains continue to exercise authority over Polynesian customary questions, while the administration and assembly handle more 'European-style' problems. In the background, the Catholic church and its priests retain much of the considerable influence they have held in Wallis and Futuna since the early nineteenth century.[24]

Wallisians and Futunans have generally participated enthusiastically in elections – for instance, in the national legislative and presidential elections in 1981, more than three-quarters of the eligible voters cast ballots, and even in the elections to the European Parliament in 1984, in which Wallisians and Futunans could also vote, just under three-quarters of the electorate went to the polling booths. There were no strictly local parties, and voters have traditionally chosen only between two parties – the PCF, the PS and the Front National have been practically inexistent in the territory. In the legislative elections of 1981, over four-fifths of the votes cast went to the conservative RPR or the centrist UDF; in the second round of voting in presidential elections earlier that year, Valéry Giscard d'Estaing scored 98 per cent of the votes. It was not surprising, therefore, that Wallis and Futuna's *député*, Benjamin Brial, affiliated with the UDF, held office for several decades, and that one of the most popular *métropolitain* politicians in the territory has been Raymond Barre, a former prime minister, UDF leader and friend of Brial.

There were occasionally, if very rarely, incidents of social action during these years. For instance, in October 1986, after threatening telephone calls to a government official and the breaking of a window by a stone thrown at an administrative building, the government declared a state of emergency and deployed troops around Mata-Utu. The confrontation soon blew over, but the kings provided only a bare minimum of ceremony for a visit by the Minister of the DOM-TOMs later in the year. 'Young Turks' in the local population charged that the administration was too closely linked with the conservative Brial.[25]

In the 1988 elections to the National Assembly, Brial again received a majority of votes, even if a reduced majority of only 52 per cent. When authorities discovered irregularities in the balloting, however, a by-election was held and Brial's opponent, Kamilo Gata, affiliated with the left-of-centre Mouvement des Radicaux de Gauche, was elected. The change did not perhaps indicate a major ideological realignment so much as a preference for a different sort of candidate. Brial was an old-style, traditional notable, whereas the younger (then thirty-year-old) Gata was a former lawyer and official in the administration who presented a more modern, professional appearance to the electorate. Gata's advisers and supporters included a number of younger Wallisians and Futunans, more highly educated and with more cosmopolitan backgrounds than many of their compatriots.

The change corresponded to an underlying social evolution in Wallis and Futuna. A new generation had emerged, often with the experience of having lived in France during military service or tertiary education or having worked in New Caledonia. The influence of the church and the customary chiefs had waned slightly. There appeared more interest in a vague sort of modernisation of Wallis and Futuna, prompted partly by the arrival of radio in Wallis in 1979 and television in 1986. *Indépendantiste* sentiment was notable by its total absence, but there have been stirrings indicating a desire for change. In late 1990, a strike by schoolteachers represented a certain *prise de position* against the Catholic church, which controls all primary schools in the territory – a situation unique in France; it also showed the potential power of the Force Ouvrière trade union which organised the strikes.[26] In the meantime, the government had admitted that the time was nigh for a reexamination of the statute of administration for Wallis and Futuna, which has not been revised since its adoption in 1962. Somewhat paradoxically, in a territory which was completely 'loyal' to France, the population already lived in a state of 'de facto independence' under the control of the kings and largely autonomous local officials.[27]

One important political change concerned the Wallisian and Futunan population of New Caledonia. Wallisians and Futunans are actually more numerous in New Caledonia than in their own islands; many are of voting age and are eligible to cast ballots there. The anti-*indépendantiste* RPCR has always counted on the support of Wallisians and Futunans in New Caledonia, largely because of their concern about what their future would hold in an independent Kanak state. For many, the lack of economic and professional prospects in Wallis and Futuna would make a return home undesirable, and many Wallisian and Futunan families have been in New Caledonia for a considerable time or even generations. In the 1980s, the RPCR was often accused of using Wallisians as a front-line at demonstrations or of engaging them for certain militant actions against the *indépendantistes*. For this very reason, Melanesians viewed Wallisians and Futunans with suspicion.

In 1989 the Union Océanienne (UO) was founded in New Caledonia by a group of Wallisians and Futunans, who announced that their party would also be open to other ethnic groups. The UO, most of whose members were young, urban Wallisians and Futunans, expressed their desire for a more equal sharing of economic and social benefits in New Caledonia and greater recognition for Pacific cultures, including those of both Melanesians and Wallisians and Futunans. Profiting from the Matignon Accord, it also asked for greater opportunities for education and professional development to be made available to the Wallisians and Futunans of New Caledonia; it proclaimed its opposition to racism and colonialism, support for democratic institutions and a preference for a modified market economy. The UO, therefore, tried to steer a course between the FLNKS and the RPCR, but the establishment of the party was a de facto declaration of Wallisian and Futunan emancipation from the influence of the anti-*indépendantistes*. Links between the UO and the victorious supporters of Kamilo Gata in Wallis and Futuna highlighted the new turn in thinking and political strategy for Wallis and Futuna. But, given the delicate demographic balance – and resulting political balance – between Melanesians and Europeans in New Caledonia, the appearance of the party could also be of significant import in that territory's political life.[28]

The election of Gata, the emergence of an active union movement and the foundation of the Union Océanienne were signal political events for Wallis and Futuna, but they might symbolise political changes in all three French territories. Gata is a new breed of politician, just as Léontieff and his former ministers in French Polynesia (and some of the *protégés* of Gaston Flosse already taking their place in the ministerial offices of Papeete); with the assassinations of Machoro, Tjibaou and Yeiwéné, a new generation of island political leaders has been pushed to the fore in New Caledonia. The activism of the teachers' union in Wallis finds parallels in the willingness of such extra-parliamentary institutions as the Protestant and Catholic churches to enter political disputes in New Caledonia and French Polynesia. And the view of the Union Océanienne on the need for compromise and collaboration between the different ethnic groups which make up the populations of the French territories is not so far removed from recent views expressed by both *indépendantistes* and anti-*indépendantistes*. The underlying sociological changes of migration, urbanisation and increased wage employment may herald a different form and content for political life over the next decades. However, such developments will not necessarily bring about the independence of France's Pacific territories.

9 Nuclear Testing, the 'New Pacific' and French International Policy

No aspect of French activity in the South Pacific since the 1960s has been so controversial as France's testing of nuclear devices in Polynesia. Critics argue that in carrying out these tests, France is poisoning the Pacific Ocean and its people and dangerously militarising the region. Defenders of the testing counter that it poses no health or environmental risks and that it is necessary for France to preserve its national defence, of which the nuclear force is an integral part. In either case, the need to test nuclear devices has often been advanced as the primary reason that France must maintain its sovereign presence in Oceania. Still other observers point out the economic and social effects the testing has wrought on French Polynesia, for better or worse, and the dislocation that might result should France discontinue the tests.

This chapter examines French nuclear policy and the history of testing in French Polynesia since the 1960s. It then looks at French military, strategic and international relations in the 1980s focusing particularly on the contours of French foreign policy and the role the South Pacific played in it; it also considers various geopolitical arguments about the present and future importance of the Pacific in world affairs and French strategic stakes in Oceania.

FRENCH NUCLEAR POLICY

In 1945 the French government established the Commissariat à l'Energie Atomique to study and develop atomic energy in France.[1] The head of the provisional government, Charles de Gaulle, signed the order setting up the commission, but a small, dedicated group of administrator-technocrats, politicians and military officers who formed an atomic lobby then and afterwards were the main promoters of the French nuclear policy.[2]

There followed seven years of research and development, and in 1952 the first construction of nuclear reactors in France. The 1950s also saw a gradual acceptance of the necessity for France to develop nuclear weapons.

Various events in the 1950s favoured the conversion of French military and political decision-makers to a nuclear option. In 1954, the North Atlantic Treaty Organisation (NATO), in which France was then an active participant, approved the principle of a tactical nuclear response to outside aggression. The same year, the defeat of the French by Indochinese rebels brought into question the efficacy of conventional French forces. The question of the future of Germany continued to preoccupy Paris, despite reasonably cordial relations between France and the two Germanies; concerns centred on German rearmament, the admission of the Federal Republic to NATO and the influence of West Germany inside the alliance. In 1956, France and its Israeli and English allies suffered another defeat, this time in the Suez Canal fiasco – perhaps a crucial turning point in France's decision to 'go nuclear'.[3] Meanwhile, France was obliged to grant full independence to its protectorates of Morocco and Tunisia, and insurrection exploded in Algeria. Ever present was the Cold War, and the acquisition of long-range bombers by the Soviet Union, already a nuclear power, followed by the successful launch of the Sputnik spacecraft in 1957, indicated clear Communist advances over the 'free world'. Politicians worried that the Soviet Union, by supporting anti-colonial movements in Africa and Asia, was outflanking the West and that it directly menaced Europe, where a power vacuum could only be filled by a nuclear force; a British government White Paper published in 1957 stated that the United Kingdom could only be defended by a nuclear deterrent. Such developments provided ample justification for France to develop a nuclear arsenal, and by the late 1950s the atomic lobby had convinced the French government that this was the appropriate course to follow. General Paul Ely coined the term '*force de frappe*', or striking force, that caught on as the designation for France's nuclear armour. The governments of the last years of the Fourth Republic hoped for military and political advantage, as well as scientific and technological benefits, from the new *force de frappe*.

In April 1958, the French prime minister signed the order for the construction of a nuclear bomb; the first tests were planned for 1960. Shortly thereafter, with the Algerian crisis threatening to divide France even further than it had already done, de Gaulle returned to power. The Fifth Republic soon replaced the Fourth Republic, but de Gaulle maintained the commitment to French nuclear weapons. In February 1960, the first French nuclear test was successfully carried out, when a nuclear device was exploded at Reggane in the Algerian Sahara. Other atmospheric tests followed, and in 1961 France also began a series of underground explosions in southern Algeria. France had joined the nuclear club of the United States, the Soviet Union and Britain, but it was losing its struggle against the Algerian nationalists.

France granted independence to Algeria in 1962; according to the Evian Accords, which ended the conflict, Algeria permitted France to use military bases in the country for a further five years, but Paris would evidently have to find other testing sites in the short or long term. Already in the 1950s, French authorities had decided that only two general locations were suitable for the nuclear experiments: the unoccupied regions of the Algerian Sahara or the remote atolls of French Polynesia (either in the Gambier or Marquesas islands). These were the sole venues which were sufficiently distant from large population centres, which could be easily defended and which were areas under complete French sovereignty. The Algerian site now gone, the Oceanic alternative remained. In 1961, the Minister for Overseas France had disavowed the government's intention to transfer testing to Polynesia, but in January 1963, de Gaulle announced to a visiting delegation of French Polynesian politicians that the testing site would indeed be relocated to the Gambiers.[4]

De Gaulle saw the establishment of a test site in French Polynesia as a way to inject capital and provide employment for France's somnolent Oceanic outpost and, in his conversations with Polynesian leaders, implied that the facility should be considered as something of a reward for the *ralliement* of Polynesians to the Free French during the Second World War and their loyalty during the 1950s. But in de Gaulle's view nuclear policy had a *raison d'état* far exceeding the needs (or protests) of a small overseas territory. Whereas under the Fourth Republic, France's nuclear policy was conceived as a vital adjunct to membership in NATO, de Gaulle used the nuclear option to distance France from its partners in the Atlantic alliance. In the late 1950s, a rift developed between the United States and France, partly because of the Americans' refusal to share their nuclear technology with the French, either by making Paris privy to that technology or by selling nuclear weapons to France. Furthermore, Washington and London declined de Gaulle's request to set up a Franco-British-American triumvirate to direct NATO. This proposal, advanced by de Gaulle in a memorandum to the American Secretary of State in 1958 and repeated on several subsequent occasions, represented an effort to elevate France to an equal footing with the United States and Britain in the Western Alliance, but it fell on deaf ears. The willingness of the Americans to share their secrets with the British reinforced de Gaulle's perception of a special relationship between Washington and London which excluded Paris. From this rift emerged de Gaulle's gradual disengagement from NATO and his determination to pursue French testing and use the *force de frappe* as both a military and political linchpin for an independent French foreign policy.[5] Thus de Gaulle declined to participate in the Geneva Disarmament Conference of 1961, and France signed neither the Nuclear Test Ban Treaty of 1963 nor the Nuclear Non-Proliferation Treaty of 1967. In 1966, France removed itself from the military command of NATO and required NATO forces to leave French territory, although it did not quit the alliance.

France's nuclear capability, demonstrated by the tests carried out in the Sahara, then in Polynesia, became the foundation for French foreign policy in the 1960s, and thereafter. Many of the main lines of that external policy, as first formulated by de Gaulle, remained unchanged after his retirement in 1969; even with the election of a Socialist president in 1981, the pillars of French foreign policy stayed in place. Among the major tenets were that France's foreign policy was global, that France exercised its foreign policy independently of the decisions made by the United States or any alliance (though without renouncing its link with the 'West'), that France should develop its role as an intermediary between the West and the Soviet Union and its allies, that France held a special position in Africa, and that France would be a leader of the European Community.[6] In the pursuit of this foreign policy, the nuclear arsenal played a variety of roles, the first of which was military.

In the 1960s, France fitted its Mirage jets with nuclear weapons, then equipped ballistic missiles with nuclear warheads; the French navy built nuclear-powered submarines, perhaps designed to carry nuclear weapons. The range of the missiles would enable France to carry out a nuclear strike anywhere in Europe, including the western Soviet Union. In the 1960s, General Charles Ailleret, the major theoretician of nuclear policy, defined a strategy in which France could attack and destroy targets in any direction; despite *rapprochement* with the Soviet Union, itself a signal achievement of de Gaulle's policy, the obvious target remained the USSR. French policy-makers claimed that since it was not certain that the United States would come to France's aid in case of a nuclear attack, France must be capable of defending itself, alone if necessary. But it was also hinted that use of France's nuclear weapons could serve as a trigger for a supportive American nuclear response. Yet another idea afloat was that of 'proportional deterrence': France's possession of a nuclear force and declaration of willingness to use it meant that any aggressor would hesitate to attack France; the potential gain offered by such an attack would be more than offset by the damage France would inflict on the aggressor. The exact conditions under which France would activate its nuclear weaponry – a conventional attack on French territory, an attack on France's allies, an attack on France's strategic interests, a nuclear attack, or some other scenario – remained an object of debate and an intentional lack of official clarification.

But France's nuclear policy had a second and perhaps more important aim, which was political. De Gaulle had been clear that nuclear weapons gave France independence and a certain status in world affairs: 'A great State which does not possess them, while others have them, does not command its own destiny'.[7] France's nuclear strength kept the world from being divided into two blocs by the superpowers. It provided France with a mandate for sitting at the negotiating table to resolve international conflicts. As de Gaulle stated at the time of the first nuclear test in 1960, the bomb not only allowed France to defend itself, the French Community and the West, but, paradoxically, gave France a stronger position from which to press for nuclear disarmament. In short, atomic weapons made France a power with which other nations had to contend. This connected with French prestige, its self-perceived role as an international power, but the view corresponded to a real determination not to withdraw from world affairs as, for example, Britain had done with the evacuation of its troops from 'east of Aden' in 1963. If France manifestly could not be in the same league as the superpowers, it could reinforce its position as a power-broker and as a major power of the second order.[8] Nuclear policy was more useful as a *political* than as a *military* asset.[9]

The nuclear force served other uses as well. Nuclear weapons and reactors displayed French technological prowess. The nuclear force provided a significant number of jobs and contracts for armaments manufacturers. It served as a symbol of near consensus in public debate. Nuclear weapons, and nuclear tests, represented a concession, or a reward, to the French military, which in the 1950s and 1960s had been disheartened by defeat in Indochina and Algeria and the loss of most of France's empire. In particular, the French Navy, which had always enjoyed a dominant position in formulating and executing colonial policy, won control of the testing site in Polynesia as a recognition of its role in French life and compensation for the end of empire.[10] This also secured the loyalty of the military to the civilian government.[11]

More recent official and quasi-official pronouncements have confirmed the outlines of French nuclear policy established earlier. A former commander of the French testing station in Mururoa stated in 1989: 'The doctrine of dissuasion which was adopted at the outset of the construction of our nuclear arsenal has not varied in twenty-five years. It is a strictly defensive doctrine', based on the idea of proportional deterrence. Henri Fages added that the nuclear arsenal is 'a trump-card in the exercise of our international responsibilities. It is also a major contribution to peace'. He concluded: 'Our entire history teaches us that it is necessary to be in a position of strength in order to guarantee peace and also to negotiate a sort of disarmament that will not be a simple pretence for capitulation. To that end, a nuclear arsenal which is continually modernised is indispensable.'[12]

In addition to the continuity of French nuclear policy, the near unanimous approval which that policy has achieved in

France holds great significance. In the mid-1960s, part of the political élite opposed de Gaulle's nuclear policy; in 1965, the presidential candidate of the united Socialist and Communist opposition, François Mitterrand, was among them. A Ligue Nationale contre la Force de Frappe and later a Mouvement contre l'Armement Atomique protested at French nuclear policy. Yet in 1966, one opinion poll showed that 46 per cent of the French approved the maintenance of a nuclear force, while 42 per cent opposed the policy (and 12 per cent expressed no opinion).[13] Since that time many opponents have converted. Mitterrand still opposed nuclear weapons and testing as a candidate for the Elysée in 1981, but after his election, he became a staunch defender of the nuclear arsenal. Anti-nuclear groups have small, but vocal, followings in France, and there are only a few prominent opponents of nuclear weapons (and nuclear energy).[14] The only mainstream political movement which has opposed nuclear policy, the Communist Party, has steadily lost votes and influence; the impact of its critique is thus muted.

No other political party (except the ecologists) has been willing to take a strong stand against atomic weapons and atomic energy for the simple reason that such a position would probably lose rather than gain votes. Explaining the solid public approval for nuclear policy is rather more difficult. It undoubtedly connects with a widely-held feeling that a nuclear arsenal does protect French independence and give Paris a greater say in world affairs than would otherwise be possible. Renunciation of nuclear potential would handicap France politically and militarily, especially without corresponding disarmament by other nuclear powers (and a forswearing of the nuclear alternative by potential nuclear powers). French politicians have repeatedly stated that nuclear resources are vital to France, and that Paris will not substantially disarm or abandon its nuclear weapons until the superpowers reduce their arsenals;[15] few seem to question these arguments. The cost of the nuclear force, and of defence in general, has not been a great item of debate in French life. An electorate accustomed to rhetoric about the nation's role in international affairs, but also a population with memories of foreign invasion three times in less than a century, defeat in two colonial wars, a tradition of military prestige and the reality of universal male military service, is perhaps not apt to question the efficacy or the morality of a nuclear force.

NUCLEAR TESTING IN POLYNESIA

Construction of the Centre d'Expérimentation du Pacifique (CEP) began in 1963; the building of the site, support facilities and auxiliary projects had immense economic and social effects on French Polynesia.[16] The first experiment took place on 2 July 1966, when a nuclear device mounted on a barge was exploded off the coast of Fangataufa atoll. As with all atmospheric tests, this initial French explosion in Oceania created some radioactive pollution. Other experiments followed, including one on 11 September 1966, during which President de Gaulle witnessed the detonation of a nuclear device suspended from a balloon. This aerial method avoided some of the maritime, although not the atmospheric, pollution. The first thermonuclear explosion took place in August 1968. France continued to carry out atmospheric tests until 1974. French authorities claimed that tests provided invaluable information for the maintenance and modernisation of France's nuclear force. They argued that pollution was minimal, basing their statements on data accumulated from numerous meteorological and biological samples. The French also pointed out that the United States had effected 213 atmospheric explosions in the Pacific from 1946 to 1963, Britain had carried out 21 between 1952 and 1957 and France had undertaken only 45 tests. The French share amounted to 11.8 megatons out of a total of 167 megatons exploded in Oceania. During this period, two foreign scientific enquiries – one by South American specialists in 1972, the other by the Australian Academy of Sciences the following year – concluded that the French tests did not create unacceptable health or pollution hazards for the South Pacific.[17]

However, atmospheric testing provoked protests in French Polynesia and the region. When de Gaulle visited Tahiti in 1966, the *député* for French Polynesia, John Teariki, proclaimed the loyalty of Polynesians to France and their desire for continued attachment to the Republic, but he stated in strong terms that the creation of the CEP and the tests, which had been carried out without consultation with the French Polynesian population, constituted a violation of the rights of local citizens. Testing endangered their health and that of their descendants, and it denied their right to an expression of opinion about the nuclear activities.[18] Anti-nuclear personalities and groups in France also voiced opposition; Jean-Jacques Servan-Schreiber, newspaper editor and well-known politician from the Parti Radical, led one anti-nuclear delegation to Tahiti. Neighbouring states raised objections to testing; the Cook Islands, the nearest state to French Polynesia, had adopted resolutions condemning French testing even before the experiments started.[19] By the early 1970s the level of protest had mounted. South American states joined those of the South Pacific in calling for the end of French atmospheric testing. Private groups entered the fray, and Greenpeace sailed a protest vessel into the waters of French Polynesia in 1972. Public demonstrations were held in Australia and New Zealand. French airline offices were attacked, and French consulates in Sydney and Auckland were fire-bombed. The Australian Council of Trade Unions forbade its members to handle French goods in Australian ports, and the Australian post office refused to carry French mail. The Australian and New Zealand governments asked the United Nations Committee on Disarmament to press for a cessation of the tests. Then New Zealand and Australia filed suit in the International Court of Justice in 1973 to have the French tests stopped. France announced its position that the court had no jurisdiction over the matter and declined even to send lawyers to plead their case. The court in The Hague nevertheless ruled against France, but Paris ignored the verdict.[20] France set off one more atmospheric explosion in 1974, then announced that henceforth only underground tests would be carried out.

The reasons for the growth of protests in the early 1970s lay both in heightened perceptions of the dangers of atmospheric testing and the general intellectual and political climate of the period. New Zealand scientists determined that each explosion left radioactive debris scattered across the South Pacific, including on inhabited islands, especially when the wind direction favoured the dissemination of particulates; Australian scientists detected increased concentrations of strontium in iodine and calcium as far away as Australia each time a nuclear device was exploded. Ecological organisations, notably Greenpeace, became more active in spreading the anti-nuclear message. Greenpeace sent another vessel to Polynesia in 1973; French Navy officials boarded the ship and allegedly roughed up the protesters. The general climate of the early 1970s was hardly conducive to French tests: protests against colonialism and strong-armed governments had rekindled the political activism of the 1968 student demonstrations, while the 'Earth Day' activities of 1970 had inspired new concern about the environment. The accession to independence of several island states in the South Pacific made the French control of its territories seem anachronistic, and French harassment of autonomists and *indépendantistes* in Tahiti hardly improved Paris's image.[21]

The new, centrist government of Valéry Giscard d'Estaing, which replaced that of de Gaulle's successor, Georges Pompidou, in 1974, decided to continue the tests, although only in their subterranean or submarine form. Regular tests have since been carried out, generally at the rate of eight per year, though the number was reduced to six in 1989. To effect the tests, engineers bore holes into the coral or the lagoon of the atoll of Mururoa. The base of each hole is lined with concrete, the explosive charge lowered into the shaft in a container, and the explosion detonated. The explosion heats the rock to such a temperature that the magma collapses in upon itself, sealing the hole. In the first few years of underground tests, holes were bored into the coral, but in more recent years, they have been bored into the lagoon of Mururoa, but otherwise tests are conducted in the same fashion.

With the advent of underground tests, criticism of France's nuclear experiments temporarily quietened; some observers hoped that testing would be gradually phased out, or that the election of a Socialist president in France in 1981 would bring them to a halt. President Mitterrand in fact ordered a review of testing policy, but the government quickly concluded that continued testing was vital to French security. Protest subsequently revived, and critics said that, contrary to French claims, radioactive materials were leaking from the holes bored into the coral and the lagoon of Mururoa. This leakage, they argued, poisoned the water and entered the food chain, and ultimately affected humans through their consumption of fish. They added that Mururoa itself resembled a Swiss cheese, full of holes from the tests, and that the entire atoll might crumble, releasing even more radioactivity. Critics also cited evidence for ciguatera poisoning in fish and data which showed that Polynesians had a higher than average incidence of certain diseases which could be linked to nuclear exposure. They pointed out that French officials either did not keep or would not release certain health figures for French Polynesia (notably on cancer), and that those statistics which were made public had all been documented by French military doctors. Finally, they said that safeguards against accidents were insufficient and that, despite French efforts, pollution and other problems had occurred both with natural disasters, such as tidal waves and cyclones, and through French dumping of radioactive materials into the ocean.[22]

The French denied dumping radioactive materials or maintaining insufficient protection against nuclear pollution. They claimed that regular tests had proved that there were no harmful effects from the testing either to French Polynesia or neighbouring island groups. Authorities said that the basalt base of Mururoa protected it against the escape of radioactivity and denied that the atoll was in danger of disintegration. To support their views, the French pointed to reports completed by the eminent geologist Haroun Tazieff in 1982, which concluded that the tests were harmless. The French also cited the evidence of a team of scientists from Australia, New Zealand and Papua New Guinea which had been invited to Mururoa in the early 1980s and allowed to carry out scientific tests to measure possible dangers from the explosions.[23] Indeed, the 'Atkinson Report' issued by the scientists judged that there existed no danger, but critics countered that the scientists had only been allowed to perform rapidly a limited range of experiments in marginal areas.

To charges that France has continued to pollute the Pacific, fouling the 'backyard' of such countries as Australia, Mexico and Chile with its tests, Paris has responded that Mururoa is 1200 kilometres from Tahiti and 6000 kilometres from the coasts of Australia and South America. Paris is closer to the Soviet testing site in Kazakhstan than is Sydney to Mururoa. Furthermore, the French have pointed out that only 200 residents live in a circle of 500 kilometres around the French testing site, whereas 1.2 million people live in the same radius from the Soviet site and 15 million live 500 kilometres or closer to the American testing range in Nevada. They have added that residents of Tahiti are exposed to less natural and artificial radioactivity than inhabitants of most regions of the northern hemisphere. The usual retort to these defences, as advanced by anti-nuclear activists and politicians, is that if the testing is so safe, then the French should transfer it to metropolitan France, perhaps to the Massif Central. The French have replied that this is impossible because an area of approximately thirty kilometres devoid of rail lines, buildings, bridges and underground conduits must exist around the test site to safeguard against any seismic damage from the explosions, and that no area of France fits this criterion. But the French have also implied that since the tests are widely *perceived* as dangerous, such a transferral would be politically unpopular.[24]

Arguments and counter-arguments have not definitively proved that the nuclear tests are either entirely safe or necessarily harmful. If much of the world remains unconcerned about French testing, in Australasia and the South Pacific there reigns a quasi-consensus that the tests are at least potentially dangerous to human life and the environment and that they should be stopped. Concern for the environment reached new heights in the region in the 1980s with debate about logging of forests, pollution of beaches, the 'greenhouse effect', the disposal of wastes (including toxic chemicals) and the depletion of maritime resources through such fishing techniques as purse-seining. Individuals and organisations ranging from rock bands to conservation groups have promoted ecological awareness. Furthermore, pro-environmental platforms have been popular with voters and thus important for electoral victories. In this context, nuclear tests in French Polynesia have provided an obvious target for criticism in the South Pacific, especially when coupled with indictments of French 'colonialism'. France has often become a scapegoat for criticism, no matter how legitimate concerns about the effects of nuclear experiments may be.

Opposition to French testing, as well as to visits by American nuclear-powered warships to Oceania, came to a head in 1985. The South Pacific Forum, an association of independent South Pacific states, including Australia and New Zealand, but excluding the French territories, adopted a proposal for a South Pacific Nuclear-Free Zone. The Rarotonga Treaty forbade nuclear testing of any sort, the storing or use of nuclear weapons and the disposal of nuclear wastes in the South Pacific. Most of the micro-states of Oceania signed the treaty, as did the regional 'superpowers' of Australia and New Zealand. France, the United States and the United Kingdom, however, declined to sign. Nor did Vanuatu, arguing that the treaty was too limited. The Soviet Union signed the Rarotonga Treaty but noted that if the international situation changed, so could Soviet policy. The treaty, without the signature of several nuclear powers and with no means of enforcement, was more useful in creating greater solidarity among the South Pacific states than in denuclearising the area concerned.[25]

Another event of the mid-1980s, directly connected to the nuclear issue and which also tarnished France's reputation in the South Pacific, was the so-called *Rainbow Warrior* affair. In May 1985, French agents sank the *Rainbow Warrior*, the flagship of the ecology organisation Greenpeace, in the harbour of Auckland, New Zealand. A Greenpeace photographer, the only person still aboard, lost his life when the ship was sunk. Greenpeace had been one of the most ardent campaigners against nuclear activities in the Pacific; in addition to sending boats to French Polynesia to protest against tests, it had also promoted the cause of Micronesian islanders suffering the effects of earlier American atomic tests. In 1985, Greenpeace intended sending the *Rainbow Warrior* once again to Mururoa. In the midst of heated debate on the French presence in the South Pacific – the violent confrontations in New Caledonia and debate on a 'nuclear-free zone' – the Greenpeace vessel was particularly unwelcome to the French.

After the sinking of the ship, New Zealand police arrested two French intelligence agents, first identified by the pseudonym of the 'Turenge' couple and later identified as Alain Mafart and Dominique Prieur. Trial testimony proved that the attack on the Greenpeace ship had been approved in Paris and launched from New Caledonia, although it has remained unclear whether the highest levels of authority, notably the French prime minister or president, had prior knowledge of the action. The French agents were sentenced to prison by the New Zealand courts. Later negotiations between New Zealand and France – which, according to New Zealand commentators, threatened European Community retaliations on New Zealand exports if the pair were not released – concluded with an arrangement for the agents to serve their sentence in protective French custody on the small island of Hao in French Polynesia. France agreed to pay reparations to New Zealand and to the family of the dead photographer, as well as to Greenpeace. Mafart and

Prieur served part of their sentence in Hao, but both were repatriated to France on grounds of ill health before the conclusion of their sentence. An international arbitration panel, including both a French and a New Zealand judge, later decided that this repatriation violated the agreement worked out between Paris and Wellington, but by the time that decision was handed down, in 1990, relations between the two countries were already healing.[26]

The nations of the South Pacific greeted the sinking of the Greenpeace ship with strident denunciations of France. Governments throughout the region condemned French trespassing in New Zealand and lamented the violence. Other commentators, then and later, spoke of French 'state terrorism'.[27] Commentators in France raised questions about the morality and usefulness of such an action, but some conservative sectors of public opinion hailed the French agents and the Minister of Defence under whose aegis the sinking took place as veritable heroes. More blinkered observers even referred to the illegality of New Zealand holding the 'Turenge' couple 'hostage' after their arrest.[28] An official French investigation was branded a whitewash by many French commentators, who wondered who precisely had ordered the attack, why the French intelligence service had decided upon it and why the effort had not been entirely successful. Such questions were never fully answered, although the head of the French intelligence bureau and the Minister of Defence were forced to resign, and President Mitterrand apologised for the incident.

The Greenpeace affair helped France's reputation in the South Pacific to plunge to an all-time low, but did not bring about a reassessment of French policy or an end to testing. To critics, the action implied disdain for the ecological concerns raised by Greenpeace and others and a total unwillingness to engage in a dialogue about the possible hazards of nuclear testing; it was also, quite obviously, a violation of the sovereignty of another nation. Those who defended the sinking of the *Rainbow Warrior* were relatively few in number, but they spoke of France's need to protect its security and France's right to carry out such activities as nuclear testing in areas under its internationally recognised sovereignty. For those able to draw back from the affair, the incident showed that France would attend to its geopolitical and strategic concerns in the South

Pacific (and elsewhere) before preoccupying itself with the concerns of local populations; in short, *raison d'état* dictated French action.[29] France's international role took precedence over strictly regional considerations, and France would brook interference in its global activities from neither private organisations nor individuals. The violence of the *Rainbow Warrior* incident showed the determination of policy-makers and intelligence services to achieve their objectives, but the bungling of the strike and the lack of clarity about final responsibility raised questions about actions of this nature.[30] Not until the visit of Michel Rocard to New Zealand in 1991 was the rift between the two countries healed, but bitterness at the French attack has not disappeared.[31]

THE NEW PACIFIC?

Controversy surrounding French nuclear testing and the Greenpeace incident pointed to a lively debate on the role of the South Pacific in world affairs in the 1980s. Seldom heretofore had Oceania seemed a region of international rivalry – the period of the 'imperial scramble' in the late nineteenth century and the years of the Second World War constitute notable (but only partial) exceptions. In the 1980s world opinion focused on the South Pacific as never before. Clashes between Caldoches and Kanaks in New Caledonia, two *coups d'état* in Fiji in 1987 and an independence movement in the Papua New Guinea province of Bougainville all indicated that the 'Pacific way of life', seemingly an exemplary form of peaceful existence and conflict resolution which writers had only a few years earlier championed as successful in the South Pacific,[32] had either lost its momentum or had never actually existed. Furthermore, the tiny island states of the Pacific, most of which had gained independence peacefully during the 1970s, now seemed targets for big power struggles. France held on to its three Pacific territories and tried to extend its influence elsewhere; the United States continued to administer American Samoa and Guam and tried to maintain the Micronesian islands, formerly the Trust Territory of the Pacific Islands, in its sphere through compacts of free association; Australia and New Zealand forged closer relationships with South Pacific states. But other powers, as well, had become interested, as Japan and China sent diplomatic delegations and offered aid to island micro-states, and Japan became the biggest aid donor to the region. The Soviet leader, Mikhail Gorbachev, made a speech in Vladivostok in 1987 in which he stated that the USSR intended to play a larger role in the Pacific region. The Soviet Union then signed fishing treaties with Vanuatu and Kiribati, although these treaties gave the Soviets no port rights and lapsed after the first years of operation. Vanuatu, something of a renegade among the micro-states, established diplomatic relations with Cuba, which for some observers threatened the penetration of the island Pacific by communism and radicalism. Meanwhile, New Zealand disallowed the visits of nuclear-powered American warships and thus broke apart the Australian/New Zealand/United States (ANZUS) security alliance. A few political figures in the South Pacific, notably several parliamentarians from Vanuatu and a fringe pro-independence group in New Caledonia, established links with Libya, and observers worried that Colonel Kaddafi would soon launch terrorist attacks in Oceania and neighbouring states.[33]

Such events (or rumours) provided reasons for the greater discussion of the South Pacific in the 1980s. But other factors also played a role. As various powers jockeyed for strengthened positions in the world, the Pacific Ocean and the islands of the Pacific represented one of the 'last frontiers' where they could acquire influence; rivalries for economic, political and military leverage created a new 'scramble for the Pacific' in which even micro-states represented real, if small, prizes. This scramble took on added import because of changes occurring in the competing countries themselves, such as *perestroika* and *glasnost* in the Soviet Union, the modernisation of China and the rise to economic power of Japan. Nations such as Libya and Cuba tried to establish influence far outside their traditional fields of activity, in locales as diverse as Africa, the Indian Ocean and the Pacific. A third reason for greater attention lay in the prospects, more mooted than proven, for economic gain from exploitation of trading routes and, particularly, maritime resources. The Law of the Sea Conference of 1982 and the establishment of 'exclusive economic zones' around coastlines implied a new maritime mercantilism. Talk of the possibility for exploiting undersea resources, notably the 'polymetallic nodules' of mineral deposits on the continental shelf or the ocean floor, or of extracting minerals from the sea itself, whetted appetites for profit. The islands of the Pacific presented relatively few land-based resources (with the exception of mineral deposits in Papua New Guinea, Nauru and New Caledonia), but they did promise potential profits from activities ranging from fishing to tourism. The 'scramble' for South Pacific influence so evident in the 1980s was not unlike the colonial rivalries of the late 1800s – efforts by competing powers to obtain a stake in distant regions possessed of potential for supposed or real economic, political or cultural gain.[34]

Finally, the island Pacific was viewed as a geographical link between the Americas and Asia, an insular annexe to Asia. As in the nineteenth century, outsiders coveted Asian markets at the same time as they feared Asian economic or political predominance. The 1980s were the decade of the Pacific, as commentators trumpeted the achievements – or warned against the dangers – of Japan, the newly industrialising states of Hong Kong, Taiwan, South Korea and Singapore, and the economic might of America's west coast.[35] 'Asia-Pacific' became a catch-phrase for both opportunities and menaces, models of successful development and threats to establish political powers and economies. In this context, the tiny islands of the South Pacific assumed an importance they could not otherwise have claimed.

French policy-makers and political theorists, especially those adopting the approach of geopolitics, were in the forefront in formulating arguments about the new Pacific. Some spoke from quasi-official positions in French public life and gained a wide audience for their theories. Replying to criticism of French policy in New Caledonia and French Polynesia and to such events as the *Rainbow Warrior* affair, they articulated new rationales for France to remain a power in the South Pacific. Military, political, economic and cultural advantages which would accrue to France from this continued presence became the themes of this new Oceanic lobby.

GEOPOLITICS AND THE OCEANIC LOBBY: THE ARGUMENTS[36]

The Pacific was in fashion in the 1980s. A 1988 report by *Newsweek* magazine argued that 'as the twentieth century draws to a close, the world is in the midst of a profound geopolitical shift' and announced the dawn of the 'Pacific century'. The previous year, writers in *Pacific Islands Monthly* affirmed that 'the Pacific basin has become the booming region in a world whose economic face has been changing rapidly'. Already in 1984, *L'Express* labelled the Pacific the 'new axis of the world'; as a 'commercial and technological superpower and a key strategic zone, the Pacific attracts admiration and excites covetousness'. A French political science review, *Politique étrangère*, titled a 1985 article 'The Pacific, a "new world"'. Protagonists representing diverse points of view hailed the region. According to a position paper of the RPR, 'The Pacific has become a crucial region in today's world. It is the Ocean of the future – a Mediterranean with planetary dimensions'. François Mitterrand spoke about 'a vision of human mass whose weight is transferring to the shores of the Pacific the traditional centres of power'.[37]

The new Pacific wave brought in its wake keen academic and political interest. New journals, books and study centres proliferated – one list counted eighty-five centres, institutions and associations concerned just with the Pacific islands. Several of these centres were in France.[38] Conferences regularly examined particular problems of the Pacific or the very phenomenon of 'the Pacific'. In Paris, for example, the Institut International Géopolitique organized a colloquium in 1984 on 'A Challenge called Pacific – Hopes and Fears of the West?', while the Ligue Internationale pour les Droits et la Libération des Peuples in 1986 sponsored a conference on 'The Pacific – Myths and Realities'. A number of books published in France during the decade examined the new Pacific. Taken together, their arguments amount to a new conservative geopolitical theory of the Pacific, one with direct relevance to France's presence in the region. The ideas had significant influence on French policymakers of the 1980s, particularly those in conservative political groups and those opposed to independence for France's territories.

Several books may be taken as representative of the new 'school' of thought. One of the first heralds of the 'new Pacific', perhaps not coincidentally, came from the French Pacific islands. In 1979 a group of New Caledonians, led by a psychiatrist, Georges Zeldine, formed the Cercle Katara in Nouméa to 'promote New Caledonians' reflection on the general problems of the contemporary world'. The club published a series of booklets on the South Pacific, the first of which, *Pacifique Sud, une paix précaire: Essai de géostrategie*, appeared in 1980.[39] It announced ideas subsequently taken up by other analysts. Three years later, the Institut du Pacifique was formed in Paris (with the Cercle Katara as an institutional member) and published a seminal work entitled *Le Pacifique, 'nouveau centre du monde'*. The Institut du Pacifique, which counts among its members academics, diplomats, business people and military personnel, became a prime lobby in France seeking to promote interest in Asia and the Pacific basin. It organised a number of seminars and published several collections of documents and articles, as well as an encyclopaedic study of Australia issued to coincide with Australia's bicentenary. Widening its ambitions, the Institut du Pacifique helped set up a European Pacific Institute and several of its members participated in establishing a Centre Européen d'Etudes Australiennes.[40]

In addition to the works of the Cercle Katara and the Institut du Pacifique, individuals published geopolitical works on the Asia-Pacific region. Notable among them was a work published in 1983 by two journalists, Gilles Etrillard and François Sureau, which charted the rising power of the Asian countries,[41] and a polemical tract written by a French conservative senator, Pierre Lacour.[42] A number of other works have looked more particularly at the issue of New Caledonia and the strategic stakes France has in that territory.[43] There were differences in perspective among these authors, but there emerged a rough theory of the 'new Pacific'.

One basic assumption of the 'new Pacific' lobby was that the Pacific formed a unit; the ocean linked rather than separated regions. Grouping together the countries of the Pacific littoral – from Asia to South and North America – the Institut du Pacifique provided impressive statistics to show that half the world's population and almost half of its gross product was produced in the 'Pacific'. Despite the multiplicity of natural resources, languages and cultures, political regimes and social organisations which characterised the Pacific basin, the authors emphasised the inter-connectedness and growing relations among the countries which border the Pacific Ocean. For the Institut du Pacifique, the countries of the Pacific shared certain traits: the Pacific was marked by 'great economic growth and technological innovation'. It formed 'a zone where, with the exception of several countries, notably the Communist ones, democracy is either well implanted or growing'. Furthermore, it was 'a zone where initiative and responsibility produce rewards' – a vague formulation of some sort of cultural dynamism.[44] Finally, it was a place where geopolitical and military tensions were growing. These traits and the links among the Pacific countries were significant because they implied that a country's presence in any part of the Pacific gave it an *entrée* into the whole basin and provided it with a legitimate reason for participating in economic, political or strategic activities which concerned the 'Pacific hemisphere'; France's overseas territories in Oceania, therefore, were seen to provide France with a toehold in a wider region.

The observers of the Pacific pointed to the great turbulence in the Asian and South American countries in the decades before the 1980s; focusing on Oceania, however, the Cercle Katara said that the Pacific islands until the 1970s were hardly touched by the economic, political and military currents which affected the rest of the world, and certainly by the big-power struggles which characterised other regions. According to the Cercle Katara:

> Such seemed to be the case from the end of the 1960s until now [the 1980s], because even the decolonisation of the Oceanic archipelagos took place in a climate of friendship, discretion and general good humour. So much so that in the middle of the unpredictable 1980s common sense led every observer of the region to affirm that it was an almost ideal sea of world peace in the present and for the future. One could judge from the evidence: no area of great agitation in these immense waters scattered with micro-archipelagos and picturesque populations, simple ambitions and more joyful [*ludiques*] than materialistic or ideological attitudes. A powerful Australo-New Zealand axis populated with descendants of Europeans, enjoying modernity and development, in fact controlled the zone, with French enclaves and a long Micronesian belt in the North which, joined to Hawaii, permitted the USA to keep out any imperialist penetration of the central or southern Pacific.[45]

Such a formulation, in retrospect, looks utopian and naive, but it corresponded to the view that the Pacific was blessed by a lack of political problems or outside interference. The assumption was, of course, that the presence of France and the United States, as well as the activities of Australia and New Zealand, were guarantees of security rather than examples of meddling.

For various authors, this situation changed dramatically in the 1980s, first of all, because of the economic ascendancy of the Asian powers, especially Japan. But, in a broader sense, the commentators felt that an increasing share of the world's population, economic power and potential military where-withal was being concentrated on the shores of the Pacific. The commercial clout of Japan and the newly industrialising countries of Asia, the growth in the economy of the Pacific seaboard of the United States and Canada and of Australia and New Zealand had shifted the centre of power away from traditional preserves towards the Pacific. The key to the observers' theory, therefore, was that the new centre of the world was or might become the 'Pacific basin'. The Cercle Katara proclaimed: 'We can only follow [the Americans] when they declare, like Toynbee, that the axis of the world will move during the next thirty years from the geographical West to the economic East.'[46] As Pierre Lacour worded the argument: 'The centre of the world is moving inexorably towards the Pacific basin, already fated to see a formidable economic development, then to become the favoured ground for the big powers' struggles for influence'.[47] Some of the writers nuanced their judgements. The Institut du Pacifique carefully noted that 'in the title of [our] book [*The Pacific, New Centre of the World*], neither the word "the" nor "a" new centre of the world is mentioned because that depends precisely on us French, on us Europeans, whether the Pacific is "the" or "a new centre of the world"'.[48] And Etrillard and Sureau cautioned that 'the vision of an inevitable and significant displacement of the centre of the world's gravity from the Atlantic to the Pacific is largely illusory'; instead they opted for a two-ocean view: 'Today, the Atlantic space *and* the Pacific space are taking a preponderant part in the creation of world wealth'.[49] Yet even they emphasised the rising power of the countries 'at the east of the world' and suggested that Asia and the Pacific, including the Pacific islands, were assuming increasing importance.

Following on from this argument, the various authors viewed the Pacific as a challenge to Europe and, more especially, to the French; these books constituted manifestos for action, not just reflections on political and economic realities. According to the Institut du Pacifique:

> If Europe weakens, the Pacific will be *the* new centre of the world, replacing the old centre based in the Atlantic. By contrast, the Pacific will be *a* new centre of the world, along with the Atlantic centre, if Europe, true to its history, its potential and its deeply-ingrained vocation, takes hold of itself and wakes up, both domestically and on an international plane, and continues to affirm and exercise its responsibilities and by doing so meets the challenge thrown down by the countries which border the Great Ocean.[50]

The challenge, the authors warned, was major and immediate; according to Zeldine, writing in 1984, 'Europe is at the present on the road to a total economic, political and social marginalisation in the Pacific hemisphere'.[51] The prospects were not rosy. The Cercle Katara sketched out four rather pessimistic scenarios for the Pacific: the 'entry of the cold war into the Pacific', especially if the Soviet Union succeeded in acquiring military bases or establishing a socialist and revolutionary regime in Fiji; the triumph of an expansionist political party in Japan which would lead to Japanese economic conquest of the region; a general 'North-South push' in which the over-populated countries of Asia, economically strong and inspired by radical ideologies, would invade the southern Pacific; or, in case of a nuclear apocalypse, a situation in which the Pacific would become a 'last refuge' for humanity, in which 'the "ends of the earth" have become the "New World" towards which the escapees of the "end of the world" will flee'.[52] The Institut du Pacifique similarly listed the various dangers threatening the Pacific: 'increasing military bi-polarisation to the profit of the two superpowers'; the 'weakening of alliances and the development of neutralist, pacifist and anti-nuclear currents' in the region; political explosions in the 'black holes' where destabilisation was most likely to occur, that is, Cambodia, Central America, Korea and the South Pacific; the strengthening of 'subversive movements' and ideas such as 'liberation theology

and Muslim fundamentalism'; and the 'problems born of economic development' and uncontrolled social metamorphosis.
The Institute outlined its three scenarios for the future: the
maintenance of a 'Nippon-American synergy' or 'triumphant
capitalism'; regional destabilisation because of the dangerous
intellectual and political currents sweeping the region; or – the
scenario preferred by the writers – the emergence of 'co-responsibility' among the nations of the Pacific which would work
together to maintain their distance from the political superpowers and the economic superpower (Japan), all the while
developing in a Western mould of democratisation and the
exchange economy. Only in this third scenario could France
play a role.[53]

France, at least as argued by a committed group of promoters, needed to meet the challenge of the Pacific. At one level, it
had to be able to compete commercially with the economic
pace-setters of the Pacific basin: 'The first lesson of the Pacific
concerns the flexibility' of the capitalist system, said Etrillard
and Sureau, adding that 'France should follow the Japanese
example': 'There is no solution for Europe except in a return
to [economic] flexibility, even to the ruggedness of economic
mechanisms which have become dilapidated'.[54] But France must
also respond to the political challenges of the Pacific – rising
nationalism, interest by outside powers, expansion by such countries as the Soviet Union, the dissemination of dangerous ideologies. Here the French territories could play a vital role. For
the Cercle Katara, in the worst-case scenario of a nuclear apocalypse, 'one of the important roles of New Caledonia . . . would
be to bear the torch of a new French civilisation or at least of
one which speaks French'.[55] But in a less catastrophic eventuality, New Caledonia and French Polynesia could be bases for
French activity and influence in the Asia-Pacific region. That
did not necessarily mean that the status quo must remain in
place, or that France must continue to administer its territories
as it had in the past. The Institut du Pacifique, for example,
favoured some sort of 'free association' between an autonomous New Caledonia and the *métropole.*

If suggestions of the Institut du Pacifique and the Cercle
Katara were relatively measured, the stand of another observer,
Pierre Lacour, was much more strident. For Lacour, France in
the mid–1980s was besieged by its adversaries in the Pacific.

Historical memories of Franco-English rivalry in the nineteenth century had not disappeared; because of the Pritchard affair,[56] in the Anglo-Saxon Pacific

> public opinion feeds on a tenacious rancour towards France, and the fires are often carefully stoked by the Protestant missions of all sects. Whence comes the hostile attitude of Australia and New Zealand, which is often expressed with extreme vehemence? We saw it only too well when France and Great Britain recognised the 'independence' of Vanuatu – in fact, an Australian protectorate by proxy which, incidentally, does not forbid landing rights to Soviet ships. Whence also the impudence with which Australia has condemned French atomic tests (after having organised ones in Australia) and the incorrectness or the culpable complacency of New Zealand in harbouring the subversive missionaries of Greenpeace.

Lacour added that Australia wanted to substitute itself for the old colonial powers in the Pacific, that Japan intended to take over the Pacific economy, that the Soviet Union had designs to penetrate the Pacific basin and even, in retrospect, that 'our eviction from Indochina was desired and prepared by President Franklin Roosevelt, obsessed by a hypocritical anti-colonialism'. France must thus reaffirm its control of its Pacific territories and defend itself against foreign incursion and domestic subversion.[57]

Certainly not all of the specialists associated with the Institut du Pacifique or the Cercle Katara, or other groups interested in the Pacific, agreed with Lacour's hysterical arguments. But many authors did extrapolate from a basic idea about the importance of the Pacific in the present and future and the fragility of France's role there to call for a reinforcement of Paris's position: continued nuclear testing in French Polynesia, the increase of military forces and material in New Caledonia, economic development to make the Pacific territories show-cases of French achievement and stepping-stones to the markets of Asia, the Americas and Australasia, and a struggle to preserve French cultural influence. Nuclear testing, efforts to combat independence and defence against real or perceived rivals became the linchpins for French policy in this view. The underly-

ing assumptions gained currency in the 1980s and, rather significantly, no opposing theory of the Pacific was formulated.
However, there existed a number of critiques for the views
expressed by the geopoliticians.

TOWARDS A CRITIQUE

The theses of the Pacific promoters were certainly not univer-
sally accepted, and their views varied – Etrillard and Sureau, for
instance, stated that 'the unity of the Pacific basin is fictitious'
and warned that 'the Pacific miracle does not exist'.[58] Hindsight
allows the detection of various errors in forecasting. None of
the authors predicted the enormous changes in the Soviet
Union and eastern Europe or the Tiananmen Square massacre
and its implications in China, but they were hardly alone in
their failure to foresee such developments. Nevertheless, much
of their argument was founded on the existence of and opposition to a monolithic and unreformed Communist ideology,
super-power rivalry and a large measure of non-cooperation
between the Communist world and other states. These realities
certainly existed in the world in the 1980s, even if they were
never significant in Oceania and have since faded. The authors
also failed to foresee the military coups in Fiji. Similarly, the
end of flirtation with such countries as Cuba and Libya by the
government of Vanuatu largely laid to rest fears of terrorism in
Oceania.

In addition to these specific failures in their works, more
substantial critiques of theses about a 'new Pacific' have been
voiced. The most succinct and cutting critique came from the
French geographer Yves Lacoste.[59] Lacoste accused the Institut
du Pacifique's book, in particular, of resorting to 'statistical
artifice', such as the inclusion of demographic and economic
figures for the entire Soviet Union and the United States, to
prove the weight of the Pacific in world affairs. Although relations between the countries of the northern Pacific were well
developed, he added, 'this does not prove that the Pacific will
henceforth be "the centre of the world"'. The Institut du
Pacifique's arguments were especially weak concerning the South
Pacific: 'The South Pacific is an immense emptiness'. Lacoste
charged that Pacific boosters resorted to grand theories of

world history such as those of Hegel, and of writers who saw an opposition between oceanic and continental empires (for example, the early twentieth century geographer Mackinder), and thus, 'The so-called geopolitical arguments are of a striking naivety'. Similarly, Régis Debray, then an adviser to President Mitterrand, dissented from the popular view. Asked if the Pacific represented the new centre of the world, he replied:

> No. In a world which fortunately has several centres, the Pacific must not become a myth. There is an economic dynamic, and the North Pacific is indeed becoming a Japanese-American condominium . . . . But the South Pacific is a different place, where the schemas of East and West and of North and South do not fit. As for strategic issues, the centres of the world will long remain the Atlantic and the Mediterranean.[60]

Lacoste and Debray agreed, however, that the Pacific had become an area of strategic sensitivity; both used the phrase 'the soft underbelly of the West' to describe the South Pacific. Lacoste added that the Soviet Union might try to benefit from the 'Balkanisation' of the South Pacific and that maritime routes had a potential usefulness for Soviet ships trying to reach a European theatre of war via the coasts of South America. Lacoste also did not reject the idea of Australian and New Zealand imperialism in the South Pacific because 'these two countries consider these waters to lie in their sphere of influence'.[61]

More specifically, military specialists disagreed with the policy implications of the Pacific geostrategists. Admiral Alexandre Sanguinetti in particular criticised the proposal of turning New Caledonia into an 'aircraft carrier' for French military forces in the Pacific basin. Sanguinetti argued that the French navy, by its very nature a mobile force equipped with long-range weapons, had no need for the sort of base Nouméa might provide. He also implied that it was unlikely that France would face military confrontations in Oceania, despite the changes taking place there and the rallying calls of Pacific promoters.[62]

Jean Chesneaux, a distinguished historian and leftist political activist, in *Transpacifiques* agreed with the geopoliticians that the Pacific had aroused growing interest and that the Pacific inspired debate on global questions. Otherwise, his views were diametrically opposed to theirs. He called the theory of the Pacific as the 'new centre of the world' 'intellectually feeble and specious' and also rejected the notions that the Pacific was the 'weak underbelly of the West', a technological Eldorado or a battlefield for confrontation between the US and the USSR. Chesneaux cast a plague on the houses of both superpowers: 'That the American order – either as a military system or a social project – hardly serves the basic interests of the peoples of the Pacific does not mean that the Soviet order is better'. Chesneaux downplayed any Soviet 'threat', emphasising the isolation of Soviet Asian bases and communications systems and Soviet lack of success in penetrating the South Pacific. What Chesneaux did fear was nuclear power; he argued that the Pacific had become 'one of the global centres of nuclear militarism', and the principle villains were the United States and France. He contested the idea that nuclear testing was either safe or necessary. Furthermore, he said, France should grant independence to New Caledonia and French Polynesia in order to preserve goodwill and France's legitimate influence: 'It is perhaps in renouncing its status as a power *in* the Pacific that France has the brightest future as an active power *of* the Pacific'. Chesneaux concluded by vaunting the Pacific style of life, based on indigenous structures and attitudes, which he termed 'an historical adventure as stimulating, but in a different way, as the docile rallying to the Japanese-American model which is unfolding on the beaches of the Great Ocean'.[63]

Various other questions and reservations could be raised about the underlying methodology and theory behind the study of the geopolitics and geostrategy of the Pacific (and about the critiques of those views). But several underlying issues in talk of a 'new Pacific' are particularly germane. First is the question of definition. For the Institut du Pacifique, the 'Pacific' comprised all countries and regions touched by Pacific waters and included the Soviet Union, Canada and the United States. Even more far-flung regions were assimilated into the Pacific, according to the Institute's book, including Burma (because of its cultural and political ties with other nations of Southeast Asia), and Bolivia (because, although the country lost its access to the Pacific shoreline, it still cherished dreams of regaining such a beachhead). Only such a broad definition permitted impressively large figures about the total population, production and trade which took place in the 'Pacific'. But the view ignored the evident lack of relations which existed among many countries of the Pacific basin. The smaller island nations, for example, had few contacts with countries other than the United States and Japan, Australia and New Zealand. Isolation has continued to be a problem in the South Pacific.

A concomitant of the absence of close relations in economics and politics has been the cultural diversity of the Pacific. Pacific promoters acknowledged the heterogeneity of the region yet assumed that it was of little importance. In the 'Pacific' are practised all the major religions; there are political systems ranging from Marxist to free-market capitalist and everything in between; literally hundreds of languages are spoken. Even in the South Pacific, where various politicians have championed an indigenous 'Pacific way', a common approach to life and politics, dissension has been more obvious than accord. The creation of a Melanesian Spearhead Group of independent nations and talks about the setting-up of a Polynesian community highlighted differences that have found echoes in varying systems of sovereignty: independent nations, freely associated states, overseas territories, dependencies of the United States, France, Britain, Chile, Australia, New Zealand and Indonesia, and disputed islands. What, after all, did a micro-state of several thousand inhabitants have in common with a country the size of China? Moreover, some countries have had very strong attachments outside the region – the dependent territories with their *métropoles*, others with ties to the Commonwealth, the EC (through the ACP group), the international Islamic or Indian communities, and so on. Such giants as the US and the USSR certainly have had interests divided between their Pacific coasts and other frontiers. In short, the Pacific in the 1980s displayed no unity and contacts were more often along a bilateral axis (for example, US-Japan, US-Australia, Japan-Australia) rather than a multi-polar one. The failures of efforts to form pan-Pacific organisations, from a Pacific Common Market to a Pacific Basin Community, gave evidence of the absence of common interests and links. 'The Pacific', which figured so largely in debates in the 1980s, was perhaps no more useful a concept than the outdated 'Levant' or 'Orient'.

Geographical reductionism did not pass unnoticed to the Pacific promoters. Etrillard and Sureau, after all, used 'Pacific' to refer to a subset of countries in the basin, while Lacour seemed to find it almost synonymous with 'Oceania'. Faced with the difficulty of defining the Pacific, various scholars have narrowed or widened the concept. The president of the Institut du Pacifique suggested the concept of the 'Southwest Pacific', including Southeast Asia, Australia and the Melanesian islands but excluding the other islands of Oceania and the Asian continent.[64] Some Indonesian scholars spoke of an Indian-Pacific 'hemisphere' stretching from the east coast of Africa to the west coast of the Americas, enclosing the areas of Indo-Malay migration which extend from Madagascar to Easter Island.[65] Neither idea, however, was particularly satisfactory. Each country in the region was liable to see its interest in a complex which included several centres, rather than in a solely Pacific framework. For instance, Australia's military planners talked about a line of defence arching from Christmas Island to Norfolk Island; the USA had a global defence system, of which the Pacific was only one element; France's defence perimeter included its overseas *départements* and territories and its neighbours in Europe and various friendly nations overseas. The islands of Oceania were only one part, albeit a significant one (because of nuclear testing), of France's strategic armour.

Along with the Pacific analysts' geographical reductionism went historical reductionism. An oft-repeated argument held that the Pacific has become the new Mediterranean. Yet the sheer size of the Pacific, disparities of development and differences in population, resources and culture in the countries concerned gave the lie to this point. The Pacific has not formed a *Weltwirtschaft* or even a cultural universe. The unity of the Mediterranean came precisely from the similarities which Fernand Braudel saw in regional structure, the constant interchange and the continuous cross-fertilisation that have been present in the Pacific only along specific axes. The expansion of civilisations, and the clash of civilisations, which Braudel found so prevalent throughout the Mediterranean, have been irregular and localised in the Pacific, not endemic. The writers quoted directly or indirectly by the geopolitical analysts, such as Hegel, Spengler, Mackinder and Toynbee, were those taken with great historical sweeps (although the geopoliticians explicitly rejected that other great systems-builder, Karl Marx); these systems have been largely discredited.

Another example of historical reductionism was the idea of the 'lessons of History' – a phrase which the Institut du Pacifique's book used, although few professional historians would have done so. Pacific geostrategists cited the precedent of Munich in 1938 to demand that Western appeasement not be repeated against, variously, Communists, the Soviet Union or the new industrial powers of Asia. Reference was frequently made to Japanese expansion – the Russo-Japanese War of 1904–1905, the invasion of Korea and Manchuria, the Japanese Greater Co-Prosperity Sphere, the Second World War; several authors called Japanese economic dynamism an economic Pearl Harbor. Similarly, the Soviet invasions of Hungary in the 1950s, Czechoslovakia in the 1960s, and Afghanistan in the 1980s led writers to speculate about future Soviet expansionism. The French withdrawal from Indochina, black Africa and the Maghreb, then from Vanuatu, was used as a warning against any abandonment of New Caledonia or the other French Pacific territories. Such examples – selectively chosen, since little reference was made to the American intervention in Korea and Vietnam, then Central America and the Caribbean – were suspect from a policy-making standpoint and simplistic from an historical one. They took no account of the changing global or national contexts, nor changes in ideology.

Ironically for the anti-Marxist Pacific promoters, economics was the key for the shift in the centre of world gravity. Furthermore, the ascendancy of one region, they suggested, must necessarily threaten or diminish the strength of another. Such intellectual mercantilism preferred neat schemas to complex designs, generalisations to nuances, grand sweeps of history to messy complexities. It further implied that economic, political and military ambitions were inextricably intertwined. Certainly they are related, but it is intellectually dubious to argue that just because Japan expanded so dramatically economically, it must also and inevitably expand politically (or militarily). The Soviet Union was not necessarily trying to effect political and military intervention just by signing a fishing treaty with Vanuatu or Kiribati. Vanuatu did not inaugurate an alliance with Cuba just because it established diplomatic relations with Havana. Nor, for that matter, just because France offered aid and technical assistance to the Polynesian states and Fiji, was it obviously trying to drive a wedge among the Oceanic nations or to buy support for its policy in New Caledonia and French Polynesia. In each of these cases, connections could be drawn, but stating that the actions were synonymous smacked of a conspiracy theory of international relations.

Many Pacific boosters did see a conspiracy, generally engineered by Anglo-Saxons (as French writers rather quaintly lumped together the Americans and British, Australians and New Zealanders), Japanese and Americans or, most often, Communists. The anti-Soviet message came out clearly in such statements as the following pronouncement from the Institut du Pacifique's book: 'The Soviet Union . . . is driven by a messianic and totalitarian impulse. She is our potential adversary in Europe, in terms of her direct strategy, and everywhere in the world, in terms of her indirect strategy'.[66] Such Cold War rhetoric gave the USSR credit for a more expansionist policy – and greater means to accomplish it – than Moscow actually possessed. It was hardly logical for the Pacific promoters to argue the community of interest in the Pacific basin, in one breath, and in the next to deny the Soviet Union an active role in the affairs of the Asia-Pacific region. Ironically, it was partly the power of the USSR's economy and demography which contributed to making the Pacific a new global centre, if such it was, and the Soviet Union has a larger Pacific shoreline than many of the states casually grouped into a 'Pacific' region. Fear of the Soviets also resurrected two older theories, the domino theory of one state or region after another falling to Communist control and the idea of containment of the Soviet menace. These ideas worked neither in theory nor in practice in the past.[67]

Anti-Communism also meant that the geopolitical views of the Pacific in the 1980s downplayed the notion of power, except as it was applied to the expansion of Communism and 'subversive' activities. For example, the Institut du Pacifique, in explaining American policy in Micronesia, said that 'the islanders' voting was always preceded by a campaign of information and explanation which allowed them to grasp that their interests and those of the United States could converge'.[68] This minimised the efforts of the United States to secure a favourable vote on a compact of free association with Palau through six referenda, marked by promises of vast government aid if islanders accepted visits of American nuclear ships; it overlooked as well the violence which resulted in the death of the president of Palau. Other examples of power relations, of course, were French activities in New Caledonia, where, irrespective of one's view on the evolution of the territory, the military and political arm of the state was strongly exercised; the *Rainbow Warrior* affair might also be invoked. Similarly, the actions of Indonesia in Irian Jaya and East Timor entered into this domain of *Realpolitik*.

Explicit in military and strategic arguments advanced by the Institut du Pacifique, Lacour, Zeldine and others was the aim of securing a French stake in the Pacific. The Institut du Pacifique's book summed it up:

> The surest way for France to keep a pre-eminent position among the nations of the Pacific zone – but also in the world at large – and to safeguard the utility of her language and the interest and universality of her culture is to put in place, in all fields, a policy of co-responsibility of which she will be the principal artisan and from which she will draw her true greatness.[69]

Underlying the programme, therefore, was the old Gaullist vision of French *grandeur* manifested on a global scale and based on military power (especially nuclear deterrence), economic wherewithal and a cultural vocation. This approach did not die with de Gaulle and was only slightly modified even by the 1980s.[70] In policy terms, this meant a continued military presence, including the nuclear testing programme. Economically, it implied, as Etrillard and Sureau pointed out, that France must learn from the Japanese economic miracle to restructure its own industry in order, as the Institut du Pacifique and Lacour emphasised, to compete with Japan and penetrate the Asian market. In principle, nothing in this programme was either surprising or particularly objectionable to most observers. When the Pacific boosters began to talk about specifics, however, their platform became more suspect. One example was the Institut du Pacifique's call for greater French cultural presence in the Pacific, certainly a laudable programme in itself. But the rhetoric (and the intention?) was compromised when the authors asked for non-French-speaking Pacific students and technicians to spend a period of study in France.

The excuse of [lack of knowledge of the] language is really inadmissible . . . . A single intelligent and open-minded non-French-speaker will quickly become a Francophone . . . . His stay in France will, in addition, make him a Francophile if he is made welcome in our country. Back in his own country, he will certainly occupy a position of responsibility in which he can influence the course of relations with France, not only in culture, but in all domains.[71]

This forthright statement seems reminiscent of the old dogma, dear to the colonial age, of assimilation of native élites into European culture and the use of cultural leverage for political gains.

This illustration reveals another basic assumption in the Pacific promoters' theory. By their own admission, their major interests were, first, global considerations and, secondly, the advantages which their own country could extract from the Pacific. French observers, therefore, looked to see what benefits France could gain from retaining control of its Pacific TOMs, developing its Asian markets or assuring itself a role in a future scenario of 'co-responsibility' in the Pacific. American observers similarly stressed the advantages of preserving the United States and its interests against the perceived onslaught of Communist ideology and Japanese technology. Australia's policymakers were concerned with finding markets and influence in Oceania and Southeast Asia and in getting a fair share of Chinese trade. Such nation-centred perspectives obscured a different view possible from inside island societies. One was an ethnographic perspective, the intention of a society to evolve within the boundaries of its own culture, even if that culture should be less than felicitous to outsiders – Melanesian and Polynesian custom, Islamic fundamentalism, varieties of Communist theory, isolationism. Like nineteenth century gunboat captains prying open the doors of China and Japan, or 1950s modernisation theorists for whom industrialisation, urbanisation and Westernisation were the benchmarks of Progress, some writers of the 1980s congratulated Asian and Oceanic countries when they opened themselves to Western ideas and products or castigated them when they established contacts which seemed less congenial to Western interests. This was not a simple question of an inside versus an outside view but rather a failure to appreciate fully the potential for each culture to assimilate, integrate or reject outside influence. Such was particularly the case with reference to the islands in the South Pacific. Whereas outside geostrategists saw the signature of a fishing deal between the Soviet Union and Kiribati or Vanuatu as a menace to regional security and the beginnings of Soviet incursion into Oceania, those in the micro-states simply saw easy revenue – or a way to force the hand of others by preying on their fears of Communism. Contacts between particular political movements in one or another island and outside powers may have held an altogether different meaning for people inside the small states than for those viewing the globe from European or American capitals.

IDEOLOGY AND POLICY

The ideas of the 'Pacific promoters' gained great credence in conservative milieux in France in the 1980s and were championed in particular by the government of Jacques Chirac and the RPR from 1986 to 1988. Yet many of the same ideas also underlined the arguments of centrist and Socialist politicians – the increasing importance of the Pacific basin, the economic and political changes in the region, the necessity for France to retain a stake in its development, the centrality of the French territories and of French nuclear power in assuring and protecting that stake. Such potent ideas were part of a Pacific mode in the 1980s which was not entirely eclipsed by the revolutions in eastern Europe at the end of the decade.

Discussion about the 'new Pacific' in the 1980s was the first time that the South Pacific had achieved such a high profile in French policy debates. Neither in the 1950s, when the independence of Indochina deprived France of a base on the Asian continent, nor with the nuclear testing debates of the 1960s and 1970s, had the case for a French strategic presence in Oceania been so strongly put as in the 1980s. For a brief time, the Pacific, and even more specifically the South Pacific, moved into the limelight of public discussion. The promoters of the Pacific seized an opportunity to broadcast their views, using arguments that sometimes had the tenor of academic analyses and at other times constituted policy recommendations. They became a new lobbying group, comparable to the colonial lobbies which had promoted European expansion and the development of empire in a different age.[72] Often the tenets of their arguments about the necessity of a sovereign French presence overseas, the importance of military defence against rivals (and now nuclear defence) and the possibilities for economic and cultural *rayonnement* sounded hauntingly familiar. Even the clarion calls about a 'new Pacific' and the move of the centre of the world's political, commercial and strategic gravity from the Atlantic to the Pacific had already been heard in the nineteenth century.[73]

The need to maintain a nuclear testing base in French Polynesia, the actual or potential role of France in the 'new Pacific' and the linkage of the Pacific outposts with France's other DOM-TOMs to form a chain of French bases encircling the globe provided the theoretical pillars for France's international policy in Oceania.[74] There have been reactions against these views, notably among those who have called for a nuclear-free and independent Pacific. Somewhat surprisingly, however, there have been very few attempts, particularly in France, to articulate a counter-theory to ideas about the importance of the Pacific and France's role there. Advocates of French withdrawal have paid little attention to the future of the Pacific islands after such a development. Some have assumed that the achievement of a nuclear free and independent Pacific would solve most of the region's problems. Still others have held a rather starry-eyed view of the realities of life in the islands of Oceania.[75] None of the dissenters to the general views which championed the significance of the Pacific, however, has succeeded in persuading governments in Paris to adopt their ideas as official policy. Therefore, it was the assumptions of defenders of the 'new Pacific' which directly or indirectly guided French action in the 1980s.

Implementation of a general Pacific policy – putting ideology into practice – was a new feature of the 1980s. Before that time, France had few links with the islands of the South Pacific other than the New Hebrides. Even after 1980, the micro-states of the South Pacific presented relatively little interest for France. France maintained ambassadors only in Papua New Guinea, Fiji and Vanuatu (although the ambassador in Vanuatu was expelled on several occasions because of disagreements between Paris and Port Vila). Nouméa hosts the South Pacific Commission, an international body set up by the colonial powers in the 1940s to carry out technical research and development projects in the region. But France has been excluded from the South Pacific Forum; the French TOMs have even been refused observer status at Forum meetings. France did not sign the Rarotonga Treaty, although it has been party to several other South Pacific agreements. French trade with the micro-states is minimal; France buys a few agricultural products, largely in the context of EC trade determined by the Lomé convention, and it sells some manufactured goods to South Pacific nations. France provides aid to the region both through the EC and bilateral arrangements; in the late 1980s, direct French aid amounted to about $A 25–30 million a year. The sum was not particularly large, but in small islands small amounts of money could be especially valuable.[76]

In the early 1980s, France made few overtures to the Pacific states and as the situation in New Caledonia worsened, France largely limited itself to defending its policy against criticism, especially from the Melanesian states.[77] The Mitterrand government established a consultative council formed of its South Pacific high commissioners and ambassadors, charged with studying Oceania, but it produced few results in French policy. Under the administration of Jacques Chirac, a more concerted effort was made to win friends in the region. Chirac created the position of Secretary of State for the South Pacific, a post filled by Gaston Flosse, the president of the French Polynesian government. Flosse served as a roving ambassador around the South Pacific, offering French aid and technical assistance and presenting France's viewpoint. French aid included grants to Solomon Islands, the Cook Islands and Tonga, as well as to Vanuatu. Flosse's missions, often criticised for being attempts to woo supporters and buttress his own political reputation, nevertheless scored successes. The Polynesian states of the Cook Islands, the closest island group to French Polynesia, and Tonga criticised France's policy on nuclear testing and on New Caledonia in only very mild terms at a time when other micro-states lambasted Paris. The Cook Islands' prime minister was fêted in Paris, and the King of Tonga visited Mururoa atoll,

which he declared appeared safe. The French were less successful with the Melanesian states, which pledged solidarity with the
Kanaks of New Caledonia. Vanuatu and Papua New Guinea
were in the front line in denouncing France and, with Solomon
Islands, formed the Melanesian Spearhead Group, whose main
vocation seemed to be to condemn Paris. (In response, Tongans
and Tahitians talked about formation of a Polynesian Community.) Fiji was a particular problem. The 1987 *coups* in Fiji lost
friends for Suva as the democratically-elected government was
overthrown, the Indian majority in the islands' population suffered attacks, and Melanesian chiefs formulated a constitution
which severely limited the rights of non-Melanesians. Most South
Pacific nations, as well as Australia and New Zealand, condemned the *coups*, and Canberra and Wellington withdrew aid.
France stepped into the breach. Flosse visited Fiji, offered aid –
rumours flew that France would supply armaments to the Fijian
army or even establish a military base in Fiji, neither of which
proved to eventuate – and awarded the Legion of Honour to
the leader of the Fiji *coups*, Sitiveni Rabuka, for his efforts in
saving a French serviceman's life when he was stationed with
United Nations troops in Lebanon. Perhaps partly as a result,
Fiji's criticism of France was muted.[78]

Even if Flosse's efforts, at least to critics, smacked of diplomatic profiteering, they represented the first concerted French
effort to shape a South Pacific policy and extend its influence to
states other than the three French territories and Vanuatu.
Flosse's initiatives were compromised by the strong-arm tactics
the Chirac government adopted in New Caledonia. After the
defeat of Chirac in the legislative elections in 1988, and especially following the signature of the Matignon Accord later that
year, relations between France and the South Pacific states
substantially improved, although the South Pacific Forum reit-
erated the independent nations' opposition to nuclear testing
and calls for New Caledonian independence. On a visit to the
South Pacific in 1990, Michel Rocard, the French prime minister, announced new aid to island states. Island leaders responded
favourably – the prime minister of the Cook Islands, expressing
his disagreement with New Zealand's withdrawal from the
ANZUS treaty, even signed an agreement with Paris whereby
French military ships and aircraft policed its territorial waters.

FRANCE IN THE SOUTH PACIFIC

In the 1980s, France attempted to develop a South Pacific policy, but it remained one attuned to safeguarding the TOMs in Oceania, continuing tests of nuclear devices and extending Paris's influence and opportunities in the wider Asia–Pacific region. Nuclear testing remained a key feature of that policy, although it would be simplistic to argue that France's entire policy was designed simply to keep Mururoa's tests going. Making friends in the South Pacific was difficult precisely because of France's insistence on nuclear testing and the maintenance of sovereignty over the TOMs. But France was also handicapped because policy-makers had made so little effort to take notice of the South Pacific in the 1960s and 1970s and because the policy which gradually emerged in the 1980s was caught up in the controversies surrounding New Caledonia and in polemics centring on the 'new Pacific'. Specific actions, none more than the *Rainbow Warrior* affair, compromised France's position and transformed it into the pariah of the South Pacific.[79] At the same time as France's star sank to its lowest level, however, other developments in Oceania – notably upheavals in Papua New Guinea, Fiji and Vanuatu – troubled the region and brought into question the heralded 'Pacific way of life', political consensus and economic development in independent island-states.[80] Furthermore, the Matignon Accord served, at least temporarily, to moderate criticism of France among island states.

In the South Pacific, France was pursuing objectives determined by both its stakes in its overseas territories and its greater global interests. Similarly, France's neighbours in Oceania and Australasia pursued objectives dictated by ideological concerns and *Realpolitik*. Opposition to French nuclear testing in the South Pacific, including condemnation in Australia and New Zealand, was far more widespread and deeply-felt than policy-makers in Paris realised; the 'green' lobbies of environmentalist groups gained great influence in the media and in government circles in the region. Opposition to an often heavy-handed French administration in Tahiti and New Caledonia was widespread and was occasionally aggravated by newspaper and television reports of violence and the disparities of wealth and opportunity for different ethnic groups in the French islands.

But individuals, groups and governments which opposed the French were also pursuing goals of their own. The 'anti-French' lobby included a number of religious groups, such as the Uniting Church in Australia, which had long championed Third World concerns and which had a century-long rivalry with Catholicism and the French administration in Oceania. Several trade union groups which supplied aid to pro-independence political parties in the French territories were generally on the left of the political spectrum in Australia and New Zealand and apt to take up the causes of nationalist or rebel groups throughout the world. The media often sensationalised developments in the French Pacific and presented one-sided views of New Caledonia and French Polynesia.[81]

At a different level, the governments of the micro-states, as well as those of Australia and New Zealand, used France as a scapegoat for criticism in attempts to improve their own fortunes. New Zealand's reformist Labour prime minister of the 1980s, David Lange, was evidently anxious to win popularity among his electorate (a tenth of which was composed of Maoris or Pacific islanders) and to make New Zealand's presence felt in Oceania. His rupture with the ANZUS alliance and promotion of the Rarotonga Treaty and of the United Nations effort to re-list New Caledonia on its roster of colonies represented efforts to gain influence among the micro-states of the Pacific. Australia's government was at the same time struggling to carve out a sphere of influence for itself in the Pacific. In the 1970s, Australia had granted independence to its South Pacific colony of Papua New Guinea and subsequently acted as big brother to the micro-states of the southwest Pacific; on the scale of Oceania, Australia was the superpower of the South Pacific, anxious to win and maintain its influence among the nations in its backyard. This explains, in part, Canberra's outspoken attitude towards French nuclear testing and more cautious support for independence movements in New Caledonia.[82]

Beneath the rhetoric about the 'Pacific way of life' and an 'independent and nuclear-free Pacific' on the one hand and defences of France's vital stakes in a critical region of the world on the other, there took place a joust for influence and profit in the Pacific. In the overheated atmosphere of the 1980s, polemics were exaggerated and the reputations of the major protagonists were tarnished as charges and counter-charges flew.[83] Such rivalries were both reminiscent of quarrels between the powers in the age of expansion, and competition for commercial advantages, political clout and military stakes in the post-colonial world. Not until the end of the 1980s did a measure of calm return to the South Pacific as developments in eastern Europe, China and the Persian Gulf dramatically overshadowed the remote islands of Oceania. After a blaze of interest just a few years before, Oceania sank again into the relative insignificance which had been its accustomed lot. Despite the opposition to French presence from outside France and from inside the territories, France remained firmly anchored in its three TOMs in Oceania.

Conclusion: The Colonial Heritage

THE FRENCH PACIFIC

Visitors to the French territories in Oceania are confronted with the awesome natural beauty of the islands, luxuriant vegetation, magnificent mountains and clear lagoons, the picture-postcard Pacific. But they are sometimes more surprised, and less delighted, to see the traffic jams of Papeete or the ugly nickel refinery on Nouméa's outskirts. They are often bemused to find French *cafés* and restaurants, chic shops with French fashions and other sights which may remind them of the Côte d'Azur. Few fail to notice the paradoxes of the contemporary Pacific islands; Wallis, one of the more remote and less well-known islands, is a fine example. The main town centre is dominated by the impressive palace of the king, which stands between an imposing Catholic cathedral and, perched on a hillside, the French prefect's residence; the streetscape provides a neat symbol of the three institutions which play a dominant role in the island's life. Across the street are the post office and the radio station, themselves symbols of the importance of modern communications to islands seemingly lost in the 'Great Ocean'. Wallis is dotted with pretty churches constructed of coral, yet in the evening the flicker of television screens seems their most obvious characteristic. It is often in the middle of the night that the huge French jets land at Wallis's tiny airport, and the planes are full to capacity with Wallisians and Futunans going to or returning from New Caledonia, islanders and *métropolitains* on their way to or from Paris on various *missions*, soldiers and students with their bags packed for sojourns overseas.

There is something palpably different between the French territories and other islands of the South Pacific. A century and a half of French rule have left a strong imprint on local cultures. Melanesians and Polynesians, as well as the Caldoches, *demis* and *métropolitains*, have indeed adopted much of French

342

culture and style – the product which Melanesian visitors to Australia most miss, it seems, is the bread to which they are accustomed in New Caledonia.[1] Even in Wallis, a meal may well begin with an *apéritif* and end with a cognac, and, unfortunately for the visitor, the prices of Tahiti's restaurants rival those of Paris. But the French imprint is deeper than just types of food or fashions in clothing or architecture. In the headiest days of the independence movement in the 1980s, Jean-Marie Tjibaou always acknowledged the importance of French culture to his own views and to the future of New Caledonia. The strength of the French Protestant and Catholic churches pervades the territories. Statements by politicians of all hues show the influence of French theory and the French concepts of the nation, politics and administration. In Vanuatu, the traces of the French presence remain visible and strong a decade after the independence of the New Hebrides.

The French presence in Oceania has indeed created a gap between what has been called '*Franconésie*'[2] and the other islands of the region. But the French islands have also witnessed many currents common to other islands: the arrival of parliamentary politics and consumer economies, urbanisation and the decline of subsistence farming, the influence of outside ways of thought and models of development. Many of the economic, social and political developments which have taken place in the French islands, in short, are common throughout the Pacific and indeed throughout the world. Some of the problems they experience, from pollution to alcohol and drug abuse, are similar to problems faced elsewhere. Furthermore, the basic remedy proposed to cure these ills – the injection of foreign capital to support development projects – differs little from remedies prescribed elsewhere.

The French territories have undergone remarkable change in the decades since the Second World War; as one writer felicitously worded it, they have gone 'from copra to the atom'.[3] The speed of change has been particularly rapid. In the 1940s and 1950s, the French territories, by all estimations, were somnolent, poor and isolated, and the lot of many of the French settlers was not markedly different from that of their Melanesian or Polynesian neighbours. The economic 'revolutions' – despite overuse, the word seems appropriate – of the 1960s in

French Polynesia and New Caledonia wrought great structural change. The problem was that economic, social and political change did not always keep up with each other. More jobs for Melanesians and Polynesians did not necessarily mean their incorporation into political life; the activism of contestatory political movements did not lead to independence or, except in French Polynesia and then only recently, to autonomy. The end of classical 'colonialism' did not efface the 'colonial' nature of France's links with its overseas territories. In fact, economic changes only reinforced the dependence of the island economies on France and on French largesse.

Public life in the French territories is particularly complex precisely because of the overlay of cultural strata. Traditional islander beliefs and customs have survived Westernisation, albeit in transmuted form, and shown themselves capable of reviving and becoming political rallying-points. Westernisation is itself a series of 'culture contacts' from the first voyages of exploration and trade, through the conversion of the islands to Christianity in the early 1800s, the effects of French takeover in the second half of that century, the impact of the Second World War, the changes of recent years. In the 1980s the islands faced new pressures and strove to create new identities in a world where old ideological certainties were being discredited.

The French territories have their own internal dynamics which concern both local problems and the contact and confrontation between local and external developments. Problems of housing, education, health and employment are the stuff of daily debate. Contests between those who hold power and those who wish to oust them form the rhythm of political life. If ethnic disputes are hardly present in Wallis and Futuna, and muted in French Polynesia, they underlie most political debate in New Caledonia. Ethnicity has been closely connected to the topic of independence for New Caledonia, an issue which dominated the political agenda during the 1980s. Certainly outside the TOMs, the French presence in the contemporary South Pacific was often – if simplisticly – reduced to two topics: the nuclear testing at Mururoa and the issue of independence. What looked to critics to be France's refusal or failure to decolonise its Pacific territories ineluctably dominated the debate on the French role in Oceania.

DECOLONISATION AND THE SOUTH PACIFIC

In the early 1980s, the programme of the Pupu Here Aia, one of French Polynesia's moderate political parties, declared that the prospect of independence for the territory was 'inscribed in the book of history', and not long afterwards, Léopold Jorédié, a leader of the FLNKS in New Caledonia, stated that the independence of New Caledonia entered into 'the logic of history'.[4] Independence has, in general, been considered the normal goal – and destiny – of the countries colonised by the expansion of European (or other) powers overseas. In the late 1940s India and Indonesia led the way to independence and by the beginning of the 1960s almost all of the major possessions of the European countries (except those of Portugal) had become independent; since that time many of the remaining smaller colonies have followed suit. The quest for independence, however, has not come to an end. An ethnic revival among such regional groups as Basques and Bretons in Western Europe began in the 1970s just as overseas decolonisation seemed to be winding up. More recently, the history of the Soviet Union and the Balkans has dramaticly shown that nationalism and the desire for sovereignty is not dead and may be the grounds for bloody dispute and great political changes.

In the early post-war years of anti-colonialism and the accession to independence of colonial areas, the Pacific islands represented an exception to decolonisation. At the end of the Second World War, the United Nations confided the former Japanese colonies to American control, for an indeterminate time, as the Trust Territory of the Pacific Islands. Although the new French constitution of 1946 included provisions for colonial independence, few imagined that France's larger overseas domains, let alone its smaller ones, would become independent; the *départementalisation* of the *vieilles colonies* of Martinique, Guadeloupe, Guyane and Réunion suggested that the fate of at least some colonies might be closer integration with the *métropole* rather than separation. The accession of Hawaii to American statehood in 1960 provided an example of such a process in Oceania. Although the Netherlands reluctantly agreed to recognise the independence of Indonesia in 1948, The Hague retained control of Irian Jaya until 1963, when that region passed under the imperial overlordship of Jakarta rather than becoming a sovereign state. Britain, for its part, did not consider granting independence to its Pacific outposts in the 1950s or 1960s.

During the late 1940s and 1950s, France was far in advance of its imperial partners in granting civil and political rights to its Pacific subjects. Paris decreed that the residents of New Caledonia, French Polynesia and Wallis and Futuna were fully-fledged French citizens, with the right of abode in France and the possibility of electing both local assemblies and representatives to the French Senate and National Assembly in Paris. (Universal suffrage came tardily only to Melanesians in New Caledonia.) The Defferre law of 1956 brought to France's Pacific territories the sort of political autonomy that existed nowhere else in the colonies of Oceania, although Paris tightened the reins only two years later. By the 1950s, vibrant and often contestatory political parties existed in the French territories, notably the Union Calédonienne and Pouvanaa's RDPT, both of which enjoyed substantial support from islander populations.

In 1962, Western Samoa became the first Pacific island colony to become independent, severing its formal ties with New Zealand. No other island nation became independent for eight years, except the minuscule Nauru in 1968. Then Fiji, the largest of Britain's colonies in the South Pacific, acceded to independence in 1970. In 1975, Australia granted independence to Papua New Guinea. Subsequently, Britain withdrew from its other Pacific colonies (with the exception of Pitcairn), as, in the late 1970s, the Solomon Islands and the Gilbert and Ellice Islands became independent, the latter colony dividing into the states of Kiribati and Tuvalu. In the case of these minor British possessions, as well as that of Papua New Guinea, it was the administering power which instigated and hurried independence rather than pressure from indigenous liberation movements.[5] The independence of the New Hebrides, in 1980, too rapidly accomplished from the French viewpoint, seemingly completed British divestment.[6]

However, not all the islands of Oceania became independent. In addition to the three French *territoires d'outre-mer*, a large number maintained formal links with overseas *métropoles*. American Samoa and Guam became 'unincorporated territories' of the United States, with elected governors and legislatures and a non-voting member of the American Congress in Washington. With the ending of the Trust Territory of the Pacific Islands, the Northern Mariana Islands became a 'commonwealth' of the United States, and the new republics of the Marshall Islands and the Federated States of Micronesia signed compacts of free association with Washington, an arrangement which may be replicated with Belau (Palau). Britain's high commissioner in New Zealand continues to administer Pitcairn, and the other former British colonies remain members of the Commonwealth of Nations, recognising the British Queen as their titular head of state and vesting certain residual powers in the British government or the Queen's representative in the islands.[7] Australia did not cede control of the Torres Straits islands, inhabited by a Melanesian population,[8] or Lord Howe and Norfolk Island, whose residents are of European ancestry. New Zealand retains indirect rule over Niue and Tokelau and has kept close relations with another former possession, the Cook Islands, through a compact of free association. Chile rules Easter Island (Rapa Nui) and Ecuador rules the Galapagos Islands.[9] The Aboriginals of Australia, the Maoris of New Zealand and the native Polynesians of Hawaii, despite movements demanding more cultural recognition, greater economic and political considerations or even outright sovereignty, have remained minorities in countries where massive waves of migration have completely changed society.[10] In short, Oceania has remained one of the least completely decolonised regions on the globe.

Elsewhere in the world, several dozen 'overseas countries and territories' (the label used by the European Community) are still under the sovereignty of countries which are generally not territorially contiguous and which are often ethnically different from these 'last colonies'. From arctic Greenland to the tropical British and Dutch West Indies, from teeming Hong Kong (at least for a few more years) to uninhabited sub-Antarctic islands, from prosperous Bermuda to poor St Helena and Tristan de Cunha, these territories retain political ties with outside countries on which they often rely for substantial economic and technical aid. The ten French *départements et territoires d'outre-mer* are only a subset of this larger cohort. They show that absolute decolonisation has not been achieved and perhaps never will be.[11]

The countries of the island Pacific, at first view, seemed to make the transition from colonialism to sovereignty in an easy manner. On closer examination, various fractures appear. A secession movement rocked New Guinea when it became independent, and the early 1990s saw a desperate attempt at secession from Papua New Guinea by the mineral-rich and ethnically-distinct island of Bougainville; Papua New Guinea, with aid from the Australian government, has campaigned to defeat the independence movement in Bougainville by both political and military means. The independence of Vanuatu was marred by a secessionist movement in Santo. In the midst of *coups d'état* and political turmoil in Fiji, the island of Rotuma – a Polynesian outlier in a country dominated by Melanesians and Indians – momentarily sought independence. Even residents of Australia's Torres Islands and New Zealand's Chatham Islands, perhaps not altogether seriously, have talked of secession or autonomy.[12]

Once independent, South Pacific countries were not immune from political, social and economic problems. Fiji suffered two *coups d'état* in 1987, followed by the adoption of a constitution which enshrined political inequalities between the Indian majority and the Melanesian minority in its population. Vanuatu saw a failed *coup d'état* in 1989 and the increasingly authoritarian rule of Prime Minister Walter Lini until his removal from office in 1991. Papua New Guinea has experienced great political in-fighting and the country is rife with charges of corruption and bribery; provincial governments have been suspended as have prominent national ministers. Tonga is run as a feudal monarchy in which political dissent is discouraged, and in Western Samoa the large chiefly class enjoys a near monopoly on political power. Violence, including the assassination of the country's president, has beset Belau. The 'Pacific way' of political consensus,[13] vaunted in the 1970s was often honoured in the breach in the following decade. Social problems also afflict the independent states of the Pacific. Papua New Guinea's capital, Port Moresby, is overrun with gangs of deracinated village youth who have migrated to the capital, the so-called 'raskols', and ranks as one of the more dangerous cities in the world.[14] Substandard living conditions exist in many countries of the South Pacific, tropical diseases cannot be completely eradicated and alcoholism is a rising problem. Many

Pacific islanders have chosen to migrate, legally or illegally, but they often have problems of adaptation in such host countries as New Zealand or Australia.

Economically, the Pacific nations have few natural resources except for minerals in some islands, and their remarkable sites – yet tourism has frequently been disrupted by world economic crises, political problems and violence, and sales of minerals are subject to the volatility of commodity markets. Aid from patron countries or international bodies, migrant remittances and a relatively small revenue from exports make up national income.[15] An extreme example of dependency is Tuvalu, the main export of which is postage-stamps (which, incidentally, are not printed in the country), and the major source of revenue is interest from a trust fund of five million dollars established by Britain, the United States and Australia. Those countries, as well as Japan, the European Community and France, are the aid donors whose financial assistance is vital for the economic survival of the independent countries of Oceania. Some of these nations have, or once possessed, sources of exports; Nauru's phosphate deposits, however, have been depleted, and mining has left the island an ecological disaster, while Papua New Guinea's income plummeted when attempted secession closed copper mines on Bougainville, the prime revenue earner for the country. In an effort to increase income, Tonga has been selling passports to foreign citizens and has offered to rent space for the storage of toxic wastes from overseas countries. Vanuatu and the Cook Islands have set up tax havens for off-shore banking. Some drug-running has occurred in both independent countries and those linked to overseas powers – the largest cash crop in Belau and Guam, it is said, is marijuana.[16]

Given various obstacles to development, including isolation, lack of resources and their small size, countries of the South Pacific have developed special relations with overseas states, generally the former administering powers – the treaties of 'free association' signed between certain islands and New Zealand or the United States are examples. Similar compacts have been suggested for other islands (including the French territories[17]). Some observers have begun to reevaluate – and question – the value of total independence, and the degree to which any real economic independence can be achieved for small, re-source-poor states such as those of the island Pacific.

These aspects of the contemporary South Pacific provide nuances to a general view of France's position in Oceania, including castigations of France as the last colonial power or, conversely, promises about the political and economic benefits which would accrue to France's territories after their accession to independence. Even were the territories to become sovereign, it is unlikely that they would escape continued 'neo-colonialism' or that they would refuse privileged economic, political and cultural relationships with Paris. The alternative would undoubtedly mean the end of the consumer society and welfare net which have existed in French Polynesia, New Caledonia and Wallis and Futuna. That fact, somewhat ironically, provides comfort both to anti-*indépendantistes* and to supporters of a gradually achieved, even French-sponsored independence.

The islands of the South Pacific have been blessedly exempt from the excruciating poverty, famines, wars and dictatorial governments which afflict parts of Africa and Asia. By comparison with residents of many parts of the Third World, Oceanians live relatively well. The fine climate, supplies of tropical food and communitarian traditions of mutual aid of the Pacific, vaunted since the first visits by European supporters, are not just myths. The Pacific is neither paradise, nor paradise lost.

FRANCE AND DECOLONISATION

It is the generally accepted view that France was not a good decoloniser, or at least that Britain decolonised more easily than did France. This idea needs revision. Portugal and Spain did not withdraw from some of their overseas possessions in Africa until the 1970s, the same decade that the Netherlands left South America. Not until 1991 did the Soviet Union see the break-up of Moscow's empire and the independence of the Baltic republics and other peripheral states which had come under Russian tsarist or Communist control through conquest, assimilation or annexation. Britain continues to control about twice as many overseas territories as France, even if some are only tiny islands; Spain, Portugal, the Netherlands and Denmark still have 'colonies'. France, in short, is not the last decoloniser it is often imagined to be.[18]

The French attitude towards its overseas domains was always considerably different from that of the British (or indeed other imperial powers). The doctrine of 'assimilation' current at the end of the nineteenth century and 'association', which replaced it at the beginning of the twentieth century, promoted a significant degree of integration between the colonies and the *métropole*. Until the decentralisation laws of the early 1980s, the overseas possessions were centrally administered by appointees from Paris, and local councils had only limited powers, but this administrative centralism prevailed in the *métropole* as well. Representation in the French parliament and the extension of French law codes to overseas areas were seen by the French as an alternative to the British model of responsible government and self-rule in the dominions. The enforcement of strict norms for education and entry into the powerful government bureaucracy were intended to impose national standards in the French overseas territories, and the *francisation* of 'natives' was thought to provide an *entrée* into French civilisation and, ultimately, guarantee eligibility for political participation. By the middle of the twentieth century, the French had stopped seriously believing that Africans, Asians, West Indians or Oceanians could simply be transformed into 'black' (or some other colour of) Frenchmen, but the ideals of integration and extension of French culture had not vanished. At least in theory, a New Caledonian or a French Polynesian of whatever ethnic background, political or religious affiliation or economic wherewithal is as much a Frenchman or Frenchwoman as a native of Paris or Marseille.

At another level of the formation and maintenance of national identity, the French long found great differences among its population difficult to accept. The centralisation of the state and the perceived universality of French culture meant that norms had to be enforced, and that all French citizens were grouped into (and made into) a homogeneous whole. Not until the 1970s, for instance, did the French government encourage the preservation of local cultures and languages (except in the debased 'folkloric' way) with, for example, authorisation for students to take regional languages as part of their *baccalauréat* examination. France has increasingly faced demands for recognition from culturally distinct groups in the body politic, and particularly it has attempted to confront the issues associated with the immigration of large numbers of Maghrebins and black Africans to France. This has raised fundamental questions about the meaning of French identity and about policy towards specific social groups, both at home and in the *outre-mer*.

In the formulation and execution of French policy, national priorities have always taken precedence over local or sectoral ones. Since the Second World War, France has displayed a determination to maintain its position as a world power, even if one of a lesser magnitude than the superpowers. The retention of overseas outposts has been championed as an important means for France to secure this objective. Politicians of all ideological colours have vaunted the advantages of France's being a sovereign power in all the world's major oceans, of its being able to have political, cultural and economic outposts and of its safeguarding the benefits of the space station in French Guiana and the nuclear testing facility in French Polynesia. France's global perspective thus outweighs the particular interests present in one or another territory: the French Pacific territories are part and parcel of the group of DOM-TOMs.[19] Recent discussion about the possibility of cessation of French atomic testing connects more with changes in the geopolitical and strategic situation in the world than with the evolution of French Polynesia. As France's real international power has been challenged, and as its 'empire' has shrunk, the remaining cards France holds – including the present-day *départements et territoires d'outre-mer* – have assumed heightened importance. In short, an answer to the question of why France has clung to its South Pacific outposts must be sought partly in the arena of international politics rather than solely at the level of the Pacific islands.

There has never existed unanimity in France about the value of empire or the usefulness of the DOM-TOMs. From the first years of French expansion in the nineteenth century onwards, there has been a vocal and large anti-colonial movement in France. Critics of colonialism charged that the government should address more pressing social problems at home or buttress its power on the European continent rather than search for distant overseas domains. In the era of decolonisation, many of the French opposed the maintenance of French rule overseas. In the 1950s, the 'Cartierists', a group of anti-colonialists who took their name from a prominent journalist who promoted their views, argued that it would be more economical for France to rid itself of its colonies. Opponents of colonialism fought against French efforts to retain Indochina and, particularly, Algeria, and the Algerian War provoked a strong burst of anti-colonialism led by a committed group of intellectuals.[20] More recently, opinion polls have shown that most of the French population would not oppose independence for the remaining DOM-TOMs, perhaps most of all for those of the South Pacific. The average French person has few stakes and relatively little interest in the South Pacific. An active, if small, minority of the French, including those who sympathise with the FLNKS and other pro-independence groups, as well as some ecologists, oppose the French role as an administering power in the South Pacific. If members of the political élite, particularly those in the neo-Gaullist movement, have campaigned ardently for the retention of ties between France and Oceania, apathy is more characteristic of the general French attitude – except, perhaps, when France is seen to be the victim of unwarranted criticism by Australia, New Zealand or the independent micro-states of the region or by international organisations, such as the United Nations decolonisation committee. In these cases, when French honour appears to be slighted, a basic nationalist reaction is apparent.

French expansion overseas, and the retention of overseas domains, has depended largely on the work of interest groups and lobbies which promote such ventures. Explorers, navy officials, traders and missionaries were instrumental in persuading Paris to hoist the flag over far-flung areas around the world in the nineteenth century, and their successors have argued for the maintenance of those realms in the French Republic. New 'post-colonial' lobbies have emerged, composed of economic, military and administrative interests and – it is very important to note – both settlers in the overseas areas and 'natives' who feel that French rule brings enough advantages to them to outweigh the disadvantages. (The majority of the electorate in no French DOM-TOM has voted for independence, even if a majority of Melanesians in New Caledonia favour it.) 'Post-colonial lobbies' thus exist both in France and in the DOM-TOMs and often coordinate their activities. Only at the risk of a direct challenge to the lobbies and interest groups in France and, particularly, in the 'colonies' – as Paris did venture at the time of the Algerian War, and as the Pisani Plan tried to do in the mid-1980s in New Caledonia – can 'decolonisation' occur. The French government, in general, has been caught between various pressure groups eager to advance their own goals; always with the cloud of elections and the search for voters hanging over it, Paris has had to choose whether to ally with one or another group or to try to mediate as an honest broker.

Decolonisation, like colonisation, is not a simple opposition of good versus bad, European versus 'indigenous', civilisation versus savagery – although it has often been so caricatured. The process of decolonisation has become even more complex with the advent of consumer societies, representative institutions, social welfare services and economic dependency; few of these existed at the time of French decolonisation in Indochina and Africa, but all are now well established in the DOM-TOMs. Decolonisation has also been complicated with proposals for arrangements which differ from absolute secession and independence, such as suggestions for 'associated states' and 'associated territories', unsuccessfully mooted in the case of Indochina in the 1940s, outlined in the 'French Union' set up by the constitution of the Fourth Republic and the 'Community' of the Fifth Republic, and revived by Pisani's proposals for New Caledonian 'independence-in-association' with France. Some observers have also spoken about the possibility of decolonisation without independence, a formula which may be either a fine turn of phrase or a legitimate alternative to other eventualities.

FRANCE AND THE SOUTH PACIFIC

The French territories of Oceania entered French political consciousness only tardily. The Second World War proved the strategic potential of the islands, just as reports of French governors after the war pointed to the economic and social underdevelopment of the territories. In the 1950s, however, Paris did relatively little to realise the potential of the islands. Some development projects were formulated, but, in general, the government simply allowed New Caledonia's major mining companies, especially the SLN, to exploit its mineral resources, and Tahiti's farmers and traders to continue production for a local market; lack of change was even more apparent in Wallis and Futuna. In political policy, France extended the suffrage to Melanesians in New Caledonia and encouraged the activities of the multi-racial and moderate Union Calédonienne, while it combated the more dangerous rhetoric and strategy of the Pouvanaa movement in French Polynesia. Strategically, France did little in Oceania, which in the 1950s still seemed a not particularly useful area of the French empire; significantly, even the Vietnamese defeat of the French at Dienbienphu and the 'loss' of the Indochinese colonies prompted no reassessment of the strategic or military use of the Pacific TOMs.[21]

Only in the 1960s did France develop a new interest in the South Pacific. The independence of Algeria created a need to relocate the nuclear testing site, and an economic boom made New Caledonia's nickel a more precious commodity on world markets. In recognition of these developments, Paris reinforced its powers over its South Pacific domains: the government disbanded the remnants of the RDPT in Tahiti, established a tighter link between Wallis and Futuna and the *métropole* with a new statute for that territory in 1962, and passed the *lois Billotte* which gave Paris more control over New Caledonia's natural resources in 1963. A period of relatively benign neglect from 1945 to 1962 – except for reaction against autonomist and nascent *indépendantiste* sentiment in French Polynesia – now gave way to a new period of intervention, economic growth and the migration of French citizens to the islands which lasted until the mid-1970s. The arrival of the CEP in French Polynesia and the boom in New Caledonia greatly transformed those two territories, and the possibilities of work for Wallisian and Futunan migrants to New Caledonia worked its effects on that territory. By the early 1970s, the Pacific TOMs seemed something of a success story, despite strong regional opposition to French nuclear testing. Yet even that criticism was momentarily muted when atmospheric testing ceased. The French Prime Minister was able to promote stepped-up migration to New Caledonia because of the good economic climate and in an effort to disarm any nationalist sentiment which might endanger the

French stronghold.[22] Meanwhile, France increased the money it invested in the New Hebrides in a rather late effort to win support among the Melanesian population in the Condominium.

From the mid-1970s through the 1980s, political questions moved to the top of the agenda in the French Pacific. The evolution towards independence in the New Hebrides, in which France finally had to bow to the wishes of its Condominium partner, created a crisis for Paris and provided a challenge to the French presence in Oceania. In New Caledonia, the contest between *indépendantistes* and anti-*indépendantistes* dominated politics, while in French Polynesia, political life saw the campaigns of *indépedantistes* against autonomists. Political questions were linked to demographic, economic and cultural issues – inequalities between ethnic groups, between urban and rural populations, between Western and islander values, between different personalities and parties in a highly fragmented political landscape. The attitude of the French government was ostensibly to safeguard national interests, to promote greater equality and justice and to respond to what it considered the legitimate demands of the population. The paradox was, however, that the very legitimacy of various demands on the French, such as the legitimacy of settler versus islander interests, was open to debate. Attempts at compromise, perhaps unsurprisingly, satisfied few of the competing groups in societies which had become highly polarised, particularly New Caledonia.

It seemed evident in the 1980s that the French government wanted the 'problems' of the South Pacific simply to go away. Different governments tried various strategies to achieve this goal. Paris suppressed nationalist dissent in New Caledonia in 1986 and 1987 and two years earlier French agents had sunk the Greenpeace vessel which compromised French nuclear testing. At other times, efforts at lessening tensions replaced strong-arm force, as in the thwarted Pisani plan for New Caledonia in 1985 and the more successful Matignon Accord of 1988 or, for French Polynesia, the 1984 statute of autonomy. It was widely believed that behind the scenes the French governments tried other manoeuvres, for example, efforts to organise a third political force between the RPCR and the FLNKS in New Caledonia or machinations to keep Flosse's Tahoeraa Huira'atira from returning to power in 1991. The benefit of 'solving' the problem of New Caledonia, or at least of seeming to do so, was obviously of electoral significance, as evidenced by the desperate effort of the Chirac government to win a French metropolitan election by attempting a *coup de force* in New Caledonia in 1988.

Many of the attempts to keep the problems of the French Pacific from spinning out of control came too late, at least in the case of New Caledonia. If there is a failure of French policy in Oceania, it must be lack of foresight both in anticipating problems which arose and in envisaging solutions to them. For instance, the French from the 1940s to the late 1970s (and certainly even more so before the Second World War) did little to incorporate the Melanesians of New Caledonia into the mainstream of economic and political life in the territory. An effort to do so, the *promotion mélanésienne*, occurred only when nationalist sentiment had begun to gain strength. A catalogue of grievances gives evidence: failure to repeal the *code de l'indigénat* until 1946, lack of enfranchisement for Melanesians until 1952 (and of universal suffrage until 1957), absence of education of Melanesians to the level of high school graduation until the 1960s and to completion of university until the next decade, continued concentration of economic and political power in the hands of the European settler élite and *fonctionnaires* sent from Paris. The failure to bring Melanesians into local institutions and the lack of development of a Melanesian élite dependent on (and perhaps loyal to) the state contrasted with the policy France pursued in the *départements* of the Caribbean and Réunion. In those *départements d'outre-mer*, a large group of islanders obtained sufficient benefits from the French presence to defuse secessionist feeling; until some very recent efforts, *in extremis*, to produce this result in New Caledonia, such has not been the case there. Put in another way, the Melanesian nationalists did not have (or were not given) enough vested interests in the presence of the French state for them to support the continuation of French rule.

At the same time, French support for the European community was one-sided and almost exclusive from the pre-1945 colonial period down until the 1980s. The 'Caldoches' established well-entrenched interests which were threatened by talk of 'Kanak independence'. Their French patriotism was not only an expression of cultural and ethnic loyalty but determination to make certain that the privileges they enjoyed as an élite were not endangered – even by the French government itself. Similarly the encouragement given to French Polynesians and Wallisians and Futunans to migrate to New Caledonia further complicated a situation of demographic imbalance to the detriment of the Melanesians, who saw settlers, Pacific migrants, *métropolitians* and the French state arrayed against them.

In the case of French Polynesia, the French lacked a long-distance view of the effects the CEP would produce when it was installed on Mururoa in the early 1960s. France underestimated the degree of opposition to nuclear testing, but also the great social and economic changes the CEP wrought on the economy of the territory. More recently, the government has not found an alternative to the testing centre as an economic mainstay for French Polynesia (no matter how 'artificial' the resulting economic structure has been). Therefore, the underlying issue in French Polynesia has essentially become economic, whereas in New Caledonia it has been political. That ties, in part, to the *métissage* of Tahitian society and the role played by the *demis* as an intermediary between France and the Polynesians.

Finally, France's policy in the South Pacific took little account of the neighbours of its territories, including Australia and New Zealand. The French view of an almost rigidly exclusive relationship between its overseas territories and the *métropole* meant that the French Pacific existed in an extreme degree of isolation from other islands of Oceania, a situation which made it particularly difficult to defuse heated criticism of France, which was imagined to be only a racist, colonial power polluting the ocean and its people with nuclear tests. In the early years of the 1990s, relations between France and other countries of the South Pacific have improved markedly, a development made possible only by the Matignon Accord and new French policy on New Caledonia. If France is perhaps no longer *persona non grata* in the South Pacific, it is still regarded with some mistrust and suspicion. The suspension, or cessation, of the nuclear tests would significantly reduce that negative view.

The 'colonial' nature of New Caledonia, French Polynesia and Wallis and Futuna is hard to dispute, although the word 'colonial' by no means provides a full explanation of the continued ties between France and its *territoires d'outre-mer* in the

South Pacific, nor of the dramatic evolution experienced by these territories since the 1960s. The nationalist movements in French Polynesia and New Caledonia in the 1980s crystallised many of the problems inherent in the special links between France and the DOM-TOMs, even if they also seemed a replay of earlier colonial confrontations. The future will show whether it will be possible to create a new relationship between France and the islands of the South Pacific which are its overseas territories, or whether they will eventually go their separate ways.

Notes and References

Introduction

1. On the French empire in this period, see Gilbert Comte, *L'Empire triomphant (1871–1936). I. Afrique occidentale et équatoriale* (Paris, 1988) and Jean Martin, *L'Empire triomphant (1871–1936). II. Maghreb, Indochine, Madagascar, Iles et Comptoirs* (Paris, 1990), and for a more interpretative approach, Jean Bouvier, René Girault and Jacques Thobie, *Impérialisme à la française* (Paris, 1986). For a new general history of French colonialism, see Jean Meyer, Jean Tarrade, Annie Rey-Goldzeiguer and Jacques Thobie, *Histoire de la France coloniale. Des Origines à 1914* (Paris, 1991) and Jacques Thobie, Gilbert Meynier, Catherine Coquery-Vidrovitch and Charles-Robert Ageron, *Histoire de la France coloniale. 1914–1990* (Paris, 1990). On the renewed importance of empire in the 1930s, Charles-Robert Ageron, 'La Perception de la puissance francaise en 1938–1939: le mythe impérial', *Revue française d'histoire d'outre-mer* 69 (1982), pp. 7–22, and on the apogee of colonialism in this period, Jacques Marseille, *L'Age d'or de la France coloniale* (Paris, 1986), and, more generally, Thomas August, 'Locating the Age of Imperialism', *Itinerario* 10 (1986), pp. 85–97.
2. The following paragraphs sum up some of the main points of my *The French Presence in the South Pacific, 1842–1940* (London, 1990).
3. See my 'European Expansion in the Island Pacific: An Historiographical Review', *Itinerario* 13 (1989), pp. 87–102, which also gives references to Japanese expansionism.

1   The Second World War in the French Pacific

1. Henri Sautot, *Grandeur et décadence du Gaullisme dans le Pacifique* (Melbourne, 1949). The best overall (but brief) account of the war period is Richard Thompson and Virginia Adloff, *The French Pacific Islands* (Berkeley, 1971), chs. 3 and 21.
2. On the *ralliement* of New Caledonia, John Lawrey, *The Cross of Lorraine in the South Pacific* (Canberra, 1982) and Georges Pisier, 'Le Ralliement de la Calédonie et l'intervention britannique (juin-octobre 1940)', *BSEHNC*, No. 62 (1985), pp. 35–47.
3. Sautot to de Gaulle, 1 October 1940, ATNC, 44 W 463.
4. Emile de Curton, *Tahiti 40* (Paris, 1973).
5. Alexandre Poncet, *Histoire de l'Ile Wallis* (Paris, 1972), ch. 20, and Robert Charbonnier, 'Aventures et Mésaventures à Wallis et Futuna', MNS 90 (manuscript), Académie des Sciences d'Outre-Mer. See also the letters of Sautot to the Free French headquarters of 12 November 1940 (on the failure of the *ralliement*), 17 February 1941 (on the possibility of the dismissal of Vrignaud), 28 March 1941 (on the use of a British or Australian ship) and 4 July 1941 (on Wallis's relations with Hanoi), ATNC, 44 W 463.

6. Quoted in Sautot to de Gaulle, 1 October 1940, ATNC, 44 W 463.

7. Margot Simington, 'Australia and New Caledonia, October 1940 – January 1941', *Royal Military College Historical Journal* 3 (1974), pp. 35–46, and 'Australia and the New Caledonia Coup d'État of 1940', *Australian Outlook* 30 (1976), pp. 73–92.

8. De Curton, *op. cit.*

9. Sautot to de Gaulle, 29 January and 28 February 1941, ATNC, 44 W 463.

10. Sautot to de Gaulle, 21 June 1941, ATNC, 44 W 463.

11. Kim Munholland, 'The Trials of the Free French in New Caledonia, 1940–1942', *French Historical Studies* 14 (1986), pp. 547–579, has been my major source for this period, supplemented by Lawrey, ch. 7, and Philippe Godard, *Le Mémorial Calédonien*, Vol. 5 (1940–1953) (Nouméa, 1975), pp. 18–33, an anti-d'Argenlieu account.

12. Sautot to de Gaulle, 25 August 1981, ATNC, 44 W 463.

13. Munholland, p. 560.

14. Quoted in Glen Barclay, *A History of the Pacific from the Stone Age to the Present Day* (London, 1978), p. 182.

15. The events of 1940–1941 in Tahiti are narrated in Philippe Mazellier (ed.), *Le Mémorial Polynésien*, Vol. V (1940–1961) (Papeete, 1977), pp. 46–83. See also Pierre-Yves Toullelan (ed.), *Encyclopédie de la Polynésie*, Vol. 7 (Papeete, 1989).

16. See Paul-Marie de la Gorce, *L'Empire écartelé* (1936–1945) (Paris, 1988).

17. The contention that the standard of living improved in the EFO is from Toullelan, *Encyclopédie*, p. 36 but seems equally valid for the other French territories, despite the early problems in New Caledonia.

18. Correspondance intérieure et extérieure du Gouverneur, 1943, ATPF.

19. *Ibid.*

20. Letters of 31 March 1941, 15 February 1941, 10 February 1941, 4 August 1943, ATNC, 44 W 463, 464, 466, 467.

21. Report by Bourgeaud, 11 August 1943, ATNC, 44 W 467.

22. *Ibid.*

23. Letter of 1 August 1941, ATNC, 44 W 463.

24. Simington, *op. cit.*

25. Barclay, p. 190.

26. Japan was already a Pacific islands power, having been entrusted with a mandate over the former German holdings in Micronesia by the League of Nations in 1919. See Mark Peattie, *Nan'yo* (Honolulu, 1987).

27. On the American troops in New Caledonia, Lawrey, ch. 6, and Henry Daly, 'La Guerre du Pacifique: "Américal" 1941–1946: Les Américains en Nouvelle-Calédonie', *BSEHNC*, No. 17 (1973), pp. 1–30; Robert G. Bowman, 'Army Farms and Agricultural Development in the Southwest Pacific', *The Geographical Review* (1946), pp. 420–46; G.F.R. [*sic*], 'New Caledonia and the War', *Pacific Affairs* 19 (1946), pp. 373–83; and Francis D. Cronin, *Under the Southern Cross: The Saga of the Americal Division* (Washington, 1951).

28. Yves Geslin, 'Les Américains aux Nouvelles-Hébrides au cours de la Seconde guerre mondiale', *JSO* 12 (1956), pp. 245–85.

29. Munholland, pp. 571–572.

30. Quoted in Munholland, p. 572.

31. However it would appear that the French fears were not entirely unjustified. President Roosevelt, the US navy and various members of Congress had at different times expressed interest in bringing New Caledonia under some form of American control; see C.J. Weeks Jr., 'An Hour of Temptation: American Interests in New Caledonia, 1935–1945', *Australian Journal of Politics and History* 35 (1989), pp. 185–200.
32. Interim Governor Laigret to Commissioner for the Colonies, 25 February 1943, AOM Nouvelle-Calédonie 163.
33. Ex-interim Governor Laigret to Commissioner for the Colonies, 1 May 1944, AOM Nouvelle-Calédonie 163.
34. According to Douglas Oliver, 'The American troops dominated the island's [New Caledonia's] life like an army of occupation. French officials held office, but American admirals and generals decided policy in critical spheres of public order, production and trade.' (*The Pacific Islands*, p. 378, quoted in Thompson and Adloff, p. 272.)
35. *Le Mémorial Calédonien.*
36. *Ibid.*
37. From the works by Lawrey, Daly and Bowman.
38. Geslin, 'Les Américains', and Jeremy MacClancy, *To Kill a Bird with Two Stones* (Port-Vila, 1980).
39. L. Picard, 'C'était comme un rêve', in Mazellier, p. 108.
40. Francis Sanford, in Mazellier, p. 116.
41. Charbonnier, 'Aventures et mésaventures'.
42. Geslin, pp. 274–75.
43. *Pacific Islands Monthly*, August 1943.
44. *Ibid.*
45. *Pacific Islands Monthly*, October 1952.
46. Siole Pilioko, personal communication, Wallis, 27 September 1990.
47. Sanford in Mazellier, p. 113.
48. Poncet, p. 170 ff.
49. Geslin on the New Hebrides; Mazellier on Bora-Bora.
50. Laigret to Commissioner for the Colonies, 25 February 1943, AOM Nouvelle-Calédonie 163. For further clashes between the Americans and French in New Caledonia, see Munholland, 'The Trials of the Free French in New Caledonia, 1940–1942'.
51. See Chapter 3, below.
52. Laigret to Commissioner for the Colonies, 1 May 1944, AOM Nouvelle-Calédonie 163.
53. For example, the pro-American sentiments voiced (and American flags prominently displayed) by some New Caledonians during the troubles of the 1980s.
54. Laigret to Commissioner for the Colonies, 1 May 1944, AOM Nouvelle-Calédonie 163. He also charged that some Americans, claiming to be soldiers, were prospecting for minerals.
55. Captain Bardet, Commander of the Third Infantry Company, report of 12 July 1943, AOM Océanie 153.
56. *Pacific Islands Monthly*, February 1946.
57. Poncet, ch. 22, and Charbonnier's manuscript, 'Aventures et mésaventures', are the basis of my account of the 1946 rebellion in

Wallis; the two differ on some minor details but largely confirm each other. On the soldiers from Nouméa in Wallis, see Bernard Brou, 'Le Corps expéditionnaire calédonien des Forces Françaises Libres à Wallis 1942–1946', *BSEHNC,* No. 55 (1983), pp. 47–59.

58. *Pacific Islands Monthly,* January, 1944.

59. Thompson and Adloff, p. 276.

60. G.F.R., 'New Caledonia and the War'; see also John Wesley Coulter, 'Impact of the War on South Sea Islands', *The Geographical Review,* July 1946, pp. 409–19.

61. *Pacific Islands Monthly,* September 1945 and October 1946.

62. Laigret to the Commissioner of Colonies, 1 May 1944, AOM Nouvelle-Calédonie 163.

63. Houssin, *commandant-supérieur des troupes par intérim,* report, 17 July 1943, AOM Océanie 153.

64. G.F.R., p. 381.

65. See Mazellier and Godard for accounts.

66. Jean Guiart, *Destin d'une église et d'un peuple* (Paris, 1959), pp. 46–48. Other sources suggest the Americans indeed paid high wages to islander labourers and also provided other compensation (food, clothing, gifts) for their work.

67. Thompson and Adloff, pp. 275–6.

68. For one example, see Stephen Henningham, 'How the Men of Maré Went to War', *Pacific Islands Monthly,* January 1989, pp. 36–37. More generally, see Geoffrey White and Lamont Lindstrom, (eds), *The Pacific Theater: Island Representations of World War II* (Honolulu, 1989) and the companion volume, Lamont Lindstrom and Geoffrey White, *Island Encounters: Black and White Memories of the Pacific War* (Washington, 1990). Although they make no reference to the French colonies, they argue that elsewhere in the South Pacific the war and the American presence had a greater effect than any foreign intervention since the arrival of the missionaries. Their evidence seems to support this conclusion, and there is no reason why the repercussions on the French islands should have been different.

69. This account is from Joël Bonnemaison, *La Dernière Ile* (Paris, 1986), ch. XII; see also Edward Rice, *John Frum You Come* (New York, 1974).

70. Alban Bensa, *Nouvelle-Calédonie: Un Paradis dans la tourmente* (Paris, 1990), p. 107.

71. *Sydney Morning Herald,* 8 November, 1940.

2   Recasting the Colonial Order

1. Lt.-Col. Maurice Myers, report to the Free French committee in London, 30 September 1943, AOM Océanie 153.

2. Wilfred G. Burchett, *Pacific Treasure Island, New Caledonia* (Melbourne, 1941), pp. 11–12, 134–135, 216.

3. Report of Governor Laigret, 24 November 1943, AOM Nouvelle-Calédonie 178.

4. Governor to Minister, 1 November 1943, AOM Nouvelle-Calédonie 178.

5. Alain Gerbault, *Un Paradis se meurt* (Paris, 1949), pp. 252, 254–5, 257, 263–9. On Gerbault, see Eric Vibart, *Alain Gerbault: Vie et voyages d'un dandy révolté des années folles* (Paris, 1989).

6. Albert T'Serstevens, *Tahiti et sa couronne* (3 vols., Paris, 1950). The quotations are from Vol. II, pp. 300 and 375, Vol. I, p. 74, Vol. II, pp. 82, 257 and 347, and Vol. I, pp. 96–97, respectively.

7. *Pacific Islands Year Book* (Sydney, 1950), pp. 145, 222, 413, 422, 432.

8. Louis-Gabriel Droux, *La France d'Outre-Mer: Guide pratique pour ceux qui veulent vivre en France d'outre-mer* (Paris, 1951).

9. Jacques Stern, *Les Colonies françaises: Passé et avenir* (New York, 1943); Charles Robequain, *Les Richesses de la France d'outre-mer* (Paris, 1949); Charles Robequain, *Madagascar et les bases dispersées de l'Union française* (Paris, 1958); Charles-André Julien, *Histoire de l'Océanie* (Paris, 1946); Jacques Bourgeau, *La France du Pacifique* (Paris, 1955).

10. Jean-Paul Faivre, *L'Expansion française dans le Pacifique de 1800 à 1842* (Paris, 1953) and Léonce Jore, *L'Océan Pacifique au temps de la Restauration et de la Monarchie de Juillet (1815–1848)* (2 vols, Paris, 1959).

11. Patrick O'Reilly, *Calédoniens* (Paris, 1953 and 1980), *Hébridais* (Paris, 1957), *Tahitiens* (Paris, 1962 and 1975).

12. For his own account, Thor Heyerdahl, *The Kon-Tiki Expedition* (New York, 1950).

13. Bengt Danielsson's first major work was *Work and Life on Raroia: An Acculturation Study from the Tuamotu Group, French Oceania* (London, 1955).

14. Maurice Leenhardt, *Do Kamo: La Personne et le mythe dans le monde mélanésien* (Paris, 1947); on Leenhardt, see James Clifford, *Person and Myth: Maurice Leenhardt in the Melanesian World* (Berkeley, 1982). Jean Guiart's first publications, which date from this period, are 'Les Effigies religieuses des Nouvelles-Hébrides', *JSO* 6 (1949); 'Sociétés, rituels et mythes du nord Ambrym', *JSO* 7 (1951), pp. 1–105. 'The Fore-runners of Melanesian Nationalism', *Oceania* 22 (1951), pp. 81–90, and 'Organisation sociale et politique du nord Malekula', *JSO* 8 (1952), pp. 150–254.

15. Hubert Deschamps and Jean Guiart, *Tahiti (La Polynésie française), Nouvelle-Calédonie, Nouvelles-Hébrides* (Paris, 1957). The section on the Melanesian islands was supposed to be written by Maurice Leenhardt, but his student took over the task after Leenhardt's death.

16. For other views on Tahiti, including some dating from this period, see Daniel Margueron, *Tahiti dans toute sa littérature* (Paris, 1989).

17. Captain Rollin to Charles de Gaulle, 'Note sur l'avenir politique de Tahiti et des EFO', 20 August 1942 and annex note, 1 August 1943, AOM Océanie 153.

18. Thierry d'Argenlieu to Commissaire des Colonies, 22 September 1943, AOM Océanie 153. The admiral's report, however, was not entirely well received, at least to judge by marginalia, perhaps written by the Commissaire himself. D'Argenlieu said that New Caledonia depended on the Americans for supplies, but, in the margin is the note 'false in part: accord between France and allies'; as for subsidies to coffee-planters: 'an old electoral story'; on d'Argenlieu's charge that divisions

were increasing: 'I believe that this is an illusion'; and, concerning the
nationalisation of SLN, 'attention to dangerous repercussions'.

19. Laurence Lader, undated article in *Far Eastern Survey*, quotations of
    copy in French, AOM Affaires Politiques 364, Dossier Nouvelle-Calédonie
    1945–46.
20. Kim Munholland, 'Yankee Farewell: The Americans Leave New Caledo-
    nia, 1945', paper presented to the French Colonial Historical Society,
    Mackinac Island, Michigan, 16–20 May 1990, provided and quoted by
    kind permission of the author.
21. A document prepared by the Vichy government on their plans for the
    Pacific, however, remains classified and unavailable for consultation in
    the Archives d'Outre-Mer.
22. This document is entitled 'Note indiquant le point de vue du
    Commissaire des colonies sur la politique que la France doit adopter et
    mettre en oeuvre dans le Pacifique' [1944], AOM Océanie 138. The
    folder is marked 'rigorously secret'. The document, incidentally, con-
    tains no mention of Wallis and Futuna or the New Hebrides.
23. 'La France devant les problèmes du Pacifique', 1 May 1944, Ministère
    des Affaires Etrangères, Asie-Océanie 1944–1955, Nouvelle-Zélande 15.
    The document exists in two slightly different versions.
24. Cabanier, 'Mémorandum sur les Possessions françaises du Pacifique',
    17 September 1943, AOM Océanie 138.
25. See Robert Aldrich, 'Le Lobby colonial de l'Océanie française', *RFHOM*
    76 (1989), pp. 411–424.
26. The fourteen-page letter from the Conseil Privé was signed by Ahnne,
    Charon, Montaron, Teriieroiterai, Viénot, Poroi, Spitz, and Maraetefau,
    all prominent political figures in Tahiti, and dated 10 February 1944.
    Pleven's reply is dated 23 May 1944. AOM Océanie 153.
27. Chargé d'affaires to Ministre des Affaires étrangères, 18 May 1953 (on
    Samoa) (annex), 16 Septembre 1953 (on resemblances between Sa-
    moa and North Africa and on American press), 19 August 1953 (on
    Chatham Islands, Tokelau and general New Zealand policy), Archives
    du Ministère des Affaires Etrangères, Paris, Asie-Océanie 1944–1955,
    Nouvelle-Zélande 15.
28. Chargé d'affaires to Ministre, 28 July 1954, Ministère des Affaires
    étrangères 1944–55 Asie-Océanie, Nouvelle-Zélande 15.
29. Charles-Robert Ageron, 'La Survivance d'un mythe: La Puissance par
    l'empire colonial (1944–1947)', *RFHOM* 73 (1985), pp. 387–403.
30. Charles-Robert Ageron, 'L'Opinion publique face aux problèmes de
    l'Union française', in Charles-Robert Ageron (ed.), *Les Chemins de la
    décolonisation de l'empire colonial français* (Paris, 1986), pp. 33–48.
31. Paul Isoart, 'L'Elaboration de la constitution de l'Union française: Les
    Assemblées constituantes et le problème colonial', in Ageron, *Les Chemins
    de la décolonisation*, pp. 15–31.
32. For further details, see Robert Aldrich and John Connell, *France's Over-
    seas Frontier* (Cambridge, 1992), Ch. 3.
33. The constitution made no provisions for the New Hebrides, which
    continued to be administered under the terms of the 1906 Franco-
    British agreement on the condominium and several later modifica-

tions. The constitution also made no special provisions for Wallis and Futuna, the legal status of which remained unclear.

34.   Many Muslims in the French *outre-mer* opted for this alternative. But all nationals of the TOMs 'enjoy the rights of citizen' – this constitutional formula was somewhat ambiguous, as the 'natives' were not declared citizens but only to have the rights of citizens. This amounted to less than a declaration of universal suffrage, which, for example, did not arrive in New Caledonia until 1957. Finally, the constitution gave the right to vote to women in France and elsewhere in the *outre-mer*. Such provisions opened access to some political participation to a much larger group of 'natives' than ever before and, through the abolition of the *code de l'indigénat*, removed one of the most 'colonial' aspects of the old system.

35.   These are discussed in detail in Chapter 5.

36.   Albert Sarraut, *La Mise en valeur des colonies françaises* (Paris, 1923).

37.   J. Bourgeau, *La France du Pacifique*, p. 184. The representative assembly of Tahiti also discussed, on 29 November 1953, the proposal for a law creating a tax on rural property which was insufficiently used, developed or built-up, but this was never enacted.

38.   Dossiers on transport, AOM Affaires économiques 137.

39.   Directeur des Affaires Politiques, 19 September 1949, Archives du Ministère des Affaires Etrangères Océanie 135, Dossier '1948–54: Communications maritimes et aériennes', which is the source of the material in the following paragraphs.

40.   Directeur des Affaires Politiques, 'Rapport au Président du Conseil', 4 August 1950, Ministère des Affaires étrangères, Océanie 135.

41.   See details in Chapter 4.

42.   Gouverneur to Ministre, 22 August 1946, AOM Affaires Politiques 364.

43.   Alan Ward, 'Labour Policy and Immigration 1945–1955', in Michael Spencer and John Connell (eds), *New Caledonia: Essays in Nationalism and Dependency* (St Lucia, Qld, 1988), pp. 81–105.

44.   P. Dareste, *Traité de droit colonial* (Paris, 1931).

3   The Economic History of the French Territories

1.   This section sums up my *The French Presence in the South Pacific, 1842–1940* (London, 1990), Ch. 4, which contains further references.

2.   'Makatéa: Bilan socio-économique d'un demi-siècle d'expérience', *JSO* 15 (1959), pp. 199–210; F. Doumenge, 'L'Ile de Makatéa et ses problèmes', *Cahiers du Pacifique*, No. 5 (1963), pp. 41–67; Colin Newbury, 'The Makatéa Phosphate Concession', in R. Gerard Ward (ed.), *Man in the Pacific Islands* (Canberra, 1972), pp. 167–188.

3.   Strategic aspects of the CEP will be treated in a later chapter of this study, so the following discussion will examine only the economic impact of the CEP. On this question, see F. Roy Willis, 'The Economic Effects of Atomic Testing in French Polynesia', in Robert Aldrich (ed.), *France, Australia and Oceania: Past and Present* (Sydney, 1992).

4.   Gilles Blanchet, *L'Economie de la Polynésie française de 1960 à 1980* (Paris, 1985), pp. 33–34.

5. Yves Signorel, 'L'Evolution de l'économie polynésienne de 1961 à 1966', (Thèse de doctorat en sciences économiques, Université de Toulouse, 1969), pp. 84–85.
6. Signorel, pp. 198 ff.
7. N.B., French francs, not French Pacific francs.
8. Signorel, pp. 310–311.
9. Blanchet, p. 196.
10. Commandement supérieur des Forces armées en Polynésie Française, Centre d'expérimentation du Pacifique, Commandement des Forces militaires et de la zone maritime du Pacifique, 'Impact des Armées et du C.E.A. sur l'économie polynésienne en 1985', Fiche 154, 20 February 1986.
11. Figures from Blanchet and Signorel.
12. Ron Hall, 'Passage through Paradise', *Condé Nast Traveler* (April 1991), pp. 106, 110.
13. Claude Robineau, 'The Tahitian Economy and Tourism', in Ben R. Finney and Karen Watson (eds), *A New Kind of Sugar: Tourism in the Pacific* (Honolulu, 1977), pp. 61–76.
14. Ben R. Finney, 'A Successful French Polynesian Co-operative?', *Journal of Pacific History* 3 (1968), pp. 65–84.
15. Victoria Joralemon, 'Collective Land Tenure and Agricultural Development: A Polynesian Case', in N. Pollock and R. Crocombe (eds), *French Polynesia* (Suva, 1988), pp. 154–180; 'Development and Inequality: The Case of Tubuai, a Welfare Economy in Rural French Polynesia', *Human Organization* 45 (1986), pp. 283–295; and, under the name Victoria S. Lockwood, 'Development, French Neocolonialism, and the Structure of the Tubuai Economy', *Oceania* 58 (1988), pp. 176–192.
16. Marie-Thérèse and Bengt Danielsson, 'The Lure of Phosphate: From Makatea to Mataiva', *Pacific Islands Monthly*, April 1984, pp. 23, 55. Incidentally, Bréaud's son was kidnapped in 1980 and killed before a $2 million ransom had been paid; the murderers' motives were unclear, but they were clients (who had gone bankrupt) of the Bréaud-owned Banque de Tahiti.
17. Information in this section, unless otherwise indicated, has been taken from the annual reports of the Institut d'Emission d'Outre-Mer.
18. A. Intes, 'La Nacre en Polynésie française: Evolution des stocks naturels et de leur exploitation', *ORSTOM Notes et Documents, Océanographie*, No. 16 (1982), and M. Cofroli, 'Développement de la production nacrière et perlière en Polynésie française', *ORSTOM Notes et Documents, Aquaculture*, No. 3 (1982).
19. Hall, 'Passage through Paradise', p. 184.
20. J. Champaud, 'Les Trucks de Tahiti', *ORSTOM, Notes et Documents de Géographie*, No. 1981/21 (1981).
21. 'Présentation économique des îles Marquises', Institut d'Emission d'outre-mer, *Exercice 1988: Rapport d'activité: Polynésie Française* (Paris, 1989), pp. 154–155. For details of one island in the Marquesas, see Gérard Cheval, *Ua Pou: Fleur des marquises* (Papeete, 1986).
22. Virginia Thompson and Richard Adloff, *The French Pacific Islands* (Berkeley, 1971), p. 405.

23. Chambre de Commerce de la Nouvelle-Calédonie, *Fluctuations de l'économie calédonienne* (Nouméa, n.d.).
24. John Connell, *New Caledonia or Kanaky?* (Canberra, 1987), p. 127.
25. Patrick Pillon, 'Développements et enjeux sociaux en Nouvelle-Calédonie: l'Opération café', *Les Temps modernes*, No. 464, March 1985, pp. 1623–1653, and J.M. Kohler and P. Pillon, *Impact de l'opération café en milieu mélanésien* (Nouméa, two volumes, 1983).
26. J.M. Kohler, *Pour ou contre le pinus: Les Mélanésiens face aux projects de développement* (Nouméa, 1984).
27. Chambre de Commerce de Nouvelle-Calédonie, pp. 73, 89.
28. On the Wallisian economy since the 1940s, see Centre de productivité et d'études économiques, *L'Archipel de Wallis* (Nouméa, 1982): Paul De Deckker, 'Mutations et développement: Wallis et Tahiti', *Civilisations* 29 (1979), pp. 312–320; J.C. Roux, 'Migration and Change in Wallisian Society', in R.T. Shand (ed.), *The Island States of the Pacific Ocean* (Canberra, 1980), pp. 167–176; John Connell, *Migration, Employment and Development in the South Pacific: Country Report No. 21, Wallis and Futuna Islands* (Nouméa, 1983); Institut d'Emission d'Outre-Mer, *Exercice 1988: Rapport d'activité: Wallis et Futuna* (Paris, 1989); and John Connell, 'Wallis and Futuna: Stability and Change at the End of Empire', in Aldrich (ed.), *France, Australia and Oceania*, pp. 91–116.
29. Falakiko Gata, interviewed in *Le Monde*, 28 June 1985.
30. Jean-Louis Andréani, 'Priorities for Wallis', *The Guardian Weekly*, 3 September 1989 (translated from *Le Monde*).
31. Karl Rensch, 'Wallis and Futuna: Total Dependency', in A. Ali and R. Crocombe (eds), *Politics in Polynesia* (Suva, 1983).
32. Centre de productivité et d'études économiques, p. 70.
33. Institut d'Emission d'Outre-Mer, *Exercice 1988: Rapport d'activité: Polynésie française*.
34. Institut d'Emission d'Outre-Mer, *Exercice 1988: Rapport d'activité: Nouvelle-Calédonie*.
35. Quoted in Myriam Dornoy, *Politics in New Caledonia* (Sydney, 1985), p. 145.

4   The Populations and Societies of the French Pacific

1.   Michel Panoff, *Tahiti métisse* (Paris, 1989).
2.   Material in this section is based on the censuses of the French territories, the most recent of which were held in New Caledonia in 1989 and in French Polynesia and Wallis and Futuna in 1983. The censuses are published by the Institut Territorial de la Statistique et des Etudes Economiques in Nouméa and Papeete. See also the reports prepared by John Connell for the South Pacific Commission on *Migration, Employment and Development in the South Pacific: Country Report No. 5: French Polynesia* (Nouméa, 1985), *No. 10: New Caledonia* (Nouméa) and *No. 21: Wallis and Futuna Islands* (Nouméa, 1983). Further information is contained in the annual reports of the Institut d'Emission d'Outre-Mer, as well as three useful atlases: Robert Brousse, *et al.*, *Atlas de Tahiti et de la*

Polynésie Française (Singapore, 1988), Frédéric Angleviel, *et al.*, *Atlas de Nouvelle-Calédonie* (Nouméa, 1989), and Benoît Antheaume and Joël Bonnemaison, *Atlas des îles et états du Pacifique-Sud* (Montpellier, 1988).

3. Panoff, *op. cit.*, To my knowledge, there exists no full-scale study of Europeans or *demis* in present-day French Polynesia.

4. On the Chinese in Tahiti, see Gérald Coppenrath, *Les Chinois de Tahiti: De l'aversion à l'assimilation, 1865–1966* (Paris, 1967) and Richard U. Moench, 'Economic Relations of the Chinese in the Society Islands' (Unpublished PhD thesis, Harvard University, n.d.).

5. Somewhat surprisingly, there has been no full-scale study of the European population in New Caledonia, although Isabelle Merle is now completing a doctoral thesis on this topic. See Isabelle Merle, 'The Trials and Tribulations of the Emancipists: The Consequences of Penal Colonisation in New Caledonia, 1864–1920', in Robert Aldrich (ed.), *France, Australia and Oceania: Past and Present* (Sydney, 1991), pp. 39–55.

6. José Barbançon, 'Le Pays du non-dit' (unpublished manuscript). I am grateful to M. Barbançon for allowing me to read his manuscript.

7. Kim Munholland, 'World War II and the End of Indentured Labor in New Caledonia' (unpublished paper). I am grateful to Professor Munholland for allowing me to read this paper. See also Alan Ward, 'Labour Policy and Immigration, 1945–1955', in Michael Spencer, Alan Ward and John Connell (eds), *New Caledonia: Essays in Nationalism and Dependency* (St. Lucia, Qld, 1988), pp. 81–105.

8. See John Connell, 'Wallis and Futuna: Stability and Change at the Ends of Empire', in Aldrich (ed.) *France, Australia and Oceania*, pp. 91–116.

9. Alain Saussol, 'Peut-on parler de créolité en Nouvelle-Calédonie?' in J.P. Doumenge, *et al.* (eds), *Iles tropicales, insularité, 'insularisme'* (Talence, 1987), pp. 157–164.

10. Several attempts to prove that the Melanesians were not the original inhabitants of New Caledonia, efforts provoked by political considerations, have not been convincing.

11. The most comprehensive recent study is Douglas Oliver, *Oceania: The Native Cultures of Australia and the Pacific Islands* (2 vols, Honolulu, 1989).

12. The notion of a full-scale destruction of islander culture was promoted in Alan Moorehead, *The Fatal Impact* (Harmondsworth, 1968), but this hypothesis has generally been rejected.

13. Michel Panoff, *La Terre et l'organisation sociale en Polynésie* (Paris, 1970); François Ravault, 'Land Problems in French Polynesia', *Pacific Perspective*, 9 (1981), pp. 31–65.

14. See Alain Saussol, *L'Héritage: Essai sur le problème foncier mélanésien en Nouvelle-Calédonie* (Paris, 1979), and Alan W. Ward, *Land and Politics in New Caledonia* (Canberra, 1982).

15. In particular, during the Polynesian wars of the 1840s in Tahiti and, in New Caledonia, in the rebellions of 1878 and 1917.

16. P. Dareste, *Traité de droit colonial* (Paris, 1931), vol. 2, pp. 333 ff.

17. *Ibid.*, pp. 498–501.

18. The idea of a 'new tradition' and the mechanisms through which it

developed are studied in Claude Robineau, *Du Coprah à l'atome* (Paris, 1984); his arguments, based on Mooréa in Polynesia, can also be applied to New Caledonia.

19. Pierre-Yves Toullelan, 'Church and State in Eastern Polynesia: Tumultuous Relations (1830–1880)', in Aldrich (ed.), *France, Oceania and Australia*, pp. 1–18.

20. See Alain Barbadzan, *Naissance d'une tradition: Changement culturel et syncrétisme religieux aux îles Australes* (Paris, 1982).

21. J.M. Kohler, 'L'Islam en Nouvelle-Calédonie', *L'Afrique et l'Asie modernes*, 135 (1982), pp. 3–11; Coppenrath, *Les Chinois de Tahiti*.

22. Jean-Claude Roux, 'Pouvoir religieux et pouvoir politique à Wallis et Futuna', in Paul De Deckker and Pierre Lagayette, *États et pouvoirs dans les territoires français du Pacifique* (Paris, 1987), pp. 54–80.

23. M.R. Charbonnier, 'Aventures et mésaventures à Wallis et Futuna', Manuscript MNS 90, Académie des Sciences d'Outre-Mer, Paris.

24. Jean-Marie Kohler, *Profil sociologique de l'église catholique de Wallis et Futuna* (Nouméa, 1985). Kohler's working paper, with its critique of the church, was controversial in religious circles.

25. Paul Hodée, *Tahiti 1834–1984: 150 ans de vie chrétienne en Eglise* (Papeete, 1983) on the Catholics, and Charles Vernier, *Au Vent des cyclones* (Paris, 1985) on the Protestants; see also Virginia Thompson and Richard Adloff, *The French Pacific Islands* (Berkeley, 1971), Ch. 15.

26. Jean-Marie Kohler, *Christianity in New Caledonia and the Loyalty Islands* (Nouméa, 1981).

27. For example, Maurice Leenhardt, who arrived in New Caledonia in 1903 as a Protestant missionary, undertook the first serious study of Melanesian beliefs. See James Clifford, *Person and Myth: Maurice Leenhardt in the Melanesian World* (Berkeley, 1982). Other clergymen who have written about the French territories include the Marist priest Patrick O'Reilly, one of France's pioneering Oceanists; Mgr Alexandre Poncet, historian of Wallis, and Paul Dubois, historian of Maré.

28. See Apollinaire Anova-Ataba, *D'Ataï à l'indépendance* (Nouméa, 1984).

29. In general, see Charles W. Forman, 'The Impact of Colonial Policy on the Churches of Tahiti and New Caledonia', *International Review of Missions*, 305 (1977), pp. 12–21.

30. See the Commission Justice et Paix report, *L'Avenir de l'outre-mer français* (Paris, 1988).

31. Forman, *op. cit.*

32. Jean-Marie Kohler, 'The Churches and the Colonial Order', in Spencer, Ward and Connell (eds), *New Caledonia*, pp. 145–174. See also the interview with the Melanesian pastor Adrien Hnangan in the same volume, pp. 198–218.

33. Brigitte Vassort-Rousset, *L'Engagement socio-politique des organisations chrétiennes dans le Pacifique* (Paris, 1985), pp. 7–10.

34. The Uniting Church (a union of the Presbyterian, Methodist and Congregational denominations in Australia), for instance, published *Kanaky Update*.

35. Daniel Mauer, *Tahiti: De la parole à l'écriture* (Paris, n.d.); Patrick O'Reilly, 'Le Français parlé à Tahiti', *JSO* (December 1962), pp. 69–81; Guy Viêt

Levilain, 'L'Académie tahitienne et la renaissance culturelle en Polynésie française', *Contemporary French Civilization*, 2/3 (1978), pp. 440–447.

36. Notably the poems of Douro Raapoto.

37. François Ravault, 'Le Français dans une société pluri-culturelle: l'exemple de Tahiti', *Anthropologie et Société*, 6 (1982), pp. 89–105.

38. For example, *station, paddock* and *creek*.

39. Stephen J. Schooling, 'A Sociolinguistic Survey of New Caledonia', unpublished paper, Summer Institute of Linguistics, 1982.

40. 'Francophonie' is the group of countries where French is used. See Robert Aldrich and John Connell, 'Francophonie: Language, Culture or Politics', in Robert Aldrich and John Connell (eds), *France in World Politics* (London, 1989), pp. 170–193. More specifically, see J.C. Roux, 'Présence et originalité du fait francophone en Mélanésie du Sud', *BSEHNC*, No. 65 (1985), pp. 19–27.

41. J.M. Kohler and P. Pillon, *Adapter l'école ou réorienter le projet social* (Nouméa, 1982), p. 9; J.M. Kohler and Loïc J.D. Wacquant, *L'Ecole inégale* (Nouméa, 1985), p. 52, n. 2.

42. In addition to the two studies cited in note 41, see J.M. Kohler and Loïc J.D. Wacquant, 'La Question scolaire en Nouvelle-Calédonie: Idéologies et sociologie' (Nouméa, 1984), reprinted in *Les Temps modernes*, No. 464 (1985), pp. 1654–87.

43. Marie-Joëlle Dardelin, *L'Avenir et le destin: Regards sur l'école occidentale dans la société kanak* (Paris, 1984).

44. Kohler and Dardelin have expressed different interpretations. Dardelin argues that 'the success or failure of Kanaks in school at the present does not depend on their economic integration in the white world' (p. 136), while Kohler insists on the inequalities caused by the economic context. See his critique of Dardelin in Kohler and Wacquant, *L'école inégale*, pp. 181–204.

45. Marie-Adèle Néchéro-Jorédié, 'A Kanak People's School', in Spencer, Ward and Connell (eds), pp. 198–218.

46. Ravault, 'Le Français dans une société pluri-culturelle: l'exemple de la Polynésie', p. 96.

47. Antoine Périni, 'L'Introduction du vernaculaire de l'enseignement du 1er degré de l'aire géographique tahitianophone: Contribution d'une reflexion' (Unpublished thesis, Université de Grenoble, 1985).

48. *Quel Avenir pour les enfants et les jeunes en Nouvelle-Calédonie? Actes d'un colloque au Lycée Jules-Garnier, 25 Juin 1988* (Nouméa, 1988).

49. The secretary-general of the government in the 1940s said that efforts to promote Melanesian work 'were viewed badly by the colonists and white employers in general, who would have preferred to see the indigenes maintained in a state of semi-servitude, so that they would constitute a reservoir of cheap labour on which all who desired could easily draw'. M. Bourgeau, 'Rapport sur la main-d'oeuvre insuffisante', 24 August 1943, ATNC 44 W 466.

50. See Patrick Pillon, 'L'Economie domestique en transition. Trois essais', *ORSTOM Rapports scientifiques et techniques, Sociologie*, No. 2 (Paris, 1987).

51. See J.M. Kohler, *Colonie ou démocratie. Elements de sociologie politique sur la Nouvelle-Calédonie* (Nouméa, 1987) and the other works of Kohler, Patrick

Pillon and Loïc Wacquant for the effects in New Caledonia. There are a number of studies on French Polynesia, including: Bengt Danielsson, *Work and Life on Raroia* (London, 1955) on the Tuamotus; Ben R. Finney, *Polynesian Peasants and Proletarians* (Cambridge, Mass., 1973) on two villages of Mai'ao and Tahiti; Robert I. Levy, *Tahitians: Mind and Experience in the Society Islands* (Chicago, 1973); Douglas Oliver, *Two Tahitian Villages: A Study in Comparison* (Honolulu, 1981); and Ron Crocombe and Pat Hereniko, *Tahiti: The Other Side* (Suva, 1985).

52. The Haussariat (Haut-Commissariat) is the residence of the French High Commissioner; Montravel is a largely Melanesian suburb of Nouméa; the Place des Cocotiers is the main public square in Nouméa, often used for political demonstrations.

53. On Melanesian attitudes, see, in particular, Jean-Marie Tjibaou, 'Recherche d'identité mélanesienne et société traditionnelle', *JSO*, 32 (1976), pp. 281–292, and 'Etre Mélanésien aujourd'hui', *Esprit*, No. 57 (1981), pp. 81–93, and Jean-Marie Tjibaou and Philippe Missotte, *Kanaké* (Papeete, 1978) and Adrien Hnangan, 'Kanak Aspirations' in Spencer, Ward and Connell (eds), *New Caledonia*, pp. 219–229. There are various pertinent articles in *Bwenando*. See also the works of Maurice Leenhardt and of Alban Bensa and Jean-Claude Rivierre. For a brief summary, Alban Bensa, 'L'Identité kanak et la colonisation', *Kanaky*, No. 16 (1988), pp. 16–18 and No. 17 (1989), pp. 11–12.

54. Emmanuel Kasarhérou, Director of the Musée Territorial de la Nouvelle-Calédonie, personal communication, 20 September 1990.

55. Déwé Gorodey, *Sous les Cendres des conques* (Nouméa, 1985).

56. A recorded collection of songs by Yata, released in 1990, is called 'Wegelelo'.

57. See Agence de Développement de la Culture Kanak, *Do I Neva: Sculpteurs et peintres kanak d'aujourd'hui* (Nouméa, 1990).

58. The Réunion des Musées Nationaux published a major exhibition catalogue, *De Jade et de nacre: Patrimoine artistique kanak* (Paris, 1990), which contains a number of important essays on Melanesian culture.

59. On Polynesian culture, see Oliver, *Oceania*.

60. Bruno Saura, 'L'Identité polynésienne: Facteurs de revendication et discours identitaires à Tahiti (Polynésie française)' (unpublished DEA Thesis, Université d'Aix-Marseille-III, 1986), Ch. 2.

61. Saura, p. 143. This section on 'Maohi' Polynesian culture is based on Part II of Saura's thesis.

62. Duro Raapoto, 'Maohi: On Being Tahitian', *Pacific Perspective*, 9 (1980), pp. 3–5, and his book of poems, *Te Pinainai o te aau – Pehepehe* (Papeete, 1980); Rui a Mapuhi, *Te hia'ai ao* (Papeete, 1985). Rui a Mapuhi, incidentally, is the *nom de plume* of a Tahitian writer who lives in France.

63. Notably the plays of Maco Tevane, such as the 1972 play 'Te Peapea hua ore o Papa Penu e a Mama Roro', a comedy about family life in Tahiti; Tevane was one of the first members of the Académie Tahitienne. Another well-known playwright is John Mairai, and the best known cinematographer is Henry Hiro.

64. Saura, pp. 192–197.

65. Saura, pp. 187–192.
66. *Le Figaro Magazine*, 12 January 1985, quoted in Saura, p. 128.
67. Quoted in Kohler and Pillon, *Adapter l'école*, p. 3.
68. J.M. Kohler, P. Pillon and L.J.D. Wacquant, *Jeunesse canaque et coutume* (Nouméa, 1985); see also Patrick Pillon, 'Jeunesse urbaine mélanésienne et différenciation sociale' (Unpublished paper, Nouméa, 1985).
69. There is unfortunately little scholarly writing on island women in the French territories. A notable exception, from which much of the material in this section is taken, is Christine Langevin-Duval, 'Traditions et changements culturels chez les femmes tahitiennes' (Third cycle doctoral thesis, EHESS, 1979). Christine Langevin has published parts of her thesis as *Tahitiennes de la tradition à l'intégration culturelle* (Paris, 1990).

5   Politics in the French Pacific, 1945–1980

1. See Robert Aldrich and John Connell, *France's Overseas Frontier: Départements et Territoires d'Outre-Mer* (Cambridge, 1992), Ch. 7, for a detailed discussion of the structure of politics in the DOM-TOMs.
2. See Chapter 2, above.
3. Paris, however, retained much power under this new legislation; see Philippe Lechat, 'Le Statut de la Polynésie Française du 6 Septembre 1984. Cinq ans après: autonomie interne ou autonomie internée?', *Annales du Centre universitaire de Pirae*, 3 (1989), pp. 69–98; for the texts of the various statutes, see Philippe Lechat (ed.), *Royaume de Tahiti et Dépendance, Etablissements Français de l'Océanie, Polynésie Française: Institutions Politiques et Administratives – Textes et Documents, 1819–1988* (Papeete, 1990).
4. The present-day overseas territories of Denmark and the Netherlands are represented in the parliaments of those countries, and the dependent territories of the United States elect non-voting members of the American House of Representatives; the British territories, however, lack representation in the House of Commons.
5. See Michel Panoff, 'Tahiti et le mythe de l'indépendance', *Les Temps modernes*, 225 (1965), pp. 1443–1471.
6. The *ta'ata Tahiti* are those who, whether are not they are 'full-blooded' Polynesians, identify themselves with Tahitian concerns, usually in opposition to the interests of Europeans or *demis*.
7. That all political parties in New Caledonia have French, rather than Melanesian, names has no significance other than indicating the lack of a common Oceanic language in New Caledonia and the Loyalty Islands.
8. See Bengt and Marie-Thérèse Danielsson, *Poisoned Reign* (Harmondsworth, second edition, 1986), for the most complete catalogue of charges of such practices, particularly during the political life of Pouvanaa a Oopa. The pro-independence parties in New Caledonia, and some outside observers, made similar charges about political activity there in later decades.

9. Afred-René Grand, 'Pouvanaa a Oopa et le nationalisme à Tahiti' (Thesis, Paris, 1981); I have drawn on Grand's thesis for much of my information about Pouvanaa and this period.

10. Letter of 'Un Groupe de volontaires', signed by Edouard Etienne Deaua to Ministre de la France d'Outre-Mer, 8 September 1946, AOM Affaires Politiques, 364.

11. Letter signed by Nemia, 3 June 1946, forwarded by the *député* Citerne to the Ministre de la France d'Outre-Mer, AOM Affaires Politiques 364.

12. Jeanne Tunica y Casas was a Frenchwoman who came to New Caledonia with her father, a medical doctor. She later married a Spanish mechanic – whence her surname. She became interested in communism during the Second World War (if not earlier), when she took part in activities in solidarity with the Soviet Union after the Nazi invasion. At the end of the war, she developed an interest in the Vietnamese independence movement and maintained contacts both with insurgents in Indochina and migrants to New Caledonia. She extended her activities to Melanesians at this time. Later, she was forced to leave New Caledonia, returned briefly to France, lived for a time in Australia – where her political sentiments made her the object of government enquiry – and finally moved to the New Hebrides, where she died. See Jean Suret-Canale, 'Nouvelle-Calédonie: Une Page oubliée de l'histoire', *Révolution* 453, 4 November 1988, pp. 45–49.

13. The manifesto is reprinted in Apollinaire Anova-Ataba, *D'Ataï a l'indépendance* (Nouméa, 1984), pp. 185–188.

14. Nemia to Ministre, *op. cit.*; Anova-Ataba, *ibid.*; Grand, *op. cit.*

15. Telegram of Governor Maestracci, 30 November 1947; Note of Commandant Supérieur, 21 January 1948; Note of Chef d'État-Major Général de la Marine, 28 November 1947; Directeur des Affaires Politiques, 8 June 1948; Ministre de la France d'Outre-Mer, 4 September 1947; Note of official from Défense Nationale, 17 June 1947; and Governor's note to minister, 5 June 1947; AOM Océanie 137. For a personal account by one demonstrator arrested in the *Ville d'Amiens* affair, see Noël Ilari, *Secrets tahitiens* (Paris, 1978), Part III, Ch. 2.

16. Lassalle-Séré, 'Rapport sur l'évolution de la situation politique', 1948–9 (after mission in 1947–48), AOM Affaires Economiques 106. See the comments by Ilari, *op. cit.*

17. Maestracci had allowed Céran-Jérusalémy to return to his government post after the acquittal despite his support for the Comité Pouvanaa. The accusation inspired Maestracci to write in the margin of Lassalle-Séré's report: 'There is a question of whether it is appropriate to undertake an open war against Pouvanaa, in which case he will appear to be a martyr, which will win him much sympathy, or whether it is not preferable to *pretend* to ignore him, meanwhile having him closely watched'. Lassalle-Séré's réponse, also in the margin, was that there existed 'support in the population for a firm policy towards Pouvanaa. In fact, Maestracci wanted to make a *tabula rasa* of his past'. Lassalle-Séré accused Maestracci elsewhere in the report of a policy 'sometimes of excessive rigour, sometimes of excessive goodwill' towards the dem-

onstrators. Another charge was that Maestracci did not nip in the bud support for Pouvanaa by a local lawyer, Weil-Curiel, and his associates (Poroi, Charon, and others); Maestracci, in his marginalia, disagreed. Such differences of opinion are indicative of the not infrequently varying attitudes and strategies of Parisian officials and administrators in the Pacific.

18. Lassalle-Séré, p. 56.
19. Lassalle-Séré, pp. 16–17.
20. On Pouvanaa, see Grand, 'Pouvanaa et le nationalisme à Tahiti'; Danielsson, *Poisoned Reign*, Ch. 3; and William Tagupa, *Politics in French Polynesia, 1945–1975* (Wellington, 1976).
21. Grand, pp. 26, 42, 53–4.
22. Grand, part 2, 'Sociologie politique, économique et religieuse du Pouvanisme'.
23. The French governor, interrupting Pouvanaa, said that it seemed that Pouvanaa either did not speak French, in which case his election was illegal – since knowledge of French was a criterion for election at this time – or that he was trying to provoke an incident. Pouvanaa defended himself, but one of his associates then said, in Tahitian, that Pouvanaa should use French in speaking before the governor as common courtesy when treating a guest. Pouvanaa replied that a previous governor had told him that 'our language is a language spoken by pigs, and today I am hearing the same thing from the mouth of another governor. But why act that way? When I left [Tahiti] to defend France [in the First World War], they did not ask me if I spoke French'. Pouvanaa's opponents charged that, in fact, he did not speak or understand French well, but his supporters said that this was untrue. The incident in the assembly is discussed in Grand, pp. 229–257.
24. Governor to Minister, 2 December 1951, AOM Océanie 136.
25. Governor to Minister, 26 June 1951, AOM Océanie 135.
26. Governor to Minister, 2 June 1951, AOM Océanie 135.
27. Petitbon to Minister, 27 August 1951, AOM Océanie 135.
28. Private letter of governor, 2 June 1951, AOM Océanie 135.
29. Note for the Director of the Cabinet of the Minister, 1951, AOM Océanie 135.
30. Governor to Minister, 9 June 1954, AOM Océanie 135.
31. Governor to Minister, 26 June 1951, AOM Océanie 135.
32. Director of Political Affairs, Ministry of Overseas France, to Governor, 23 March 1951, AOM Océanie 135.
33. See Danielsson, *op. cit.*
34. Report of the head of security services to the secretary-general of the territory, 29 October 1953, AOM Océanie 135. (Pouvanaa's statement was provided to the authorities by one of the secret informers in his group.)
35. Written in red in the margin of the comment just quoted, presumably by the secretary-general of the territory, is the comment: 'The day will come when Tahiti will no longer be French, because such is the wish of the RDPT'.

36. In a private dinner with Governor Angeli in 1966, Pouvanaa was asked: 'What is the best political solution for Polynesia?'. He replied: '*Départementalisation*, an income tax and a judicial review of my conviction [of 1959]'. Quoted in Grand, p. 331.

37. The only other major politician to oppose de Gaulle on this issue was Sékou Touré, who led Guinea to independence in 1958.

38. See Danielsson, *op. cit.*, for details.

39. The most comprehensive study of the trial is in Grand, pp. 80–114.

40. Quoted in Grand, appendix.

41. Quoted in Mazellier, pp. 542–543.

42. John Connell, *New Caledonia or Kanaky?* (Canberra, 1987), pp. 243–244.

43. Bernard Brou, *Trente ans d'histoire politique et sociale de la Nouvelle-Calédonie de 1945 à 1977* (Nouméa, n.d.), p. 51, charges that the party and its leaders were 'launched in an underhanded way by the staff of Governor Counarie in 1950–1951, and the political party was organised and directed by diverse administrators and heads of administrative bureaus'. The head of the agriculture service, a prominent Caldoche, was Jacques Barrau; the ethnologist was Jean Guiart, who, incidentally, was the brother-in-law of Maurice Lenormand.

44. On the political history of New Caledonia, see Myriam Dornoy, *Politics in New Caledonia* (Sydney, 1984), as well as Brou and Connell, *op. cit.*

45. Union Calédonienne, *Pourquoi oui à l'Union Calédonienne, oui à l'autonomie?* (Nouméa, 1972), p. 1.

46. Quoted in Connell, p. 246.

47. Connell, p. 247.

48. Quoted in Dornoy, p. 170.

49. Quoted in Virginia Thompson and Richard Adloff, *The French Pacific Islands* (Berkeley, 1971), p. 326.

50. See Tagupa, *op. cit.*, and the *Encyclopédie de la Polynésie*, Ch. 7.

51. See Chapter 9, below.

52. In French electoral practice, each candidate is seconded, on the same ticket, by a *suppléant*; in the case of a victorious candidate being unable to serve, or being removed from office by reason of health, judicial conviction, resignation or death, the *suppléant* automatically assumes his seat for the remainder of his term.

53. On Teariki and Sanford, *Encyclopédie de la Polynésie*, pp. 117–118.

54. Ibid., pp. 106–107, 119–120.

55. The rather complicated history of political parties in New Caledonia is discussed in detail by Dornoy, pp. 170–215, and Connell, *op. cit.*

56. The name of the group was a reference to a red scarf given by the Communard Louise Michel, who had been exiled to New Caledonia in the 1870s, to the Melanesian chief Ataï, leader of the islander revolt in 1878.

57. Quoted in Dornoy, p. 276.

58. Association pour la Fondation d'un Institut Kanak d'Histoire Moderne, *Contribution à l'histoire du pays kanak* (Nouméa, 1983), p. 91.

59. The Front Indépendantiste included the Union Calédonienne, the Front Uni de Libération Kanake, the Parti Socialiste Calédonien, the Union Progressiste Mélanésien and the Parti de Libération Kanake.

60. See Jean-Marie Tjibaou and Philippe Missotte, *Kanaké: The Melanesian Way* (Papeete, 1978); also, the previous chapter.
61. In the Comoros, however, the island of Mayotte voted against independence and remains a French territory.
62. In French Polynesia, the RDPT and its successor organisations never officially pronounced themselves in favour of independence, although certain leaders, such as Pouvanaa, Teariki and Sanford at various times certainly indicated that this was their long-term goal.
63. An under-class which, however, depended for its employment on the jobs provided by the élite and the possibility of remaining in a territory where their presence was not welcomed by the Melanesians.

6 From the New Hebrides to Vanuatu

1. The only general history of the New Hebrides in English is Jeremy MacClancy, *To Kill a Bird with Two Stones* (Port-Vila, 1980), although Howard Van Trease, *The Politics of Land in Vanuatu* (Suva, 1987) is also a comprehensive account. It should be noted that even in the 1980s spellings of New Hebrides place-names varied. Thus, to use examples of locales discussed in this chapter, Efate or Vaté, Malakula or Mallicolo, Tanafo or Vanafo or Fanafo. Espiritu Santo is usually referred to simply as Santo. Personal names also vary: thus, Jimmy Stevens or Stephens.
2. There was a Spanish judge for the simple reason that the island group was discovered by a Spanish explorer – a neat way negotiators in 1906 found of resolving possible disagreements between the French and British judges.
3. The New Hebrides is a fine example of the way in which colonial powers (and observers of imperial rivalries) could contemplate selling or exchanging territories. For instance, in 1906, the Paris newspaper *Le Figaro* suggested that Britain cede the Indian Ocean island of Mauritius (which had been a French colony from the 1600s until the defeat of Napoleon) to France in return for full rights over the New Hebrides. At the same time, the *Journal des Débats* and *Le Temps* recommended that the archipelago be divided between the two colonial powers; the *Mois colonial* opposed any French withdrawal. Across the Channel, the *Globe* thought that Britain should leave the New Hebrides to France in return for France's giving up the fishing rights the residents of Saint-Pierre et Miquelon enjoyed in the waters of neighbouring Newfoundland. The *Morning Post* opted for Britain's giving France 'some corner of land in Africa' in exchange for the New Hebrides. In the event, no such exchanges eventuated. (Freddy Drilhon, *Le Peuple inconnu* (Paris, 1955)). In the 1920s, proposals for partition or exchange were again put forward and talks were held between London and Paris. Yet the French Minister of Colonies displayed little interest; by the time a new French minister showed greater enthusiasm, the British were no longer willing to consider cession.
4. William Edgell and Fred Kalo (eds), 'The New Hebrides: A Doubly Oppressed Colony' (pamphlet, no publication details); 'pandemonium' as a play on 'Condominium', was a term popularised by Walter Lini,

future president of Vanuatu, who later used it in the title of his book *Beyond Pandemonium: From the New Hebrides to Vanuatu* (Wellington, 1980).

5. Aimé Louis Grimald, *Gouverneur dans le Pacifique* (Paris, 1990), pp. 148–149.

6. *Ibid.*, pp. 146–147.

7. *Ibid.*, Pt I, Ch. 2, and Maurice Delauney, *De la Casquette à la jaquette, ou de l'administration coloniale à la diplomatie africaine* (Paris, 1982), pp. 99–140.

8. Christiane Delpech and Félix Bellaïche, *Hier les Nouvelles-Hébrides* (n.p., 1987), a series of interviews with French residents of the islands.

9. Personal communication; the source prefers to remain anonymous. For recently published accounts of French life in the New Hebrides, see Guy Lacam, *Souvenirs des Nouvelles-Hébrides* (Nouméa, 1990), and Jacques Gédéon, 'Le Condominium des Nouvelles-Hébrides', *BSEHNC*, No. 89 (1991), pp. 61–80.

10. For a comprehensive discussion of agriculture and colonisation, see Joël Bonnemaison, 'Passions et misères d'une société coloniale: Les Plantations au Vanuatu entre 1920 et 1980', *JSO*, No. 82–83 (1986), pp. 65–84, and Jean Guiart, 'La Conquête et le déclin: Les Plantations, cadre des relations sociales et économiques au Vanuatu (ex Nouvelles-Hébrides)', *JSO*, No. 82–83 (1986), pp. 7–40.

11. Bonnemaison, 'Passions et misères', p. 75.

12. The extent to which the British pressured the French in the New Hebrides to support de Gaulle is unclear. One Frenchman testified: 'One must admit . . . that the decision [to support de Gaulle] was a little influenced, first of all, by the presence of the English, and then by our need to eat. In order to receive provisions, we had to stay on their good side . . . . You have to admit that this influenced the decision of three-quarters of the population. When people say that we were the first to rally [to de Gaulle], that's true but it was a little bit by force. It happened that the Resident, Sautot, under pressure from the British, broke off relations with the French governor in Nouméa and declared his total independence from the French authorities so that the settlers might continue to receive provisions from Australia and that things could continue to work.' (M. Desmoulières, quoted in Delpech and Bellaïche, pp. 85–86). As he recorded in his autobiography *Gentleman Pauper* (Bognor Regis, 1984), pp. 89–91, Sir Ronald Garvey, as Acting British Resident Commissioner in Vila, had no difficulty in persuading the fiercely patriotic Sautot to take over. Sautot's successor, Robert Kuter, was also strongly Free French.

13. The only casualty of the Japanese bombardment of Santo was a cow; a group of American GIs erected a plaque: 'Here lies Bossy. Tojo got her, 11 p.m. 9/9/43 because she was walking around during a blackout'. (Reece Discombe, 'The New Hebrides at War' (unpublished manuscript, 1979, Vanuatu Cultural Centre, Port-Vila), which provides one account of the war years).

14. MacClancy, p. 107.

15. Yves Geslin, quoted in Bonnemaison, 'Passions et misères', p. 78.

16. Jean-Marc Colardeau (quoted in Delpech and Bellaïche, pp. 44–45) added that when he saw the American medical teams, 'It was the first time in my life that I saw doctors worthy of the name' – a measure of the isolation and underdevelopment of the New Hebrides. The problem of health in the Condominium, particularly malaria, was so severe that a Frenchman sent to the islands in 1942 recalled: 'When you left New Caledonia for the New Hebrides, people said you were going to the cemetery. The New Hebrides had a bad reputation not only because of the life you could lead there, but also because there were so many mosquitoes. It was said that it would not be long before any European or New Caledonian who went there would end up in the cemetery' (Rémy Delaveuve, quoted in Delpech and Bellaïche, p. 51).

17. See in particular the interview with Mr Harris, an Australian in the New Hebrides, in Delpech and Bellaïche, pp. 111–117.

18. On the John Frum cult, see Chapter 1, above, and the account in Joël Bonnemaison, *La Dernière île* (Paris, 1986), as well as the older work by Jean Guiart, *Un Siècle et demi de contacts culturels à Tanna, Nouvelles-Hébrides* (Paris, 1956). (Guiart is also author of a classic work on *Espiritu Santo* (Paris, 1958).) For a recent reappraisal, see Ron Adams, 'Homo Anthropologicus and Man-Tanna: Jean Guiart and the Anthropological Attempts to Understand the Tannese', *Journal of Pacific History*, 22 (1987), pp. 3–14.

19. The most famous account of the American presence in the New Hebrides is a work of fiction, James Michener, *Tales of the South Pacific* (New York, 1947).

20. Report from Britain to the United Nations, 1949, AOM Affaires politiques 932.

21. Yves Le Treunt, 'Les Terres françaises et le futur des Hébrides', 1948, AOM Nouvelles-Hébrides 19. This file also contains a list of the shareholders in the SFNH and other notes critical of the SFNH.

22. Delauney, pp. 106, 113. On the relations between the French Residents and other Frenchmen – and thus, on the power relations in the colony – compare the views of M. Desmoulières, an accountant: 'There was always a very good collaboration [by the SFNH] with the administration, and the Resident, at that time considered the agents of the Comptoirs [SFNH] as a sort of technical counsellor, especially from the commercial point of view. I won't say that the Residents did nothing without us, far from that, but, well, an important decision was never taken without their speaking to us'. (Quoted in Delpech and Bellaïche, p. 79).

23. *Ibid.*, p. 100.

24. In general, see J.S.G. Wilson, *Economic Survey of the New Hebrides* (London, 1966); Centre de productivité et d'études économiques, *Les Nouvelles-Hébrides: Document d'information générale* (Nouméa, 1977); H. C. Brookfield, 'Multum in Parvo: questions about diversity and diversification in small developing countries', in Percy Selwyn (ed.), *Development Policy in Small Countries* (London, 1975), pp. 54–76; and Margaret C. Rodman, *Masters of Tradition: Consequences of Customary Land Tenure in Longana, Vanuatu* (Vancouver, 1987).

25. Quoted in Bonnemaison, *op. cit.*
26. See Bonnemaison's and Guiart's articles on plantations and Wilson's report for more details.
27. See Wilson. Only about 250 New Hebrideans were employed in the fishing plant and the manganese mine.
28. Bedford, p. 206.
29. Brookfield, p. 67.
30. Centre de productivité et d'études économiques, pp. 57–59.
31. On land speculation, see Selwyn, Bonnemaison, MacClancy and Guiart, as well as John Beasant, *The Santo Rebellion* (Honolulu, 1984).
32. *Ibid.*
33. Quoted in *Nabanga*, 1975. *Nabanga* was the newsletter of the French Residency.
34. Brookfield, p. 66, and Bob Hering (ed.), *The Political Economy of the South Pacific* (Canberra, 1983), p. 192.
35. Wilson, pp. 98 and 101.
36. On the land question, see Van Trease, *Politics*, Barak Sope, *Land and Politics in the New Hebrides* (Suva, 1975) and (ed.) *Land Tenure in Vanuatu* (Suva, 1984), Joël Bonnemaison, 'Cultural Aspects of Systems of Land Tenure in Vanuatu', *Report of the Regional Conference on Land Management* (Port-Vila, 1981), pp. 17–23; Howard Van Trease, 'Historical Background to the Problem of Land Alienation in Vanuatu', *ibid.*, pp. 24–40; Selwyn Arutangai, 'Vanuatu: Overcoming the Colonial Legacy', in R. Crocombe (ed.), *Land Tenure in the Pacific* (Suva, 1977), pp. 261–302; and Peter Larmour, 'Alienation of Land and Independence in Melanesia', in *Evolving Cultures in the Pacific Islands: Proceedings of the 1982 Politics Conference* (Laie, 1982), pp. 185–231.
37. The question is explored further in Van Trease, *Politics.*
38. Hubert Benoist, *Le Condominium des Nouvelles-Hébrides et la société mélanésienne* (Paris, 1972), pp. 159–176.
39. Benoist, pp. 191–192.
40. On Stephens, see Van Trease, *Politics*; Bonnemaison, *La Dernière île*; Beasant, *Santo*; and Jean Leder, *Les Cent jours du bout du monde* (Nouméa, 1981). On the role of 'custom' in politics: Bernard Hours, 'Custom and Politics in the New Hebrides', *Pacific Perspectives* 8 (1979), pp. 15–20; James Jupp, 'Custom, Tradition and Reform in Vanuatu Politics', in *Evolving Cultures*, pp. 143–158; Robert Tonkinson, 'Vanuatu Values: A Changing Symbiosis', in R.J. May and Hank Nelson (eds), *Melanesia: Beyond Diversity*, Vol. 1 (Canberra, 1982), pp. 74–90; Margaret Jolly, 'Birds and Banyans of South Pentecost: Kastom in Anti-Colonial Struggle', *Mankind* 13 (1982), pp. 338–355; Lamont Lindstrom, 'Cultural Politics: National Concern in Bush Areas on Tanna (Vanuatu)', in *Evolving Cultures*, pp. 232–246; R. Tonkinson, 'National Identity and the Problem of Kastom in Vanuatu', *Mankind*, 13 (1982), pp. 305–315; and Joël Bonnemaison, 'Les Lieux de l'identité: Vision du passé et identification culturelle dans les îles du sud et du centre de Vanuatu (Mélanésie)', *Cahiers de l'ORSTOM, Série Sciences humaines* 21 (1985), pp. 151–170.

41. On the John Frum movement, see Ch. 1. In brief, it was a 'cargo cult' of Melanesians which combined traditional ideas with hopes for the arrival of a powerful and generous patron, a kind of messiah, from overseas.

42. On party politics, see James Jupp, 'The Development of Party Politics in the New Hebrides', *Journal of Commonwealth and Comparative Politics*, 27 (1979), pp. 263–282; James Jupp, 'Elections in Vanuatu', *Political Science*, 35 (1983), pp. 1–15; James Jupp and Marian Sawer, 'Colonial and Post-Independence Politics: Vanuatu', in R.J. May and Hank Nelson (eds), pp. 549–570; J.V. MacClancy, 'From the New Hebrides to Vanuatu, 1979–1980', *Journal of Pacific History*, 16 (1981), pp. 91–104; R.A.S. Forster, 'Vanuatu: The End of an Episode of Schizophrenic Colonialism', *Round Table* 70 (1980), pp. 367–373. I have also drawn on a detailed unpublished report by Keith Woodward, 'Historical Summary of Constitutional Advance in the New Hebrides, 1954–1977', written in 1978 and kindly supplied by Mr Woodward.

43. Keith Woodward, personal communication, 30 May 1991. Woodward served in the British administration from 1953 to 1978, and for the last 10 years of his career was political secretary at the British Residency. I would like to thank Mr Woodward for making a lengthy cassette recording of his impressions of the history of the Condominium.

44. Alain Bigard, *Vanuatu: Chronique d'une décolonisation* (Nouméa, 1984), p. 15.

45. *Ibid.*, pp. 21–26.

46. Guiart, 'Les Plantations'; cf. Jupp, p. 147.

47. The composition of the local councils and the Representative Assembly were partially determined by the constitution of the electorate and the method of voting. Three years of residence in the New Hebrides was necessary for an inhabitant to obtain voting rights; all islanders were enfranchised. In the municipal elections, the French pressured the British not to divide voting areas into distinct wards with separate representation; the result on Santo was the overwhelming victory of the MANH and Nagriamel, although the coalition won only 52 percent of the popular vote. In the Assembly the French aimed at preserving a certain parity between islanders and settlers despite the great disparity in population numbers; Melanesians particularly resented the granting of seats to the Chamber of Commerce. Election of chiefs to the Assembly also posed problems, both in determination of how they were selected and because of their VAP tendencies. In general, there were also challenges to voting results, and the Joint Court obliged two by-elections to be held. The Representative Assembly first met in June 1976, without all four chiefs who were to be members. For the first meeting of the Assembly at its full strength, in November 1976, after the by-elections, the VAP held 21 seats, the UCNH 12, and the 'independents' (including MANH/Nagriamel) 9. (Woodward, 'Historical Summary'.)

48. Bonnemaison, *La Dernière île*, pp. 310–318.

49. Woodward, 'Historical Summary', p. 13.

50. See Beasant, Jupp and MacClancy for accounts.
51. Bigard, pp. 54, 72, 73.
52. The most comprehensive brief treatment is Joël Bonnemaison, 'Un Certain refus de l'Etat: Autopsie d'une tentative de sécession en Mélanésie', *International Political Science Review*, 6 (1985), pp. 230–247. For more detailed coverage of Tanna, Bonnemaison, *La Dernière île*.
53. Quoted in Bonnemaison, *La Dernière île*, p. 348.
54. *Ibid.*, p. 351.
55. On Santo, see Beasant and Leder. Beasant, a member of the leftist wing of the British Labour Party and an unsuccessful candidate for election to the British Parliament, was Lini's press secretary from 1977 to 1982. Leder, a French New Caledonian lawyer, defended Stephens and the other Santo rebels at their trial. The personal and political opinions of both writers very much colour their accounts.
56. Robert's speech is reprinted in Leder, pp. 249–265.
57. Many of the Anglo-Saxon writers of the time took this view, and analysts such as Jupp, Clark and MacClancy stress the role of the French.
58. Leder, *Les Cent jours du bout du monde*.
59. Alain Bigard, *Vanuatu*. Bigard was the editor of a French language newspaper in the New Hebrides, *Jeune Mélanésien*, closed down by the VAP government. He argues that in the 1970s 'it would be the French Governments, in the persons of its Secretaries of State for the DOM-TOMs, MM. Olivier Stirn and Paul Dijoud, who would be the best allies of the *indépendantistes*' (p. 29). He also criticises several Frenchmen who favoured the independence of the archipelago, notably the ethnologist Jean Guiart, whose broadcasts on Radio Vanuatu he characterises as being the work of the 'tortuous spirit of the impotent moralist that is M. Guiart' (p. 166).
60. Notably Bonnemaison in his various writings. (Bonnemaison was a French researcher who lived in the New Hebrides in the 1970s.)
61. Personal communication from a resident who prefers to remain anonymous, Port-Vila, 11 September 1990.
62. Jean Guiart maintains: 'Inspector-General Robert, the French Resident Commissioner, was tightly reined in by his Minister. In public he only said and did what he had been ordered to do and say'. (Guiart's review of Leder's book, *JSO*, No. 72–73 (1981), p. 312.)
63. Pierre Anthonioz, personal communication, letter of 28 April 1991.
64. This is the interpretation of Anne-Gabrielle Thompson, 'John Higginson, Patriot or Profiteer?', (Unpublished PhD Thesis, University of Queensland, 1982).
65. There were official censuses in the New Hebrides only in 1967 and 1979, and they did not clearly divide French from English residents. This figure, therefore, is not entirely reliable.
66. Anthonioz, personal communication, 28 April 1991.
67. Quoted in Bonnemaison, 'Passions et misères', p. 77.
68. Robert Oliver Turnbull, *Tin Roofs and Palm Trees* (Canberra, 1977), p. 87.
69. Jean-Claude Guillebaud, *Un Voyage en Océanie* (Paris, 1980), p. 195.
70. *Ibid.*, p. 204.

71. Woodward, personal communication, 30 May 1991. See also Van Trease, *The Politics of Land in Vanuatu*, esp., pp. 108–116.

72. Cf. Clark, p. 14; Jupp and Sawer, pp. 557–558; Julie-Anne Ellis and Michael Parsons, 'Vanuatu: Social Democracy, Kastom and "Melanesian Socialism"', in Peter Davis (ed.), *Social Democracy in the South Pacific* (Auckland, 1983), p. 118, argue that France wanted to install a puppet government in the New Hebrides; MacClancy, p. 126, stresses French interest in protecting the rights of the Francophone minority; Beasant, p. 32, says France wanted to protect the economic interests of French citizens and to preserve Francophonie in post-independence Vanuatu.

73. Excerpts from the report are printed in *PIM*, May 1982, pp. 32–37.

74. Quoted in Turnbull, *Tin Roofs*, p. 87.

75. Anthonioz, personal communication, 28 April 1991.

76. Personal communications with various residents of Vanuatu, September 1990.

77. On French education efforts and its achievements, Ian L. Gray, 'The Emergence of Leaders in the New Hebrides' (Unpublished MA Thesis, University of Auckland, 1971).

78. Quoted in Turnbull, *Tin Roofs*, p. 79.

79. Quoted in Gray, p. 125.

80. On benefits given to French bureaucrats, Guillebaud, pp. 77, 125.

81. Jean-Marc Philibert, 'Living under Two Flags: Selective Modernisation in Erakor Village, Efate', in M. Allen (ed.), *Politics, Economics and Ritual in Island Melanesia* (Sydney, 1981), pp. 316, 323, 333.

82. Excerpts from the reports of Mouradian, Langlois and Gauger quoted in the following paragraphs are printed in *PIM*, with a commentary by Howard van Trease, July 1982, pp. 31–35; August 1982, pp. 27–29; and September 1982, pp. 27–30. Van Trease found these reports in a carport, abandoned by the French authorities, along with other papers, in their hurry to leave Port Vila in July 1980. He also makes great use of the reports in *The Politic of Land in Vanuatu*.

83. Keith Woodward, personal communication, 30 May 1991.

84. Van Trease, p. 115.

85. French Resident's report. See Note 82, above.

86. Woodward, personal communication, 30 May 1991. Woodward adds that the French administration considered the holding of court the most important activity of the district agents, a view the British did not share. The British considered other tasks, notably the organisation of local councils, more pressing.

87. French Resident's report.

88. *Ibid.*

89. *Ibid.*

90. Guiart, in his review of Leder's book, however, argues: '*Vis-à-vis* the French Residency, M. Robert and his close collaborators, the attitude of the Vemerana chiefs . . . was absolute suspicion. M. Robert was considered by them as one of their most dangerous adversaries.' (*JSO*, No. 72–73 (1981), p. 313).

91. Bonnemaison, *La Dernière île*, p. 320.

92. As outlined by M. Limousi, the French Secretary of State in the prime

minister's department; quoted in Bigard, p. 199.

93. Bigard, p. 215. The payments were 16 364 CFP for a single person or 27 272 CFP for a couple, plus 8182 CFP per child, as well as moving costs of 45 454–318 181 CFP.

94. Silas C. Hakwa, 'Land and the Constitution', in *Report of the Regional Conference*, pp. 41–47. See also Charles Zorgbibe, *Vanuatu: Naissance d'un Etat* (Paris, 1981).

95. W. Lini, *Beyond Pandemonium*, p. 62.

96. J.V. MacClancy, 'Vanuatu since Independence, 1980–1983', *Journal of Pacific History*, 19 (1984), pp. 84, 100–101. Cf. Alan Clark, 'Vanuatu: Independence but still the French Connection', *New Zealand International Review*, 5 (1980), pp. 12–15.

97. MacClancy, pp. 108–109.

98. Letter of Vanuatu Secretary of State for Foreign Affairs, 30 May 1983, National Archives of Vanuatu, Ministry of Home Affairs HA 804/1.

99. Prime Minister of Vanuatu to French Ambassador, 1 September 1980, *ibid.*

100. Note from First Secretary, Vanuatu National Planning and Statistics Office, Office of the Prime Minister, *ibid.*

101. Fred Timakata to French Ambassador, 8 August 1980, *ibid.*

102. Bigard, p. 202.

103. 'Le Déclin de la Francophonie', *La Dépêche de Tahiti*, 18 December 1987 and 'Un Député de l'opposition dénonce la suppression de toute liberté d'expression', *La Dépêche de Tahiti*, 10 February 1987. See, more particularly, 'Le Déclin économique de Santo', *La Dépêche de Tahiti*, 22 January 1988, and Marc Charuel, 'Triste Vanuatu', *Le Spectacle du Monde*, No. 307, October 1987. (I am grateful to Philippe Lechat for providing me with copies of these articles.) It should be noted that the conservative, anti-independence press of France and its overseas territories was anxious to highlight the lack of achievements of the Vanuatu government and promote the views of the opponents of Lini and the VAP.

104. *PIM*, April 1986, p. 17, September, pp. 21, 35, April 1987, p. 22.

105. *PIM*, November 1987, pp. 16–17.

106. *PIM*, January 1988, pp. 13–14, July, pp. 10–12, September, pp. 10–13, November, p. 14, January 1989, pp. 24–26, March, pp. 10–13. Lini's hold on power was severely weakened, however; during 1990, there were intense struggles against him inside the Vanuaaku Party, and in 1991, Lini was forced to relinquish his leadership of the party and the prime ministership. Subsequently the Francophone Maxime Carlot was elected prime minister and relations between Vanuatu and France have been strengthened.

107. Information supplied by M. Pain, French Vice-Consul in Port Vila, 10 September 1990.

108. Information from M. Rousse, a French *coopérant* in the Vanuatu Ministry of Education.

7 The Crisis in New Caledonia in the 1980s

1. In English, the most comprehensive account of events down to 1987 is

John Connell, *New Caledonia or Kanaky?* (Canberra, 1987), supplemented by his 'New Caledonia: The Matignon Accord and the Colonial Future', Research Institute for Asia and the Pacific, University of Sydney, Occasional Paper No. 5, 1988 and various press reports. See also Helen Fraser, *New Caledonia: Anti-Colonialism in a Pacific Territory* (Canberra, 1988). French sources will be noted later in this chapter.

2. A useful chronology of events down until 1983 is Association pour la Fondation d'un Institut Kanak d'Histoire Moderne, *Contribution à l'histoire du pays kanak* (Nouméa, 1983).

3. See the long polemical *dossier*, Gérard Lacourrège, *Qui a tué Pierre Declercq?* (Nouméa, 1986).

4. The declaration is reprinted in Claude Gabriel and Vincent Kermel, *Nouvelle-Calédonie: La Révolte Kanake* (Paris, 1985), p. 130.

5. Detailed data on election results in New Caledonia are provided in Connell, *New Caledonia or Kanaky*, which also discusses the multitude of political parties in the territory.

6. The charter is reprinted in Connell, *New Caledonia or Kanaky*, pp. 447–450.

7. Connell, p. 331.

8. Pisani's speech of 7 January 1985, in which he presented the plan, is reprinted in Connell, pp. 451–459.

9. In the eighteenth century, both the French and other explorers referred to people whom they first encountered as 'Indians' or 'naturals'. 'Natives', more often used in English than French, has alternately been considered offensive and appropriate by the people to whom it refers. 'Indigenes', and the cumbersome 'autochthones' which to some extent succeeded it, were meant to be more scientific and neutral labels.

10. '*Métros*' is short for *métropolitains* and the origin of '*z'oreilles*' ('the ears') may relate to sunburned faces of foreigners in the tropics or the gossip and eaves-dropping they were thought to practise. *Niaouli*, the name of an indigenous tree in New Caledonia, was applied to those of Asian origin born in the territory, while the *z'Arabes* were descendants of political prisoners (most of whom, in fact, were Berber) transported from North Africa to New Caledonia in the 1870s, and the *Viets* are Vietnamese.

11. Thierry Desjardins, in *Le Figaro*, 29–30 November 1984, quoted in Connell, p. 332.

12. See, for example, Bernard Brou, *Peuplement et population de la Nouvelle-Calédonie: La Société pluriethnique* (Nouméa, n.d.).

13. Alan Clark, 'Mitterrand, Matignon and the Role of the Republican State in New Caledonia', in Robert Aldrich (ed.), *France, Oceania and Australia: Past and Present* (Sydney, 1991), pp. 137–42.

14. Maurice Satineau, *Le Miroir de Nouméa* (Paris, 1987).

15. Frédéric Bobin, 'Kanak Activism and Political Cycles in New Caledonia', in Aldrich (ed.), *France, Oceania and Australia*, pp. 127–35.

16. Yet *Les Nouvelles* also experienced the effects of the crisis when it was purchased by the French newspaper magnate Robert Hersant, and its former editor – allegedly no friend of Chirac and even too conservative for the RPR – was dismissed from his job.

17. J.M. Kohler, 'Colonie ou Démocratie', *Le Monde Diplomatique*, July 1987, published in English as 'Colony or Democracy: The New Caledonian Dilemma, *Australian Journal of Politics and History* 33 (1987), pp. 47–59; for other works by Kohler, see notes to Ch. 3.

18. Jean Guiart, *La Terre est le sang des morts: La Confrontation entre blancs et noirs dans le Pacifique sud français* (Paris, 1983); 'What immediate future for New Caledonia?', *Pacific Perspective* 8 (1979), pp. 21–25; 'One of the Last Colonies: New Caledonia', *Journal of International Affairs* 36 (1982), pp. 105–112; 'Nouvelle-Calédonie 1985: Commentaires', *Les Temps modernes* May 1985, pp. 2126–2140; see also notes to Ch. 2. For the Latham-Guiart exchange, see the insert to *Bulletin de la Société des Etudes Historiques de la Nouvelle-Calédonie* 14 (1979).

19. A. Saussol, *L'Héritage: Essai sur le problème foncier mélanésien en Nouvelle-Calédonie* (Paris, 1979).

20. Jean Chesneaux, *Transpacifiques* (Paris, 1987).

21. One example is the Association pour l'Information et le Soutien au Droits du Peuple Kanak (AISDPK), founded in Paris in 1982, which organises meetings, exhibits and demonstrations and publishes a review, *Kanaky*. Among those who have contributed articles are Bensa, Chesneaux and Kohler.

22. Such as *Kanaky* and *Kanaky Update*.

23. The present author is one such example.

24. Marie-France Pisier, *Le Bal du Gouverneur* (Paris, 1984); Jacqueline Sénès, *Terre violente* (Paris, 1987) and her non-fiction *La Vie quotidienne en Nouvelle-Calédonie de 1850 à nos jours* (Paris, 1985); Richard Hall, *Noumea* (Sydney, 1990). On earlier works, see Anne-Marie Nisbet, *Littérature néo-calédonienne* (Montréal, 1985).

25. See Isabelle Merle, 'Les Australiens et la Nouvelle-Calédonie. Bilan des recherches en sciences sociales', *Revue française d'histoire d'outre-mer* 76 (1989), pp. 583–596.

26. John Connell, 'Trouble in Paradise: the perception of New Caledonia in the Australian Press', *Australian Geographical Studies* 25 (1987), pp. 54–65.

27. Helen Fraser, *New Caledonia: Anti-Colonialism in a Pacific Territory* (Canberra, 1988) and *Your Flag's Blocking Our Sun* (Sydney, 1990).

28. David Robie, *Blood on Their Banner: Nationalist Struggles in the South Pacific* (London, 1989).

29. See Chapter 4, above.

30. Gérard Lacourrège, *Les Heures noires de la Calédonie* (Nouméa, 1985); 'Isabelle Doisy', *Chronique des années de cendres* (Paris, 1988); Maurice Delarge, '*La France Australe':Nouvelle-Calédonie: 'Ile de Lumière'* (Nouméa, 1985).

31. For example, Antoine Sanguinetti, *et al.*, *Enquête sur Ouvéa* (Paris, 1989).

32. Alain Rollat, *Tjibaou le Kanak* (Lyon, 1989) and, with Edwy Plenel, *Mourir à Ouvéa. Le Tournant Calédonien* (Paris, 1988).

33. Gilbert Picard, *L'Affaire d'Ouvéa* (Paris, 1988).

34. Claude Gabriel and Vincent Kermel, *Nouvelle-Calédonie: La Révolte Kanake* (Paris, 1985); Claude Gabriel and Vincent Kermel, *Nouvelle-Calédonie:*

Les Sentiers de l'Espoir (Montreuil, 1988); Thierry Desjardins, *Nouvelle-Calédonie: Iles veulent rester Français* (Paris, 1985).

35. Antonio Raluy, *La Nouvelle-Calédonie* (Paris, 1990).
36. Among others are Marc Coulon, *L'Irruption Kanak: De Calédonie à Kanaky* (Paris, 1985); Marc Weitzmann, *Nouvelle-Calédonie: Un Siècle de Balles Perdues* (Paris, 1985); Daniel Veill, *Opération Victor* (Paris, 1989); and Patrick Forestier, *Les Mystères d'Ouvéa* (Paris, 1988).
37. Desjardins; Gabriel and Kermel, *op. cit.*
38. Satineau, *Le Miroir de Nouméa.*
39. This was also the conclusion of Connell, *New Caledonia or Kanaky*, p. 445. Cf. R. Aldrich, 'New Caledonia: The Current Crisis in Historical Perspective', *Contemporary French Civilization* 10 (1986), pp. 175–209.

8 French Polynesia and Wallis and Futuna in the 1980s

1. For a general survey of politics in French Polynesia, see Pierre-Yves Toullelan, *Tahiti et ses archipels* (Paris, 1991), Ch. VIII. The information in this chapter is taken largely from articles in *Pacific Islands Monthly* (hereafter *PIM*) and *Islands Business*, supplemented by material from other periodicals, such as *Le Monde*. Many of the articles in *Pacific Islands Monthly* were written by Bengt and Marie-Thérèse Danielsson, and some of their reports were drawn together in *Poisoned Reign* (Ringwood, Vic., revised ed., 1986). I have also drawn on conversations with various residents of Tahiti during a two-week stay there in 1990.
2. *PIM*, July 1983, pp. 12–14.
3. See *Le Nouvel Observateur*, 2 August 1990, pp. 42–45.
4. *Sydney Morning Herald*, 11 September 1987; *Le Nouvel Observateur*, 22 March 1990.
5. The nuclear question is examined in more detail in Ch. 9 and is also the particular focus of the Danielssons' book cited above.
6. *PIM*, May 1991, pp. 19–20.
7. In 1977, for instance, a small group called Te Toto Tupuna had bombed the Tahiti telephone exchange. In later years, the Pomaré Party was alleged to be trying to import weapons into Tahiti.
8. This was the opinion of French Polynesia's senator, Daniel Millaud, as expressed in his electoral brochure '1980–1989: Neuf ans à votre service'.
9. Speech of François Mitterrand, kindly provided by the Présidence de la République.
10. On the electoral sociology of the territory, see the *Encyclopédie de la Polynésie*, Vol. 8, pp. 110–118.
11. Oscar Temaru, 'Maohinui (French Polynesia): The Need for Independence', in Nancy J. Pollock and Ron Crocombe (eds), *French Polynesia: A Book of Selected Readings* (Suva, 1988), pp. 275–283.
12. See *Islands Business*, April 1986.
13. *Les Nouvelles de Tahiti*, 11 October 1990.
14. See Toullelan, p. 191.
15. The new statute is printed in Philippe Lechat, *Royaume de Tahiti et*

Dépendances, Etablissements Français de l'Océanie, Polynésie Française: Institutions Politiques et Administratives Textes et Documents, 1819–1988 (Papeete, 1990), pp. 433–471. For a critical commentary, see Philippe Lechat, 'Le Statut de la Polynésie Française du 6 Septembre 1984. Cinq ans après: autonomie interne ou autonomie internée?', *Annales du Centre Universitaire de Pirae*, No. 3 (1988–1989), pp. 69–98.

16.   Oscar Temaru, 'Tahitians Stir to Plight of New Caledonia's Kanaks', *PIM*, May 1985, pp. 52–53; on Flosse and Ukeiwé, *PIM*, April 1985, pp. 28–29.

17.   *Tahiti Sun Press*, quoted in *Islands Business*, March 1987, p. 37.

18.   *Le Monde*, 23 July 1987.

19.   *Le Monde* (3 November 1987) interpreted the riots as a result of rising unemployment, social tension and the plight of the poor; *Le Figaro* (12 November 1987) rejected this explanation and blamed the *indépendantistes*, who, the newspaper hinted, were financed by Australia and New Zealand.

20.   Several of Léontieff's ministers resigned from their appointments in order to cast votes in the assembly and give Léontieff a solid majority for adoption of the territory's budget. When Léontieff reappointed the ministers, there resulted a challenge to the legality of his action.

21.   Barry Shineberg, 'The Image of France: Recent Developments in French Polynesia', *Journal of Pacific History* 21 (1986), p. 165.

22.   *Le Point*, 14 August 1989.

23.   On recent developments, see John Connell, 'Wallis and Futuna: Stability and Change at the Ends of Empire', in Robert Aldrich (ed.), *France, Australia and Oceania: Past and Present* (Sydney, 1991), pp. 91–116. I have drawn heavily on this article, as well as my conversations with Wallisians during my visit to the island in September 1990.

24.   'Le Kava, La Crosse et l'Etat', *La Croix*, 25 August 1989.

25.   *Le Monde*, 15 April 1987.

26.   *Les Nouvelles Calédoniennes*, 28 September 1990, p. 71.

27.   *Le Monde*, 15 April 1987.

28.   Platform of the Union Océanienne and other information kindly supplied by M. Michel Héma, the head of the party. See also *The Dominion* (Wellington, NZ), 5 December 1991.

9   Nuclear Testing, the 'New Pacific' and French International Policy

1.   Much of this section is based on Wilfrid L. Kohl, *French Nuclear Diplomacy* (Princeton, 1971).

2.   Lawrence Scheinman, 'Euratom: Nuclear Integration in Europe', *International Conciliation*, No. 563 (May 1967), quoted in Kohl, p. 19.

3.   Kohl, p. 36.

4.   Greenpeace, *French Polynesia: The Nuclear Tests: A Chronology, 1967–1981* (Auckland, 1981).

5.   This is at least the interpretation of Kohl.

6.   See Robert Aldrich and John Connell, 'Beyond the Hexagon', in Robert Aldrich and John Connell (eds), *France in World Politics* (London, 1989), pp. 1–15.

7. Quoted in Kohl, p. 129.
8. This phrase of a '*puissance moyenne*' was often used in the 1970s and 1980s.
9. See, for example, Alfred Grosser, *Affaires extérieures* (Paris, 1984).
10. Jean-Pierre Gomane, *Les Marins et l'outre-mer* (Paris, 1988), p. 111.
11. *Ibid.*
12. Henri Fages, 'Un intérêt majeur de la France en Océanie. Le Centre d'Expérimentation du Pacifique', *JSO*, No. 87 (1989), pp. 11, 12, 19.
13. Kohl, *French Nuclear Diplomacy.*
14. Jean Chesneaux, *Transpacifiques* (Paris, 1987).
15. *Pacific Islands Monthly*, June 1991, pp. 10–11.
16. See Chapter 3, above.
17. Yves Le Baut, 'Les Essais nucléaires français de 1966 à 1974', *Relations Internationales*, No. 59 (Autumn 1989), pp. 359–370.
18. J.W. Davidson, 'French Polynesia and the French Nuclear Tests: The Submission of John Teariki', *Journal of Pacific History* 2 (1967), pp. 149–154.
19. David Stone, 'The Awesome Glow in the Sky: The Cook Islands and the French Nuclear Tests', *Journal of Pacific History* 2 (1967), pp. 154–159.
20. Stewart Firth, *Nuclear Playground* (Sydney, 1987), pp. 96–97.
21. See Chapter 5, above.
22. For critical views, see for example Bengt Danielsson, 'Under a Cloud of Secrecy: the French Nuclear Tests in the South Pacific', in Nancy J. Pollock and Ron Crocombe, *French Polynesia* (Suva, 1988), pp. 260–274.
23. Pierre Thireaut, head of the testing centre, interviewed in *Islands Business*, November 1986, pp. 24–25.
24. Thireaut, pp. 24–25.
25. *PIM*, September 1985, pp. 10–13. For the Australian viewpoint, see the speech by the then Australian Minister of Foreign Affairs, Bill Hayden, *PIM*, June 1987, pp. 16–17, and for the French view, the remarks by the French Minister for Overseas Departments and Territories, Bernard Pons, *PIM*, September 1987, pp. 21–22. More generally, see Michael Hamel-Green, 'The Rarotonga South Pacific Nuclear-Free Zone Treaty', in Ranginui Walker and William Sutherland (eds), *The Pacific: Peace, Security and the Nuclear Issue* (Tokyo, 1988), pp. 93–122.
26. Richard Shears and Isobelle Gidley, *The Rainbow Warrior Affairs* (Sydney, 1985) was the first of several 'instant books' on the drama – which also sparked a television 'mini-series'. It was quickly followed by J. Dyson, *Sink the Rainbow! An Enquiry into the 'Greenpeace Affair'* (London, 1986); M. King, *Death of the Rainbow Warrior* (Auckland, 1986); D. Robie, *Eyes of Fire: The Last Voyage of the Rainbow Warrior* (Auckland, 1986); and Sunday Times Insight Team, *Rainbow Warrior: The French Attempt to Sink Greenpeace* (London, 1986).
27. Stewart Firth, *Nuclear Playground*; 'State Terror', *Arena*, No. 73 (1985), p. 3.
28. Pierre Lacour, *De l'Oceanie au Pacifique* (Paris, 1987).
29. Firth, *op. cit.*, discusses various views.
30. See Richard Deacon, *The French Secret Service* (London, 1990), and Roger Faligot, *La Piscine: The French Secret Service since 1989* (Oxford,

390 *Notes and References*

1989) for general introductions to the history of French intelligence activities.

31. *Pacific Islands Monthly,* June 1991, pp. 10–11. The arrest of a third agent involved in the affair, in Switzerland in 1991, threatened new tensions.

32. See Ron Crocombe, *The South Pacific* (Auckland, 1983).

33. See John Ravenhill (ed.), *No Longer an American Lake?* (Berkeley, 1989) for various articles on geopolitical concerns, as well as R. Walker and W. Sutherland (eds), *The Pacific: Peace, Security and the Nuclear Issue* (Tokyo, 1988); on nationalism, see David Robie, *Blood on Their Banner: Nationalist Struggles in the South Pacific* (London, 1989); on Papua New Guinea, see Sean Dorney, *Papua New Guinea: People, Politics and History since 1975* (Sydney, 1990), and Mark Turner, *Papua New Guinea: The Challenge of Independence* (Melbourne, 1990); on Fiji, Robert T. Robertson and Akosita Tamanisau, *Fiji: Shattered Coups* (Sydney, 1988).

34. I have underlined certain parallels between the 1880s and the 1980s in my 'L'Australie et la France dans le Pacifique: contentieux actuel et arrière-plan historique', *JSO,* No. 84 (1987), pp. 93–98.

35. See, for example, Simon Winchester, *The Pacific* (London, 1991), especially the section 'The Great Ocean', pp. 31–62.

36. This section is taken largely from my 'Rediscovering the Pacific: A Critique of French Geopolitical Analysis', *JSO,* No. 87 (1989), pp. 5–24, which contains a more extensive treatment of these themes and the works discussed.

37. *Newsweek,* 22 February 1988; M.T. Daly and John Connell, 'The New Pacific Pirates', *Pacific Islands Monthly,* December 1987, p. 38; 'Le Pacifique, nouvel axe du monde', *L'Express,* 6 April 1984: René Servoise, 'Le Pacifique, "nouveau monde"', *Politique étrangère,* January 1985, pp. 101–117; RPR, *Le RPR vous parle de la Nouvelle-Calédonie* (RPR, Paris, 1985); François Mitterrand, *Réflexions sur la politique extérieure de la France* (Paris, 1986), p. 13.

38. Ron Crocombe, 'Studying the Pacific: Past Experiences and Future Potentials', in Anthony Hooper, *et al.,* *Class and Culture in the South Pacific* (Auckland, 1987), pp. 115–138.

39. Cercle Katara, *Pacifique Sud, une paix précaire: Essai de géostratégie* (Nouméa, 1980). Later publications included Georges Zeldine, *L'Hémisphère pacifique: Réalités et avenirs* (Nouméa, 1984).

40. Institut du Pacifique, *Le Pacifique, 'nouveau centre du monde'* (Paris, 1983; 2nd ed., 1986). The informally published collections of articles included volumes on the Pacific, ASEAN and Antarctica. The book on Australia, edited by Georges Ordonnaud and Alain Sérieyx, is *Australie 88: Bicentennaire ou Naissance?* (Paris, 1988).

41. Gilles Etrillard and François Sureau, *A l'Est du monde* (Paris, 1983).

42. Pierre Lacour, *De l'Océanie au Pacifique: Histoire et enjeux* (Paris, 1987).

43. See Chapter 7, above.

44. Institut du Pacifique, *Le Pacifique,* Chap. 1.

45. Cercle Katara, *Pacifique Sud.*

46. Cercle Katara, *Pacifique Sud,* p. 10.

47. Lacour, p. 17.

48. Institut du Pacifique, *Le Pacifique,* Chap. 1.

49. Etrillard and Sureau, p. 32.
50. Institut du Pacifique, *Le Pacifique.*
51. Zeldine, p. 31.
52. Cercle Katara, *Pacifique Sud.*
53. Institut du Pacifique, *Le Pacifique.*
54. Etrillard and Sureau, p. 202.
55. Cercle Katara, *Pacifique Sud.*
56. The 'Pritchard affair' pitted English and French interests against one another and indirectly led to the declaration of a French protectorate over Tahiti. Pritchard, the English consul in Papeete and a Protestant missionary, tried successfully in the 1830s to keep French and Catholic influence out of Tahiti. In 1842, however, those efforts were thwarted by French takeover of the island.
57. Lacour, pp. 52, 71. In the 1950s, Britain carried out nuclear tests in the Australian desert, to which Lacour refers.
58. Etrillard and Sureau, p. 140.
59. Yves Lacoste, 'Le Pacifique, est-il vraiment le "nouveau centre du monde"?', *Les Nouvelles littéraires*, December 1984, pp. 169–172 and interview in *Libération*, 12 September 1985.
60. Interview in *Libération*, 14 February 1986.
61. Lacoste in *Libération*.
62. Alexandre Sanguinetti, 'Nouvelle-Calédonie: Summum jus, Summa injuria', *Politique d'aujourd'hui*, June 1985.
63. Chesneaux, *Transpacifiques*, pp. 118, 120, 138.
64. Georges Ordonnaud, 'Pacifique sud-ouest: un nouveau théâtre?', *Le Monde*, 22 August 1985.
65. John Connell and Michael van Langenberg, 'Indonesia: A Giant Awakens', *Pacific Islands Monthly*, March 1988, p. 27, discuss this view.
66. Institut du Pacifique, *Le Pacifique*, p. 264.
67. On this point, see 'La Théorie des dominos', *Le Monde*, 29 November 1984.
68. Institut du Pacifique, *Le Pacifique*, p. 113.
69. Institut du Pacifique, *Le Pacifique*, p. 299.
70. See the introduction, 'Beyond the Hexagon', and other articles in Aldrich and Connell (eds), *France in World Politics*. For a fuller discussion, see Robert Aldrich and John Connell, *France's Overseas Frontier: Départements et Territoires d'Outre-Mer* (Cambridge, 1992), especially Chapter 9.
71. Institut du Pacifique, *Le Pacifique*, p. 293.
72. Robert Aldrich, 'Le Lobby colonial de l'Océanie française', *Revue Française d'Histoire d'Outre-Mer* 76 (1989), pp. 411–424, and 'Rediscovering the Pacific: A Critique of French Geopolitical Analysis', pp. 68–71, which discusses 'The Pacific Lobby: Old and New'.
73. Particularly in the works of Paul Deschanel, *La Politique française en Océanie à propos du canal de Panama* (Paris, 1884) and *Les Intérêts français dans l'Océan Pacifique* (Paris, 1888).
74. See Aldrich and Connell, *France's Overseas Frontier*, and Robert Aldrich, 'France in the South Pacific', in Ravenhill (ed.), *American Lake No Longer?*, pp. 76–105.

75. Chesneaux, *Transpacifiques*.
76. See Stephen Henningham, *France and the South Pacific* (Sydney, 1992), Chapter 8. I would like to thank Dr Henningham for allowing me to read an early version of the manuscript of his book before its publication.
77. Stephen Bates, *The South Pacific Island Countries and France: A Study in Inter-State Relations* (Canberra, 1990).
78. P. De Deckker, unpublished conference paper.
79. Roland Perrigueux, 'France, la mal-aimée du Pacifique', *Le Monde*.
80. Jean Chesneaux, 'Le Pacifique Sud rongé par une modernité destructrice', *Le Monde diplomatique*, July 1990, pp. 26–27.
81. See John Connell, '"Trouble in Paradise": The Perception of New Caledonia in the Australian Press', *Australian Geographical Studies* 25 (1987), pp. 54–65.
82. Robert Aldrich, 'Le Pacifique français vu d'Australie', *ENA International: Bulletin des Anciens Elèves de l'Ecole Nationale d'Administration* (forthcoming). See also Xavier Pons, *Le Géant du Pacifique* (Paris, 1988).
83. See Paul De Deckker, 'The Perception of France in the Pacific Islands', pp. 167–89 and Xavier Pons, 'Neighbours and Strangers: Perceptions of Australia in New Caledonia', pp. 143–65, in Robert Aldrich (ed.), *France, Australia and Oceania: Past and Present* (Sydney, 1991).

Conclusion

1. Xavier Pons, 'Neighbours and Strangers: Perceptions of Australia in New Caledonia', in Robert Aldrich (ed.), *France, Oceania and Australia: Past and Present* (Sydney, 1991), pp. 143–65.
2. A term used by Jean Chesneaux, *Transpacifiques* (Paris, 1987).
3. Claude Robineau, *Du Coprah à l'atome* (Paris, 1984).
4. Quoted in *Pacific Islands Monthly*, February 1984, p. 34.
5. See, for example, Judith H. Bennett, *Wealth of the Solomons: A History of a Pacific Archipelago, 1800–1978* (Honolulu, 1987), Ch. 14.
6. On the general history of the South Pacific, see I.C. Campbell, *A History of the Pacific Islands* (St Lucia, Qld, 1989) and Deryck Scarr, *The History of the Pacific Islands: Kingdoms of the Reefs* (South Melbourne, 1990).
7. After the *coups d'état* of 1987, Fiji became a republic and was expelled from the Commonwealth.
8. On the Torres Strait Islands, see Jeremy Beckett, *Torres Strait Islanders: Custom and Colonialism* (Cambridge, 1987).
9. Stewart Firth, 'Sovereignty and Independence in the Contemporary Pacific', *The Contemporary Pacific*, 1 (1989), pp. 75–96.
10. See, for instance, Donna Awatere, *Maori Sovereignty* (Auckland, 1984).
11. John Connell and Robert Aldrich, 'The Last Colonies: Failure of Decolonisation?', in Chris Dixon and Michael Heffernan, *Colonialism and Development in the Contemporary World* (London, 1991), pp. 183–203.
12. John Connell, 'Chatham Wants Better Deal from New Zealand', *Pacific*, 13 (1988), p. 60.
13. See, for example, Ron Crocombe, *The South Pacific: An Introduction* (Auckland, 1983).

14. Sean Dorney, *Papua New Guinea: People, Politics and History since 1975* (Sydney, 1990).

15. John Connell, 'Island Microstates: The Mirage of Development', *The Contemporary Pacific* 3 (1991), pp. 251–287, and Benoît Antheaume and Peter Lawrence, 'A l'Aide ou trop d'aide? Evolution des économies vivrières dans le Pacifique insulaire', *Etudes rurales*, No. 99–100 (1985), pp. 367–387. See also Benoît Antheaume and Joël Bonnemaison, *Atlas des îles et états du Pacifique-Sud* (Montpellier, 1988).

16. John Connell, *Sovereignty and Survival: Island Microstates in the Third World* (Sydney, 1988).

17. This suggestion has been made by, among others, Senator Daniel Millaud for French Polynesia and the Institut du Pacifique for New Caledonia.

18. See H.L. Wesseling, 'Towards a History of Decolonisation', *Itinerario* 9 (1987), pp. 95–106. Particularly useful are R.F. Holland, *European Decolonisation, 1918–1981: An Introductory Survey* (London, 1985) and Miles Kahler, *Decolonisation in Britain and France: The Domestic Consequences of International Relations* (Princeton, 1984). More recently, see Charles-Robert Ageron, *La Décolonisation française* (Paris, 1991) and Raymond F. Betts, *France and Decolonisation, 1900–1960* (London, 1991).

19. Robert Aldrich and John Connell, *France's Overseas Frontier: Départements et Territoires d'Outre-Mer* (Cambridge, 1992).

20. Raoul Girardet, *L'Idée coloniale en France* (Paris, 1972).

21. The present author, at least, has found no archival evidence to suggest such a reappraisal in 1954 or immediately afterwards.

22. Pierre Messmer's letter of 1972 concerning migration to New Caledonia; quoted in Claude Gabriel and Vincent Kermel, *Nouvelle-Calédonie: La Révolte Kanake* (Paris, 1985), p. 51.

Bibliography

ARCHIVES

Académie des Sciences d'Outre-Mer (Paris).
  Robert Charbonnier, 'Aventures et mésaventures à Wallis et Futuna', MNS 90 (manuscript).
Archives d'Outre-Mer (Aix-en-Provence).
  Affaires économiques 106, 137.
  Affaires politiques 364, 932.
  Nouvelle-Calédonie 178, 263.
  Nouvelles-Hébrides 19.
  Océanie 135, 136, 137, 138, 153.
Archives Territoriales de la Nouvelle-Calédonie (Nouméa).
  Series 44 W 463, 466 and 467.
Archives Territoriales de la Polynésie Française (Papeete).
  Correspondance intérieure et extérieure du Gouverneur, 1943.
Ministére des Affaires Etrangéres (Paris).
  Asie-Océanie 1944–1955, Nouvelle-Zélande 15.
  Asie-Océanie 1944–1955, Océanie 135.
National Archives of Vanuatu (Port Vila).
  Ministry of Home Affairs HA 804.

THESES AND OTHER UNPUBLISHED MATERIAL

Barbançon, José, 'Le Pays du non-dit' (Unpublished manuscript).
Commandement supérieur des Forces armées en Polynésie Française; Centre d'expérimentations du Pacifique, Commandement des Forces militaires et de la zone maritime du Pacifique, 'Impact des Armées et du C.E.A. sur l'économic polynésienne en 1985', Fiche 154, 20 February 1986.
Discombe, Reece, 'The New Hebrides at War' (Unpublished manuscript, 1979).
Grand, Alfred-René, 'Pouvanaa a Oopa et le nationalisme à Tahiti' (Unpublished Thesis, Paris, 1981).
Gray, Ian L., 'The Emergence of Leaders in the New Hebrides' (Unpublished MA Thesis, University of Auckland, 1971).
Langevin-Duval, Christine, 'Traditions et changements culturels chez les femmes tahitiennes' (Third cycle doctoral thesis, EHESS, 1979).
Moench, Richard U., 'Economic Relations of the Chinese in the Society Islands' (Unpublished PhD Thesis, Harvard University, n.d.).
Munholland, Kim, 'Yankee Farewell: The Americans Leave New Caledonia, 1945', paper presented to the French Colonial Historical Society, Mackinac Island, Michigan, 16–20 May 1990.
Munholland, Kim, 'World War II and the End of Indentured Labor in New Caledonia' (Unpublished paper).

Perini, Antoine, 'L'Introduction du vernaculaire de l'enseignement du 1er degré de l'aire géographique tahitianophone: Contribution d'une reflexion' (Unpublished Thesis, Université de Grenoble, 1985).

Pillon, Patrick, 'Jeunesse urbaine mélanésienne et différenciation sociale' (Unpublished paper, Nouméa, 1985).

Saura, Bruno, 'L'Identité polynésienne: Facteurs de revendication et discours identitaires à Tahiti (Polynésie française)' (Unpublished DEA Thesis, Université d'Aix-Marseille-III, 1986).

Schooling, Stephen J., 'A Sociolinguistic Survey of New Caledonia' (Unpublished paper, Summer Institute of Linguistics, 1982).

Signorel, Yves, 'L'Evolution de l'économie polynésienne de 1961 à 1966' (Thèse de doctorat en sciences économiques, Université de Toulouse, 1969).

Thompson, Anne-Gabrielle, 'John Higginson, Patriot or Profiteer?' (Unpublished PhD Thesis, University of Queensland, 1982).

Woodward, Keith, 'Historical Summary of Constitutional Advance in the New Hebrides, 1954–1977' (Unpublished report).

NEWSPAPERS

(Various issues unless otherwise indicated)
Bwenando (Nouméa)
Islands Business (Suva)
Kanaky (Paris)
Kanaky Update (Melbourne)
La Croix (Paris), 25 August 1989
La Dépêche de Tahiti (Papeete)
Le Monde (Paris)
Le Nouvel Observateur (Paris)
Le Point (Paris)
Le Spectacle du Monde (Paris), October 1987
Les Nouvelles Calédoniennes (Nouméa)
Les Nouvelles de Tahiti (Papeete)
Libération (Paris)
Pacific Islands Monthly (Suva)
Sydney Morning Herald
The Dominion (Wellington), 5 December 1991

BOOKS AND ARTICLES

Adams, Ron, 'Homo Anthropologicus and Man-Tanna: Jean Guiart and the Anthropological Attempts to Understand the Tannese', *Journal of Pacific History*, 22 (1987), pp. 3–14.

Agence de Développement de la Culture Kanak, *Do I Neva: Sculpteurs et peintres kanak d'aujourd'hui* (Nouméa, 1990).

Ageron, Charles-Robert, 'La Survivance d'un mythe: La Puissance par l'empire colonial (1944–1947)', *RFHOM* 73 (1985), pp. 387–403.

Ageron, Charles-Robert, 'L'Opinion publique face aux problèmes de l'Union française', in Charles-Robert Ageron (ed.), *Les Chemins de la décolonisation de l'empire colonial français* (Paris, 1986), pp. 33–48.

Ageron, Charles-Robert, *La Décolonisation française* (Paris, 1991).

Ageron, Charles-Robert, 'La Perception de la puissance française en 1938–1939: le mythe impérial', *RFHOM* 69 (1982), pp. 7–22.

Aldrich, Robert, 'European Expansion in the Island Pacific: An Historiographical Review', *Itinerario* 13 (1989), pp. 87–102.

Aldrich, Robert, 'Le Lobby colonial de l'Océanie française', *RFHOM* 76 (1989), pp. 411–424.

Aldrich, Robert, 'Le Pacifique français vu d'Australie', *ENA International: Bulletin des Anciens Élèves de l'Ecole Nationale d'Administration* (forthcoming).

Aldrich, Robert, 'New Caledonia: The Current Crisis in Historical Perspective', *Contemporary French Civilization* 10 (1986), pp. 175–209.

Aldrich, Robert, 'Rediscovering the Pacific: A Critique of French Geopolitical Analysis', *JSO*, No. 87 (1989), pp. 57–71.

Aldrich, Robert, *The French Presence in the South Pacific, 1842–1940* (London, 1990).

Aldrich, Robert (ed.), *France, Australia and Oceania: Past and Present* (Sydney, 1991).

Aldrich, Robert, 'France in the South Pacific', in J. Ravenhill (ed.), *No Longer an American Lake? Alliance Problems in the South Pacific* (Berkeley, 1989), pp. 76–105.

Aldrich, Robert and Connell, John, *France's Overseas Frontier: Départements et Territoires d'Outre-Mer* (Cambridge, 1991).

Aldrich, Robert and Connell, John (eds), *France in World Politics* (London, 1989).

Allen, M. (ed.), *Politics, Economics and Ritual in Island Melanesia* (Sydney, 1981).

Angleviel, Frédéric, *et al.*, *Atlas de Nouvelle-Calédonie* (Nouméa, 1989).

Anova-Ataba, Apollinaire, *D'Ataï à l'indépendance* (Nouméa, 1984).

Association pour la Fondation d'un Institut Kanak d'Histoire Moderne, *Contribution à l'histoire du pays kanak* (Nouméa, 1983).

Antheaume, Benoît and Bonnemaison, Joël, *Atlas des îles et états du Pacifique-Sud* (Montpellier, 1988).

Antheaume, Benoît and Lawrence, Peter, 'A l'Aide ou trop d'aide? Evolution des économies vivrières dans le Pacifique insulaire', *Etudes rurales*, No. 99–100 (1985), pp. 367–387.

August, Thomas, 'Locating the Age of Imperialism', *Itinerario* 10 (1986), pp. 85–97.

Awatere, Donna, *Maori Sovereignty* (Auckland, 1984).

Barbadzan, Alain, *Naissance d'une tradition: Changement culturel et syncrétisme religieux aux îles Australes* (Paris, 1982).

Barclay, Glen, *A History of the Pacific from the Stone Age to the Present Day* (London, 1978).

Bates, Stephen, *The South Pacific Island Countries and France: A Study in Inter-State Relations* (Canberra, 1990).

Beasant, John, *The Santo Rebellion* (Honolulu, 1984).

Beckett, Jeremy, *Torres Strait Islanders: Custom and Colonialism* (Cambridge,

1987).

Bedford, R., Migration, Employment and Development in the South Pacific (Nouméa, 1986).

Bennett, Judith H., *Wealth of the Solomons: A History of a Pacific Archipelago, 1800–1978* (Honolulu, 1987).

Benoist, Hubert, *Le Condominium des Nouvelles-Hébrides et la société mélanésienne* (Paris, 1972).

Bensa, Alban, *Nouvelle-Calédonie: Un Paradis dans la tourmente* (Paris, 1990).

Betts, Raymond F., *France and Decolonisation, 1900–1960* (London, 1991).

Bigard, Alain, *Vanuatu: Chronique d'une décolonisation* (Nouméa, 1984).

Blanchet, Gilles, *L'Economie de la Polynésie française de 1960 à 1980* (Paris, 1985).

Bonnemaison, Joël, *La Dernière Ile* (Paris, 1986).

Bonnemaison, Joël, 'Passions et misères d'une société coloniale: Les Plantations au Vanuatu entre 1920 et 1980', *JSO*, No. 82–83 (1986), pp. 65–84.

Bonnemaison, Joël, 'Cultural Aspects of Systems of Land Tenure in Vanuatu', *Report of the Regional Conference on Land Management* (Port-Vila, 1981), pp. 17–23.

Bonnemaison, Joël, 'Les Lieux de l'identité: Vision du passé et identification culturelle dans les îles du sud et du centre de Vanuatu (Mélanésie)', *Cahiers de l'ORSTOM, Série Sciences humaines* 21 (1985), pp. 151–170.

Bonnemaison, Joël, 'Un Certain refus de l'Etat: Autopsie d'une tentative de sécession en Mélanésie', *International Political Science Review*, 6 (1985), pp. 230–247.

Bourgeau, Jacques, *La France du Pacifique* (Paris, 1955).

Bouvier, Jean, Girault, René and Thobie, Jacques, *Impérialisme à la française* (Paris, 1986).

Bowman, Robert G., 'Army Farms and Agricultural Development in the Southwest Pacific', *The Geographical Review* (1946), pp. 420–46.

Brou, Bernard, *Trente ans d'histoire politique et sociale de la Nouvelle-Calédonie de 1945 à 1977* (Nouméa, n.d.).

Brou, Bernard, *Peuplement et population de la Nouvelle-Calédonie: La Société pluriethnique* (Nouméa, n.d.).

Brousse, Robert, *et al.*, *Atlas de Tahiti et de la Polynésie Française* (Singapore, 1988).

Burchett, Wilfred G., *Pacific Treasure Island, New Caledonia* (Melbourne, 1941).

Weeks Jr., C.J., 'An Hour of Temptation: American Interests in New Caledonia, 1935–1945', *Australian Journal of Politics and History* 35 (1989), pp. 185–200.

Campbell, I.C., *A History of the Pacific Islands* (St Lucia, Qld, 1989).

Centre de productivité et d'études économiques, *Les Nouvelles-Hébrides: Document d'information générale* (Nouméa, 1977).

Centre de productivité et d'études économiques, *L'Archipel de Wallis* (Nouméa, 1982).

Cercle Katara, *Pacifique Sud, une paix précaire: Essai de géostratégie* (Nouméa, 1980).

Chambre de Commerce de la Nouvelle-Calédonia, *Fluctuations de l'économie calédonienne* (Nouméa, n.d.).

Champaud, J., 'Les Trucks de Tahiti', *ORSTOM, Notes et Documents de Géographie,*

No. 1981/21 (1981).

Chesneaux, Jean, *Transpacifiques* (Paris, 1987).

Chesneaux, Jean, 'Le Pacifique Sud rongé par une modernité destructrice', *Le Monde Diplomatique*, July 1990, pp. 26–27.

Cheval, Gérard, *Ua Pou: Fleur des Marquises* (Papeete, 1986).

Clark, Alan, 'Vanuatu: Independence but still the French Connection', *New Zealand International Review*, 5 (1980), pp. 12–15.

Clifford, James, *Person and Myth: Maurice Leenhardt in the Melanesian World* (Berkeley, 1982).

Cofroli, M., 'Développement de la production nacrière et perlière en Polynésie française', *ORSTOM Notes et Documents, Aquaculture*, No. 3 (1982).

Commission Justice et Paix, *L'Avenir de l'outre-mer français* (Paris, 1988).

Comte, Gilbert, *L'Empire triomphant (1871–1936). I. Afrique occidentale et équatoriale* (Paris, 1988).

Connell, John, *New Caledonia or Kanaky?* (Canberra, 1987).

Connell, John, 'New Caledonia: The Matignon Accord and the Colonial Future', Research Institute for Asia and the Pacific, University of Sydney, Occasional Paper No. 5 (1988).

Connell, John, 'Trouble in Paradise: the perception of New Caledonia in the Australian Press', *Australian Geographical Studies* 25 (1987), pp. 54–65.

Connell, John, 'Chatham Wants Better Deal from New Zealand', *Pacific*, 13 (1988), p. 60.

Connell, John, 'Island Microstates: The Mirage of Development', *The Contemporary Pacific* 3 (1991), pp. 251–287.

Connell, John, *Sovereignty and Survival: Island Microstates in the Third World* (Sydney, 1988).

Connell, John, *Commission on Migration, Employment and Development in the South Pacific: Country Report No. 5: French Polynesia* (Nouméa, 1985), *No. 10: New Caledonia* (Nouméa, 1985) and *No. 21: Wallis and Futuna Islands* (Nouméa, 1983).

Coppenrath, Gérald, *Les Chinois de Tahiti: De l'aversion à l'assimilation, 1865–1966* (Paris, 1967).

Coulon, Marc, *L'Irruption Kanak: De Calédonie à Kanaky* (Paris, 1985).

Coulter, John Wesley, 'Impact of the War on South Sea Islands', *The Geographical Review*, July 1946, pp. 409–19.

Crocombe, R. (ed.), *Land Tenure in the Pacific* (Suva, 1977).

Crocombe, Ron, *The South Pacific* (Auckland, 1983).

Crocombe, Ron, 'Studying the Pacific: Past Experiences and Future Potentials', in Anthony Hooper, *et al.*, *Class and Culture in the South Pacific* (Auckland, 1987), pp. 115–138.

Crocombe, Ron and Hereniko, Pat, *Tahiti: The Other Side* (Suva, 1985).

Cronin, Francis D., *Under the Southern Cross: The Saga of the Americal Division* (Washington, 1951).

Daly, Henry, 'La Guerre du Pacifique: "Americal" 1941–1946: Les Américains en Nouvelle-Calédonie', *BSEHNC*, No. 17 (1973), pp. 1–30.

Danielsson, Bengt, *Work and Life on Raroia* (London, 1955).

Danielsson, Bengt and Marie-Thérèse, *Poisoned Reign* (Harmondsworth, second edition, 1986).

Dardelin, Marie-Joëlle, *L'Avenir et le destin: Regards sur l'école occidentale dans la société kanak* (Paris, 1984).

Dareste, P., *Traité de droit colonial* (Paris, 1931).

Davidson, J. W., 'French Polynesia and the French Nuclear Tests: The Submission of John Teariki', *Journal of Pacific History* 2 (1967), pp. 149–154.

De Curton, Emile, *Tahiti 40* (Paris, 1973).

De Deckker, Paul, 'Mutations et développement: Wallis et Tahiti', *Civilisations* 29 (1979), pp. 312–320.

De la Gorce, Paul-Marie, *L'Empire écartelé (1936–1945)* (Paris, 1988).

Deacon, Richard, *The French Secret Service* (London, 1990).

Delarge, Maurice, *'La France Australe': Nouvelle-Calédonie: 'Ile de Lumière'* (Nouméa, 1985).

Delauney, Maurice, *De la Casquette à la jaquette, ou de l'administration coloniale à la diplomatie africaine* (Paris, 1982).

Delpech, Christiane and Bellaïche, Félix, *Hier les Nouvelles-Hébrides* (n.p., 1987).

Deschamps, Hubert and Guiart, Jean, *Tahiti (La Polynésie française), Nouvelle-Calédonie, Nouvelles-Hébrides* (Paris, 1957).

Deschanel, Paul, *La Politique française en Océanie à propos du canal de Panama* (Paris, 1884).

Deschanel, Paul, *Les Intérêts français dans l'Océan Pacifique* (Paris, 1888).

Desjardins, Thierry, *Nouvelle-Calédonie: Ils veulent rester Français* (Paris, 1985).

Dixon, Chris and Heffernan, Michael, *Colonialism and Development in the Contemporary World* (London, 1991).

Doisy, Isabelle, *Chronique des années de cendres* (Paris, 1988).

Dorney, Sean, *Papua New Guinea: People, Politics and History since 1975* (Sydney, 1990).

Dornoy, Myriam, *Politics in New Caledonia* (Sydney, 1984).

Doumenge, F., 'L'Ile de Makatéa et ses problèmes', *Cahiers du Pacifique*, No. 5 (1963), pp. 41–67.

Drilhon, Freddy, *Le Peuple inconnu* (Paris, 1955).

Droux, Louis-Gabriel, *La France d'Outre-Mer: Guide pratique pour ceux qui veulent vivre en France d'outre-mer* (Paris, 1951).

Dyson, J., *Sink the Rainbow! An Enquiry into the "Greenpeace Affair"* (London, 1986).

Edgell, William and Kalo, Fred (eds), 'The New Hebrides: A Doubly Oppressed Colony' (pamphlet, no publication details).

Ellis, Julie-Anne and Parsons, Michael, 'Vanuatu: Social Democracy, Kastom and "Melanesian Socialism"', in Peter Davis (ed.), *Social Democracy in the South Pacific* (Auckland, 1983).

Encyclopédie de la Polynésie, Vol. 8 (Papeete, 1989).

Etrillard, Gilles and Sureau, François, *A l'Est du monde* (Paris, 1983).

Fages, Henri, 'Un Intérêt majeur de la France en Océanie. Le Centre d'Expérimentation du Pacifique', *JSO*, No. 87 (1988), pp. 10–19.

Faivre, Jean-Paul, *L'Expansion française dans le Pacifique de 1800 à 1842* (Paris, 1953).

Faligot, Roger, *La Piscine: The French Secret Service since 1989* (Oxford, 1989).

Finney, Ben R., 'A Successful French Polynesian Co-operative?', *Journal of Pacific History* 3 (1968), pp. 65–84.

Finney, Ben R., *Polynesian Peasants and Proletarians* (Cambridge, Mass., 1973).

Firth, Stewart, *Nuclear Playground* (Sydney, 1987).

Firth, Stewart, 'Sovereignty and Independence in the Contemporary Pacific', *The Contemporary Pacific*, 1 (1989).

Forestier, Patrick, *Les Mystères d'Ouvéa* (Paris, 1988).

Forman, Charles W., 'The Impact of Colonial Policy on the Churches of Tahiti and New Caledonia', *International Review of Missions*, 305 (1977), pp. 12–21.

Forster, R.A.S., 'Vanuatu: The End of an Episode of Schizophrenic Colonialism', *Round Table* 70 (1980), pp. 367–373.

Fraser, Helen, *New Caledonia: Anti-Colonialism in a Pacific Territory* (Canberra, 1988).

Fraser, Helen, *Your Flag's Blocking Our Sun* (Sydney, 1990).

Gabriel, Claude and Kermel, Vincent, *Nouvelle-Calédonie: La Révolte Kanake* (Paris, 1985).

Gabriel, Claude and Kermel, Vincent, *Nouvelle-Calédonie: Les Sentiers de l'Espoir* (Montreuil, 1988).

Gédéon, Jacques, 'Le Condominium des Nouvelles-Hébrides', *BSEHNC*, No. 89 (1991), pp. 61–80.

G.F.R. [*sic*], 'New Caledonia and the War', *Pacific Affairs* 19 (1946), pp. 373–83.

Gerbault, Alain, *Un Paradis se meurt* (Paris, 1949).

Geslin, Yves, 'Les Américains aux Nouvelles-Hébrides au cours de la Seconde guerre mondiale', *JSO* 12 (1956), pp. 245–85.

Girardet, Raoul, *L'Idée coloniale en France* (Paris, 1972).

Godard, Philippe, *Le Mémorial Calédonien, Vol. 5 (1940–1953)* (Nouméa, 1975).

Gomane, Jean-Pierre, *Les Marins et l'outre-mer* (Paris, 1988).

Gorodey, Déwé, *Sous les Cendres des conques* (Nouméa, 1985).

Greenpeace, *French Polynesia: The Nuclear Tests: A Chronology, 1967–1981* (Auckland, 1981).

Grimald, Aimé Louis, *Gouverneur dans le Pacifique* (Paris, 1990).

Grosser, Alfred, *Affaires extérieures* (Paris, 1984).

Guiart, Jean, *Destin d'une église et d'un peuple: Nouvelle-Calédonie 1900–1959*, (Paris, 1959).

Guiart, Jean, 'La Conquête et le déclin: Les Plantations, cadre des relations sociales et économiques au Vanuatu (ex-Nouvelles-Hébrides)', *JSO*, No. 82–83 (1986), pp. 7–40.

Guiart, Jean, *Un Siècle et demi de contacts culturels à Tanna, Nouvelles-Hébrides* (Paris, 1956).

Guiart, Jean, *Espiritu Santo* (Paris, 1958).

Guiart, Jean, *La Terre est le sang des morts: La Confrontation entre blancs et noirs dans le Pacifique sud français* (Paris, 1983).

Guiart, Jean, 'What immediate future for New Caledonia?', *Pacific Perspective* 8 (1979), pp. 21–25.

Guiart, Jean, 'One of the Last Colonies: New Caledonia', *Journal of International Affairs* 36 (1982), pp. 105–112.

Guiart, Jean, 'Nouvelle-Calédonie 1985: Commentaires', *Les Temps modernes* May 1985, pp. 2126–2140.

Guiart, Jean, 'Les Effigies religieuses des Nouvelles-Hébrides', *JSO* 6 (1949), pp. 51–86.

Guiart, Jean, 'Sociétés, rituels et mythes du nord Ambrym', *JSO* 7 (1951), pp. 1–105.

Guiart, Jean, 'The Forerunners of Melanesian Nationalism', *Oceania* 22 (1951), pp. 81–90.

Guiart, Jean, 'Organisation sociale et politique du nord Malekula', *JSO* 8 (1952), pp. 150–254.

Guillebaud, Jean-Claude, *Un Voyage en Océanie* (Paris, 1980).

Hall, Richard, *Noumea* (Sydney, 1990).

Hall, Ron, 'Passage through Paradise', *Condé Nast Traveler* (April 1991), pp. 102–15.

Hamel-Green, Michael, 'The Rarotonga South Pacific Nuclear-Free Zone Treaty', in Ranginui Walker and William Sutherland (eds), *The Pacific: Peace, Security and the Nuclear Issue* (London, 1988), pp. 93–122.

Henningham, Stephen, *France and the South Pacific* (Sydney, 1992).

Hering, Bob (ed.), *The Political Economy of the South Pacific* (Canberra, 1983).

Heyerdahl, Thor, *The Kon-Tiki Expedition* (New York, 1950).

Hodée, Paul, *Tahiti 1834–1984: 150 ans de vie chrétienne en Eglise* (Papeete, 1983).

Holland R.F., *European Decolonisation, 1918–1981: An Introductory Survey* (London, 1985).

Hours, Bernard, 'Custom and Politics in the New Hebrides', *Pacific Perspectives* 8 (1979), pp. 15–20.

Ilari, Noël, *Secrets tahitiens* (Paris, 1978).

Institut d'Emission d'Outre-Mer, *Exercice 1988: Rapport d'activité: Nouvelle-Calédonie* (Paris, 1989).

Institut d'Emission d'Outre-Mer, *Exercice 1988: Rapport d'activité: Wallis et Futuna* (Paris, 1989).

Institut d'Emission d'Outre-Mer, *Exercice 1988: Rapport d'activité: Polynésie Française* (Paris, 1989).

Institut du Pacifique, *Le Pacifique, 'nouveau centre du monde'* (Paris, 1983; 2nd ed., 1986).

Intes, A., 'La Nacre en Polynésie française: Evolution des stocks naturels et de leur exploitation', *ORSTOM Notes et Documents, Océanographie*, No. 16 (1982).

Jolly, Margaret, 'Birds and Banyans of South Pentecost: Kastom in Anti-Colonial Struggle', *Mankind* 13 (1982), pp. 338–355.

Joralemon, Victoria, 'Collective Land Tenure and Agricultural Development: A Polynesian Case', in N. Pollock and R. Crocombe (eds), *French Polynesia* (Suva, 1988), pp. 154–180.

Joralemon, Victoria, 'Development and Inequality: The Case of Tubuai, a Welfare Economy in Rural French Polynesia', *Human Organization* 45 (1986), pp. 283–295.

Jore, Léonce, *L'Océan Pacifique au temps de la Restauration et de la Monarchie de Juillet (1815–1848)* (2 vols, Paris, 1959).

Julien, Charles-André, *Histoire de l'Océanie* (Paris, 1946).

Jupp, James, 'Custom, Tradition and Reform in Vanuatu Politics', in *Evolving Cultures in the Pacific Islands: Proceedings of the 1982 Politics Conference* (Laie, 1982), pp. 143–158.

Jupp, James, 'The Development of Party Politics in the New Hebrides', *Journal* of *Commonwealth and Comparative Politics*, 27 (1979), pp. 263–282.

Jupp, James, 'Elections in Vanuatu', *Political Science*, 35 (1983), pp. 1–15.

Jupp, James and Sawer, Marian, 'Colonial and Post-Independence Politics: Vanuatu', in R.J. May and Hank Nelson (eds), *Melanesia: Beyond Diversity* (Canberra, 1982), pp. 549–570.

Kahler, Miles, *Decolonisation in Britain and France: The Domestic Consequences of International Relations* (Princeton, 1984).

King, M., *Death of the Rainbow Warrior* (Auckland, 1986).

Kohl, Wilfrid L., *French Nuclear Diplomacy* (Princeton, 1971).

Kohler, J.M., *Pour ou contre le pinus: Les Mélanésiens face aux projets de développement* (Nouméa, 1984).

Kohler, J.M., 'L'Islam en Nouvelle-Calédonie', *L'Afrique et l'Asie modernes*, 135 (1982), pp. 3–11.

Kohler, J.M., *Colonie ou démocratie. Elements de sociologie politique sur la Nouvelle-Calédonie* (Nouméa, 1987).

Kohler, J.M., Pillon, P. and Wacquant, L.J.D., *Jeunesse canaque et coutume* (Nouméa, 1985).

Kohler, J.M., 'Colonie ou Démocratie', *Le Monde Diplomatique*, July 1987, published in English as 'Colony or Democracy: The New Caledonian Dilemma', *Australian Journal of Politics and History* 33 (1987), pp. 47–59.

Kohler, J.M. and Pillon, P., *Adapter l'école ou réorienter le projet social* (Nouméa, 1982).

Kohler, J.M. and Pillon, P., *Impact de l'opération café en milieu mélanésien* (Nouméa, 2 volumes, 1983).

Kohler, J.M. and Wacquant, Loïc J.D., *L'Ecole inégale* (Nouméa, 1985).

Kohler, J.M. and Wacquant, Loïc J.D., *La Question scolaire en Nouvelle-Calédonie: Idéologies et sociologie* (Nouméa, 1984).

Kohler, Jean-Marie, *Profil sociologique de l'église catholique de Wallis et Futuna* (Nouméa, 1985).

Kohler, Jean-Marie, *Christianity in New Caledonia and the Loyalty Islands* (Nouméa, 1981).

Lacam, Guy, *Souvenirs des Nouvelles-Hébrides* (Nouméa, 1990).

Lacoste, Yves, 'Le Pacifique, est-il vraiment le "nouveau centre du monde"?', *Les Nouvelles littéraires*, December 1984, pp. 169–172.

Lacour, Pierre, *De l'Océanie au Pacifique: Histoire et enjeux* (Paris, 1987).

Lacourrège, Gérard, *Qui a tué Pierre Declercq?* (Nouméa, 1986).

Lacourrège, Gérard, *Les Heures noires de la Calédonie* (Nouméa, 1985).

Langevin, Christine, *Tahitiennes de la tradition à l'intégration culturelle* (Paris, 1990).

Larmour, Peter, 'Alienation of Land and Independence in Melanesia', in *Evolving Cultures in the Pacific Islands: Proceedings of the 1982 Politics Conference* (Laie, 1982), pp. 185–231.

Lawrey, John, *The Cross of Lorraine in the South Pacific* (Canberra, 1982).

Le Baut, Yves, 'Les Essais nucléaires français de 1966 à 1974', *Relations Internationales*, No. 59 (Autumn 1989), pp. 359–370.

Lechat, Philippe, 'Le Statut de la Polynésie Française du 6 Septembre 1984. Cinq ans après: autonomie interne ou autonomie internée?', *Annales du Centre universitaire de Pirae*, 3 (1989), pp. 69–98.

Lechat, Philippe (ed.), *Royaume de Tahiti et Dépendances, Etablissements Français de l'Océanie, Polynésie Française: Institutions Politiques et Administratives – Textes et Documents, 1819–1988* (Papeete, 1990).

Leder, Jean, *Les Cent jours du bout du monde* (Nouméa, 1981).

Leenhardt, Maurice, *Do Kamo: La Personne et le mythe dans le monde mélanésien* (Paris, 1947).

Levy, Robert I., *Tahitians: Mind and Experience in the Society Islands* (Chicago, 1973).

Lindstrom, Lamont, 'Cultural Politics: National Concern in Bush Areas on Tanna (Vanuatu)', in *Evolving Cultures in the Pacific Islands: Proceedings of the 1982 Politics Conference* (Laie, 1982), pp. 232–246.

Lindstrom, Lamont and White, Geoffrey, *Island Encounters: Black and White Memories of the Pacific War* (Washington, 1990).

Lini, W., *Beyond Pandemonium: From the New Hebrides to Vanuatu* (Wellington, 1980).

Lockwood, Victoria S., 'Development, French Neocolonialism, and the Structure of the Tubuai Economy', *Oceania* 58 (1988), pp. 176–192.

Lyons, Martyn, *The Totem and the Tricolour: A Short History of New Caledonia* (Sydney, 1986).

MacClancy J.V., 'From the New Hebrides to Vanuatu, 1979–1980', *Journal of Pacific History*, 16 (1981), pp. 91–104.

MacClancy, J.V., 'Vanuatu since Independence, 1980–1983', *Journal of Pacific History*, 19 (1984), pp. 100–102.

MacClancy, Jeremy, *To Kill a Bird with Two Stones* (Port-Vila, 1980).

'Makatéa: Bilan socio-économique d'un demi-siècle d'expérience', *JSO* 15 (1959), pp. 199–210.

Margueron, Daniel, *Tahiti dans toute sa littérature* (Paris, 1989).

Marseille, Jacques, *L'Age d'or de la France coloniale* (Paris, 1986).

Martin, Jean, *L'Empire triomphant (1871–1936). II. Maghreb, Indochine, Madagascar, Iles et Comptoirs* (Paris, 1990).

Mauer, Daniel, *Tahiti: De la parole à l'écriture* (Paris, n.d.).

Mazellier, Philippe (ed.), *Le Mémorial Polynésien, Vol. V (1940–1961)* (Papeete, 1977).

Merle, Isabelle, 'Les Australiens et la Nouvelle-Calédonie. Bilan des recherches en sciences sociales', *Revue Française d'histoire d'outre-mer* 76 (1989), 583–596.

Meyer, Jean, Tarrade, Jean, Rey-Goldzeiguer, Annie and Thobie, Jacques, *Histoire de la France coloniale. Des Origines à 1914* (Paris, 1991).

Michener, James, *Tales of the South Pacific* (New York, 1947).

Mitterrand, François, *Réflexions sur la politique extérieure de la France* (Paris, 1986).

Moorehead, Alan, *The Fatal Impact* (Harmondsworth, 1968).

Munholland, Kim, 'The Trials of the Free French in New Caledonia, 1940–1942', *French Historical Studies* 14 (1986), pp. 547–579.

Newbury, Colin, 'The Makatéa Phosphate Concession', in R. Gerard Ward (ed.), *Man in the Pacific Islands* (Canberra, 1972), pp. 167–188.

Nisbet, Anne-Marie, *Littérature néo-calédonienne* (Montréal, 1985).

O'Reilly, Patrick, *Calédoniens* (Paris, 1953 and 1980).

O'Reilly, Patrick, *Hébridais* (Paris, 1957).
O'Reilly, Patrick, *Tahitiens* (Paris, 1962 and 1975).
O'Reilly, Patrick, 'Le Français parlé à Tahiti', *JSO* (December 1962), pp. 69–81.
Oliver, Douglas, *Oceania: The Native Cultures of Australia and the Pacific Islands* (2 vols, Honolulu, 1989).
Oliver, Douglas, *Two Tahitian Villages: A Study in Comparison* (Honolulu, 1981).
Ordonnaud, Georges and Sérieyx, Alain (eds), *Australie 88: Bicentennaire ou Naissance?* (Paris, 1988).
Pacific Islands Year Book (Sydney, 1950).
Panoff, Michel, *Tahiti métisse* (Paris, 1989).
Panoff, Michel, *La Terre et l'organisation sociale en Polynésie* (Paris, 1970).
Panoff, Michel, 'Tahiti et le mythe de l'indépendence', *Les Temps modernes*, 225 (1965), pp. 1443–1471.
Peattie, Mark, *Nan'yo* (Honolulu, 1987).
Picard, Gilbert, *L'Affaire d'Ouvéa* (Paris, 1988).
Pillon, Patrick, 'Développements et enjeux sociaux en Nouvelle-Calédonie: l'Opération café', *Les Temps modernes*, No. 464, March 1985, pp. 1623–1653.
Pillon, Patrick, 'L'Economie domestique en transition. Trois essais', *ORSTOM Rapports scientifique et techniques, Sociologie*, No. 2 (Paris, 1987).
Pisier, Georges, 'Le Ralliement de la Calédonie et l'intervention britannique (juin-octobre 1940)', *BSEHNC*, No. 62 (1985), pp. 35–47.
Pisier, Marie-France, *Le Bal du Gouverneur* (Paris, 1984).
Pollock, Nancy J. and Crocombe, Ron (eds), *French Polynesia: A Book of Selected Readings* (Suva, 1988).
Poncet, Alexandre, *Histoire de l'Ile Wallis* (Paris, 1972).
Pons, Xavier, *Le Géant du Pacifique* (Paris, 1988).
Quel Avenir pour les enfants et les jeunes en Nouvelle-Calédonie? Actes d'un colloque au Lycée Jules-Garnier, 25 Juin 1988 (Nouméa, 1988).
Réunion des Musées Nationaux, *De Jade et de nacre: Patrimoine artistique kanak* (Paris, 1990).
Raapoto, Duro, 'Maohi: On Being Tahitian', *Pacific Perspective*, 9 (1980), pp. 3–5.
Raapoto, Duro, *Te Pinainai o te aau – Pehepehe* (Papeete, 1980).
Raluy, Antonio, *La Nouvelle-Calédonie* (Paris, 1990).
Ravault, François, 'Le Français dans une société pluri-culturelle: l'exemple de Tahiti', *Anthropologie et Société*, 6 (1982), pp. 89–105.
Ravault, François, 'Land Problems in French Polynesia', *Pacific Perspective*, 9 (1981), pp. 31–65.
Ravenhill, John (ed.), *No Longer an American Lake? Alliance Problems in the South Pacific* (Berkeley, 1989).
Rensch, Karl, 'Wallis and Futuna: Total Dependency', in A. Ali and R. Crocombe (eds), *Politics in Polynesia* (Suva, 1983).
Rice, Edward, *John Frum You Come* (New York, 1974).
Robequain, Charles, *Les Richesses de la France d'outre-mer* (Paris, 1949).
Robequain, Charles, *Madagascar et les bases dispersées de l'Union française* (Paris, 1958).

Robertson, Robert T. and Tamanisau, Akosita, *Fiji: Shattered Coups* (Sydney, 1988).

Robie, D., *Eyes of Fire: The Last Voyage of the Rainbow Warrior* (Auckland, 1986).

Robie, David, *Blood on Their Banner: Nationalist Struggles in the South Pacific* (London, 1989).

Robineau, Claude, 'The Tahitian Economy and Tourism', in Ben R. Finney and Karen Watson (eds), *A New Kind of Sugar: Tourism in the Pacific* (Honolulu, 1977), pp. 61–76.

Robineau, Claude, *Du Coprah à l'atome* (Paris, 1984).

Rodman, Margaret C., *Masters of Tradition: Consequences of Customary Land Tenure in Longana, Vanuatu* (Vancouver, 1987).

Rollat, Alain, *Tjibaou le Kanak* (Lyon, 1989). Rollat, Alain and Plenel, Edwy, *Mourir à Ouvéa. Le Tournant Calédonien* (Paris, 1988).

Roux, J.C., 'Présence et originalité du fait francophone en Mélanésie du Sud', *BSEHNC*, No. 65 (1985), pp. 19–27.

Roux, J.C., 'Migration and Change in Wallisian Society', in R.T. Shand (ed.), *The Island States of the Pacific Ocean* (Canberra, 1980), pp. 167–176.

Roux, Jean-Claude, 'Pouvoir religieux et pouvoir politique à Wallis et Futuna', in Paul De Deckker and Pierre Lagayette, *États et pouvoirs dans les territoires français du Pacifique* (Paris, 1987), pp. 54–80

RPR, *Le RPR vous parle de la Nouvelle-Calédonie* (Paris, 1985).

Rui a Mapuhi, *Te hia'ai ao* (Papeete, 1985).

Sénès, Jacqueline, *Terre violente* (Paris, 1987).

Sénès, Jacqueline, *La Vie quotidienne en Nouvelle-Calédonie de 1850 à nos jours* (Paris, 1985).

Sanguinetti, Alexandre, 'Nouvelle-Calédonie: Summum jus, Summa injuria', *Politique d'aujourd'hui,* June 1985.

Sanguinetti, Antoine, *et al.*, *Enquête sur Ouvéa* (Paris, 1989).

Sarraut, Albert, *La Mise en valeur des colonies françaises* (Paris, 1923).

Satineau, Maurice, *Le Miroir de Nouméa* (Paris, 1987).

Saussol, A., *L'Héritage: Essai sur le problème foncier mélanésien en Nouvelle-Calédonie* (Paris, 1979).

Saussol, Alain, 'Peut-on parler de créolité en Nouvelle-Calédonie?' in J.P. Doumenge, *et al.* (eds), *Iles tropicales, insularité, 'insularisme'* (Talence, 1987), pp. 157–164.

Sautot, Henri, *Grandeur et décadence du Gaullisme dans le Pacifique* (Melbourne, 1949).

Scarr, Deryck, *The History of the Pacific Islands: Kingdoms of the Reefs* (South Melbourne, 1990).

Scheinman, Lawrence, 'Euratom: Nuclear Integration in Europe', *International Conciliation*, No. 563 (May 1967).

Selwyn, Percy (ed.), *Development Policy in Small Countries* (London, 1975).

Servoise, René, 'Le Pacifique, "nouveau monde"', *Politique étrangère,* January 1985, pp. 101–117.

Shears, Richard and Gidley, Isobelle, *The Rainbow Warrior Affair* (Sydney, 1985).

Shineberg, Barry, 'The Image of France: Recent Developments in French Polynesia', *Journal of Pacific History* 21 (1986), pp. 153–68.

Simington, Margot, 'Australia and New Caledonia, October 1940 – January 1941', *Royal Military College Historical Journal* 3 (1974), pp. 35–46.

Simington, Margot, 'Australia and the New Caledonia Coup d'État of 1940', *Australian Outlook* 30 (1976), pp. 73–92.

Sope, Barak, *Land and Politics in the New Hebrides* (Suva, 1975).

Spencer, Michael and Connell, John (eds), *New Caledonia: Essays in Nationalism and Dependency* (St Lucia, Qld, 1988).

Stern, Jacques, *Les Colonies françaises: Passé et avenir* (New York, 1943).

Stone, David, 'The Awesome Glow in the Sky: the Cook Islands and the French Nuclear Tests', *Journal of Pacific History* 2 (1967), pp. 154–159.

Sunday Times Insight Team, *Rainbow Warrior: The French Attempt to Sink Greenpeace* (London, 1986).

Suret-Canale, Jean, 'Nouvelle-Calédonie: Une Page oubliée de l'histoire', *Révolution* 453, 4 November 1988, pp. 45–49.

T'Serstevens, Albert, *Tahiti et sa couronne* (3 vols., Paris, 1950).

Tagupa, William, *Politics in French Polynesia, 1945–1975* (Wellington, 1976).

Thobie, Jacques, Meynier, Gilbert, Coquery-Vidrovitch, Catherine and Ageron, Charles-Robert, *Histoire de la France coloniale. 1914–1990* (Paris, 1990).

Thompson, Richard and Adloff, Virginia, *The French Pacific Islands* (Berkeley, 1971).

Tjibaou, Jean-Marie, 'Recherche d'identité mélanesienne et société traditionnelle', *JSO* 32 (1976), pp. 281–292.

Tjibaou, Jean-Marie, 'Etre Mélanésien aujourd'hui', *Esprit*, No. 57 (1981), pp. 81–93.

Tjibaou, Jean-Marie and Missotte, Philippe, *Kanaké* (Papeete, 1978).

Tonkinson, R., 'National Identity and the Problem of Kastom in Vanuatu', *Mankind*, 13 (1982), pp. 305–315.

Tonkinson, Robert, 'Vanuatu Values: A Changing Symbiosis', in R.J. May and Hank Nelson (eds), *Melanesia: Beyond Diversity*, Vol. 1 (Canberra, 1982), pp. 74–90;

Toullelan, Pierre-Yves, *Tahiti et ses archipels* (Paris, 1991).

Toullelan, Pierre-Yves (ed.), *Encyclopédie de la Polynésie*, Vol. 7 (Papeete, 1989).

Turnbull, Robert Oliver, *Tin Roofs and Palm Trees* (Canberra, 1977).

Turner, Mark, *Papua New Guinea: The Challenge of Independence* (Melbourne, 1990).

Union Calédonienne, *Pourquoi oui à l'Union Calédonienne, oui à l'autonomie?* (Nouméa, 1972).

Van Trease, Howard, *The Politics of Land in Vanuatu* (Suva, 1987).

Vassort-Rousset, Brigitte, *L'Engagement socio-politique des organisations chrétiennes dans le Pacifique* (Paris, 1985).

Veill, Daniel, *Opération Victor* (Paris, 1989).

Vernier, Charles, *Au Vent des cyclones* (Paris, 1985).

Viêt Levilain, Guy, 'L'Académie tahitienne et la renaissance culturelle en Polynésie française', *Contemporary French Civilization*, 2/3 (1978), pp. 440–447.

Vibart, Eric, *Alain Gerbault: Vie et voyages d'un dandy révolté des années folles* (Paris, 1989).

Walker, R. and Sutherland, W. (eds), *The Pacific: Peace, Security and the Nuclear Issue* (Tokyo, 1988).

Ward, Alan W., *Land and Politics in New Caledonia* (Canberra, 1982).

Weitzmann, Marc, *Nouvelle-Calédonie: Un Siècle de balles perdues* (Paris, 1985).

Wesseling, H.L., 'Towards a History of Decolonisation', *Itinerario* 9 (1987), pp. 95–106.

White, Geoffrey and Lindstrom, Lamont, (eds), *The Pacific Theater: Island Representations of World War II* (Honolulu, 1989).

Wilson, J.S.G., *Economic Survey of the New Hebrides* (London, 1966).

Winchester, Simon, *The Pacific* (London, 1991).

Zeldine, Georges, *L'Hémisphère pacifique: Réalités et avenirs* (Nouméa, 1984).

Zorgbibe, Charles, *Vanuatu: Naissance d'un Etat* (Paris, 1981).

Index